MW00783604

# A DIABOLICAL VOICE

A VOLUME IN THE SERIES

*Medieval Societies, Religions, and Cultures*
Edited by M. Cecilia Gaposchkin and Anne E. Lester

A list of titles in this series is available at cornellpress.cornell.edu.

# A DIABOLICAL VOICE

## HERESY AND THE RECEPTION OF THE LATIN *MIRROR OF SIMPLE SOULS* IN LATE MEDIEVAL EUROPE

## JUSTINE L. TROMBLEY

CORNELL UNIVERSITY PRESS

*Ithaca and London*

First published 2023 by Cornell University Press

Library of Congress Cataloging-in-Publication Data

Names: Trombley, Justine L., 1987– author.
Title: A diabolical voice : heresy and the reception of the
    Latin Mirror of simple souls in late medieval Europe /
    Justine L. Trombley.
Description: Ithaca : Cornell University Press, 2023. |
    Series: Medieval societies, religions, and cultures |
    Includes bibliographical references and index.
Identifiers: LCCN 2022053348 (print) | LCCN 2022053349
    (ebook) | ISBN 9781501769610 (hardcover) |
    ISBN 9781501769627 (pdf) | ISBN 9781501769634
    (epub)
Subjects: LCSH: Porete, Marguerite, approximately
    1250–1310. Miroir des simples âmes. | Porete,
    Marguerite, approximately 1250–1310—Translations
    into Latin—History and criticism. | Mysticism—
    France—History—Middle Ages, 600–1500. | Christian
    literature, French—Translations into Latin—History
    and criticism. | Christian heresies—France—History—
    Middle Ages, 600–1500. | Soul—Christianity—History
    of doctrines—Middle Ages, 600–1500.
Classification: LCC BV5077.F8 T76 2023 (print) |
    LCC BV5077.F8 (ebook) | DDC 248.2/20944—dc23/
    eng/20230111
LC record available at https://lccn.loc.gov/2022053348
LC ebook record available at https://lccn.loc.
    gov/2022053349

*To Grandad, my first intellectual hero.*
*And to Mom, Dad, Lee, Tiffany, Cambria, and Vivien,*
*who mean so much to me, and who always cheer me on.*

# Contents

# ACKNOWLEDGMENTS

I am grateful to the staff of several libraries who allowed me to view manuscript material in person and provided help during my visits, or who provided me with photos of manuscripts: the Biblioteca universitaria in Padua, the Vatican Library, the Bodleian Library, the Biblioteca nazionale centrale in Florence, the Universitätsbibliothek in Eichstätt, the Universitätsbibliothek in Würzburg, the Forschungsbibliothek in Gotha, the Domstiftsbibliothek in Bautzen, the British Library, and the Kongelige Bibliotek in Copenhagen; and thanks to Dr. Filippo Sedda for providing me with photographs of documents from the Capestrano Archive. Thanks also to the anonymous reviewers for their excellent comments and insights, and to my series editors Cecilia Gaposchkin and Anne Lester, as well as Mahinder Kingra at Cornell University Press, who have all been pleasantly enthusiastic, patient, and helpful throughout the publication process. Thank you also to the excellent and thorough copyeditors.

This book has been a long time in the making, which means that there are quite a lot of people who deserve thanks for their help, advice, and support during its creation. My thanks go especially to Sean Field, who not only first introduced me to Marguerite Porete and *The Mirror of Simple Souls* back when I was an undergraduate but who has since been an unfailing source of advice, support, encouragement, editorial feedback, and numerous cups of coffee. Thank you also to Frances Andrews and Chris Given-Wilson, who expertly guided this book in its earliest stages. Exchanges with and comments over the years from Robert Lerner, Sylvain Piron, John Arnold, Pablo Acosta García, Walter Simons, Dávid Falvay, Miri Rubin, Danielle Dubois, John Arblaster, Zan Kocher, Elodie Pinel, and Elizabeth A. R. Brown have all helped to improve this book. Thank you to Wolfgang Mieder, who with characteristic kindness bought me a copy of the Latin edition of *The Mirror of Simple Souls* when I couldn't afford it myself as a PhD student. Thank you also to Delfi I. Nieto-Isabel for always being ready with both encouragement and analogies between medieval heresy and various action films. I am grateful to Cecilia Gaposchkin and Walter Simons at Dartmouth College for inviting me to the 2018 Dartmouth History Institute, where I was able to workshop chapter 4 of this book and where I received excellent feedback. This book was also greatly improved by my time at the Pontifical Institute of Mediaeval Studies in Toronto, especially through discussions with staff at seminars, feedback from and conversations with Greti Dinkova-Bruun, Fred Unwalla, and Jonathan Black, and conversations with my fellow fellows Magda Hayton, Robert Shaw, and Giovanni Gasbarri. Thanks also to Bob Sweetman for suggesting the title for chapter 4.

I finished this book while a member of the Department of History at the University of Nottingham, a wonderful department in which to work. The friendship and support I received there were crucial to finishing this book—especially during the lockdowns of 2020. Comic relief from Matt Hefferan, Matt Ward, Matt Raven, and Dan O'Neill in A7 was a welcome morale booster. Conversations with Rob Lutton about the cult of the Holy Name provided crucial insight, and Richard Goddard kindly offered helpful comments and suggestions from the "nonspecialist" viewpoint, along with plenty of jokes. My marvelous Coffee Club comrades Dan Hucker and Dean Blackburn helped me finish this book more than they probably think.

Although it did not become a book until long after I left, this will always be my St. Andrews book. The Department of Mediaeval History at the University of St. Andrews is where this project began. The wonderful community (*conventiculum*, perhaps?) of medievalists that I was a part of there played an enormously important role. The lively, weird, and delightful atmosphere of the Osgood Room—birthplace of the cult of St. Hippo of Augustine—was an especially crucial foundation to this work. So, thank you to all my St. Andrews friends and partners in PhD-ing, not just for your friendship and moral support but also for all the medieval jokes that only we could find funny, the creative cocktail recipes, Leeds discos, cloister runs, and all-around good times. Thank you especially to Rob Houghton, Varan Houghton, Maxine Esser, Trish Stewart, Eilidh Harris, Richard Meyer Forsting, Jane Edwards, Mike French, Anna Peterson, Will Eves, Jo Thornborough, Nicole Peterson, Andrew Alliger, Steve Ling, and Liz Mincin.

Finally, this book would never have been possible without the boundless support and love of my family, who never questioned why I would want to dedicate all my time to reading and writing about an obscure book written in the fourteenth century, even when I sometimes questioned it myself. Thank you so much to Mom, Dad, Lee, Tiffany, Cambria, and Vivien.

# ABBREVIATIONS

| | |
|---|---|
| *1241 Errors* | Theological errors condemned in Paris in 1241, printed in E. Chatelain and H. Denifle, eds., *Chartularium Universitatis Parisiensis*, vol. 1 (Paris: Ex typis fratrum Delalain, 1889), 170–172. English translation in Dana Carleton Munro, ed., *Translations and Reprints from the Original Sources of European History*, vol. 2.3 (Philadelphia: University of Pennsylvania Press, 1895), 17–19. |
| AN | Archives nationales de France |
| BAV | Biblioteca apostolica vaticana (known in English as the Vatican Library) |
| *Middle English Mirror* | Marguerite Porete, *The Mirror of Simple Souls: A Middle English Translation*, ed. Marilyn Doiron, in *Archivio italiano per la storia della pietà* 5 (1968): 243–382. |
| *PL* | *Patrologia Latina*, https://patristica.net/latina/ |
| Sargent, "Latin and Italian" | Michael Sargent, "Medieval and Modern Readership of Marguerite Porete's *Mirouer des simples âmes anienties*: The Manuscripts of the Continental Latin and Italian Tradition," in *The Medieval Translator/Traduire au Moyen Age 15: In Principio Fuit Interpres*, ed. Alessandra Petrina (Turnhout: Brepols, 2013), 85–96. |
| *Speculum CCCM* | Marguerite Porete, *Le mirouer des simples âmes/Speculum Simplicium Animarum*, ed. Romana Guarnieri and Paul Verdeyen, in *Corpus Christianorum: Continuatio Mediaevalis* 69 (Turnhout: Brepols, 1986). |

Stieber, *Supreme Authority*      Joachim Stieber, *Pope Eugenius IV, The Council of Basel, and the Secular and Ecclesiastical Authorities in the Empire: The Conflict over Supreme Authority and Power in the Church* (Leiden: Brill, 1978).

# A DIABOLICAL VOICE

# Introduction

> O my Lover, what will beguines say,
> And the religious,
> When they shall hear the excellence of your
> divine song?
> Beguines say that I err,
> priests, clerics, and Preachers,
> Augustinians, and Carmelites,
> and the Friars Minor,
> Because I wrote about the being of Pure Love.
>
> —Marguerite Porete, *The Mirror of Simple Souls*

In these lines from her book, *The Mirror of Simple Souls*, Marguerite Porete both conveys her own frustration and concern over the reception of her work and ominously foreshadows the events about to unfold around her. Marguerite, who lived in the county of Hainaut at the end of the thirteenth century, wrote the *Mirror* as a mystical dialogue, in which various allegorical characters discuss how a human soul becomes completely annihilated in love and union with the divine. While plenty of other writers of her time—women and men—outlined similar spiritual journeys, Marguerite expressed herself in bold, paradoxical, and at times shocking terms that, as shown here, even she acknowledged might unsettle her readers and listeners. Eventually, her *Mirror* was to be condemned by ecclesiastical authorities not once but twice: first in the town of Valenciennes and again several years later

---

"Amis, que diront beguines / et gens de religions / Quant ilz orront l'excellence / de vostre divine chançon? / Beguines dient que je erre / prestres, clers, et prescheurs, / Augustins, et carmes / et les freres mineurs / Pource que j'escri de l'estre / de l'affinnee Amour." Marguerite Porete, *Le mirouer des simples âmes/Speculum simplicium animarum*, ed. Romana Guarnieri and Paul Verdeyen, in *Corpus Christianorum: Continuatio Mediaevalis 69* (Turnhout: Brepols, 1986) (hereafter *Speculum CCCM*), 342. This verse appears only in the French version. The English here is a slightly modified translation taken from Marguerite Porete, *The Mirror of Simple Souls*, trans. Ellen L. Babinsky (New York: Paulist Press, 1993), 200, and supplemented with the translation in Marguerite Porete, *The Mirror of Simple Souls*, trans. Edmund Colledge, Judith Grant, and J. C. Marler (South Bend, IN: University of Notre Dame Press, 1999), 152–153.

1

in Paris. The above verse hints that, even while Marguerite was still writing, storm clouds were already gathering. When these clouds finally burst in 1310, Marguerite Porete was tried, condemned, and burned at the stake for heresy in the Place de Grève in Paris. The *Mirror* was meant to share her fate.

But the *Mirror*, like so many banned books, was not so easily stamped out. It was not destroyed but instead shed its association with Marguerite's name and fate and circulated across late medieval Europe. It was translated out of its original Old French *picard* dialect into three languages: Latin, Italian, and Middle English. It was transcribed into Middle French. It was read, copied, and valued by a wide range of people, some of whom were the very types of people Marguerite had previously counted among her critics. It moved across not only France but also Italy, Germany, England, and Bohemia, appearing in the hands of monks, vicars, priests, and even apothecaries. Many of these readers showed little concern over what they saw in the *Mirror*. Notes in the margins of a French copy point to the "beauty" of its passages and the "marvelous" things it says; another note in a Latin copy exclaims, "O, how well said!" (*O quam bene dicit!*).[1] A fifteenth-century Tuscan monk copied a Latin *Mirror* into a manuscript made for the edification of his brothers, tucked into a codex alongside not only works by Bonaventure and Ambrose but also one of his own compositions.[2]

This acceptance was not always wholehearted. Closer scrutiny shows the slight tarnish of unease on the bright surfaces of these later versions of the *Mirror*. The same monk in Tuscany who included the *Mirror* alongside his own work also included a warning in its incipit: *Caute legendus, et non ab omnibus*— "To be read cautiously, and not by everyone."[3] The Middle English translator of the *Mirror* added explanatory glosses to some parts of their translation after they learned that "some wordis þerof have be mystake."[4] One copyist of a Latin *Mirror* referred to it as *speculatissimus*, implying that it was extremely

---

1. Pablo Acosta García, "'Notez bien, bonnes pucelles': A Complete Transcription of the French and Continental Latin Annotations of the *Mirror of Simple Souls*," *Sacris Erudiri: Journal of Late Antique and Medieval Christianity* 56 (2017): 22 and 37. The manuscripts in question are Chantilly, Musée Condé, MS F XIV 26 and Vatican City, Biblioteca apostolica vaticana (hereafter BAV), MS Vat. lat. 4355.

2. Justine L. Trombley, "New Frontiers in the Late Medieval Reception of a Heretical Text: The Implications of Two New Latin Copies of Marguerite Porete's *Mirror of Simple Souls*," in *Late Medieval Heresy: New Perspectives: Studies in Honor of Robert E. Lerner*, ed. Michael D. Bailey and Sean L. Field (Woodbridge, UK: Boydell and Brewer, 2018).The manuscript is Florence, Biblioteca nazionale centrale, MS Conv. soppr. G.3.1130.

3. MS Conv. soppr. G.3.1130, f. 103r; Trombley, "New Frontiers," 167.

4. Marguerite Porete, *The Mirror of Simple Souls: A Middle English Translation* (hereafter *Middle English Mirror*), ed. Marilyn Doiron, *Archivio italiano per la storia della pietà* 5 (1968): 9, and Kathryn Kerby-Fulton, *Books under Suspicion: Censorship and Tolerance of Revelatory Writing in Late Medieval England* (South Bend, IN: University of Notre Dame Press, 2006), 280. "Mystake" could mean either misunderstood or taken amiss.

speculative or unclear; another Latin copyist at the Benedictine monastery in Subiaco believed the *Mirror* was unsuitable for printing because it was "too high for the simple" and *quasi scandalosus*. The same copyist noted places where the *Mirror* seemed to contradict "all the doctors of the Church."[5] Another monk, a French Celestine in Ambert, penned a work entitled *La discipline d'amour divine*, which aimed to correct and clarify some of the *Mirror*'s more "dangerous" assertions.[6] But, despite these misgivings and feelings of uncertainty, these readers and copyists still brought the *Mirror* into their spiritual lives. They did not throw the wheat out with the chaff. Its difficulties could be glossed, rather than burned. To all appearances, then, the *Mirror* had made it into the realm of orthodoxy—or had at least made a delicate treaty with it.

For many years, the remarkable success of the *Mirror*—its positive acceptance into late medieval spiritual reading—has been the dominant story in scholarship of its post-1310 career. It is a fascinating story of a book that triumphed over initial adversity and escaped the censor's hand. But this book focuses on another, more troubled story that has been less visible. Where some readers saw passages that merely needed additional explanation, others, like those who burned Marguerite Porete, saw the "pestilential sickness" of heresy. Late medieval theologians, preachers, inquisitors, and canon lawyers—none of whom knew of the *Mirror*'s 1310 condemnation or the identity of its author—preached or wrote against the *Mirror* as a heretical text; some even physically destroyed it. Their attention this time was trained on copies of the *Mirror* in Latin, a linguistic tradition that was often regarded as the "ultimate accolade" for a vernacular work.[7] These Latin manuscripts tell another side of the *Mirror*'s story: they reveal renewed persecution and condemnation of the *Mirror*, entirely in ignorance of its earliest troubles, and in some cases more than a century after those took place. In just eight lines, then, the verse from the *Mirror* with which I began not only foreshadows Marguerite's original run-in with authorities but also encapsulates the

5. Justine L. Trombley, "The Latin Manuscripts of *The Mirror of Simple Souls*," in *A Companion to Marguerite Porete and "The Mirror of Simple Souls*," ed. Robert Stauffer and Wendy R. Terry (Leiden: Brill, 2017), 194–195.

6. Geneviève Hasenohr, "La seconde vie du *Miroir des simples âmes* en France: Le livre de la discipline d'amour divine (XVᵉ-XVIIIᵉ s.)," in *Marguerite Porete et le "Miroir des simples âmes": Perspectives historiques, philosophiques et littéraires*, ed. Sean L. Field, Robert E. Lerner, and Sylvain Piron (Paris: Vrin, 2013), and also Hasenohr, "La tradition du *Miroir des simples âmes* au XVᵉ siècle: De Marguerite Porete (†1310) à Marguerite de Navarre," *Comptes rendus des séances de l'Academie des Inscriptions et Belles-Lettres* 143, no. 4 (1999): 1349–1352 and 1365–1366. An English translation of this latter article is Hasenohr, "The Tradition of the *Mirror of Simple Souls* in the Fifteenth Century: From Marguerite Porete (†1310) to Marguerite of Navarre (†1549)," trans. Zan Kocher, in *A Companion to Marguerite Porete and "The Mirror of Simple Souls*," ed. Robert Stauffer and Wendy R. Terry (Leiden: Brill, 2017).

7. The phrase is from S. S. Hussey, "Latin and English in the *Scale of Perfection*," *Mediaeval Studies* 35 (1973): 476.

longer history of opposition that dogged her *Mirror* both in the days leading up to her execution and long after those events as well.

This, then, is a book about a book and the history of the opposition that book faced. It details a series of attacks on *The Mirror of Simple Souls*, attacks that existed alongside its positive reception in other circles and that were aimed almost entirely at its Latin version. This book primarily uses manuscripts within the *Mirror* tradition itself to tell this story, supplemented with contemporary sermons, monastic records, and letters. Some of these sources have long been known but are understudied, while others are newly discovered. This evidence fundamentally challenges how we perceive Marguerite Porete, the *Mirror*, and both of their places within late medieval intellectual and spiritual life. It demonstrates that the *Mirror* was a controversial work in its own right and provoked charges of heresy in multiple different times and places, completely separated from Marguerite's name and fate. Many late medieval intellectuals took the *Mirror* seriously, on its own terms, and saw in it ideas that they found deeply troubling. This means that, whatever other circumstances were at play in the trial of Marguerite Porete, her and her book's fate in 1310 should not be attributed solely to clerical prejudices, politics, or misrepresentation of her work. As this book will show, fear over the implications of Marguerite's ideas was very real and produced real consequences. Uncovering this other side of the *Mirror*'s reception also has larger implications, furthering our understanding of the variety of medieval spiritual life and the ambiguity of heresy and orthodoxy, and also raising crucial questions about the condemnation of texts in the late Middle Ages.

## The Beguine and the Burned Book: Introducing *The Mirror of Simple Souls* and the Trial of Marguerite Porete

Most scholars who have spent time studying the *Mirror* can probably remember the first time they read it. Usually, the memory involves a combination of bafflement, surprise, incredulity, fascination, and probably a certain amount of despair. Fittingly, all of those emotions also appear within the pages of the *Mirror* itself, suggesting that even its own author wrestled with it in some way. It is not a book that lends itself easily to summarization. There is no plot or even a clear linear progression. It often contradicts, doubles back on, and repeats itself. Given that Marguerite was attempting to communicate the uncommunicable—the soul's complete union with God himself—this is perhaps understandable and may even have been deliberate.

Although, as Sean Field has remarked, "nothing can replace the experience of reading the *Mirror* oneself," what follows is a rough summary of its ideas and form. *The Mirror of Simple Souls* (*Le mirouer des simples âmes/Speculum simplicium animarum/Specchio delle anime semplici*) revolves around the concept of *anéantissement/adnihilatio*, or "annihilation" of the soul, which Marguerite presents as the height of spiritual perfection. An annihilated soul is one with God in a state of nonbeing, in which the soul has no will, no desire, and no self of its own. The union is indistinct and immovable: the self has so completely dissolved that there is no distinction between soul and God, and no concern, either internal or external, can shake the soul out of the state of annihilation once it has been attained, not even sin. This is best expressed by one of Marguerite's more (in)famous passages: "Such a Soul neither desires nor despises poverty nor tribulation, neither mass nor sermon, neither fast nor prayer, and gives to Nature all that is necessary, without remorse of conscience."[8]

The attainment of *anéantissement* is achieved through the negation of the will; no thought for the material world or the self can remain. This includes leaving behind not only personal thoughts and desires but also *anything* that has to do with the created world. This means that church-prescribed actions such as penances, prayers, charitable works, and even the practice of the virtues have no place on the path to annihilation. Marguerite is careful to note, however, that she is not advocating for a life of immorality and sin; rather, the annihilated soul perfectly embodies and rules over the virtues. For Marguerite, one must not strive for God but should rather dissolve and melt into God by destroying one's own identity and one's will. While the journey to becoming annihilated permeates the entire book, near the end it is laid out in a linear fashion for the reader as being achievable through seven specific stages or steps, which culminate in the soul's complete disintegration into God.[9]

Marguerite was not an equal opportunist. She makes it clear that the spiritual life she describes in her book is one superior to all others and is not open to everyone. She makes a distinction between "the Lost" and "the Sad," the former being those who carry on using their will and participate in church works who are oblivious to the higher spiritual life and the latter being those who know that there is a better spiritual path but do not know how to attain it.[10] Those souls who do know the path to annihilation and have achieved it belong to "Holy Church the Greater" (*Sancta Ecclesia Maior*), which is superior to the institutional church, dubbed "Holy Church the Lesser" (*Sancta Ecclesia Minor*).[11] Marguerite

---

8. Porete, *Mirror of Simple Souls*, ed. Babinsky, 87.
9. *Speculum CCCM*, 317–333.
10. See *Speculum CCCM*, 159–160 and 165–167.
11. *Speculum CCCM*, 75, 132–133.

does not make these distinctions in a punitive sense—the Lost, the Sad, and all those in *Ecclesia Minor* may not achieve the highest and best form of spiritual life, but they will live a good life and be saved. Marguerite does, however, write that they will be saved in a lesser way than those who are annihilated: in an "uncourtly" way, to use her words.[12]

The *Mirror* is set up in a dialogic format. The main voices of Love, the Soul, and Reason discuss the Soul's path to annihilation, with other minor characters, such as Christ or Pure Courtesy, occasionally speaking at random intervals. Reason is the unenlightened voice who is held up as the main obstacle to annihilation. She constantly questions and exclaims over what Love and the Soul say about the life of spiritual perfection (her favorite phrase is "O God! What are you saying?"). Reason cannot comprehend what she is told and mocking Reason for her stupidity is one of Love and the Soul's favorite pastimes. At one point, Reason even dies of shock at what she hears from Love and the Soul—an event that the Soul celebrates.[13] Marguerite specifically links Reason with the world of the lesser institutional church. She makes it clear that those who adhere to Reason are too preoccupied with worldly things and the self to be able to achieve or understand annihilation and dismisses them as "beasts and asses."[14] Set up in opposition to Reason are Love and the Soul, who discuss the pathway to annihilation and teach the reader what is necessary to achieve such a state.[15] The Soul acts as narrator, describing her experiences and spiritual progress. Love is the teacher, guiding and bringing the Soul to *anéantissement* and admonishing Reason for her frequent questions and "foolishness." Love is a divine force of "nothingness" that binds the Soul to God, containing no will and no desire.

Marguerite Porete, the author of this swirling, paradoxical text, is almost as mysterious as the *Mirror* itself. We know very little about her life. The story of her trial has received a flurry of attention in the last two decades, and a steady cascade of both new evidence and reconsideration of existing evidence means it is in an almost constant state of change. Marguerite Porete's life and trial comes to us through only two main primary sources: her trial documents, all contained in carton J428 held in the Archives nationales de France in Paris, and what hints can be gleaned from the pages of the *Mirror*. Brief descriptions of her execution are also found in four fourteenth-century chronicles of French origin.[16] Margue-

---

12. *Speculum CCCM*, 181–183.
13. *Speculum CCCM*, 247.
14. *Speculum CCCM*, 193.
15. Robin Anne O'Sullivan has argued that the structure and content of the *Mirror* suggests that it was meant as an instructional spiritual work for beguines. See O'Sullivan, "The School of Love: Marguerite Porete's *Mirror of Simple Souls*," *Journal of Medieval History* 32 (2006).
16. These are the "Continuer of Guillaume de Nangis," the *Grandes Chroniques de France*, the *Ly Myreurs des Histors* of Jean d'Outremeuse, and the *Chronicle of Gerard Frachet*. The passages mentioning

rite, perhaps born around 1260, was a laywoman who came from the county of
Hainaut and lived either in or near the vicinity of Valenciennes in what would
today be northern France, right on the border with modern Belgium.[17] In the
thirteenth century, Hainaut belonged to the German empire, though Valenciennes lay in an area that was more politically ambiguous.[18] Although she wrote
in French and was tried in Paris, John Van Engen has pointed out that culturally
Marguerite would have been more Netherlandish than French.[19] Nothing certain
is known of her family or background, though it is quite likely that she came
from or at least had connections to a well-off, possibly noble family, since evidence from the *Mirror* indicates that she was highly literate and familiar with
courtly culture.[20] In her trial documents she is referred to as a "beguine" (*beguina*),
which usually denoted a laywoman living a semireligious, uncloistered life of
poverty and chastity, a form of life that was most popular in the Low Countries
and in Germany from the thirteenth to the sixteenth centuries.[21] While there has
been some debate over whether or not Marguerite was "really" a beguine—that
is, associated with an established community—Sean Field has pointed out that
this point is moot, as the "fluidity" of the term in the early fourteenth century
meant that it was used to describe a woman's self-presentation as much as her
links to a formal community, or as a pejorative.[22]

Marguerite—along with her trial documents from J428—are transcribed in Paul Verdeyen, "Le procès
d'inquisition contre Marguerite Porete et Guiard de Cressonessart," *Revue d'histoire ecclesiastique* 81
(1986): 88–93. For English translations of these passages and Marguerite's trial documents see Sean L.
Field, *The Beguine, the Angel, and the Inquisitor: The Trials of Marguerite Porete and Guiard de Cressonessart*
(South Bend, IN: University of Notre Dame Press, 2012), 209–238.

17. The most detailed account of Marguerite Porete's life and trial is Field, *The Beguine*.

18. John Van Engen, "Marguerite of Hainaut and the Low Countries," in *Marguerite Porete et le "Miroir
des simple âmes": Perspectives historiques, philosophiques et littéraires*, 27. See also Field, *The Beguine*, 28.

19. Van Engen, "Marguerite and the Low Countries," 25.

20. Van Engen, "Marguerite and the Low Countries," 28–33, and Field, *The Beguine*, 29. On Marguerite's use of metaphors of nobility, see in general Joanne Maguire Robinson, *Nobility and Annihilation in Marguerite Porete's "Mirror of Simple Souls"* (New York: SUNY Press, 2001), and Suzanne [Zan]
Kocher, *Allegories of Love in Marguerite Porete's "Mirror of Simple Souls"* (Turnhout: Brepols, 2009).

21. There is a vast historiography on beguines. For an overview of the movement, see Walter Simons, *Cities of Ladies: Beguine Communities in the Medieval Low Countries, 1200–1565* (Philadelphia: University of Pennsylvania Press, 2001). See also Tanya Stabler Miller, *The Beguines of Medieval Paris: Gender,
Patronage, and Spiritual Authority* (Philadelphia: University of Pennsylvania Press, 2014). On historiographical issues see Jennifer Kolpacoff Deane, "Did Beguines Have a Late Medieval Crisis? Historical Models
and Historiographical Martyrs," in *Early Modern Women* 8 (2013). For perspectives on persecution see
Elizabeth Makowski, *A Pernicious Sort of Woman: Quasi-Religious Women and Canon Lawyers in the Later
Middle Ages* (Washington, DC: Catholic University of America Press, 2005), and Anne E. Lester, "'Women
Behind the Law: Lay Religious Women in Thirteenth-Century France and the Problem of Textual Resis-
tance," in *Jews and Christians in Thirteenth-Century France*, ed. Elisheva Baumgarten and Judah D. Galinsky
(New York: Palgrave Macmillan, 2015).

22. Field, *The Beguine*, 31–32. A summary of the debate is given on p. 31. On the complexities of
the term "beguine" see also the essays in Letha Böhringer, Jennifer Kolpacoff Deane, and Hildo van
Engen, eds., *Labels and Libels: Naming Beguines in Northern Medieval Europe* (Turnhout: Brepols, 2014).

Recently, however, evidence has emerged that indicates that Marguerite was a member of the beguine community at Valenciennes, the beguinage of St. Elizabeth.[23] Huanan Lu has examined archival documents that stem from the investigation of the beguines of St. Elizabeth, conducted by the Premonstratensian abbot of Vicogne in 1323 on the orders of Bishop Peter of Cambrai.[24] When the abbot, Godefridus, asked the beguines whether they knew of anyone who had "disputed on the highest trinity and divine essence," preached, or introduced any opinions contrary to the sacraments or the faith, the beguines responded there was only one, named "Marghoneta," but that she had been executed and had not gained any followers.[25] As Lu argues, this, surely, is a reference to Marguerite Porete; it seems too great a coincidence to be anyone else. While the reference is brief, it nevertheless shows that Marguerite had indeed belonged to a beguinage at some point, and it definitively places her as a resident of Valenciennes.[26]

Marguerite probably composed the *Mirror* in the 1290s, though no certain date can be given. There is evidence to suggest that she most likely composed it in stages, revisiting and rewriting pieces here and there, rather than creating it all in one go.[27] Between the years 1297 and 1305—perhaps around 1300—the *Mirror* came to the attention of Guido de Collemezzo, the bishop of Cambrai from 1297 to 1305.[28] He "publicly and solemnly" condemned the *Mirror* and ordered for it to be burned in public in Valenciennes.[29] Marguerite herself was not condemned, but Guido set down in a letter that, should she recirculate

---

23. Huanan Lu, "Marguerite Porete et l'enquête de 1323 sur le béguinage Sainte-Élisabeth de Valenciennes," *Revue du Nord* 440 (2021): 451–485. Jörg Voigt, "Margarete Porete als Vertreterin eines freigeistig-häretischen Beginentums? Das Verhältnis zwischen den Bischöfen von Cambrai und den Beginen nach dem Häresieprozess gegen Margarete Porete (+1310)," in *Meister Eckhart und die Freiheit*, ed. Janina Franzke, Christine Büchner, and Freimut Löser (Stuttgart: Verlag W. Kohlhammer, 2018).

24. Lu, "Marguerite Porete et l'enquête". These documents were first published by Jörg Voigt, "Margarete Porete als Vertreterin eines freigeistig-häretischen Beginentums? Das Verhältnis zwischen den Bischöfen von Cambrai und den Beginen nach dem Häresieprozess gegen Margarete Porete (+1310)," in *Meister Eckhart und die Freiheit*, ed. Janina Franzke, Christine Büchner, and Freimut Löser (Stuttgart: Verlag W. Kohlhammer, 2018). 48–50. The text mentioning Marguerite is one of twelve published by Voigt that deal with investigations of beguines in the Low Countries in the years following the Council of Vienne.

25. Lu, "Marguerite Porete et l'enquête," 468, and Voigt, "Margarete Porete als Vertreterin," 49.

26. Lu, "Marguerite Porete et l'enquête."

27. Sylvain Piron, "Marguerite in Champagne," *Journal of Medieval Religious Cultures* 43 (2017): 136–138.

28. Field, *The Beguine*, 54. Given Marguerite's comment that "beguines" said that she erred, and the new evidence suggesting her residence at the Valenciennes beguinage, it is possible that Marguerite had shared her work with her sisters there, and knowledge of her book could have eventually reached the bishop through the beguinage.

29. Paris, Archives nationales de France (hereafter AN), J428 no. 19bis, edited in Verdeyen, "Le procès," 78–79, and translated in Field, *The Beguine*, 225–226.

her book in any way, she would be relaxed to the secular arm for execution.[30] Sometime around this first condemnation—there is some debate as to whether it took place before or after—Marguerite showed her work to three church-men in order to garner their opinions on it. As it turned out, these three men praised the *Mirror* rather than condemned it.[31] These appraisals are found within the *Mirror* itself, in the Middle English, Latin, and Italian (following the Latin) traditions only; they are not first-person, personal accounts but are re-ported secondhand by Marguerite herself.[32] The three men consulted were John of Quérénaing, a Franciscan; Franc, a cantor of the abbey of Villers; and Godfrey of Fontaines, a master theologian at the University of Paris.[33] Of the three, only Godfrey is identifiable, as he was a famous theologian of his time; Franc and John have yet to be identified.[34] Each one praised the *Mirror*'s so-phisticated spirituality and did not find it heretical, although both John and Godfrey advised that Marguerite not circulate it widely.[35]

These warnings, however, were not taken on board. It eventually came to the attention of Jean of Châteauvillain, the bishop of Châlons-sur-Marne, that Mar-guerite had rewritten or recirculated her book in some way.[36] It was Jean who in all likelihood alerted inquisitorial authorities to her defiance of Bishop Guido's order.[37] She was interrogated first by Ralph de Ligny, the inquisitor of Lorraine, to whom she admitted recirculating her book, and then she confessed again in the presence of Philip of Marigny, the new bishop of Cambrai (from 1306 to 1309) who had been appointed after Guido de Collemezzo was transferred to

---

30. Verdeyen, "Le procès," 78–79; Field, *The Beguine*, 225–226. This letter has not survived; its existence is merely reported in the trial document.

31. See Field, *The Beguine*, 48–54. The debate over the timing of this event runs as follows: Some, such as Winfried Trusen, Paul Verdeyen, Ellen Babinsky, and Robert Lerner, believe that no churchman would have risked contradicting the official judgment of a bishop on a matter of heresy. See Winfried Trusen, *Der Prozess gegen Meister Eckhart: Vorgeschichte, Vorlauf, und Folgen* (Paderborn: Ferdinand Schöningh, 1988), 35; Verdeyen, "Le procès," 52; Ellen L. Babinsky, Introduction to *The Mirror of Simple Souls*, 22–23; and Robert E. Lerner, "New Light on the *Mirror of Simple Souls*," *Speculum* 85 (2010): 99. Field believes this episode to have taken place after the first burning of the *Mirror* at Valenciennes. See his full argument in "The Master and Marguerite: Godfrey of Fontaines' Praise of *The Mirror of Simple Souls*," *Journal of Medieval History* 35 (2009).

32. For the Middle English see *Middle English Mirror*, 249–250. For the Latin see *Speculum CCCM*, 405–409.

33. The identification of John as hailing from Quérénaing comes only from the Middle English version, describing him as from "Querayn." In the Latin he is merely "John." See *Middle English Mir-ror*, 249, and *Speculum CCCM*, 405.

34. See discussions in Kocher, *Allegories of Love*, 34–36; Field, "The Master and Marguerite," 140–142; and Field, *The Beguine*, 49–54.

35. See *Middle English Mirror*, 249 and 250, and *Speculum CCCM*, 407.

36. Sylvain Piron has suggested that Marguerite may have left Hainaut for Champagne after her book's condemnation, which might explain how she came to the attention of Bishop Jean. See Piron, "Marguerite in Champagne."

37. See Field, *The Beguine*, 55–56.

the bishopric of Salerno.[38] Philip then, in the autumn of 1308, sent Marguerite to Paris, into the custody of William of Paris, Dominican inquisitor and personal confessor to the king of France, Philip IV the Fair (r. 1285–1314).[39] This meant that Marguerite had now entered the custody of a man who was essentially an agent of the Capetian court; it therefore also meant she was thrust into a highly charged environment of political-religious wrangling over the fate of the Knights Templar, who had been arrested by Philip IV in 1307, an effort that William of Paris had led.[40] Marguerite's trial also involved multiple other figures who had close ties to the Capetian court, indicating that Capetian interests influenced how her trial was both conducted and recorded.[41]

In a strange turn of events, shortly after Marguerite entered William's custody, a man named Guiard of Cressonessart publicly came to her defense.[42] Guiard called himself the "Angel of Philadelphia" and seems to have been a proponent of Joachite ideas similar to those adopted by certain followers of the Spiritual Franciscans.[43] No concrete connection between him and Marguerite Porete has yet been established, and while we do not know exactly how Guiard defended her, it was enough to attract the attention of William of Paris, who arrested and imprisoned him. Both Marguerite and Guiard refused to take

---

38. Field, *The Beguine*, 57–60. On Ralph of Ligny see Sean L. Field, "The Inquisitor Ralph of Ligny, Two Germany Templars, and Marguerite Porete," *Journal of Medieval Religious Cultures* 39 (2013). As Field notes, Philip of Marigny was "the king's man," that is, King Philip IV of France. His brother Enguerran was a rising star in Philip's service at this time, and Philip IV likely lobbied Pope Clement V for Philip of Marigny to be installed as bishop after Guido. See Field, *The Beguine*, 59–60.

39. Field, *The Beguine*, 60.

40. On William's involvement see Sean L. Field, "The Heresy of the Templars and the Dream of the French Inquisition," in *Late Medieval Heresy: New Perspectives*, 14–34, and Field, *The Beguine*, 63–84. On the larger history of the Templar affair, see Malcolm Barber, *The Trial of the Templars*, 2nd ed. (Cambridge: Cambridge University Press, 2006).

41. Sean Field has argued that William's careful handling of the case was influenced by his official reprimand by the papacy over his actions in the arrests of the Templars three years earlier, which meant he needed to rehabilitate his reputation with the pope with a clear-cut and unquestionable condemnation of a heretic. The difficulty over the Templar affair similarly meant that the Capetian court more broadly may have had a vested interest in prosecuting a "real" heretic who was unequivocally guilty. The various political intricacies surrounding Marguerite's trial are laid out in more detail in Field, *The Beguine*, 73–84 and 85–166. See also Field, "William of Paris's Inquisitions against Marguerite Porete and Her Book," and William Courtenay, "Marguerite's Judges: The University of Paris in 1310," both articles found in *Marguerite Porete et le "Miroir des simple âmes": Perspectives historiques, philosophiques et littéraires*. Another perspective on how her trial was conducted is offered by Henry Ansgar Kelly, "Inquisitorial Deviations and Cover-Ups: The Prosecutions of Margaret Porete and Guiard of Cressonessart, 1308–1310," *Speculum* 89 (2014).

42. Field, *The Beguine*, 89.

43. On Guiard see Robert E. Lerner, "An 'Angel of Philadelphia' in the Reign of Philip the Fair: The Case of Guiard of Cressonessart," in *Order and Innovation in the Middle Ages: Essays in Honor of Joseph Strayer*, ed. William Chester Jordan, Teofilo F. Ruiz, and Bruce McNab (Princeton: Princeton University Press, 1976); Field, *The Beguine*, 105–124; and Lerner, "Addenda on an Angel," in *Marguerite Porete et le "Miroir des simples âmes": Perspectives historiques, philosophiques, et littéraires*.

the inquisitorial oath and confess. Although she could have been immediately condemned as a relapsed heretic, William of Paris instead left Marguerite (and Guiard) in custody for a year and a half. Then, in the spring of 1310, William moved their cases forward. He initiated a meticulous process against both Marguerite and Guiard, involving several legal and theological consultations.

First, in March, William gathered together a group of five canon lawyers and fifteen master theologians to consult them on whether each prisoner could be considered a heretic on the basis of their continuing refusal to confess; the theologians in this case declined to offer an opinion on the grounds that the case as it stood was more relevant to the canon lawyers.[44] The written opinions of the five canon lawyers were issued on 3 April, in which they declared that both prisoners could be considered heretics and could be condemned on the basis of their contumacy.[45] Shortly after this, Guiard finally confessed to William, which led the canon lawyers to pronounce him a heretic a second time, on the basis of his testimony.[46] Then, on 11 April 1310, William brought the *Mirror* into the proceedings for the first time. He took several extracts from it and presented them to twenty-one master theologians from the University of Paris for assessment, a process not unlike how the university policed the works of its own members.[47] No details about the book—its title, author, or that it was written in the vernacular—are mentioned in the document that recounts the consultation. William submitted at least fifteen articles to the panel; the precise number is unknown. This is noted in the response of the theologians, which cited two of the articles, labeled the "first" and the "fifteenth." These articles read as follows:

[1] That the annihilated soul gives license to the virtues and is no longer in servitude to them because it does not have use for them, but rather the virtues obey its command.

---

44. Field, *The Beguine*, 96–100. The record of this meeting is in AN J428 no. 16, printed in Lerner, "An Angel of Philadelphia," 361–362; Verdeyen, "Le procès," 56–58. The English translation can be found in Field, *The Beguine*, 211–214. Though the document of this meeting only mentions Guiard's case, Field argues that there must have been another similar document regarding consultation on Marguerite's case made at the same time, which is now lost. See Field, *The Beguine*, 98.

45. Field, *The Beguine*, 96–103. AN J428 no. 17 is printed in Lerner, "An Angel of Philadelphia," 363–364. Both the decision regarding Marguerite and the one regarding Guiard are printed in Verdeyen, "Le procès," 62–63 and 60–61, respectively. For the English see Field, *The Beguine*, 214–218.

46. See AN J428 no. 18, printed in Lerner, "An Angel of Philadelphia," 363–364, and Verdeyen, "Le procès," 65–67. The English translation can be found in Field, *The Beguine*, 219–222.

47. This point is made by Field, *The Beguine*, 131, who also notes that a consultation of this kind on a vernacular work, much less the work of a laywoman, was almost entirely without precedent. On the process of examining the suspect works of university theologians, see J. M. M. H. Thijssen, *Censure and Heresy at the University of Paris, 1200–1400* (Philadelphia: University of Pennsylvania Press, 1998), and William Courtenay, "Inquiry and Inquisition: Academic Freedom in Medieval Universities," *Church History* 58 (1989).

[15] That such a soul does not care about the consolations of God or his gifts, and ought not to care and cannot, because such a soul has been completely focused on God, and its focus on God would then be impeded.[48]

An additional article is quoted in the chronicle of the "Continuer of Guillaume de Nangis" as part of an account of Marguerite's execution:

That the Soul annihilated in love of the Creator, without blame of conscience or remorse, can and ought to concede to nature whatever it seeks and desires.[49]

The theologians judged the *Mirror* to be heretical and, after a final consultation with the canon lawyers, this time revealing to them the details of Marguerite's first transgression in Valenciennes and the judgment of her book, William publicly sentenced and condemned both Marguerite Porete and Guiard de Cressonessart in the Place de Grève on 31 May 1310.[50] Guiard, who had confessed, was sentenced to perpetual imprisonment, but Marguerite was relaxed to the secular arm for execution as a relapsed heretic. The next day, on 1 June 1310, she was burned at the stake. The "Continuer of Guillaume de Nangis," based at the abbey of St. Denis, reported that "she showed . . . many signs of penitence at her end, both noble and devout, by which the hearts of many were piously and tearfully turned to compassion."[51] While sentencing Marguerite, William of Paris also condemned the *Mirror*, ordering for it "to be exterminated and burned" and declaring that—on pain of excommunication—any who possessed the work were required to turn it in to the Dominican convent of St. Jacques in Paris by the end of the month.[52]

While the *Mirror* was burned, it was certainly not exterminated. As Kathryn Kerby-Fulton has observed, manuscript culture "was not much amenable even to *authorial* control, let alone authoritarian control."[53] As already noted, the *Mirror* survived and went on to have a spectacular afterlife in late medieval Europe, one that demonstrated just how limited the medieval church's scope for effective "censorship" was. While this book focuses mainly on the Latin tradition, a basic knowledge of the other linguistic versions of the *Mirror* helps to clarify the bigger picture of its reception. The different versions

---

48. Verdeyen, "Le procès," 50–51. English from Field, *The Beguine*, 223–224.
49. Verdeyen, "Le procès," 88. English from Field, *The Beguine*, 234.
50. The text of the canon lawyers' final consultation is in AN J428 no. 19bis, printed in Verdeyen, "Le procès," 78–79; English in Field, *The Beguine*, 225–226. The text of the sentences is in AN J428 no. 15b, printed in Verdeyen, "Le procès," 81–83. English in Field, *The Beguine*, 226–231.
51. Verdeyen, "Le procès," 89. English from Field, *The Beguine*, 234.
52. AN J428 no. 15b, in Verdeyen, "Le procès," 82, and Field, *The Beguine*, 229.
53. Kerby-Fulton, *Books under Suspicion*, 17.

resonate with one another not just linguistically and philologically but also historically. The reception the *Mirror* received in its vernacular versions is both the backdrop to the Latin's circulation and the main springboard for the argument of this book, as they represent the positive side of the *Mirror's* reception and have been the dominant focus of *Mirror* scholarship. It will be useful, therefore, to trace what the *Mirror's* post-condemnation incarnations looked like.

## The Many Faces of the *Mirror* in Late Medieval Europe

The best known and most studied tradition of the *Mirror*, as one might expect, is the French version. Despite being the language in which Marguerite would have originally written the *Mirror*, the French tradition in fact has the fewest surviving manuscripts. There is only one complete surviving manuscript of a French *Mirror*: Chantilly, Musée Condé, MS F XIV 26, which was copied at the end of the fifteenth century in the region of Orléans. Its text is broken up into 139 chapters with explanatory titles. There is also a poem, inserted before the main text begins, which cautions scholars and "men of reason" that they will not understand the book's contents.[54] Since Romana Guarnieri's publication of an edition of this manuscript—first in 1961, and then twice more in 1965 and 1986—the Chantilly copy has been the main reference text for scholars of the *Mirror*.[55] Literary and theological studies of the *Mirror* use its French vocabulary, and most of the modern *Mirror* translations have been made from the Chantilly text.[56] But scholars have observed that the language of the Chantilly codex is deceptive. Although it was initially considered the closest approximation of Marguerite's work, it is written in Middle French, which is significantly different to the *picard* dialect in which Marguerite would originally have thought and written.[57]

Although only one complete French copy survives, other evidence shows that the French *Mirror* enjoyed a fairly diverse circulation. Pieces of the French

---

54. For the poem see *Speculum CCCM*, 8.

55. Marguerite Porete, *Le mirouer des simples âmes anienties et qui seulement demeurent en vouloir et désir* d'amour, ed. Romana Guarnieri (Rome: Storia e Letteratura, 1961. The 1965 edition was published in Guarnieri, "Il movimento del libero spirito," *Archivio italiano per la storia della pietà* 4 (1965). References to the *Mirror's* chapters in wider scholarship are always based upon the Chantilly reckoning—this is the convention that is used in this book, unless otherwise noted.

56. The main modern English translations are *The Mirror of Simple Souls*, trans. Ellen L. Babinsky, and *The Mirror of Simple Souls*, trans. Edmund Colledge, Judith Grant, and J. C. Marler.

57. This point has been made by Povl Skårup, "La langue du *Miroir des simples âmes* attribué à Marguerite Porete," *Studia Neophilologica* 60 (1998); Hasenohr, "La tradition," 1358; and Kocher, *Allegories of Love*, 47.

text show up in other manuscripts. One of the most significant finds of the past twenty years has been Geneviève Hasenohr's discovery of fragments of the *Mirror* embedded in a text found in Valenciennes, Bibliothèque municipale, MS 239, a fifteenth-century manuscript.[58] These fragments are in the Old French *picard* dialect in which Marguerite would have written and therefore represent excerpts from an early fourteenth-century *Mirror*, close to the original.[59] Hasenohr and Zan Kocher have shown that the *Mirror* had a *seconde vie* in late medieval France. Their work has uncovered its appearance in miscellanies and its appropriation by one Celestine monk in Ambert as a way of teaching readers what should and should not be pursued or believed in the course of mystical contemplation.[60] Hasenohr's work, alongside that of Kocher's, also shows that the *Mirror* was owned, read, and copied by various other readers in Sens and Dijon, including monks, nuns, and lay readers.[61]

While the single French manuscript has been the basis for most of the literary and theological studies of the *Mirror*, its Middle English translation has also received a great deal of attention.[62] The Middle English *Mirror* survives in three fifteenth-century codices: Oxford, Bodleian Library, MS Bodley 505; Cambridge, St. John's College, MS 71; and London, British Library, MS Additional 37790. All three were owned by the Carthusians or had close Carthusian connections. The Oxford and Cambridge codices belonged to the London Charterhouse, and, as Marleen Cré has shown, the British Library copy exhibits strong associations with Carthusian spiritual interests and includes annotations by the sixteenth-century Carthusian James Grenehalgh.[63] A single Latin translation was also made from the Middle English. This version was done in 1491 by Richard Methley (ca. 1450–ca. 1528), a Carthusian monk of the Mount Grace Charterhouse in Yorkshire, and it survives in a sixteenth-century copy found in Cambridge, Pembroke College, MS 221.[64] These versions of the *Mirror* contain a prologue and several glosses from its original translator, who notes that they translated it from French. The translator-cum-commentator is known only by the initials "M. N.," which are appended to

---

58. The fragment is printed in Hasenohr, "La tradition," 1361–1363.

59. Hasenohr, "La tradition."

60. Hasenohr, "La tradition," 1349–1352, and Hasenohr, "La seconde vie."

61. See Hasenohr, "La tradition," 1347–1366; Hasenohr, "La seconde vie," 263–317; Zan Kocher, "The Apothecary's *Mirror of Simple Souls*: Circulation and Reception of Marguerite Porete's Book in Fifteenth-Century France," *Modern Philology* 111, no. 1 (2013).

62. *Middle English Mirror*, 247–355.

63. Marleen Cré, *Vernacular Mysticism in the Charterhouse: A Study of London, British Library, MS Additional 37790* (Turnhout: Brepols, 2006).

64. For an edition of the Methley manuscript see Richard Methley, *Speculum Animarum Simplicium: A Glossed Latin Version of "The Mirror of Simple Souls,"* ed. John Clark, in *Analecta Cartusiana* 266 (Salzburg: Institut für Anglistik und Amerikanistik, 2010).

each of the glosses. As M. N. notes, each gloss is meant to clarify a particularly confusing or difficult point in the text.[65] The identity of M. N. has been the subject of some debate; recently, Robert Stauffer has suggested that it could have been the nun Mathilda Newton, of Syon Abbey.[66] M. N.'s prologue and glosses make the Middle English version an ideal case study in the *Mirror*'s reception, as their glosses reveal a simultaneous fascination with and slight concern over the *Mirror*'s "high spiritual feelings," as the translator described it.[67] But despite this unease, the Middle English *Mirror* still found a comfortable place among other popular translations and original compositions within late medieval English spirituality, keeping company with the works of such authors as Julian of Norwich, Jan van Ruusbroec, and Bridget of Sweden.[68]

The Italian version of the *Mirror* was made from the Latin, and there are two separate recensions.[69] Although it was the Italian version that first drew scholarly attention to the *Mirror* in the early twentieth century, it remains the tradition about which we know the least. It survives in four manuscripts: Florence, Biblioteca Riccardiana, MS 1468 (fourteenth century); Naples, Biblioteca nazionale, MS XII F 5 (fourteenth century); Vienna, Österreichische Nationalbibliothek, MS Palatino 15093 (1400–1449); and Budapest, Országos Széchényi Könyvtár, MS Oct. Ital. 15 (1450–1500).[70] A unique characteristic of the Italian is that three of the manuscripts attribute the work to Blessed Margarita of Hungary, a thirteenth-century princess who lived in a Dominican

---

65. *Middle English Mirror*, 248.

66. Robert Stauffer, "Possibilities for the Identity of the English Translator of *The Mirror of Simple Souls*," in *A Companion to Marguerite Porete and "The Mirror of Simple Souls*," 282–288. Given the different possibilities for the translator's identity, I will hereafter use "they" to refer to M. N. rather than either "he" or "she."

67. *Middle English Mirror*, 247.

68. See John Arblaster, "Iste liber aliter intitulatur Russhbroke: Unanswered Questions Concerning Marguerite Porete and John of Ruusbroec in England," *Ons Geestelijk Erf* 90 (2020); Marleen Cré, *Vernacular Mysticism in the Charterhouse*, and "Women in the Charterhouse? Julian of Norwich's Revelations of Divine Love and Marguerite Porete's Mirror of Simple Souls in British Library, MS Additional 37790," in *Writing Religious Women: Female Spiritual and Textual Practices in Late Medieval England*, ed. Denis Renevey and Christina Whitehead (Toronto: University of Toronto Press, 2000); and Nicholas Watson, "Melting into God the English Way: Deification in the Middle English Version of Marguerite Porete's *Mirouer des simples âmes anienties*," in *Prophets Abroad: The Reception of Continental Holy Women in Late-Medieval England*, ed. Rosalyn Voaden (Woodbridge, UK: Boydell and Brewer, 1996).

69. Michael Sargent, "Medieval and Modern Readership of Marguerite Porete's *Mirouer des simples âmes anienties*: The Manuscripts of the Continental Latin and Italian Tradition," in *The Medieval Translator/Traduire Au Moyen Age 15: In Principio Fuit Interpres*, ed. Alessandra Petrina (Turnhout: Brepols, 2013) (hereafter Sargent, "Latin and Italian"), 89, and Guarnieri, "Il movimento," 506–508. That the Latin was made from the Italian was first noted by Florio Banfi (pseudonym of Hungarian scholar Ladislao Holik-Barabàs) in "*Lo specchio delle anime semplici dalla B. Margarita d'Ungaria scripto*," *Memorie Domenicane* 57 (1940): 137.

70. Romana Guarnieri published an edition of the Riccardiana manuscript: Romana Guarnieri, Giovanna Fozzer, and Marco Vannini, eds., *Lo specchio delle anime semplici* (Milan: San Paolo, 1994).

convent and whose cult became popular in Italy after 1270.[71] These manuscripts also contain a prologue, which relates the story of Margarita receiving the stigmata. Whether this attribution was meant to lend legitimacy to a suspect work or whether it was a more organic attribution is uncertain, but either way it is an indication that the name "Margarita" somehow remained with certain versions of the *Mirror*, a characteristic that the manuscript examined in chapter 2, MS Laud Latin 46, shares.[72] Another notable characteristic of the Italian is the fact that at least two codices—Naples and Budapest—have possible connections to the Franciscan Giovanni of Capestrano, who carried out an inquisition against the *Mirror*, which is discussed in chapter 1.

In many ways, the reception of the Italian version is bound up with that of the Latin, in that a majority of the Latin manuscripts were also copied on the Italian peninsula. The Italian context of the *Mirror* is the focus of chapter 1 and is discussed at length throughout the book. For now, suffice it to say that the *Mirror* appears to have been very popular on the peninsula, not only because the largest number of surviving manuscripts originated there—four Italian and five Latin—but also because it is mentioned in multiple contemporary sources from the region, particularly from Tuscany and northeastern areas. As will be seen, these sources show that it circulated widely and was in the hands of men and women across the societal spectrum.

## The Latin Manuscript Tradition

The Latin *Mirror of Simple Souls* represents the largest corpus of surviving *Mirror* manuscripts, outnumbering the other linguistic traditions by a significant margin. It currently comprises nine manuscripts, five of which contain complete copies of the *Mirror*, one of which contains roughly 60 percent of the text, and three of which contain fragments or excerpts. These comprise the continental Latin tradition, which circulated exclusively on mainland Europe and which was originally made from the French.[73] Distinct from this tradition is the Latin translation produced in England by Richard Methley. As this Latin copy was made from the Middle English translation, it is in a separate tradition to the rest of the Latin manuscripts. My focus in this book is solely on the continen-

---

71. Gábor Klaniczay, *Holy Rulers and Blessed Princesses: Dynastic Cults in Medieval Central Europe*, trans. Éva Pálmai (Cambridge: Cambridge University Press, 2000), 225 and 375–376.

72. On this relationship see Dávid Falvay, "The Italian Version of the *Mirror*: Manuscripts, Diffusion and Communities in the 14–15th Century," in *A Companion to Marguerite Porete and "The Mirror of Simple Souls,"* 229–233.

73. Kocher, *Allegories of Love*, 49–50.

tal Latin tradition and therefore Methley's translation does not feature in my analysis.

The six complete (or mostly complete) *Mirror* copies are Vatican City, Biblioteca apostolica vaticana (BAV), MS Vat. lat. 4355, MS Rossianus 4, MS Chigianus B IV 41, and MS Chigianus C IV 85; Florence, Biblioteca nazionale centrale, MS Conv. soppr. G.3.1130; and Bautzen, Domstiftsbibliothek Sankt Petri, MS M I 15.[74] One manuscript, Oxford, Bodleian Library, MS Laud Latin 46, addressed in chapter 2, once contained a complete *Mirror*, but most of its pages were removed from the codex, leaving behind only a few fragments. Two codices, Vatican City, BAV, MS Vat. lat. 4953 and Padua, Biblioteca universitaria di Padova, MS 1647, both contain lists of verbatim extracts taken from (now lost) copies of Latin versions of the *Mirror*; these extracts are presented and refuted as errors. These two codices are the focus of chapters 3 and 4, respectively.

The Latin tradition is arguably the most diverse of the *Mirror* traditions in both chronological and geographical scope, as one might expect, given Latin's lingua franca status. Three of the Vatican manuscripts—Vat. lat. 4355, Rossianus 4, and Chigianus B IV 41—have been roughly dated to the mid-to-late fourteenth century. The Oxford manuscript, Vat. lat. 4953, the Paduan manuscript, the Florence manuscript, and the Bautzen copy are all from the first half of the fifteenth century. MS Chigianus C IV 85 is the latest, copied in 1521. In terms of geography, for many years the Latin was believed to be almost entirely confined to Italy, with the exception of the Oxford manuscript, which might have come from southern Germany, although that, too, is thought by some to be Italian in origin.[75] The recent discovery of the Bautzen codex, however, shows that the *Mirror* also made it into Bohemia and then from there to eastern Germany (to the town of Bautzen itself).[76] The ownership of many of these manuscripts is unknown, but what information we do have again paints a fairly diverse picture. The Florentine manuscript was copied by a Camaldolese monk; the Paduan codex was owned by a university canon lawyer; MS Chigianus C IV 85 was copied in the famed Benedictine monastery of Subiaco; and the Bautzen codex was owned by a *vicarius* in the city of Bautzen.[77] Outside of the manuscripts, we can discern more readers and scrutinizers of

74. Descriptions of the Vatican codices can be found in Verdeyen, Introduction to *Speculum CCCM*, viii–xii, and in Trombley, "Latin Manuscripts," 186–217. The Florence and Bautzen codices are described in Trombley, "New Frontiers." The Bautzen codex contains about 60 percent of the text, missing both the beginning and the end.

75. This is addressed in chapter 2.

76. Trombley, "New Frontiers," 158–164.

77. See Trombley, "Latin Manuscripts"; Trombley, "New Evidence on the Origins of the Latin *Mirror of Simple Souls* from a Forgotten Paduan Manuscript," *Journal of Medieval History* 43, no. 2 (2017): 138–139; and Trombley, "New Frontiers," 163–164.

the Latin *Mirror* in contemporary evidence—these are discussed in the succeeding chapters, particularly in chapter 1.

The exact origins of the Latin tradition are for the most part still obscure, but there has been significant progress made in recent years in guessing the *where* and the *when*. Sylvain Piron has noted that the language of the Latin denotes a translator who would have been French-speaking but unfamiliar with Marguerite's northern dialect; he therefore theorizes that the Latin may have originated somewhere in the Rhône Valley sometime between the years 1310 and 1330.[78] This is based on the dissemination of the word *philocapta*, which appears in the *Mirror* and which originated in the work of the Catalan theologian Ramon Llull between 1273 and 1283.[79] Piron theorizes that the Latin *Mirror* may have been brought to the Rhône Valley when attendees at the Council of Vienne were constructing the decree *Ad nostrum*.[80] An origin in the Rhône would also help to explain the *Mirror*'s swift appearance in Italy by the mid-fourteenth century.[81] Piron also suggests that the translator was a cleric, since some theological concepts are more precisely expressed in the Latin version than in the French, and that he may have been translating for a clerical audience.[82] My own work—which agrees with Piron's suggestion of the Rhône Valley—has argued that the latest possible date for composition of the Latin is 1317. This is drawn from evidence from the Paduan text discussed in chapter 4, evidence that suggests it is a later copy of a work written prior to 1317.[83]

In all the *Mirror*'s traditions, Marguerite's authorship and her fate remained distinctly separate from her book.[84] With the exception of the Italian manuscripts attributed to Margarita of Hungary, in all its manuscript copies the *Mirror* circulated as an anonymous text. While Marguerite's name could have been deliberately removed from surviving copies of her work in the immediate aftermath of her execution, it is also possible that her name never appeared prominently in the work to begin with. Similarly, the memory of the *Mirror*'s condemnation in Paris did not endure over time; even those who attacked the *Mirror* later did so without knowing it had been previously condemned. No

---

78. Sylvain Piron, "Marguerite, entre les béguines et les maîtres," in *Marguerite Porete et le "Miroir des simples âmes": Perspectives historiques, philosophiques et littéraires*, 88.

79. Piron, "Marguerite, entre," 87.

80. Piron, "Marguerite, entre," 88.

81. Piron, "Marguerite, entre," 88. The Latin *Mirror*'s date of origin is discussed further in chapter 4.

82. Piron, "Marguerite, entre," 88.

83. Trombley, "New Evidence," 149–150. I also suggest that Piron's evidence on the word *philocapta* indicates that the earliest possible date could even be pushed back to 1308. The details of my argument for the Paduan text are summarized in chapter 4.

84. The name *Margarita* did appear in some manuscripts later on but not in explicit reference to Marguerite Porete. This will be discussed further in chapters 1 and 2.

one really reunited the *Mirror* with Marguerite Porete and her fate until the twentieth century. Perhaps the most amusing example of how far the *Mirror* had drifted from the story of Marguerite came in 1927, when Clare Kirchberger, under the auspices of the Downside Benedictines—a monastic community in Somerset, England—published a modern English version of the book and the Vatican gave it the *nihil obstat* and *imprimatur*, the official stamps of approval allowing it to be published.[85] It was not until 1945 that the Italian scholar Romana Guarnieri, seeing connections between the excerpts quoted in Marguerite's trial documents and certain passages in the *Mirror*, finally brought the two together again, announcing that Marguerite Porete was the author of *The Mirror of Simple Souls*.[86] Within the last ten years some have questioned the certainty of this attribution.[87] But Sean Field, Robert Lerner, and Sylvain Piron, after a reappraisal of the evidence, have convincingly reaffirmed Marguerite's authorship of the *Mirror*.[88]

# The Orthodox Heretic? Marguerite, *The Mirror of Simple Souls*, and the Latin *Mirror* in Scholarship

The twin stories of Marguerite Porete and her *Mirror* are undoubtedly compelling, peppered as they are with tragedy, mystery, and unexpected success. Since Guarnieri announced in 1945 that *The Mirror of Simple Souls* was authored by a woman burned at the stake for heresy, there has been a surge in studies of both, to the point that "Marguerite studies" or "*Mirror* studies" are almost a field unto themselves. Literary and theological analyses of the *Mirror* have undoubtedly been the dominant focus. Scholars have examined its relationship to and affinity with other mystical writings (both "beguine" and otherwise), its borrowing

---

85. Marguerite Porete, *The Mirror of Simple Souls, by an Unknown French Mystic of the Thirteenth Century, Translated into English by M.N.*, ed. Clare Kirchberger (London: Orchard Books, 1927).

86. Romana Guarnieri, "Lo 'Specchio delle anime semplice' e Margherita Porete," *L'Osservatore Romano*, 16 June 1946. Reprinted in Guarnieri, "Il movimento," 661–663.

87. Lydia Wegener, "Freiheitsdiskurs und Beginenverfolgung um 1308—der Fall der Marguerite Porete," in *1308: Eine Topographie historischer Gleichzeitigkeit*, ed. Andreas Speer and David Wirmer (Berlin, De Gruyter, 2010), 205–207; and Elizabeth A. R. Brown, "Marguerite Porète, une béguine brûlée pour hérésie," in *L'affaire des Templiers, du procès au mythe*, ed. Ghislain Brunel (Paris: Archives Nationale de France, 2011), 50; Brown, "Jean Gerson, Marguerite Porete, and Romana Guarnieri: The Evidence Reconsidered," *Revue d'histoire ecclésiastique* 108, no. 3–4 (2013); and Brown, "Veritas à la cour de Philippe le Bel de France: Pierre Dubois, Guillaume de Nogaret et Marguerite Porete," in *La vérité: Vérité et crédibilité: Construire la vérité dans le système de communication de l'Occident (XIIIᵉ–XVIIᵉ siècle)*, ed. Jean-Philippe Genet (Paris-Rome, Éditions de la Sorbonne/École française de Rome, 2015).

88. Sean L. Field, Robert E. Lerner, and Sylvain Piron, "A Return to the Evidence for Marguerite Porete's Authorship of *The Mirror of Simple Souls*," *Journal of Medieval History* 43, no. 2 (2017).

from the literary tradition of courtly love poems, and its various philosophical and theological concepts.[89] For many years historical studies of Marguerite Porete were few and far between, but the past fifteen years or so have seen a flurry of new research on the topic, with Sean Field's book-length examination of Marguerite's trial and execution among the most substantial.[90] But when it comes to historical—rather than literary, theological, or philological—studies of the *Mirror*, there remain many significant gaps. This is particularly acute in the areas of codicology and the reception of the various *Mirror* manuscripts. In other words, while the words of the *Mirror* have been examined in meticulous detail, the actual vessels of those words, the manuscripts, have yet to receive the same level of scrutiny. This has begun to be remedied in the French tradition through excellent studies by Geneviève Hasenohr, Zan Kocher, and Pablo Acosta García.[91] Marleen Cré has done significant work on the Middle English manuscripts, and Dávid Falvay on the Italian.[92] These scholars have shown just how much even an initial foray into these manuscripts can offer when it comes to enriching our understanding of not just the *Mirror* and Marguerite Porete but also late medieval spirituality, readership, and textual circulation.

89. The literature is too vast to be fully recounted here; on theological studies and beguine mystics see footnote 105. A few notable examples on Marguerite's courtly themes are Barbara Newman, "The Mirror and the Rose: Marguerite Porete's Encounter with the *Dieu d'Amours*," in *The Vernacular Spirit: Essays on Medieval Religious Literature*, ed. Renate Blumenfeld-Kosinski, Duncan Robertson, and Nancy Bradley Warren (New York: Palgrave Macmillan, 2002); Newman, *Medieval Crossover: Reading the Secular against the Sacred* (South Bend, IN: University of Notre Dame Press, 2013), chapter 3; Kocher, *Allegories of Love*; Maguire Robinson, *Nobility and Annihilation*. For an excellent overview of theological and literary studies, see Sean L. Field, Robert E. Lerner, and Sylvain Piron, "Marguerite Porete et son *Miroir*: Perspectives historiographiques," in *Marguerite Porete et le "Miroir de simples âmes": Perspectives historiques, philosophiques et littéraires*, 9–23.

90. Field, *The Beguine*. Other notable historical studies of Marguerite and her trial have been Field, "The Master and Marguerite"; Van Engen, "Marguerite and the Low Countries"; Ansgar Kelly, "Inquisitorial Cover-Ups"; Courtenay, "Marguerite's Judges"; Piron, "Marguerite in Champagne"; and Danielle Dubois, "Transmitting the Memory of a Medieval Heretic: Early Modern French Historians on Marguerite Porete," *French Historical Studies* 41, no. 4 (2018).

91. Hasenohr, "La tradition"; Hasenohr, "Retour sur les caractères linguistiques du manuscrit de Chantilly et de ses ancêtres," in *Marguerite Porete et le "Miroir des simples âmes": Perspectives historiques, philosophiques et littéraires*; Hasenohr, "La seconde vie"; Kocher, "Apothecary's Mirror"; Pablo Acosta García, "The Marginalia of Marguerite Porete's *Le Mirouer des simple âmes*: Towards a History of the Reading of the Chantilly Manuscript," *Critica del testo* 15, no. 1 (2012); Acosta García, "Forgotten Marginalia and the French and Latin Manuscript Tradition," *Anuario de estudios medievales* 44, no. 1 (2014); and Acosta García, "Notez bien, bonnes pucelles."

92. Cré, *Mysticism in the Charterhouse*; Cré, "Women in the Charterhouse?"; Cré, "Contexts and Comments: The Chastising of God's Children and Marguerite Porète's *Mirour of Simple Souls* in Oxford, MS Bodley 505," in *Medieval Texts in Context*, ed. Graham D. Caie and Denis Reveney (London: Routledge, 2008); Falvay, "Italian Version of the *Mirror*"; Falvay and Konrád Eszter, "Osservanza francescana e letteratura in volgare dall'Italia all'Ungheria: Richerche e perspettive," in *Osservanza francescana e cultura tra Quattrocento e primo Cinquecento: Italia e Ungheria a confronto: [Atti del Convegno (Macerata-Sarnano, 6–7 dicembre 2013)]*, ed. Francesca Bartolacci and Roberto Lambertini (Rome: Viella, 2014).

When it comes to the Latin tradition, there was—and to a large extent still is—an even bigger gap in the scholarship.[93] The Latin has mostly played a supporting role in the study of the French tradition, being used as part of the effort to reconstruct what an original *Mirror* may have looked like and to trace the *Mirror*'s various metamorphoses into the texts we have now.[94] Apart from these brief mentions, there have previously been only two major publications that treat the Latin tradition in its own right. The first came from Guarnieri in 1965, when she published her landmark "Il movimento del libero spirito." This publication included a vast chronology detailing what Guarnieri believed to be the history of free spiritism as a cohesive doctrine in medieval Europe. It is in this chronology that Guarnieri assembled and brought attention to the incidents surrounding the Latin and Italian *Mirror* in fifteenth-century Italy, which are discussed at length in this book.[95] She also edited and published important primary sources in the appendix, including letters relating to an inquisition against the *Mirror* in Venice (discussed in chapter 1) and the list of errors from MS Vat. lat. 4953 (discussed in chapter 3).[96]

The second major publication appeared in 1986, when Paul Verdeyen published a standard edition of the Latin, printed page-facing with Guarnieri's edition of the Chantilly codex. Verdeyen made his edition using the readings of five of the six surviving *Mirror* copies that were known to exist at that time (excluding the excerpts from MS Vat. lat. 4953) and with MS Vat. lat. 4355 (his manuscript "A") as the main basis.[97] In this edition, Verdeyen included an introduction in which he listed and briefly described the six known codices.[98] Verdeyen's introduction and edition of the Latin remained the main historical and textual sources of information on the Latin tradition for over thirty years. In 2013, Michael Sargent published an overview of the Latin tradition, summing up some of Guarnieri's arguments, putting forth some of his own suggestions as to its original translation and audience, and discussing its linguistic relationship to the

---

93. Such a large gap also exists for the Italian tradition; to my knowledge the work of Dávid Falvay is the only scholarship to focus on the Italian since Guarnieri. See preceding note.

94. Hasenohr noted that the Latin was probably made from an ancestor of the Valenciennes text. "La tradition," 1358. In examining Hasenohr's findings, Robert Lerner has suggested that the Latin tradition is a doctrinally tamer version of the *Mirror* than some of its vernacular counterparts. "New Light on the *Mirror of Simple Souls*," *Speculum* 85 (2010): 110–111. This position is questioned in Trombley, "Latin Manuscripts," 193–194.

95. Guarnieri, "Il movimento," 466–477.

96. Guarnieri, "Il movimento," 645–660.

97. *Speculum CCCM*. The manuscripts unknown at the time were Padua, Biblioteca universitaria di Padova, MS 1647; Bautzen, Domstiftsbibliothek Sankt Petri, MS M I 15; and Florence, Biblioteca nazionale centrale, MS Conv. soppr. G.3.1130.

98. Paul Verdeyen, Introduction to *Speculum CCCM*, viii–xii.

Italian version.[99] In 2017 Pablo Acosta García published a full transcription of the marginalia found in each of the then-known Latin manuscripts.[100] Also in 2017 I published an overview of the Latin manuscripts that modified or updated some of Verdeyen's descriptions.[101] A few of my own publications have investigated some aspects of the Latin's origins and late medieval reception.[102] Perhaps because many studies of the *Mirror*'s linguistic traditions have been focused on reconstructing what an original *Mirror* would have looked like, the Latin often features as a distant and only supporting actor in the story. Perhaps, too, because it is in Latin, it is less exciting than the rich narrative of the new and innovative vernacular spiritual writings that exploded into view in the later Middle Ages. Latin is "old school." One basic aim of this book, then, is to partially fill in this gap and provide in-depth analysis of the Latin tradition in its own right, examining both its manuscripts and the history of its reception.

Of course, studying something because it is unstudied is not necessarily a virtue on its own, although knowledge for knowledge's sake should also not be considered a vice. But the Latin, when taken alongside the larger backdrop of the *Mirror*'s various traditions, feeds into some important historiographical questions surrounding both the *Mirror* and Marguerite Porete herself. Overall, the impression of the *Mirror*'s post-1310 reception has been a positive one. The *Mirror* seemingly overcame its initial difficulties and became orthodox, leaving behind the stain of heresy. Much of the aforementioned scholarship on the *Mirror*'s reception has highlighted this success. While largely occupying a supporting role, the existence of the Latin has at the same time been seen as the crowning achievement of the *Mirror*'s escape from condemnation, its official stamp of approval. When viewed alongside the positive reception the *Mirror* had in its vernacular traditions, the Latin solidifies the compelling narrative of success for the *Mirror*.

This apparent success creates a disconnect between Marguerite Porete's brutal fate and the later history of her book. Why did Marguerite burn at the stake for a book that was later accepted by so many? Or, to reverse the question, why did so many accept a book for which its author had been burned as a heretic? Compounding the issue is the fact that the master theologians who judged her book in Paris left behind no indication of their reasoning or their deliberations

---

99. Sargent, "Latin and Italian."

100. Acosta García, "Notez bien, bonnes pucelles."

101. Trombley, "The Latin Manuscripts," 186–217.

102. Trombley, "New Evidence"; Trombley, "New Frontiers"; Trombley, "The Text as Heretic: Mixed Genres and Polemical Techniques in a Refutation of the *Mirror of Simple Souls*," *Medieval Worlds* 7 (2018); and Trombley, "Self-Defence and Its Limits in Marguerite Porete's *Mirror of Simple Souls*," *Nottingham Medieval Studies* 63 (2019).

on the *Mirror*'s orthodoxy; we are left only with their judgment that the articles they had seen were heretical. This tension is then heightened further when studies show the influences on the *Mirror* and its affinity with other orthodox theological and mystical writings, both early and contemporary.[103] If the *Mirror* contained the same ideas as texts by Augustine, or Bernard of Clairvaux, or other beguines such as Hadewijch of Brabant and Mechthild von Magdeburg— neither of whom ended at the stake—then its condemnation begins to look less like a reaction to heresy and more like a misunderstanding, or even a deliberate misreading. There have been several studies that on some level have tried to reconcile this seemingly disparate history. One strain of scholarship, particularly in the immediate decades after Guarnieri's announcement, debated whether or not Marguerite was a "real" heretic after all. Some were adamant that her ideas were undoubtedly heretical, while others were more ambivalent.[104] This debate over the *Mirror*'s orthodoxy has now largely subsided, with most scholars seeing it as something of a moot point, at least in terms of its relevance to historical inquiry.

In a related vein, the contrast between Marguerite's fate and her *Mirror*'s success has also influenced scholarly views of the reasons for both of their condemnations in 1310. Such condemnations, when compared with the later reception of the *Mirror*, seem anomalous. That is, if so many later readers of the *Mirror* embraced it as good and useful, or only had slight misgivings about it, then those who condemned Marguerite and her *Mirror* could not have really done so because they truly believed the *Mirror* was heretical; other factors must have been at play. A number of factors have been suggested: the narrow-minded judgment of her persecutors, who were unable (or unwilling) to "properly" understand Marguerite's words as they were meant; the Parisian theologians being given an out-of-context compilation of the *Mirror*'s errors,

---

103. To mention just a few works in this area (of which there are many): Kurt Ruh, "Beginenmystik: Hadewijch, Mechthild von Magdeburg, Marguerite Porete," *Zeitschrift für Deutsches Altertum und Deutsche Literatur* 106 (1977); Bernard McGinn, *The Flowering of Mysticism: Men and Women in the New Mysticism, 1200–1350* (New York: Crossroad, 1998), 199–265; Wendy R. Terry, *Seeing Marguerite in the Mirror: A Linguistic Analysis of Porete's "Mirror of Simple Souls"* (Leuven: Peeters, 2011); Danielle Dubois, "Natural and Supernatural Virtues in the Thirteenth Century: The Case of Marguerite Porete's *Mirror of Simple Souls*," *Journal of Medieval History* 43, no. 2 (2017).

104. For the "heretical" camp, see Stephanus Axters, *Geschiedenis van de Vroomheid in de Nederlanden*, vol. 2 (Antwerp: De Sikkel, 1953), 466–469; Edmund Colledge and Romana Guarnieri, "The Glosses by 'M. N.' and Richard Methley to 'The Mirror of Simple Souls,'" appendix to *Middle English Mirror, Archivio italiano per la storia della pietà* 5 (1968): 381–382. See also the quotation of Colledge in Michael Sargent, "Medieval and Modern Readership of Marguerite Porete's *Mirouer des simples âmes anienties*: The French and English Traditions," in *Middle English Religious Writing in Practice: Texts, Readers, and Transformations*, ed. Nicole Rice (Turnhout: Brepols, 2013), 65. For the "ambivalent" camp, see Jean Orcibal, "Le 'Miroir des simples âmes' et la 'secte' du Libre Esprit," *Revue de l'histoire des religions* 176 (1969); Robert E. Lerner, *The Heresy of the Free Spirit in the Later Middle Ages* (Berkeley: University of California Press, 1972), 208.

making them look more heretical than they actually were; the composition of her book in the vernacular (and therefore automatically suspicious); and the political machinations of the Capetian court, committed to condemning Marguerite so that they might have a "true" heretic to burn as an example.[105] Marguerite is also seen as having been condemned mainly on the basis of her actions, rather than her ideas.[106] All of these in some way—whether consciously or unconsciously—set the *Mirror* itself to one side, rendering the question of its perceived heresy as either irrelevant or only tangentially important to it and Marguerite's condemnation in 1310.

It is undeniable that some or all of the above factors played a role in Marguerite's condemnation.[107] There is also no doubt that the *Mirror* enjoyed a great deal of popularity in the late Middle Ages. My goal here is not to discount these factors but to add another layer to the story. The main aim of this book is to argue that heresy did play an important part in the *Mirror*'s history, that it never fully left behind the controversy that marked its earliest circulation. To be clear, I am not reviving the old argument over the *Mirror*'s orthodoxy. The question is not, was the *Mirror* heretical? Instead, I want to ask, did *medieval readers* believe that the *Mirror* was heretical? This book shows that some certainly did, and did so with firm conviction. What is more, the evidence for this comes not from the vernacular but from the Latin tradition. The new evidence examined here provides what is missing from the Parisian theologians' condemnation: the reasons the *Mirror*'s critics thought it was heretical. It shows that those who attacked the *Mirror* saw in it ideas that they believed went against fundamental Christian tenets and church doctrine. Furthermore, their arguments reveal that they launched these criticisms entirely in ignorance of the *Mirror*'s previous condemnations in Paris and Valenciennes. This was not a case of the past coming back to haunt the *Mirror*. Instead, this book shows that the *Mirror* was a text that could provoke condemnation repeatedly—and entirely separately from all the forces that surrounded it in Valenciennes and Paris.[108]

---

105. For example, see Lerner, *The Heresy of the Free Spirit*, 75–77; Georgette Epiney-Burgard and Emilie Zum Brunn, *Women Mystics in Medieval Europe*, trans. Sheila Hughes (New York: Paragon, 1989), 144–145; Michael G. Sargent, "The Annihilation of Marguerite Porete," *Viator* 28 (1997): 266–268; and Else Marie Wiberg Pedersen, "Heterodoxy or Orthodoxy of Holy Women's Texts: What Makes a Holy Woman's Text Holy?", in *Cultures of Religious Reading: Instructing the Soul, Feeding the Spirit, and Awakening the Passion*, ed. Sabrina Corbellini (Turnhout: Brepols, 2013), 25 and 30.

106. Field, *The Beguine*, 163; Field, "Debating the Historical Marguerite Porete," in *A Companion to Marguerite Porete and "The Mirror of Simple Souls*," 19.

107. Field's work in particular has shown how carefully Marguerite's case was crafted by William of Paris and the interest that Capetian agents took in her case. Ansgar Kelly argues for an even higher level of interference and "abuse"; see Kelly, "Inquisitorial Deviations."

108. As Kathryn Kerby-Fulton has put it, "The *Mirror* was a book under suspicion that, even in *utter anonymity*, re-created new suspicions." *Books under Suspicion*, 276.

# The Late Medieval Heretical Landscape

The treatment of the *Mirror* as a heretical book played out against the larger back-drop of late medieval heresy and persecution. Heresy in the late Middle Ages, as Sean Field and Michael Bailey have recently pointed out, is often dominated in scholarship by the English Lollards and the Bohemian Hussites, but the fourteenth and fifteenth centuries saw a broad range of dissident intellectuals, groups, proph-ets, and visionaries.[109] The initial tribulations of Marguerite and her *Mirror* came at a turning point in the history of medieval heresy. By the early decades of the fourteenth century, the sect that had been seen as the main enemy of orthodoxy for centuries, the so-called Cathars, had been largely stamped out in Languedoc in the South of France, its main stronghold.[110] The other large-scale heretical movement of the twelfth and thirteenth centuries, the Waldensians, had been driven out of sight into a more clandestine existence.[111] New threats, however—or, perhaps more accurately, new fears—were beginning to emerge. Most were not cohesive mass movements—although they were certainly perceived as such by those in power—but were rather intellectual and spiritual groups and trends that had been developing for decades within the church itself.

In many ways, heresies in the fourteenth and fifteenth centuries came from the church turning in on itself in an attitude of fear and increased suspicion over visions, revelations, intellectual errors, and diabolical influences. The def-inition of heresy expanded to include an ever more diverse range of actions and beliefs, and many of these new heresies came from groups previously con-sidered to be pillars of orthodoxy. For example, roughly contemporarily with Marguerite's travails, the Franciscan Order saw itself torn into various pieces over the issue of poverty, a crisis that developed out of the decades-long tension between the strict "Spirituals" and the more pragmatic "Conventuals."[112] The Spirituals' zeal for absolute poverty eventually melded with a strain of Joachite apocalypticism, which made for a potent mixture.[113] In 1318 four Spiritual

109. Michael D. Bailey and Sean L. Field, Introduction to *Late Medieval Heresy: New Perspectives*, 1–13. Without intending to diminish their importance in any way, I will not discuss the Lollard and Hussite movements here, given how well known and well documented they are.

110. For a clear summary of the chronology of medieval heresy, again see Bailey and Field, Intro-duction to *Late Medieval Heresy: New Perspectives*, 2–3

111. While the Waldensians were "down," they were by no means "out"; they continued to be persecuted throughout the fourteenth and fifteenth centuries. See Peter Biller, *The Waldenses: 1170–1530* (Ashgate: Aldershot, 2001), and also recent work by Reima Välimäki on large-scale inquisitions against Waldensians in Germany at the end of the fourteenth century. Välimäki, *Heresy in Late Medieval Ger-many: The Inquisitor Petrus Zwicker and the Waldensians* (Woodbridge, UK: Boydell and Brewer, 2019).

112. These were by no means neat categories, but I use these terms for the sake of simplicity.

113. This particular conflict also touched Marguerite's trial; as noted earlier, Marguerite's sole defender was Guiard of Cressonessart, whose self-conception and worldview were rooted in a

Franciscans were burned at the stake in Marseilles for refusing to yield on their position over poverty; this touched off decades of inquisitions aimed at crushing their lay followers, known to scholarship as "Beguins."[114] Once again, Languedoc was the site of these persecutions. Here, too, we find a burned book. The Apocalypse commentary of the Narbonne Franciscan Peter of John Olivi provocatively combined the two issues of poverty and apocalypticism, and his book played a starring role in the conflict, having taken on a quasi-scriptural meaning for those being persecuted in Languedoc. Also like the *Mirror*, it was condemned as heretical twice, by panels of theologians commissioned by Pope John XXII: once in 1318 and again in 1326.[115] The pursuit of the rebel Spirituals and their followers lasted decades, beginning in Languedoc and then moving to Italy. A main persecutor of this group in Italy in the fifteenth century—where they were known as the *Fraticelli*—was the Franciscan Giovanni of Capestrano, whom we will meet in chapter 1, as he also turned his inquisitorial eye to the *Mirror*.

Another growing fear in this era was the influence of diabolical forces, which manifested itself in two distinct areas: that of magic and sorcery, and that of visions and revelations. The former grew in intensity over the course of the fourteenth century, famously gaining momentum in the pontificate of John XXII, who linked sorcery to heresy in his bull *Super illius specula*, a bull that was subsequently included several decades later in the inquisitor Nicholas Eymerich's inquisitors' manual, the *Directorium inquisitorum*.[116] Sorcerers, necromancers, and witches, thought to make willing pacts with demons and other diabolical forces in order to gain power, riches, or (particularly in the case of witches) to engage in carnal depravities, were brought into inquisito-

Joachite conception of church history that closely echoed the Spirituals' worldview. See Field's contextualization in *The Beguine*, particularly chapter 5, "Philadelphia Story."

114. Overviews of both the intra-Franciscan conflict and the persecutions in Languedoc can be found in David Burr, *The Spiritual Franciscans: From Protest to Persecution in the Century After Saint Francis* (University Park: Penn State University Press, 2001), and Louisa Burnham, *So Great a Light, So Great a Smoke: The Beguin Heretics of Languedoc* (Ithaca, NY: Cornell University Press, 2008). Delfi I. Nieto Isabel has done pioneering work on the transmission of beliefs and the intricate social networks of the Beguin movement, in addition to other heretical movements. See "Communities of Dissent: Social Network Analysis of Religious Dissident Groups in Languedoc in the Thirteenth and Fourteenth Centuries" (PhD diss., University of Barcelona, 2018); see also Nieto Isabel, "Beliefs in Progress: The Beguins of Languedoc and the Construction of a New Heretical Identity," *SUMMA: Revista de Cultures Medievals* 15 (2020); Nieto Isabel, "Overlapping Networks: Beguins, Franciscans, and Poor Clares at the Crossroads of a Shared Spirituality," in *Clarisas y dominicas: Modelos de implantación, filiación, promoción y devoción en la Península Ibérica, Cerdeña, Nápoles y Sicilia*, ed. Gemma Teresa Colesanti, Blanca Garí, and Núria Jornet-Benito (Florence: Firenze University Press, 2017).

115. David Burr, *Olivi's Peaceable Kingdom: A Reading of the Apocalypse Commentary* (Philadelphia: University of Pennsylvania Press, 1993), 198–239.

116. Michael D. Bailey, "Magic, Mysticism, and Heresy in the Early Fourteenth Century," in *Late Medieval Heresy: New Perspectives*, 71–72.

rial jurisdiction as threats to Christendom. Meanwhile, fears of less overt, more deceitful diabolical influences through visions and revelations also increased in intensity. Revelatory and visionary experiences—particularly those experienced by women—were subjected to increasing suspicion. Fearing that an "angel of Satan" could masquerade as an "angel of light" and deceive those who had such experiences and, by association, those who listened and accorded authority to such figures, visionary activity was subjected to intensifying scrutiny and "testing."[117] The discernment of the veracity of such experiences became more codified over the course of the fourteenth century, so that by the fifteenth century it was nearly its own discipline. This was arguably exacerbated by the Great Schism (1378–1417), a time in which competing papal courts and their supporters each had their own visionaries, prophets, and saints who all claimed divine favor for their respective sides.[118]

But the most significant development regarding perceptions of the *Mirror* was the church's fear over the so-called "heresy of the free spirit." The *Mirror*'s ideas of achieving a state of spiritual perfection in this lifetime, where one has no care for church works or virtuous practices and claims freedom from sin, were solidified in the fourteenth and fifteenth centuries into the doctrine of a coherent "sect" of free spirits. While this fear was not immediately born out of the *Mirror*'s persecution in 1310—suspicions had arisen over similar ideas between 1307 and 1308 in Cologne—the century after Marguerite's condemnation saw numerous inquisitions directed against just these concepts, and there is reason to believe that the *Mirror* was a main source for the church's legislation against this perceived sect.[119] A little over a year after Marguerite Porete was burned at the stake, the decree *Ad nostrum* was drawn up at the Council of Vienne (1311–1312), a council attended by a number of figures who had been involved in Marguerite's case.[120] This decree attributed eight errors to the sect of the beghards and beguines, which read as follows:

1. That a person in this present life can acquire a degree of perfection, which renders him utterly impeccable and unable to make further progress in grade.

---

117. The "angel of Satan/angel of light" metaphor is from 2 Corinthians 11:14. On increased suspicion of women visionaries and the discernment of spirits, see Dyan Elliott, *Proving Woman: Female Spirituality and Inquisitional Culture in the Later Middle Ages* (Princeton: Princeton University Press); Nancy Caciola, *Discerning Spirits: Divine and Demonic Possession in the Middle Ages* (Ithaca, NY: Cornell University Press, 2003); and Wendy Love Anderson, *The Discernment of Spirits: Assessing Visions and Visionaries in the Late Middle Ages* (Tübingen: Mohr Siebeck, 2011).

118. Renate Blumenfeld-Kosinski, *Poets, Saints, and Visionaries of the Great Schism, 1378–1417* (Philadelphia: University of Pennsylvania Press, 2006).

119. Lerner, *Heresy of the Free Spirit*, 66, 67, and 78–181.

120. See Field, *The Beguine*, 193–204.

2. That it is not necessary to fast or pray after gaining this degree of perfection, for then the sensitive appetite has been so perfectly subjected to the spirit and to reason that one may freely grant the body whatever pleases it.

3. That those who have reached the said degree of perfection and spirit of liberty are not subject to human obedience, nor obliged to any commandments of the church.

4. That a person can gain in this life final beatitude in every degree of perfection that he will obtain in the life of the blessed.

5. That any intellectual nature in itself is naturally blessed, and that the soul does not need the light of glory to elevate it to see God and enjoy him blissfully.

6. That the practice of the virtues belongs to the state of imperfection and the perfect soul is free from virtues.

7. That to kiss a woman is a mortal sin since nature does not incline one to it, but the act of intercourse is not a sin, especially in time of temptation, since it is an inclination of nature.

8. That at the elevation of the body of Jesus Christ, they ought not to rise or show reverence to it; it would be an imperfection for them to come down from the purity and height of their contemplation so far as to think about the ministry or sacrament of the Eucharist, or about the passion of Christ as man.[121]

Scholars have long believed that *The Mirror of Simple Souls* was one of the main sources used in constructing this list, at least for the first six errors, which bear a close resemblance to several of the *Mirror*'s main concepts.[122] But this association has been critiqued in the past. Michael Sargent has argued that the textual relationship between the *Mirror* and *Ad nostrum* is weaker than many scholars have thought.[123] More recently Olivier Boulnois has suggested that *Ad nostrum* seems to be a conglomeration of errors from several different theologi-

---

121. Clementines 5.3.3. Emil Friedberg, ed., *Clementis Papae V Constitutiones*, in *Corpus Iuris Canonicis*, vol. 2 (Leipzig: C. Focke, 1888), cols. 1183–1184. The English translations here—which also appear alongside a transcript of the Latin—are taken from Elizabeth Makowski, "When is A Beguine Not a Beguine?" in *Labels and Libels: Naming Beguines in Northern Medieval Europe*, ed. Letha Böhringer, Jennifer Kolpacoff Deane, and Hildo van Engen (Turnhout: Brepols, 2014), 94–95. On the modifications made to *Ad nostrum* between its inception and publication, see Jacqueline Tarrant, "The Clementine Decrees on the Beguines: Conciliar and Papal Versions," *Archivum Historiae Pontificae* 12 (1974).

122. For a discussion of these similarities, see Lerner, *The Heresy of the Free Spirit*, 81–83; Kent Emery Jr., Foreword to *The Mirror of Simple Souls*, trans. Colledge, Grant, and Marler, ix and xi; Field, *The Beguine*, 197–199; and Trombley, "New Evidence," 147–148.

123. Michael Sargent, "'Le Mirouer des simples âmes' and the English Mystical Tradition," in *Abendländische Mystik im Mittelalter*, ed. Kurt Ruh (Stuttgart: Springer, 1986), 461.

cal issues of the day, issues that included doctrine similar to Marguerite's but also comprised errors from Joachimism and errors found in Cologne and Strasbourg.[124] As this book will show, however, several of the *Mirror*'s medieval critics did closely associate the *Mirror* with the heresy of the free spirit and *Ad nostrum*.

Robert Lerner has famously demonstrated that *Ad nostrum* effectively created the doctrine of a coherent sect of free spirits where there in fact was none.[125] Instead, what we find is a loose conglomeration of individuals who held ideas or had experiences that were then connected to those errors listed in the decree. The persecution that followed *Ad nostrum*'s formal publication as part of the Clementine decrees in 1317 was very real, however, with Richard Kieckhefer dramatically describing it as a "war" against beghards and beguines.[126] The fourteenth century saw many investigations and repressions of beghards and beguines in Germany, and *Ad nostrum* became a standard interrogatory used in inquisitorial processes.[127] Also caught up in this controversy were certain mystics whose writings and sermons were perceived to contain elements of free spirit doctrines. The most famous example is that of the Dominican Meister Eckhart, who had a list of twenty-nine articles taken from his writings and sermons condemned in the 1329 bull *In agro dominico*. Many of the propositions in this bull resembled errors found in *Ad nostrum*, and like *Ad nostrum* it, too, was used as an inquisitorial interrogatory.[128] It should also be said that many of Meister Eckhart's concepts, metaphors, and modes of expression bear a striking resemblance to those found in the *Mirror*, so much so that several scholars have speculated that Eckhart may have read the *Mirror* himself.[129] While large-scale persecutions of beguines and beghards had largely

---

124. Olivier Boulnois, "Qu'est-ce que la liberté de l'esprit? La parole de Marguerite et la raison du théologien," in *Marguerite Porete et le "Miroir de simples âmes": Perspectives historiques, philosophiques et littéraires*, 130–131.

125. Lerner, *Heresy of the Free Spirit*. Lerner describes *Ad nostrum* as the heresy's "birth certificate" (83).

126. Richard Kieckhefer, *The Repression of Heresy in Medieval Germany* (Liverpool: University of Liverpool Press, 1979), 19.

127. For an overview of this repression see Lerner, *Heresy of the Free Spirit*, 65–163, and Kieckhefer, *Repression of Heresy*, 19–51. On the use of *Ad nostrum* in inquisition, see in general Lerner, *The Heresy of the Free Spirit*; Kieckhefer, *Repression of Heresy*, 21–32; and Lerner, "Meister Eckhart's Specter: Fourteenth-Century Uses of the Bull *In agro dominico* Including a Newly Discovered Inquisitorial Text of 1337," *Mediaeval Studies* 70 (2008).

128. Lerner, "Meister Eckhart's Specter."

129. On the similarities between Eckhart and the *Mirror*, and the possibility that Eckhart may have read the *Mirror*, see Edmund Colledge and J. C. Marler, "'Poverty of the Will': Ruusbroec, Eckhart, and *The Mirror of Simple Souls*," in *Jan van Ruusbroec: The Sources, Content, and Sequels of His Mysticism*, ed. Paul Mommaers and N. De Paepe (Leuven: Leuven University Press, 1984); the essays in Bernard McGinn, ed., *Meister Eckhart and the Beguine Mystics: Hadewijch of Brabant, Mechthild of Magdeburg, and Marguerite Porete* (New York: Continuum, 1994); Justine L. Trombley, "The Master and the Mirror: The Influence of Marguerite Porete on Meister Eckhart," *Magistra: A Journal of Women's Spirituality in History* 16, no. 1 (2010); Élodie Pinel, "Forme et sens chez Eckhart et Marguerite Porete," in *Maître Eckhart, une écriture inachevée:*

subsided by the fifteenth century, the threat of the errors of *Ad nostrum* and "free spirit" mysticism continued to linger in the minds of churchmen.[130] We will see this lingering fear directed at the *Mirror* throughout this book.

The heresy of the free spirit is the one most obviously linked to the *Mirror*, but the other late medieval heresies mentioned here—along with Lollardy and Hussitism—provided a background hum that overlapped and intertwined with some of the same ideas. The Olivian-Joachite apocalypticism that imbued the rebel Spiritual Franciscans contained the ideal of a new age of spiritual renewal and elevation that would render the reigning church hierarchy irrelevant, and in which humans could experience divine truth directly. This is akin to the *Mirror's* concept of annihilation—and one of the errors of *Ad nostrum*—in which the soul achieves the highest state of spiritual perfection and surpasses the need to practice ordinary prayers, sacraments, and virtues. In fact, none other than the famed bishop-inquisitor (and eventual Pope Benedict XII) Jacques Fournier linked the two concepts directly, saying that Olivi's new "spiritual intelligence" was a state of "impeccability" also espoused by those condemned in *Ad nostrum*.[131] In a similar vein, other critics of Olivi's commentary declared that his new spiritual age would mean humans would have direct knowledge of the divine in this lifetime; as we will see, the exact same charge would be made against the *Mirror*.[132] Furthermore, within her broader philosophy of rejecting anything and all to do with the self and the created world, Marguerite, too, advocated radical rejection of material goods. Michael Bailey has pointed out that the "inscrutability" of both mystical experiences and magical rites produced similarly troubled reactions from ecclesiastical authorities.[133] The charge that diabolical voices could deceive humans into believing they were performing good and divine acts, along with a fear of those who believed themselves to be above sin and who indulged in natural desires, appears in a few of the attacks on the *Mirror* discussed in this book. The list of connections between these various currents could go on, but such a study would probably fill another book. These examples serve merely to underscore the importance of viewing the *Mirror* and its nega-

---

*Nouvelles perspectives théologiques, philosophiques et littéraires*, ed. Élisabeth Boncour (Grenoble: Jérôme Millon, 2017).

130. See Lerner, *Heresy of the Free Spirit*, 164–181.

131. Sylvain Piron, "Recovering a Theological Advice by Jacques Fournier," in *Pope Benedict XII (1334–1342): The Guardian of Orthodoxy*, ed. Irene Bueno (Amsterdam: Amsterdam University Press, 2018), 63. The canonist Alvarus Pelagius (ca. 1280–1352), who served in the papal court of John XXII, also accused the Spiritual Franciscans and the Beguins of adhering to the articles of *Ad nostrum, in his De statu et planctu ecclesiae*. See Alfredo Cocci, "Alvaro Pais e il Libero Spirito: i capitoli 51 e 52 del libro secondo del 'De statu et planctu Ecclesiae,'" *L'Italia francescana: rivista trimestrale di cultura francescana* 58 (1983).

132. On these criticisms of Olivi see Burr, *Olivi's Peaceable Kingdom*, 226–227.

133. Bailey, "Magic and Mysticism."

tive receptions as one piece in the larger jigsaw of late medieval heresy, rather than as an isolated element that only belonged to one single heretical sphere. Those who attacked the *Mirror* had a number of heretical threats on their minds and saw many of those threats within its pages.

## Plan of the Book

This book is primarily organized around three manuscript case studies, with one chapter providing context and evidence from other contemporary sources. A general sense of chronology underlies the order in which they are presented, but it does not strictly dictate how the analysis proceeds. Instead, it is structured more around the different kinds of attacks the *Mirror* received: theological and canon-legal refutation, "character assassination" through tropes and heretical stereotypes, and physical destruction. Chapter 1 provides context to the three manuscripts, detailing the reception of the *Mirror* in Italy and Germany in the first half of the fifteenth century as it appears in contemporary records. The chapter analyzes the *Mirror's* numerous appearances in sermons, letters, monastic records, and inquisitions. These appearances demonstrate the complicated reception of the *Mirror*, highlighting both hostility and popularity, and the chapter outlines the implications of these appearances. Chapter 2 examines Oxford, Bodleian Library, MS Laud Latin 46, a manuscript that once contained a complete Latin *Mirror* but now holds only a few fragments, as the rest of the work was cut out of and/or unbound from the codex. In addition to providing new codicological information on the manuscript, this chapter shows the process of and reasons behind this *Mirror's* removal. It demonstrates how its textual company points toward an attitude of suspicion toward the codex as a whole and argues that it potentially has connections to both southern Germany and northern Italy. Chapter 3 looks at Vatican City, BAV, MS Vat. lat. 4953, which contains a theological refutation of several extracts taken from the *Mirror*, compiled as a list of errors. The chapter argues for the potential origins of this list in an inquisition against the *Mirror* conducted in Venice in 1437 and that it also likely had connections to debates between the Greek and Latin churches at the Council of Florence in 1439. It then examines the contents of the list itself, detailing the arguments and sources that were used to denounce the *Mirror's* doctrine. Chapter 4 examines the recently rediscovered Padua, Biblioteca universitaria di Padova, MS 1647 and gives the first in-depth analysis of its contents. This manuscript, like MS Vat. lat. 4953, contains a number of refuted errors taken from a Latin *Mirror* but takes a decidedly canon-legal approach to its refutations and employs vitriolic rhetoric that paints the *Mirror* as diabolical.

Throughout the book, I present examples of the *Mirror* being treated not just with unease or slight suspicion but as an undoubtedly heretical text. These examples show that the *Mirror* was considered heretical on both theological and legal grounds, but they also reveal that these attacks did not remain within the dry boundaries of purely academic refutation. The Latin *Mirror* was also assailed as diabolical and dangerous and attacked with classics from the antiheretical toolkit that had been used more often against people than against texts. The aim is not to discount or dismiss the positive reception of the *Mirror* but rather to show that a parallel thread of opposition ran alongside this acceptance. Following such a thread reveals the power the *Mirror* had, how its descriptions of self-negation and divine union could simultaneously compel and repel readers. Tracing the dark side of the *Mirror's* reception adds yet another layer of complexity to its multifaceted history and solidifies its place as one of the most intriguing and important mystical works of the late Middle Ages.

# CHAPTER 1

# "Worthless, Deceptive, and Dangerous"

Controversies over *The Mirror of Simple Souls*
in the Fifteenth Century

Religious life in the fourteenth and fifteenth cen-
turies was once defined by a narrative of decline, decadence, and stagnation.[1]
Freed from this narrative over the past several decades, the period is now shown
to be a vibrant, multifaceted world in which anxiety and restriction moved side-
by-side with enthusiasm and innovation.[2] Disruptions such as the Great Schism,
the emergence of Lollardy and Hussitism, the Hundred Years' War, and the
ensuing power struggle between papal and conciliar authorities in the years following the Schism contributed to an atmosphere of crisis, decline, and suspicion. But growing with and in some ways out of these upheavals were also
currents of renewed spiritual fervor, devotional practices, and intellectual activity. The period saw a deepening of participation in contemplative, ascetic, and
penitential practices and new spiritual movements, the expansion of universities and with them the emergence of humanism (and its opponents) and "public intellectuals," and an explosion in the production and consumption of

---

1. Johan Huizinga, *The Autumn of the Middle Ages*, trans. Rodney J. Payton and Ulrich Mammitzsch
(Chicago: University of Chicago Press, 1996); see also Howard Kaminsky's historiographical essay, "From
Lateness to Waning to Crisis: The Burden of the Middle Ages," *Journal of Early Modern History* 4, no. 1
(2000).
2. John Van Engen, "Multiple Options: The World of the Fifteenth Century Church," *Church History* 77, no. 2 (2008); see also Van Engen, "A World Astir: Europe and Religion in the Early Fifteenth
Century," in *Europe After Wyclif*, ed. J. Patrick Hornbeck II and Michael Van Dussen (Fordham, NY: Fordham University Press, 2016).

religious texts, both Latin and vernacular.[3] Alongside the expansion of lay devotion, religious orders were caught up in the "Observant" movement, which made impassioned calls for reform, emphasizing a return to their original spiritual foundations and strict observance of institutional rules.[4] Each of these developments—lay devotion, humanism, textual production, reform—met with and fostered both enthusiasm and hostility, as each one trod the fine and subjective line of what was and was not considered acceptable. To borrow from John Van Engen, the world of late medieval religion was "astir" with growth and decay, celebration and demonization, innovation and restriction.[5]

The circulation of *The Mirror of Simple Souls* was caught up in these currents, and its reception can almost be seen as a microcosm of this varied spiritual world. Particularly within fifteenth-century Italy, there is abundant evidence that the *Mirror* provoked not just suspicion but outright hostility, often from luminaries of the Observant movement. This atmosphere, however, coexisted with—and perhaps was fed by—a parallel one in which the *Mirror* was read and accepted with little or no concern, in a wide range of reading circles: lay, semi-religious, and even within some of the most eminent and distinguished Observant religious houses and congregations. This chapter sets these controversies in a new light.[6] While most of the events described here take place in Italy, the chapter shows that hostility to the *Mirror* can also be glimpsed in Germany. It also provides the broader contextual background to the manuscripts that are analyzed in the following chapters, detailing the environments out of which they may have been created and in which they may have been used.

## The Preacher: Bernardino of Siena

In the existing summaries, the *Mirror*'s fifteenth-century troubles always begin with Bernardino of Siena, one of the four "pillars" of the Franciscan Obser-

---

3. Van Engen, "Multiple Options"; Van Engen, "A World Astir"; Van Engen, *Sisters and Brothers of the Common Life: The Devotio Moderna and the World of the Later Middle Ages* (Philadelphia: University of Pennsylvania Press, 2008); Daniel Hobbins, "The Schoolman as Public Intellectual: Jean Gerson and the Late Medieval Tract," *The American Historical Review* 108 (2003); Hobbins, *Authorship and Publicity in the Age Before Print: Jean Gerson and the Transformation of Late Medieval Learning* (Philadelphia: University of Pennsylvania Press, 2009).

4. On the various incarnations of Observant reform see James D. Mixson, *Poverty's Proprietors: Ownership and Mortal Sin at the Origins of the Observant Movement* (Leiden: Brill, 2009); James D. Mixson and Bert Roest, *A Companion to Observant Reform in the Late Middle Ages and Beyond* (Leiden: Brill, 2015); Robert L. J. Shaw, *The Celestine Monks of France: Observant Reform in an Age of Schism, Council, and War* (Amsterdam: Amsterdam University Press, 2018).

5. Van Engen, "A World Astir."

6. Short summaries of some of these controversies have previously appeared in Guarnieri, "Il movimento," 466–476; Sargent, "Latin and Italian," 85–96; and Trombley, "Latin Manuscripts," 186–217.

vance. Bernardino was the rock-star Franciscan preacher of his time, arguably one of the most influential figures of the early fifteenth century.[7] As Franco Mormando has shown, Bernardino saw society as being under constant attack from the diabolical influences of sin and vice; this led him to repeatedly and forcefully target those he believed were vessels or agents of such forces, namely those branded as witches, usurers, heretics, and sodomites.[8] Bernardino was immensely popular: his sermons would attract huge crowds, and as a result he wielded significant influence.[9] It is striking, therefore, not only that the *Mirror* caught his attention but that it did so enough that he felt the need to attack it not just once but multiple times. In approximately seven of his works—six sermons in Latin, one in Italian—he singles out the *Mirror* for criticism.[10] While Bernardino's Latin sermons are not "sermons" in the sense of representing texts that he preached live but rather are treatises on certain topics that could be used for preaching or for personal study, they still demonstrate Bernardino's thinking on the *Mirror* and his attempts to disseminate his views.

While a majority of Bernardino's references to the *Mirror* appear in his Latin sermons, the first alarm that he sounds about it is in one of his vernacular sermons, given in Siena in 1427. In a sermon on the annunciation of the Virgin Mary, Bernardino touches upon the topic of sin. He cites 1 John 1:8, "If we say that we do not sin, we deceive ourselves."[11] He goes on to say that no one can say they are not a sinner and that being righteous means sinning. He then addresses the audience directly: "Look, is there anyone who owns that book *Of the simple soul* [*Libro dell'anima semplice*], the one that says, at the end, that there is no way to sin, neither venially nor mortally? Do you know what I am saying to you? Do not believe it, because it is not true. Do you not see that it goes against the apostolic saying? Because the apostle says that one cannot help but sin, and this book says that it is not possible to sin."[12] He calls the book heretical and says to his listeners, "My suggestion to the owner is

---

7. For an overview of Bernardino's career, see Franco Mormando, *The Preacher's Demons: Bernardino of Siena and the Social Underworld of Early Renaissance Italy* (Chicago: University of Chicago Press, 1999), 1–51.

8. Mormando, *Preacher's Demons.*

9. Mormando, *Preacher's Demons,* 1; Cynthia Polecritti, *Preaching Peace in Renaissance Italy: Bernardino of Siena and His Crowd* (Washington, DC: Catholic University of America Press, 2000).

10. Guarnieri, "Il movimento," 467–469, and Trombley, "The Latin Manuscripts," 206–208.

11. Bernardino quotes this in Latin: "Si dixerimus quod peccatum non fecimus, ipsi nos seducimus." Bernardino of Siena, *Prediche volgari sul Campo di Siena,* ed. Carlo Delcorno (Milan: Rusconi, 1989), Predica XXIX, 825.

12. Bernardino of Siena, *Prediche volgari,* 825. "Ècci niuno che abbi quello Libro dell'anima semplice, che ne la fine dice che non si può peccare per niuno modo né venialmente né mortalmente? Sai che ti dico? Non gli credare, ché elli non è vero. Non vedi tu che egli dà contro al detto apostolico? Ché l'Apostolo dice che non si può fare che non si pecchi, e questo libro dice che non si può peccare."

that he puts it into the fire."[13] Only two people have been without sin in this life, he says, and they are Christ and the Virgin Mary.[14]

The first reference to the *Mirror* in Bernardino's Latin sermons appears in the third sermon of his *Quadragesimale de christiana religione*, a series of Lenten sermons composed between 1430 and 1436.[15] In this sermon, Bernardino dedicates an entire section—entitled "On the Faith Necessary to Prelates and Learned Men"—to describing different texts and writings, categorizing them in various ways. First, there are the three essential texts of the New Testament, the Old Testament, and the decrees and decretals of the Roman Church. But outside of these, there are three other types of texts, "and these various [others] ought to be understood, for some are approved and some are rejected" (*Et de hiis varie sentiendum est, nam quaedam sunt approbate, quaedam autem reprobate*).[16] Bernardino distinguishes the first type as those writings that are approved by the church: those of the Four Doctors and many other early authorities, as well as the authentic works of figures like Bernard of Clairvaux, Alexander of Hales, Peter Lombard, and "many others," which he says are too long to recount.

Bernardino's second category are those writings that are rejected and condemned by the church. He notes those texts that are condemned in Gratian's fifteenth distinction, a section of Gratian that reproduces the sixth-century Gelasian decree, which lists several books that are rejected by the church.[17] Occupying the third chapter of the fifteenth distinction, it states that "the Catholic and Apostolic Roman Church in no way receives the works of heretics or schismatics."[18] After the fifteenth distinction, he names a text that is almost certainly *The Mirror of Simple Souls*: "The doctrine of a book that is called *On the Simple Soul* [*De anima simplici*] is condemned in *Extra, de hereticis, capitulo unico*, in the Clementines [i.e., the decree *Ad nostrum*], in which many errors of that book are set forth."[19] After the *Mirror*, Bernardino names books of necromancy, divi-

---

13. "e do per consiglio a colui che l'ha, che elli il riponga in sul fuoco." Bernardino of Siena, *Prediche volgari*, 825. I am grateful to Dr. Alessandro Salvador for his help in translating these passages.

14. Bernardino of Siena, *Prediche volgari*, 825.

15. Guarnieri (and Trombley, following Guarnieri) states that these were composed between 1417 and 1429, but the Quaracchi edition of these sermons puts 1430 as the earliest date. Guarnieri, "Il movement," 467, and Trombley "Latin Manuscripts," 206.

16. Bernardino of Siena, *Opera Omnia I: Quadragesimale de Christiana Religione (Sermones I-XLVI)* (Florence: Quaracchi, 1950), 29–37.

17. D. 15, c. 3, in Emil Friedberg, ed., *Decretum Magistri Gratiani*, in *Corpus Iuris Canonici*, vol. 1 (Leipzig: C. Focke, 1879), 36.

18. D. 15, c. 3, in Friedberg, *Decretum*, 36. "Ceterum, que ab hereticis, siue scismaticis conscripta uel predicata sunt, nullatenus recipit catholica et apostolica ecclesia Romana." English from Augustine Thompson and James Gordley, trans. and ed., *Gratian: The Treatise on Laws, Decretum DD. 1–20, with the Ordinary Gloss* (Washington, DC: Catholic University of America Press, 1993), 57.

19. Bernardino of Siena, *Quadragesimale de Christiana Religione*, 28. "In Extra, de hereticis, cap. unico, in Clementinis*, condemnatur doctrina libri qui *De anima simplici* nuncupatur, ubi explicantur

nation, and also "lewd" (*lascivus*) poems and writings of pagans, which also belong to this second category.[20] The third category—works considered "dubious" or "doubtful" (*dubitate*) by the church—is worthy of mention, for reasons that will become clear both later in this chapter and in subsequent ones. Among these doubtful works are those whose authorship is unknown; this refers again to the Gelasian decree in Gratian's fifteenth distinction, where it lists several works deemed "apocryphal" that "Catholics ought to avoid" (*a catholicis vitanda sunt*).[21] Bernardino singles out a few titles of books included on this list, and two of the works he mentions are the *Liber de infantia salvatoris*—apocryphal stories about Jesus as a child—and the *Penitentia Origenis*, which allegedly recorded the final words of Origen. These two apocryphal works appear alongside the *Mirror* in at least two other contexts, both of which will be discussed later.

In another series of sermons, his *Quadragesimale de evangelio aeterno*, composed between 1430–1444, Bernardino singled out the *Mirror* twice more. In a sermon for the Thursday after Ash Wednesday, Bernardino describes three types of fear that drive people to produce good works but yet contain no inward piety or true faith: the fear of losing one's essence (*substantia*), the fear of losing one's reputation (*fama*), and the fear of losing life (*vita*). The first belongs to those who avoid blaspheming, vanities, and frivolities, not on account of God but so that they may avoid being damned. The second belongs to those who habitually go to church, frequent masses, attend sermons, and regularly confess and receive the sacrament, not because they truly believe but so that they are not thought less of by others and to maintain a good reputation. The third, says Bernardino, is the fear of losing life, and he expounds upon them as follows:

> There are many, certainly, who are full of errors and heresies, and yet in outward appearance are just; those who, if they showed outwardly what they believed in their hearts, would be justly destroyed by fire. Among these are counted certain [people] who are lapsed into the damned heresy of the free spirit [*haeresim de spiritu libertatis*], the doctrine of which is set down in a book which is usually entitled *On the Simple Soul*. Those who use it universally fall into this heresy, although such people, when they are infected with such a pestilential sickness, *making excuses in sins* [Psalms 141:4], and attacking the spirit of truth, may say such a book and status is not understood by their attackers. And in such a way they judge and damn the Church, which condemned this doctrine in sacred

---

plurimi illis libri errores." Quoted also in Guarnieri, "Il movimento," 467, and Trombley, "The Latin Manuscripts," 206.

20. Bernardino of Siena, *Quadragesimale de Christiana Religione*, 29.

21. D. 15, c. 3, in Friederg, *Decretum*, 36.

council, as is clear in *Extra, de hereticis, capitulo unico*, in the Clementines [*Ad nostrum*], where many condemned articles of this heresy and this book are enumerated.[22]

To these falsely pious "free spirits" Bernardino adds "many other heretics," as well as schismatics, baptized Jews, Dolcinites, and those from the "Anti-Christ sect" (*anti-christiana secta*). All three of the aforementioned types of people adhere to Catholic works out of fear, like children obeying a schoolmaster, and appear to live honest lives but are inwardly full of error.[23] We are warned against this by Christ, says Bernardino, using a phrase familiar to the antiheretical toolkit: "Beware of false prophets, who come to you in the clothing of sheep, but are inwardly ravening wolves: by their fruits you shall know them [Matthew 7:15]."[24]

In the same compilation of sermons, sermon LVI, *De passione domini*, Bernardino again takes on the *Mirror*. In a section that talks of the "nine fruits" of the cross, Bernardino notes that those who do not have the fruits of the cross or the merit of grace arrive at "remarkable annihilation" (*admirabilem annihilationem*), which is experienced by those who follow the "spirit of love and the free spirit, or the heretical book which is called *Of the Simple Souls* [*Animarum simplicium*], who are condemned in their errors in [*Ad nostrum*]."[25] He then casts these people as the enemies of Christ mentioned in Philippians 3:18 and Galatians 5:24, who mock and deceive with their "many errors." He then notes that he is familiar with these people and their errors through personal experience.[26]

In another sermon on the Virgin Mary, composed between 1430 and 1440, Bernardino shows a bit more knowledge of the *Mirror*'s contents. In a section that deals with the tranquility of the Virgin, in which she is able to perfectly control her feelings and her will, Bernardino compares it to the immovability of those in rapture. Those in rapture are able at the highest point of contemplation

---

22. Bernardino of Siena, *Opera Omnia III: Quadragesimale de Evangelio Aeterno* (Florence: Quaracchi, 1956), 109. "Multi utique sunt erroribus et haeresibus pleni, extra tamen in apparentia iusti; qui, si extra ostenderent quod intus in corde credunt, iuste comburerentur. Inter quos numerandi sunt quidam qui lapsi sunt in damnatam haeresim de spiritu libertatis, quae doctrina ponitur in libro qui *De anima simplici* intitulari solet; quo qui utuntur in illam haeresim communiter prolabuntur, licet tales, quando tali pestifero morbo infecti sunt, *ad excusandas excusationes in peccatis* et ad impugnandum spiritum veritatis, dicant talem librum et statum non intelligi ab impugnatoribus suis; et sic iudicant et damnant Ecclesiam, quae talem doctrinam in sacro concilio condemnavit, sicut patet Extra, *De haereticis*, unico capitulo in *Clementinis*, ubi illius haeresis atque libri plures condemnati articuli numerantur." My translation, which is modified from the translation appearing in Trombley, "Latin Manuscripts," 207.

23. Mormando provides a translation of this section in *Preacher's Demons*, 200.

24. Bernardino of Siena, *Quadragesimale de Evangelio Aeterno*, 109–110.

25. Bernardino of Siena, *Opera Omnia V: Quadragesimale de Evangelio Aeterno*, 153. ". . . qui sequuntur spiritum amoris et spiritum libertatis, aut librum haereticum qui dicitur *Animarum simplicium*, qui in erroribus suis damnatus est, Extra, *De haereticis*, cap. unico, in *Clementinis*."

26. Bernardino of Siena, *Quadragesimale de Evangelio Aeterno* (*Opera Omnia V*), 153.

to control their feelings so perfectly that they are not in any way inclined toward "a fall" (*casum*).[27] This state, Bernardino notes, "is spoken of in the book *On the Simple Soul* or *On the Free Soul*, although many worthless, deceptive, dangerous, and erroneous [things] are contained in that book."[28] Bernardino even brings the *Mirror* into his discussion of spiritual discernment in a sermon, *De inspirationum discretione*. In discussing the value of works and describing how the merit of works depends on the inner intention of those performing them, he notes that those who focus only on temporal works will not be remunerated for them eternally. Such discourse, Bernardino says, also reveals the error of those who are tormented and deceived "by the errors of the free spirit and of the simple soul" (*ab erroribus spiritus libertatis et animae simplicis*).[29] Such people "flee works and dread [them], since they may not be more perfect [by doing them]."[30]

There are many interesting layers to Bernardino's attacks on the *Mirror*. First, it is clear that, even if he may not have read it cover-to-cover, he was at least passingly familiar with its contents. His specific use of the term *annihilatio*, his references to immovability, and the connections he makes with it to *Ad nostrum* suggest that he knew a fair amount about its contents and probably saw and at least partially read a physical copy of the *Mirror*. Second, the level of importance that Bernardino accords to the *Mirror* in these sermons is notable. It is not merely a book to be avoided, but rather the foundational text of an entire heresy. The *Mirror* is a text that in fact *causes* its readers to fall into heresy, as seen in his vernacular sermon from Siena, and his sermon on false piety: no one who reads the book can help but fall into the heresy it advocates. The *Mirror* to Bernardino is essentially a bible of free spirit heresy. Indeed, as seen in *De inspirationum*, the "errors of the simple soul" is used interchangeably as a descriptor for the "errors of the free spirit." But the most striking example of this is in the third sermon from the *Quadragesimale*, where Bernardino specifically discusses good and bad books. There, he not only prominently places the *Mirror* among texts that are rejected by the church but he also states that the *Mirror* itself is condemned in *Ad nostrum*, as if it is mentioned by name in that decree (which, of course, it is not). In doing this, Bernardino in a sense creates a specific "official" condemnation of

27. Bernardino of Siena, "De Immaculata Conceptione Beatae Mariae Virginis," in *Sancti Bernardini Senensis Ordinis Seraphici Minorum Sermones Eximii de Christo Domino, Augustissimo Eucharistiae Sacramento Deipara Virgine, de Tempore Necnon de Sanctis*, vol. 4, ed. Johannes de la Haye (Venice, 1745), 84.

28. Bernardino of Siena, "De Immaculata," 84. "Et de hoc statu et de illo tempore loquitur libro *de anima simplici* atque *de anima libera*, licet in illo libro multa nugatoria et plurium deceptiva atque periculosa et erronea contineantur."

29. Bernardino of Siena, "De Inspirationum Discretione," in *Sancti Bernardini Senensis*, vol. 3, 127.

30. Bernardino of Siena, "De Inspirationum Discretione," 127. "labores fugiunt atque horrent, quum perfectiores non sint."

the *Mirror* in canon law where one did not actually exist. This, too, indicates a more than passing knowledge of the *Mirror*, if he sees its contents and the errors of *Ad nostrum* as indistinguishable from one another. Therefore, the *Mirror* to Bernardino is the font and foundation of an entire heresy, condemned in canon law, and deserves to be reckoned alongside not only other heretics like the Dolcinites but also other "corrupters" of society, as he demonstrates in his sermon from the *Evangelio aeterno*. Furthermore, the themes that Bernardino focuses on are telling. He fixates on what he sees as the *Mirror*'s emphasis on achieving a state of perfection that accords freedom from sin, or freedom from the need to do penance or good works. Given the broader nature of Bernardino's sermons, with their heavy focus on the threat of sin and the need for constant vigilance against and purgation of sin, it is easy to see why, given his interpretation of its contents, Bernardino might have considered the *Mirror* to be a dangerous book. He was also not alone: as we will see, other critics of the *Mirror* shared his concerns about sin and perfection.

Clearly, the *Mirror* kept returning to Bernardino's mind, and not just in reference to heretics and other societal "deviants" but also in sermons concerned with spiritual fruits, spiritual labors, and the Virgin. This seems to indicate that the *Mirror* was a fairly popular text and that Bernardino frequently encountered or heard about it. Perhaps most telling in this regard is the way he refers to it in his vernacular sermon in Siena in 1427. "That book *Of the Simple Soul*," he says, as if expecting his audience to know what he is referencing, or to be likely to come upon it. But in each reference he makes to it in all of his sermons, there is little elaboration on the *Mirror*'s contents, perhaps implying that he expected his audience and/or readers to have at least heard of the text in question. Additionally, it is not the *Mirror* alone that is discussed in these sermons and treatises; he also refers to "those people" who are "lapsed" into the *Mirror*'s heresy. Bernardino clearly believed that the *Mirror* was influential, that it fostered heresy in its readers, and that there was a sect who followed its precepts. Were there in fact sects of people reading the *Mirror* who genuinely organized their way of life around its tenets? It is difficult to tell how Bernardino is constructing his views here. While it is certainly possible that Bernardino had encountered sects of *Mirror* followers, he could also have assumed the existence of these adherents to the *Mirror*'s doctrine purely on the basis of the *Mirror* itself. The book does set up its teachings as belonging to a "church," that is, "Holy Church the Greater" (*Sancta Ecclesia Maior*), and its various references to those souls who have achieved annihilation give the impression of a select group of people attempting to live the life it describes. It creates a further sense of division by pointing out those who are *not* a part of the *Mirror*'s doctrines, where it describes "the Lost" and "the Sad" as those who are either unaware of or unable to attain the spiritual state described within its pages.[31] It is possible that Bernardino could have inferred the existence of the *Mirror*'s adherents from these references. It is also possible that Bernardino was given the impression of a sect through *Ad nostrum*. If he believed that the *Mirror* was the foundation of the errors listed there, then he would also likely have believed that the "abominable sect" of beghards and beguines mentioned in that decree were also adherents of the *Mirror*. In other words, just as it more broadly conjured up the sect of the heresy of the free spirit, so too could it have conjured up the "sect" of *The Mirror of Simple Souls* in Bernardino's mind.

But it is also perfectly possible that Bernardino did encounter people who, while not part of an actual sect, still read and valued the *Mirror*. As we will see, the *Mirror* was found to be in the hands of several people in Venice and Padua and was also circulating in his native Tuscany. Bernardino surely would not feel compelled to attack it multiple times if he had not seen the *Mirror* being read. Importantly, he referred to it in both Latin and vernacular sermons. This means he directed his warnings to both Latinate and non-Latinate audiences, scholarly and popular, clerical and lay. It follows, then, that he believed it to be circulating in multiple contexts and that it was not solely a risk to any one particular group. It perhaps even suggests that Bernardino knew the *Mirror* was circulating in both Latin and Italian versions. At any rate, as the *Mirror* was circulating in different languages, so, too, were warnings against reading it. Bernardino could, therefore, have believed it to be a text all the more dangerous because of its broad appeal.

## The Monks: The Congregation of Santa Giustina

Bernardino's fears were not necessarily unfounded. There were influential and well-respected religious communities in Italy that were reading and copying the *Mirror*. One such community was the Benedictine Congregation of Santa Giustina. The congregation had its beginnings in the Paduan Benedictine house of Santa Giustina, the abbacy of which was given *in commendam* in 1408 to Ludovico Barbo (1381–1443), the then prior of the Augustinian Canons of San Giorgio in Alga in Venice.[32] San Giorgio was, incidentally, the religious community set up in 1402 by the two cousins Antonio Correr and Gabriel Condulmer, the latter of whom was the future Pope Eugenius IV; we will meet both

---

31. See *Speculum CCCM*, 159–167.

32. On Barbo's career, see Ildefonso Tassi, *Ludovico Barbo (1381–1443)* (Rome: Edizioni di storia e letteratura, 1952), and Luigi Pesce, *Ludovico Barbo: Vescovo de Treviso (1437–1443)* (Padua: Antenore, 1969).

Antonio and Eugenius shortly in two other *Mirror*-related incidents.[33] Upon taking over Santa Giustina, Barbo implemented a program of reform, establishing strict observance of the Benedictine rule. Over the next thirty years, the congregation would become a major center of Benedictine Observant reform, and its reputation prompted other Italian Benedictine houses to seek affiliation, creating a network of houses that became the "Congregation" of Santa Giustina.[34] When their general chapter met in 1433, it included houses in Venice, Milan, Mantua, Genoa, Verona, Bassano, Bologna, Perugia, and Rome.[35] At this chapter meeting—roughly contemporary with Bernardino's references to the *Mirror* in his Latin sermons—some concerns surfaced over the brothers' reading material: "The governing president [*presidens regiminis*] should inquire throughout the entire congregation about a book which is called *Of the Simple Souls* [*Simplicium Animarum*], and in any place where he finds books of this sort he will seize it himself, and let him keep it away so that our brothers may not use it."[36]

This passage, though brief, reveals a great deal. It has most often been described as a "ban" on the *Mirror*, but a closer reading and clearer translation shows that more was going on here.[37] This is, in reality, as much a commission as a ban. The passage does not say merely that the brothers should not read the *Mirror*, but that the president of the congregation must *seek it out* and confiscate it from them. Such a commission must have been based on more than just rumor. This implies an expectation that there was something there to be found. Note, too, that it says the president should inquire "throughout the entire congregation"; in other words, not in one house in one city, but in all the houses that belong to the network. Furthermore, there is a strong impression of concern over the *Mirror*'s influence in these words. The *Mirror* is to be seized and kept away "so that our brothers may not use it." This indicates a belief that the *Mirror* appealed to the brothers and that if they did "use it" it would be to their detriment. This echoes Bernardino of Siena in his statements that those who

33. Giorgio Cracco, "La fondazione dei canonici secolari di S. Giorgio in Alga," *Rivista di storia della chiesa in Italia* 13 (1959): 73. Barbo had held San Giorgio *in commendam* from Pope Boniface IX since 1397. Gabriel (Eugenius IV) was related by marriage to Barbo through his sister, who had married Ludovico's brother Nicolaus. See Joseph Gill, *Eugenius IV: Pope of Christian Union* (Maryland: Newman Press, 1961), 15 and 17.

34. On the beginnings of Santa Giustina see Tassi, *Ludovico Barbo*, 27–74.

35. Barry Collett, *Italian Benedictine Scholars and the Reformation* (Oxford: Clarendon Press, 1985), 3–5; Guarnieri, "Il movimento," 469.

36. "Presidens regiminis debeat inquirere per totam congregationem de libro qui dicitur *Simplicium Animarum*, et ubicumque reperit huiusmodi libros capiet apud se, et prohibeat ne fratres nostri eo utantur." T. Leccisotti, ed., *Congregationis S. Iustinae de Padua O.S.B. Ordinationes Capitulorum Generalium*, vol. 1 (Montecassino: Badia di Montecassino, 1939), 36. This is a modified translation to that which appears in Trombley, "Latin Manuscripts," 208.

37. Trombley, "Latin Manuscripts," 216.

"make use" of the *Mirror* "universally fall into this heresy." Such a fear is in many ways remarkable. The monks of Santa Giustina were known not only for their spiritual rigor but also for their erudition and learning; they were hardly an untutored, naive audience believed to fall easily into error. Therefore, to worry about their use of a book like the *Mirror* suggests that there was something in it that could appeal strongly to them, and that use of it had been observed. And, indeed, in a similar way to how Bernardino would have feared the *Mirror* in relation to the danger of sin, it is also fitting that the *Mirror*, with its focus on total relinquishment of the self in order to dissolve into divine love, may have found appeal among a religious community that emphasized ascetic rigor, contemplation, and rejection of the material world.[38] As to where and how the *Mirror* came to circulate within the congregation, there is the possibility that it made the jump from another order, the Camaldolese. As will be discussed in more detail later, the *Mirror* was being copied and circulated within Camaldolese houses in Florence and Venice, and there was frequent contact between the Camaldolese houses and those of Santa Giustina.[39]

## The Inquisition: Venice and Padua, 1437

The clearest example of the *Mirror*'s popularity appears in one of the most interesting—and convoluted—episodes surrounding it in the fifteenth century. In the autumn of 1437, the Franciscan friar Giovanni of Capestrano and the then bishop of Castellano, Lorenzo Giustiniani, encountered the *Mirror* while investigating heresy in Venice on commission from Pope Eugenius IV. Here again we find prominent figures of Observance and reform. Giovanni of Capestrano was another hugely influential figure of the Observant Franciscans, another of the four "pillars," who traveled and preached extensively across Italy, central Europe, and Germany.[40] He was a close associate of Bernardino of Siena; indeed, he was a fervent advocate for Bernardino's canonization.[41] Lorenzo Giustiniani had been prior of San Giorgio in Alga and would become the patriarch of Venice in 1451; he would be canonized in the seventeenth century.[42] Together, these two

---

38. See Tassi, *Ludovico Barbo*, 95–140.

39. Tassi, *Ludovico Barbo*, 44–45.

40. The scholarship on Giovanni is vast. For a brief overview, see Michael J. P. Robson, *The Franciscans in the Middle Ages* (Woodbridge, UK: Boydell and Brewer, 2006), 213–216.

41. Daniele Solvi, "Giovanni of Capestrano's Liturgical Office for the Feast of Saint Bernardino of Siena," *Franciscan Studies* 75 (2017): 49.

42. On Lorenzo's influence see Silvio Tramontin, "La cultura monastica del Quattrocento dal primo patriarca Lorenzo Giustiniani ai Camaldolesi Paolo Giustiniani e Pietro Quirini," *Storia della cultura veneta* 3, no. 1 (1980).

figures pursued an inquisition that would eventually snag the *Mirror* in its net. The sequence of events in this episode have been laid out multiple times.[43] Rather than try to reconstruct them again, I will instead give a brief recap and then analyze the *Mirror*'s appearances in this episode.

In a letter dated 9 August 1437, Pope Eugenius IV commissioned Giovanni and Lorenzo to investigate rumors of heresy in Venice.[44] In the course of this investigation, which saw the lay-religious order of the Gesuati come under suspicion, the *Mirror* was also discovered. The *Mirror* then, it seems, attracted special attention in this case. As indicated by a letter written to Eugenius by Giovanni of Capestrano a month later on 10 September, Giovanni and Lorenzo clearly felt the *Mirror* was heretical, and it was one of many "little books" (*multi libelli*) that were handed over to them during the investigation.[45] Seven days before Giovanni wrote to Eugenius, the bishop of Ferrara, Giovanni Tavelli of Tossignano, wrote to Giovanni of Capestrano protesting the investigation of the Gesuati, among whom he had lived for twenty-five years.[46] Tavelli also mentions an (unnamed) book, which he was surprised to hear contained errors; it is possible that the book he was referring to was *The Mirror of Simple Souls*. The next piece of evidence comes from a letter of 13 September sent by Antonio Correr, the cardinal of Bologna (and cousin to Eugenius IV), to Giovanni of Capestrano. In this letter, Correr mentions that Eugenius commissioned Giovanni and Lorenzo to look into the matter of the *Mirror* specifically.[47] Correr also said that he was sending a messenger, Marco Donato, to speak to Giovanni and Lorenzo specifically about the matter of the *Mirror*;

---

43. Guarnieri, "Il movimento," 470–474; Sargent, "Latin and Italian"; Trombley, "Latin Manuscripts," 209–214.

44. The letter commissioning Giovanni and Lorenzo can be found in Ulricus Hüntemann, ed., *Bullarium Franciscanum: Continens Constitutions, Epistolas, et Diplomata Romanorum Pontificum: Eugenii IV et Nicolai V, ad Tres Ordines S.P.N. Francisci Spectantia: 1431–1455*, vol. 1 (Florence: Quaracchi, 1929), 145–146. Also in Luke Wadding, *Annales Minorum seu Trium Ordinum a S. Francisco Institutorum*, ed. Rocco Bernabo and José María Fonseca y Ebora, vol. 11 (Rome, 1734), 13 and 14. Accessed via the Hathi Trust, http://babel.hathitrust.org/cgi/pt?id=ucm.5319085016;view=1up;seq=33 (accessed October 2020). While it has frequently been said that Eugenius specifically asked them to investigate the order of the Gesuati and *The Mirror of Simple Souls*, his letter makes no mention of either, merely "several persons of both sexes, both ecclesiastical and secular," whose reputations had been "blackened" (*denigratur*). See discussion in Trombley, "Latin Manuscripts," 209–210.

45. The letter is edited and printed in Guarnieri, "Il movimento," 645–647. A copy can be found in Capestrano, Biblioteca Ordini Frati Minori, MS 19, f. 19r. I am grateful to Dr. Filippo Sedda for providing me with photographs of this document.

46. Published in Wadding, *Annales Minorum*, 14. Partially cited in Guarnieri, "Il movimento," 473, and partially translated and quoted in Sargent, "Latin and Italian," 95. See also Trombley, "Latin Manuscripts," 211–212.

47. A printed edition of this letter can be found in Guarnieri, "Il movimento," 647. Transcribed from Capestrano, Archivio di Frati Minori, carta 91. I thank Dr. Filippo Sedda for providing me with a photograph of this document.

whether such a meeting ever happened, and what was discussed, is for now a mystery. Five days after Correr sent his letter, on 18 September, Giovanni was sent another letter, this time from Antonio Zeno, the *vicarius* of the bishop of Padua, who at that time was Pietro Donato. Zeno tells Capestrano that he dealt with a *conventiculum* of people fleeing Venice and that he found copies of the *Mirror* in their possession.[48] Zeno then ordered, under pain of excommunication, that anyone who possessed the book must turn it in to him, and furthermore anyone who knew of others who possessed the book must reveal this to him or others in his office. Zeno told Capestrano that he had sent a list of propositions taken from the *Mirror*, along with a full copy of the book, to the theologians at the University of Padua and had asked them to examine it. While the outcome of this assessment is not mentioned in any known contemporary sources, chapter 3 will argue that a partial copy of the theologians' assessment may be the error list found in Vatican City, BAV, MS Vat. lat. 4953. Giovanni and Lorenzo's inquisition came to a close on 2 October 1437, and the Gesuati were absolved of any suspicion of heresy.[49] It is here that the trail of evidence regarding the *Mirror* in this episode mostly disappears, and there is no indication as to what the final judgment upon it was.

The only known sources we have for this episode—with one small exception—are the letters exchanged between Giovanni of Capestrano and Eugenius IV, Tavelli, Correr, and Zeno. While what precisely was going on behind these letters is a mysterious knot that resists easy untying, they still cast some interesting light on the *Mirror's* circulation.

Let us proceed in chronological order. The letter of 3 September, in which Giovanni Tavelli protested the investigation of the Gesuati, is, according to Wadding, only a fragment: the beginning of the letter is missing. The letter begins with the words, "I am greatly surprised about the book, that if there are errors in it, about that it is said that it was read by many servants of God, [who] did not perceive such obvious errors."[50] The book mentioned here has frequently been taken to be the *Mirror*, but, since other books were also found during the inquisition in Venice, the identification is not certain.[51] Closer scrutiny, however, hints

48. Letter printed in Guarnieri, "Il movimento," 647–648. Transcribed from Capestrano, Archivio di Frati Minori, carta 331. I thank Dr. Filippo Sedda for providing me with a photograph of this document.

49. The letter in which Lorenzo Giustiniani clears the Gesuati of any wrongdoing is found in Wadding, *Annales Minorum*, 15. It is also excerpted in Isabella Gagliardi, *I Pauperes Yesuati: Tra esperienze religiose e conflitti istituzionali* (Rome: Herder, 2004), 330.

50. Wadding, *Annales Minorum*, 14; Guarnieri, "Il movimento," 473. "De libro miror valde, quod si in illo sunt errores, de quibus dicitur, quod per plures servos Dei legatur, nec percipiant tam manifestos errores."

51. Gagliardi, *Pauperes Yesuati*, 326; Trombley, "Latin Manuscripts," 212.

that it might in fact be the *Mirror* to which Tavelli refers. The use of *dicitur* combined with *quod* and a subjunctive verb indicates indirect speech, that Tavelli is reporting something that has been said about the book's contents. This is where his use of "many servants of God" (*plures servos Dei*) catches the eye. In one surviving late fourteenth-century copy of the *Mirror* (copied in Italy), Vatican City, BAV, MS Chigianus B IV 41, the chapter heading of the *approbatio*—the section containing the opinions of the three churchmen whom Marguerite consulted on her book—reads, "Approval of this book made by many reverend doctors in Christ" (*Approbatio libri huius facta per multos in christo reverendos doctores*). But, unlike all the other Latin manuscripts, the text of the *approbatio* that follows does not contain the names of John, Franc, and Godfrey but merely notes the opinions of "servants of God who heard this book, who were of great name, life, and sanctity" (*dei servorum qui audierunt istum librum qui fuerunt magni nominis, vite, et sanctitatis*). Tavelli's echoing of the "servants of God" phrase tentatively suggests that he could have been referring to a copy of the *Mirror* that contained this nameless version of the *approbatio*. This would then in turn explain his surprise at hearing that it was considered erroneous, given the presence of this "approval" within its pages.

If the *Mirror* is the book in question here, it is worth noting what exactly Tavelli says in this brief sentence. It has been described as a defense of the *Mirror* or a rejection of the opinion that it is heretical, but the wording is not so emphatic.[52] He is merely expressing surprise at what seems to be an allegation—which comes to us only secondhand through Tavelli—that "the book" contained "obvious errors," since "servants of God" had read it and found nothing wrong with it. He then spends the rest of the letter defending the morals and life of the Gesuati, among whom he had previously lived. This segue suggests that the Gesuati had been reading the book in question. Tavelli's defense can be taken one of two ways. He could be using his defense of the Gesuati as a way of proving that the book in question is not heretical, since their way of life is to him beyond reproach.[53] But it could also be that Tavelli is trying to distance the Gesuati from the book. His expression of surprise at the book's errors indicates that someone has informed him of these errors. His statement expresses only surprise and does not necessarily indicate his belief or disbelief in the allegations. It could be that Tavelli had previously not perceived the errors himself but that they had then been pointed out to him. By following with a defense of the Gesuati's life and morals, then, Tavelli could in fact have been trying to demonstrate that they were good *in spite of* their reading of the book that was

---

52. Guarnieri, "Il movimento," 473; Sargent, "Latin and Italian," 95.
53. Sargent, "Latin and Italian," 95.

now said to be erroneous. Given what we saw with Bernardino and Santa Giustina, where the *Mirror* was believed to cause its readers to fall into heresy, this
may have been a particularly important point for Tavelli to make.

Either way, Tavelli's surprise fits with what we saw in the case of Santa Giustina: that there were plenty of readers, particularly in religious or semireligious
congregations, who read the *Mirror* without perceiving any heresy. While there
is no mention of the *Mirror* in the letter of Eugenius's original commission, it is
perhaps for the above reason that he at some point—we do not know exactly
when—requested that Giovanni of Capestrano and Lorenzo Giustiniani launch
an inquisition into the *Mirror* specifically. We unfortunately know this only indirectly, through the letter dated 13 September that Antonio Correr sent to
Giovanni of Capestrano. That letter opens with Correr saying, "We understand
our lord to have committed to you an inquisition into the matter of a foolish
and erroneous little book, which is called *The Book of the Simple Souls* [*Liber simplicium animarum*]."[54] But an earlier indication of Eugenius's requested inquisition into the *Mirror* can be seen in the only letter we have from Giovanni of
Capestrano in this matter, the one he sent to Eugenius IV on 10 September.
That letter opens with Giovanni referring to a "short message" (*succincto sermone*) that he had written to Eugenius the day before "about *The Mirror of
Simple Souls*, in which many obvious errors, already condemned by the Church,
quite clearly appear."[55] It is possible that the "short message," a copy of which
is unfortunately lost, was written as a report for Eugenius, as a result of the
pope's request that he look into the *Mirror*. We can only guess what this message might have said. It is possible, since he mentions the "errors" of the *Mirror*,
that Giovanni outlined said errors for Eugenius. Of note is Giovanni's comment that these errors had "already been condemned by the Church" (*ab ecclesia iam damnati*). While not certain, this is likely a reference to *Ad nostrum*, since,
as we saw with Bernardino, the errors of that decree were easily linked to the
*Mirror*'s contents. At any rate, it seems likely that Eugenius had already ordered
Giovanni to look into the *Mirror* by the time he wrote his "short message"
about it, given that Antonio Correr seemed to already know about such a commission just three days later.[56] Again, that the pope made such a commission is
the strongest indication yet that the *Mirror* was both well known and deeply

---

54. Capestrano, carta 91. Printed in Guarnieri, "Il movimento," 647. "Intelleximus dominum nostrum commisisse vobis inquisitionem materiae libelli fatui et erronei, qui dicitur *Liber simplicium
animarum*."

55. Capestrano, MS 19, f. 19r; Guarnieri, "Il movimento," 645. "Pridie Vestrae Sanctitati succinto
sermone scribebam de *Speculo simplicium animarum*, in quo multi patentes errores, ab ecclesia iam
damnati, luculenter apparent."

56. Eugenius was in Bologna at the time; Correr was in Verona.

troubling. Important to note is that it was around this time that Eugenius was locked in one of his many fierce struggles with the Council of Basel, attempting to have it moved to Italy, which he formally did on 18 September with the bull *Doctoris gentium*, so it is not as if there were no other pressing matters on his agenda at the time.[57]

What the rest of Giovanni's letter reveals is that the *Mirror* was not the only "erroneous" book that Giovanni and Lorenzo had discovered in the course of their inquisition. "We recently found still others which are no lesser danger against the faith, for when we interrogated others, the Lord of Castellano and I, we discovered certain books, written from the dictation of a certain Lady Mina. In these clearly appear the illusions of demons and fantastical revelations."[58] In these books, Mina claimed that she was pregnant with two children, a male and a female. The male would be pope and the female would "defend the faith of women" (*mulierum fidem defendet*).[59] She claimed that the keys to the kingdom of heaven had been given to her by divine authority, and this made others show signs of obedience to her, through kneeling and the kissing of her hand. Many other "immense and wicked things" (*multa enormia et nefandissima*) were contained in these books, Giovanni says, which he cannot lay out in full. Apparently Mina's books were not discovered by Giovanni and Lorenzo's inquisition but rather via an accusation made against the parish priest of the church of Sant'Eufemia in the Giudecca, attesting that he falsified Mina's books, for which he was condemned and incarcerated. The priest's own books were handed over to his examiners, who then gave them to Giovanni and Lorenzo.[60]

Near the end of the letter, Giovanni mentions that other *libelli* were also turned in, one a text called *Lucidario* in which Giovanni says, like the *Mirror*, "there are many errors," and another entitled *De infantia salvatoris*, which Giovanni notes is condemned in the fifteenth distinction of Gratian's *Decretum*.[61] *Lucidario* was probably an Italian translation of the *Elucidarium*, an eleventh-century work by Honorius Augustodunensis, which takes the form of a dialogue between an anonymous master and his pupil, where the pupil

---

57. Joachim Stieber, *Pope Eugenius IV, The Council of Basel, and the Secular and Ecclesiastical Authorities in the Empire: The Conflict Over Supreme Authority and Power in the Church* (Leiden: Brill, 1978) (hereafter Stieber, *Supreme Authority*), 446. Eugenius, the *Mirror*, and the council are discussed further in chapter 3.

58. MS 19, f. 19r; Guarnieri, "Il movimento," 645. "Nonnulla etiam nuper invenimus non minora pericula contra fidem; nam cum alia quaereremus, Dominus Castellanus et ego, reperimus quosdam libros, conscriptos ex dictatu cuiusdam dominae Minae. In quibus expressisime patent daemonum illusiones et revelationes phantasticae."

59. MS 19, f. 19r; Guarnieri, "Il movimento," 645. See also Trombley, "Latin Manuscripts," 211.

60. MS 19, f. 19r; Guarnieri, "Il movimento," 646.

61. MS 19, f. 19r; Guarnieri, "Il movimento," 645.

expresses a desire to acquire "hidden knowledge."[62] Although this work was immensely popular in the Middle Ages—more than three hundred manuscripts survive today—it also fell into gray areas of acceptability and aroused suspicion among some. A Provençal translation was made in which its contents were adapted to fit with Catharism, and the fourteenth-century inquisitor Nicholas Eymerich wrote a refutation of it in 1393.[63] The *De infantia salvatoris* was probably one of the many apocryphal stories circulating about Jesus's childhood, which, like the *Mirror*, had a tradition of both acceptance and rejection.[64] As Giovanni noted, it is included in the Gelasian decree as a text deemed "apocryphal" and therefore not accepted by the church.[65] This is the second time that the *Infantia salvatoris* appears alongside the *Mirror*. Bernardino of Siena referenced this same text and decree in the sermon in which he included the *Mirror* in a list of works rejected by the church.

Although unfortunately Giovanni's letter to Eugenius that was solely concerned with the *Mirror* is lost, this surviving letter still provides useful insight into his mindset. Obviously, he saw the *Mirror* as erroneous, as the opening of his letter clearly states. But other parts of the letter add more. In introducing Mina's books, he writes that this discovery is "no lesser danger to the faith" (*non minora pericula contra fidem*). This comparative indirectly highlights the *Mirror*'s "danger" as well, a danger on par with "wicked" books like Mina's, which in his view contained demonic deceptions and fantasies.

That the *Mirror* had attracted attention throughout the course of this inquisition is emphasized further in the letter sent by the cardinal Antonio Correr just three days later, on 13 September. Antonio—cousin and close associate of Eugenius IV, with whom he had founded San Giorgio in Alga and with whom he had lived there—must have been in touch with Eugenius about the affair. Antonio's letter, which is only seven lines long in its extant form in the Capestrano Archive, does not say much. As already mentioned, Antonio opens the letter by saying he knows Eugenius has commissioned Giovanni and Lorenzo to look into the matter of the *Mirror*. But he then goes on to say that Marco

---

62. Isabella Gagliardi has identified a fifteenth-century Italian version of this work in Florence at the Biblioteca Riccardiana, MS Ricc 1307. See Gagliardi, *Pauperes Yesuati*, 327n135.

63. Yves Lefèvre, *L'Elucidarium et les Lucidaires: Contribution, par l'histoire d'un texte, à l'histoire des croyances religieuses en France au moyen âge* (Paris: E. de Boccard, 1954), 259. On some of Eymerich's objections to *Elucidarium*, see also Caroline Walker Bynum, *Resurrection of the Body* (New York: Columbia University Press, 1995), 152–153. On the Provençal translation, see Marcel Dando, "L'adaptation provençale de l'Elucidarium d'Honoré d'Autun et le catharisme," *Cuadernos de estudios Gallegos* 28 (1977).

64. For an overview of the career of *De infantia salvatoris*, see Mary Dzon, "Cecily Neville and the Apocryphal *Infantia salvatoris* in the Middle Ages," *Mediaeval Studies* 71 (2009).

65. D. 15, c. 3, in Friedberg, *Decretum*, 36.

Donato will be coming to talk to Giovanni about the matter on his (Antonio's) behalf, and that Giovanni and Lorenzo should give full credence to Donato's report, "as if it were his [Antonio's] own, if we spoke the same to you."[66] That is the end of the letter.

This is an intriguing little episode. First, it establishes with certainty that Eugenius asked Giovanni to look into the *Mirror*. But there are a lot of unanswered questions here. Suddenly, Marco Donato arrives on the scene, with information on the *Mirror*. It is slightly unclear whether Marco Donato is relating information given to him by Antonio or whether Marco is being sent by Antonio to relate information that he, Marco, has acquired himself and that he told to Antonio. Marco's background suggests that it could be the latter. Marco (ca. 1415–ca. 1465) was the nephew of Pietro Donato, bishop of Padua at the time of the letter.[67] He would later serve in various ambassadorial roles, but at the time of this letter Marco was a student of law at the University of Padua.[68] What was Marco going to tell the two investigators about the *Mirror*, and how did he come to know it? There is no known record of Marco's meeting with Giovanni and Lorenzo, so it is impossible to say with certainty. There are, however, a few clues. Marco's connection to both Pietro Donato and the University of Padua may be the key. As we will see in more detail in chapter 4, a canon lawyer named Giacomo de Zocchi was a professor at the university at this time and had been since 1428. De Zocchi had himself copied a polemical treatise that attacked the *Mirror* and bound it into a codex with multiple other legal texts he would have used in the course of his work. De Zocchi was a popular and well-known professor at the time; it is entirely possible that he taught Marco. Marco certainly knew de Zocchi in some way, as he was present when de Zocchi was awarded his second degree in civil law in Padua on 8 May 1436.[69] It is possible, then, that some of what Marco knew about the *Mirror* could have come from de Zocchi. Or de Zocchi's knowledge of the *Mirror* could have come indirectly to Marco, via his uncle Pietro's administration. Antonio Zeno, Pietro's *vicarius*, also undoubtedly knew Giacomo de Zocchi:

---

66. Capestrano, carta 91; Guarnieri, "Il movimento," 647. I thank Dr. Filippo Sedda for providing me with a photograph of this document.

67. Pietro was yet another ally of Eugenius IV, having been one of Eugenius's conciliar presidents at the Council of Basel in 1434–1435. See Stieber, *Supreme Authority*, 36, and Thomas M. Izbicki and Luke Bancroft, "A Difficult Pope: Eugenius IV and the Men Around Him," in *Nicholas of Cusa and the Making of the Early Modern World*, ed. J. G. Burto, Joshua Hollman, and Eric M. Parker (Leiden: Brill, 2019), 59.

68. See the brief biographical sketch in Margaret L. King, *Venetian Humanism in an Age of Patrician Dominance* (Princeton: Princeton University Press, 1986), 369–370.

69. Caspare Zonta and Iohanne Brotto, eds., *Acta Graduum Academicorum Gymnasii Patavini: Ab Anno 1406 A.D. Annum 1450: 1435–1450* Vol. 1.2 (Padua: Antenore, 1970), 28, no. 1121. Marco and de Zocchi had also been present together at another degree granting ceremony, at the episcopal palace on 19 April 1435. Zonta and Brotto, *Acta Graduum II*, 5, no. 1039.

they were involved in numerous university examinations and degree granting ceremonies together, often at the episcopal palace.[70] One can easily imagine knowledge of the *Mirror* as a dangerous book finding its way from de Zocchi to Antonio and Pietro Donato, and then on to Marco.

We do not know what Marco said to Giovanni and Lorenzo—or if the planned meeting ever took place—but Marco's connection to Padua may provide the link between this letter and the final one that survives concerning the *Mirror* in this episode. This is a letter dated 18 September, five days after the one sent by Antonio Correr, and it was sent by Antonio Zeno to Giovanni of Capestrano and Lorenzo Giustiniani. The letter is in extremely poor condition and many sections are totally illegible, meaning that reconstructing Antonio's words is very difficult; I therefore have relied heavily on Guarnieri's transcription of this document. The letter seems to inform Giovanni of the detection of a *conventiculum* of men and women in Padua who had fled Venice out of fear of the inquisition there. It appears that these men and women had with them copies of the *Mirror* as well as other books. Antonio tells Giovanni that he commanded that anyone possessing such books, or knowing such books to be in the hands of others, must hand them over to the office of the *vicarius* under pain of excommunication.[71] So far, one copy had been turned in that was found in the hands of "a certain priest" (*quendam presbyterum*) and another that was found in the possession of a "certain Venetian woman" (*penes quandam mulierem venetam*). Other copies had not yet appeared. Antonio relates that a list of propositions from the *Mirror* had been drawn up "point-by-point" (*articulatim conscripsi*) and sent along with a copy of the book to the theologians at the University of Padua for examination. The final lines of the document are almost impossible to decipher in full, but Antonio might have promised to provide Giovanni and Lorenzo with the theologians' judgment, as the word *transmittam* ("I will send over") seems to appear at the end of this section.[72]

Connecting these episodes requires some historical imagination. If, as indicated in Antonio Correr's letter, an inquisition into the *Mirror* specifically was launched in Venice, then we can imagine a scenario along the following lines: Giovanni and Lorenzo put out an order of confiscation in Venice, which included both the *Mirror* and possibly other "suspect" books, perhaps those mentioned in Giovanni's letter to Eugenius. Such an order could then have prompted some of those who owned these books to flee rather than turn them over or

---

70. For several examples see the entries in Zonta and Brotto, *Acta Graduum II*, for the years 1435–1437.

71. Capestrano, carta 331; Guarnieri, "Il movimento," 647. I thank Filippo Sedda for providing me with a photograph of this document.

72. Capestrano, carta 331; Guarnieri, "Il movimento," 648.

admit to owning them; some of these people were then apprehended in Padua. It seems unlikely that Antonio Zeno would have sent a letter out of the blue to Giovanni and Lorenzo that just happened to concern similar actions against the *Mirror*, so it could be that Giovanni got in touch with him—or with the bishop, Pietro Donato, Antonio's superior—first, perhaps prompted by information from Marco Donato on the *Mirror* in Padua. Or it could be that the reason Marco was sent to Giovanni and Lorenzo in the first place was to inform them of the actions being taken in Padua, since Marco would have likely known the actions his uncle was taking. This means that perhaps Zeno's letter is an update of some sort, to follow on from Donato's information. It is difficult, however, to decipher the sequence of the events in Padua in relation to the timeline of composition for both Correr's and Zeno's letters.

The picture we get from Zeno's letter is unlike any other episode in the *Mirror*'s history. It seems to indicate that there was a group of men and women fleeing Venice with the *Mirror* in their possession. This is the first—and only—known evidence of the *Mirror* being tracked down and confiscated from a group of people.[73] Zeno uses the word *conventiculum*, a standard phrase used to describe groups of heretics, often with a semi-sinister, secretive implication. But it is uncertain whether there was an actual "sect" of those reading and adhering to the *Mirror* as a core text or whether it was merely a popular text read and owned by a number of different people.

This is the final substantial piece of evidence that we know of relating to the *Mirror* in the Venetian inquisition. Curiously, when the inquisition was concluded in October of 1437, we know only that the Gesuati were cleared of any wrongdoing and their reputation was restored.[74] There is no substantial evidence that points to the *Mirror*'s fate in this affair, but a small, overlooked postscript provides a hint. In a *vita* of Giovanni of Capestrano produced by Nicolao of Fara (d. 1477), in which he lists Giovanni's accomplishments and miracles, there is a section dedicated to his antiheretical activities. Sandwiched in between his efforts against the Fraticelli and the Hussites, there is this brief line: "As a witness, all the people of Venice, where, by the command of Pope Eugenius, he uprooted with great effort the pernicious *heresy of the simple soul*, which had sprung up [there]."[75] This is undoubtedly a reference to the *Mirror*. It is further

---

73. William of Paris called for the *Mirror* to be turned in during the sentencing of Marguerite Porete in 1310, but there is no evidence of how—or whether—this occurred.

74. Gagliardi, *Paupere Yesuati*, 330.

75. My emphasis. "Testis est omnis Venetorum populus, ubi animae simplicis exortam pestiferam haeresim, Eugenio papae mandante, grandi labore extirpavit." Nicolae de Fara, *Vita Clarissimi Viri Fratris Joannis de Capistrano*, ed. Johannes Bolland, Godefridus Henschenius, and Daniel Papebrochius, in *Acta Sanctorum*, vol. 10 (Brussels: Societé des Bollandistes, 1861), 449. See also Trombley, "Latin Manuscripts," 214.

proof that there must have been a formal inquisition against the *Mirror* and those who read it in Venice, and that the *Mirror* probably received some sort of noticeable condemnation. It also explicitly ties Eugenius IV to such an event. While there is no mention of this episode in other *vitae* of Giovanni, its inclusion here does indicate that some knowledge of the Venice inquisition circulated and that some considered it a noteworthy episode in Giovanni's career.

Some of the surviving *Mirror* manuscripts—in both the Latin and the Italian traditions—may also carry connections to the Venice inquisition, or the Paduan theological assessment. A manuscript of the Italian translation of the *Mirror*, Naples, Biblioteca nazionale, MS XII F 5, carries an *ex libris* showing that it belonged to Giovanni's home convent of Capestrano: *Pertinet ad conventum S. Francisci Capistrani.*[76] This may indicate that this copy was a *Mirror* confiscated during Giovanni's inquisition in Venice that he kept for future reference.[77] But another copy can be connected to these events with even more certainty. MS Rossianus 4 is a Latin copy of the *Mirror* held in the Vatican Library (Biblioteca apostolica vaticana). It has some particularly interesting characteristics that strongly indicate that it may have been the copy Antonio Zeno sent to the Paduan theologians. First, several characteristics of MS Rossianus 4 point to a readership along the lines of what Giovanni and Lorenzo may have investigated in Venice, and Antonio Zeno in Padua. MS Rossianus 4 is perhaps one of the smallest *Mirror* manuscripts—measuring about $13.5 \times 17$ cm ($5 \times 7$ in)—giving the impression of portability, or perhaps easy concealment.[78] It is written in large, easily legible script and uses very few abbreviations. It is also the only Latin codex that provides the character designations of "Love," "Reason," and so on before each voice in the text, making it easier to distinguish who is speaking, and there is more signposting in general using red pilcrows.[79] It is also a bilingual codex, as the last four folios of the manuscript contain excerpts from Pseudo-Dionysius that are written in Italian. These factors all suggest that this codex was perhaps owned not by a highly educated cleric but by someone of lesser Latin literacy, perhaps a literate lay reader, or was perhaps shared by a mixed clerical-lay reading community.[80] This fits with the fact that Giovanni in his letter to Eugenius indicates that they had found a mixture of vernacular and

---

76. Falvay and Konrád, "Osservanza francescana," 164.

77. Falvay and Konrád, "Osservanza francescana," 164–165.

78. Guarnieri describes the Rossianus codex as "da bisaccia"—i.e., small enough to be carried in a sack like a *vade mecum*. Guarnieri, Introduction to *Lo specchio delle anime semplici*, 46.

79. Trombley, "Latin Manuscripts," 190.

80. On the "religious sociability" of texts in Italy, crossing lay-clerical boundaries, see Sabrina Corbellini, "Beyond Orthodoxy and Heterodoxy: A New Approach to Late Medieval Religious Reading," in *Cultures of Religious Reading in the Late Middle Ages: Instructing the Soul, Feeding the Spirit, and Awakening the Passion*, ed. Sabrina Corbellini (Turnhout: Brepols, 2013).

Latin texts, *Lucidario* perhaps written in Italian and the *Liber infantia salvatoris* in Latin. Antonio Zeno notes that he found the *Mirror* in the hands of a woman, as well as a priest.

But there is even more explicit evidence. MS Rossianus 4 contains twenty-one marginal marks, which indicate that it was scrutinized for errors. There are nineteen crosses written next to particular passages in this *Mirror* copy. Two factors suggest that these crosses were put there to denote errors, rather than someone merely marking them out of interest. One is the fact that there are two marks in the margins of the manuscript that say either *error* or *nota errorem*. The second is the fact that eighteen of these marks—both crosses and *error* notes—correspond exactly to extracts from the *Mirror* that are listed as errors in both MS Vat. lat. 4953 and MS 1647, both of which refute the *Mirror* as heretical.[81] Both Guarnieri and Verdeyen also noted that the readings of the errors in MS Vat. lat. 4953 match very closely with those of MS Rossianus 4; Guarnieri commented that MS Vat. lat. 4953 even reproduces some of the errors and inconsistencies of the Rossianus copy, although the extracts in the Vatican list do contain their own small variations.[82] But there is more. Several of the errors found in the list in MS Vat. lat. 4953 are said to come from certain "chapters" (*capitula*) in the *Mirror*. These chapters are not identified by numbers but by their opening lines. For example, the eighth error on the Vatican list starts, "The eighth error is in the chapter which begins: 'The fourth point is, that this Soul does nothing on account of God.'"[83] Subsequent errors are then said to be "in the same chapter" as the one mentioned previously, until a new chapter is mentioned.[84] At first glance, MS Rossianus 4 does not appear to be broken up into chapters, at least not as we would imagine a chapter to look. But it does have places in the text where a large decorated initial appears, written in red or blue. This seems to denote a new section. Every chapter mentioned in MS Vat. lat. 4953 corresponds to these places in MS Rossianus 4. That is, in MS Vat. lat. 4953, each line that is cited as the line with which a particular chapter begins corresponds *exactly* to a line that begins with one of the decorated initials in MS Rossianus 4. There is no opening chapter line cited in MS Vat. lat. 4953 that is *not* begun with a decorated initial in MS Rossianus 4. Each error that is then said to be "in the same chapter" as one cited

---

81. Trombley, "Latin Manuscripts," 197–198, only counted the passages that appeared in MS Vat. lat. 4953.

82. Guarnieri, "Il movimento," 650, and Verdeyen, Introduction to *Speculum* CCCM, xii. See appendix 1 for some remarks on the variants in MS Vat. lat. 4953. MS Rossianus 4 (B) more often matches with D (MS Chigianus C IV 85) and H (MS M I 15) than with C (MS Chigianus B IV 41) and J (MS Conv. soppr. G. 3.1130).

83. "Octavus error est in capitulo quod incipit: 'Quartus punctus est, quod hec Anima nichil facit propter Deum.'" MS Vat. lat. 4953, f. 29v, and Guarnieri, "Il movimento," 653.

84. See appendix 1 for a transcription and translation of the MS Vat. lat. 4953 errors.

previously consistently appears within that "chapter" or section in MS Rossianus 4. Most of the marginal crosses that appear in these sections also match up to the errors in the list that are said to come from that particular chapter. Finally, these initialed section breaks in MS Rossianus 4 eventually stop appearing in the latter half of the work, around the same place that the list in MS Vat. lat. 4953 stops citing chapters. This cannot be a coincidence. It is almost certain, therefore, that MS Rossianus 4 is the copy that was used to create the error list in MS Vat. lat. 4953. Since the list in MS Vat. lat. 4953 is very likely a copy of the Paduan theologians' assessment of the *Mirror*, this means that MS Rossianus 4 is one of the copies of the *Mirror* that was confiscated or handed in to Antonio Zeno and is in all likelihood the copy that he gave to the theologians to examine. This also means that MS Rossianus 4 is the first *Mirror* copy we can firmly identify as one that was confiscated as part of an inquisition.

The Venice inquisition reveals a remarkable amount of interest in the *Mirror*, and it is not merely a case of local authorities showing concern. A point in need of emphasis is that it was *papal* interest that drove these events. Whatever Eugenius knew of the *Mirror*, he found it concerning enough to commission an inquisition to deal with it, as indicated by the line from Giovanni's *vita*, where the heresy of the simple soul is "uprooted" at his express command. Granted, Eugenius was a Venetian himself and had begun his religious life there with the founding of the community of San Giorgio in Alga, so it is reasonable that he would be concerned with Venice's religious affairs. It could also be the case that, similar to the position that the Capetian court was in during Marguerite Porete's trial, Eugenius felt he needed to burnish his image by proving his zeal in defending orthodoxy, as the autumn of 1437 was the exact time in which his relationship with the Council of Basel once again began to deteriorate, as we will see shortly. Whatever the reason, it is noteworthy that it was the *Mirror* upon which he trained his attention.

## The Heretic Pope: The *Mirror* at the Council of Basel

Eugenius's directive against the *Mirror* in Venice makes its next appearance both striking and puzzling. As noted earlier, while the inquisition in Venice was taking place, Eugenius was locked in the latest of a string of bitter struggles with the Council of Basel. From its inception in 1431, Eugenius IV had engaged in a battle of wills with the council, attempting to assert the supreme authority of the papacy over the church against that of the councils, which had been established at the Council of Constance (1415–1417) in the aftermath of the Great Schism.[85] Eugenius's first clash with Basel had ended with his capitulation to the council in 1433, but in 1437, nearly concurrent with the inquisition in Venice, events once again came to a head. Eugenius had from the beginning attempted to move the council to Italy, which would allow him greater control over the proceedings. On the exact day that Antonio Zeno composed his letter to Giovanni of Capestrano about the *Mirror*, 18 September 1437, Eugenius issued the bull *Doctoris gentium*, which transferred the council to Ferrara and reasserted papal supremacy over general councils.[86] This move prompted the Council of Basel to split from Eugenius and to initiate legal proceedings against him.[87] The proceedings began as charges of misconduct and disobedience, but by the spring of 1439 they had become charges of heresy.[88] On 25 June 1439 the Council of Basel formally deposed Eugenius, on grounds of being, among other things, "a schismatic," "an apostate from the faith," and "an obstinate heretic."[89]

A little over a month after his deposition, an additional charge of heresy was made against Eugenius IV in a strange incident recorded by the council historian—and stanch conciliarist—John of Segovia.[90] In late July of 1439, on a day when the council was not in session, a certain "James" (whose last name the editors F. Palacky and E. von Birk omitted from their edition), master in arts and medicine, who was dressed in ragged clothing in the manner of a hermit, appeared at the house of the president and spoke to the conciliar committee. Apparently James had already written to the *procurator fidei* (a judicial official responsible for orthodoxy and the council's rights) in order to inform the council of thirty erroneous extracts that he had drawn up from the book *Of the Simple Souls* (*simplicium animarum*), a book to which he said Eugenius IV had shown favor (*favebat*).[91] James went on to say that after Eugenius had been deposed by the council, he had set up three bishops as judges: the bishop of Venice (Lorenzo Giustiniani), the bishop of Recanati (Tommaso Tomasini Paruta), and Fantino

---

85. The main Constance bulls on this topic were *Haec sancta* and *Frequens*, establishing councils as the supreme ruling authority in the church. For a full account of the clash between Eugenius IV and the Council of Basel, see Stieber, *Supreme Authority*. For general background and an overview of the struggles between pope and council, see Steven Ozment, *The Age of Reform (1250–1550): An Intellectual and Religious History of Late Medieval and Reformation Europe* (New Haven, CT: Yale University Press, 1980), 173–185.

86. Stieber, *Supreme Authority*, 38–39.

87. Stieber, *Supreme Authority*, 39–40.

88. Stieber, *Supreme Authority*, 53–55.

89. Stieber, *Supreme Authority*, 55–56.

90. Guarnieri writes that the incident took place on 31 July ("Il movimento," 474), but Edmund Colledge sets the date as 22 July. See Colledge, Introduction to *The Mirror of Simple Souls*, lxiv.

91. John of Segovia, *Monumenta Conciliorum Generalium Seculi Decimi Quinti: Concilium Basiliense*, ed. F. Palacky and E. von Birk, vol. 3.3 (Vienna: C.R. Officinae Typographicae aulae et status, 1873), 341. James refers to Eugenius by his "civilian" name, Gabriel Condulmer.

Dandolo (the future bishop of Padua).[92] These three proceeded to imprison certain people who were prosecuting "those holding the errors of the said book" (*tenentes errores dicti libri*).[93] Feeling that he was at risk of imprisonment, presumably because of his role in compiling the list of errors, James's relatives asked for his safe conduct to explain himself. This request was refused, and so James, fearing for those who were incarcerated, entered the prison in disguise and led them out. He apparently had many other things to say about Eugenius's support of the *Mirror* and support for those who adhered to the errors of the *Mirror*. For this reason, James said, the pope ought to be judged a heretic. He had recorded sixteen cases of Eugenius's support for the book, and he petitioned the council to free those who were still incarcerated. The episode ends with the information that thirty-six copies of the *Mirror* had been discovered by the council commissioners, and these were brought to Basel to be burned.[94]

What are we to make of this episode? There are more questions than answers. The *Mirror* does not appear again in John of Segovia's record, and it does not appear in other accounts.[95] If the council acted upon any of James's accusations, there is no known record of it. Some have questioned this event's authenticity, suggesting that it might have been a fabrication on the part of John of Segovia.[96] But the peculiarity of the story, with the hermit "James" appearing from nowhere with accusations involving Eugenius and the *Mirror*, seems too unusual to be entirely made-up.[97] The first part of it seems to be a strange, garbled version of the 1437 Venice inquisition. It is entirely likely that the events in Venice were manipulated and spun in a way that would fit the purpose of attacking Eugenius. It was, after all, instigated by Eugenius and partially conducted by Eugenius's friend Lorenzo Giustiniani, and it involved numerous other close friends and associates of the pope. But in this version, the roles are reversed: Eugenius is the supporter of the *Mirror*, and those who oppose it are arrested at his direction. The cast of characters has also changed: Giovanni of Capestrano has disappeared, as well as Antonio Correr and Antonio Zeno, to be replaced by the Dominican Tommaso Tomasini Paruta and Fantino Dandolo,

---

92. John of Segovia, *Concilium Basiliense*, 341.

93. John of Segovia, *Concilium Basiliense*, 341.

94. John of Segovia, *Concilium Basiliense*, 342.

95. Aeneas Sylvius Piccolomini does not note this episode in his *De gestis Concilii Basiliensis*. See *De Gestis Concilii Basiliensis Commentarium Libri II*, ed. and trans. Denys Hay and W. K. Smith (Oxford: Oxford University Press, 1967).

96. Colledge, Introduction to *The Mirror of Simple Souls*, lxvi. See also Trombley, "Latin Manuscripts," 215.

97. Guarnieri identified James the hermit with Giacomo (James) de Zocchi, who copied and owned the polemical treatise discussed in chapter 4, but examination of this manuscript seems to discount this. Trombley, "New Evidence," 141n19. Guarnieri's identification is in "Il movimento," 474–476.

who would succeed Pietro Donato as the bishop of Padua in 1448.[98] Lorenzo
Giustiniani notably still makes an appearance. Oddly, the events have now been
shifted from 1437 to the summer of 1439, after Eugenius was deposed as a heretic by the council.

Worthy of note is that the text does not say the judges imprisoned those
working against the *Mirror* itself but those working against the *tenentes*, the
*people* who adhered to its errors. Here, again, we find the impression of a group,
a circle of people thought to be "followers" of the *Mirror's* words. This echoes
Bernardino's sermons and Antonio Zeno's description of a *conventiculum* who
possessed the *Mirror*, as well as the "heresy of the simple soul" found in the *vita*
of Giovanni of Capestrano. The use of the group image in this context was
perhaps meant to give the impression that Eugenius himself was part of such a
group and therefore imprisoned their detractors to protect them and himself.
The evocation of a group may also be another garbled reference to the treatment of the Gesuati. As Gagliardi points out, the inquisition against the Gesuati, which resulted in their exoneration, may have been perceived as too
lenient, or the perception may have been that whatever evidence of heresy it
found was hushed up.[99] Adding to this perception was probably the fact that
Eugenius IV and his circle had close ties to the Gesuati from the years when
they belonged to the community of San Giorgio in Alga; in fact, Antonio Correr was said to be a part of the Gesuati before joining San Giorgio.[100] Therefore,
it could potentially have looked like a less than an impartial inquiry. But, whatever reports circulated of the Venice inquisition, the stand-out component was
that it targeted a group of people who were readers and "followers" of *The
Mirror of Simple Souls.*

The motive was obviously to discredit Eugenius IV further, but the timing is
unusual. By the time this accusation arose, Eugenius's deposition had already
been formally declared. Additionally, Eugenius's main offenses fell under the category of disobedience to the council and not of holding or practicing any particular heresy or belief.[101] Why the additional accusation? Perhaps it was meant to
solidify the image of Eugenius as a heretic and to further justify the council's
actions, as the debate over whether Eugenius should be accused as a heretic had
been highly contentious.[102] John of Segovia could also have decided to include it
as an extra heresy ascribed to Eugenius, one that added doctrinal and spiritual
transgressions to the existing charges of disobedience and obstinacy.

98. King, *Venetian Humanism*, 358.
99. Gagliardi, *Pauperes Yesuati*, 331. Guarnieri also makes this point in "Il movimento," 650.
100. Gagliardi, *Pauperes Yesuati*, 332.
101. See Stieber, *Supreme Authority*, 55.
102. See, for example, the debates recorded in Piccolomini, *De Gestis Concilii Basiliensis*, 21–31.

Once again we find the *Mirror* singled out as a marker of heresy. It seems, however, an odd choice of a black mark against Eugenius's name, Venice inquisition or no. This might be the strongest indication yet that the *Mirror* had attracted a fair amount of notoriety. This was not, however, the first time that Eugenius had been accused of favoring or participating in a "free spirit"-esque lifestyle. In May 1431, during Eugenius's first clash with the council, the Swiss scholar and conciliarist Felix Hemmerlin (ca. 1388–1460) alleged that Eugenius had been a "helper and supporter of beghards" and that Eugenius had himself been a beghard once.[103] This almost certainly stems from Eugenius's bull of 1431, *Audientiam nostram*, which protected the rights of "orthodox" beguines and beghards (a bull which Hemmerlin had glossed and attacked).[104] But it could also be a reference to the secular religious community that Eugenius—then Gabriel Condulmer—had founded in Venice along with his cousin Antonio Correr, San Giorgio in Alga. Before formal recognition in 1404, this community had begun as merely a group of Eugenius's associates all living an ascetic lifestyle together, without a formal rule (although the community would later take the rule of the Augustinian canons).[105] This loose, semireligious way of life could have appeared to some as a beghardian lifestyle, and Eugenius's later support of beghards would have only cemented this impression. If a later opponent were looking to build upon this accusation of beghardism, it would not be a great leap to make an association between being a beghard and being a supporter of the *Mirror*, since, as we saw with Bernardino of Siena and as we will see with the text in chapter 3, *Ad nostrum*, describing the "errors of the beghards," was frequently associated with the *Mirror*. Eugenius's association with the *Mirror* through the Venetian inquisition—and his own Venetian origins—could have provided the link.

Then we have the intriguing mention of thirty-six copies of the *Mirror* brought to Basel to be burned. According to John of Segovia, it was not James who brought these copies, but they were discovered by the council commissioners, who had them brought to Basel. This seems to add an extra chronological layer to the incident recorded here. Presumably the discovery and collection of these copies were prompted by James's accusation and did not take place beforehand. This means that the commissioners did take some kind of action and that they sent people to seek out copies. Where exactly these copies were found is unclear, but as they were brought *to* Basel, perhaps they were found in outlying areas nearby. If true, this means that the *Mirror* was

---

103. Rudolf Haubst, *Studien zu Nikolaus von Kues und Johannes Wenck aus Handschriften der Vatikanischen Bibliothek* (Münster: Aschendorff, 1955), 118.

104. Haubst, *Studien*, 118.

105. Cracco, "La fondazione."

circulating in and around Basel. Perhaps it even arrived there as a consequence of the council, since the Council of Basel was a massive center of textual exchange.[106] Given the number and range of attendees at the council, it would in fact be more surprising if it *hadn't* made its way there, through one avenue or another, given the diversity of its readership, as this chapter shows.

"If true" is the key phrase here, however. Was this part of the story also a fabrication of John of Segovia? Perhaps, though it is difficult to say. Like with the figure of James himself, it seems unlikely that John would have completely fabricated these copies of the *Mirror*. True or not, it does serve an additional rhetorical purpose. In a way, it provides a neat capstone to the narrative of Eugenius's heresy given in this account, by indicating that the *Mirror* was circulating on a large scale. This would have made it a prevalent—and therefore more threatening—carrier of heresy, perhaps even implying that it was flourishing *because* Eugenius had tried to thwart those who worked against it. Therefore the mention of the thirty-six copies was perhaps meant to lend more weight and urgency to James's accusation.

In a way, the use of the *Mirror* here is the culmination of all the condemnations and attacks that came before. A little more than a decade after Bernardino of Siena first attacked it, by 1439 the *Mirror* seems to have attracted enough attention and censure to become a well-known example of heresy, enough so that it could become a ready political weapon. If the accuser expected his accusation to carry any weight, then he must have felt the *Mirror* to have such a reputation that to accuse someone of being its *fautor* would carry with it the stain of heresy.

## Warnings to Women: Cecilia Gonzaga and Diodata degli Adimari

Two more brief criticisms of the *Mirror* in Italy appear a few years after the incident at the Council of Basel. In 1443, Gregorio Correr wrote a letter to Cecilia Gonzaga. Gregorio was the nephew of Antonio Correr, and he was made an apostolic notary by Eugenius IV in 1433. By 1443 he was the commendatory

---

106. In the words of Daniel Hobbins, "Probably no single event was more important than this council for the spread of late medieval texts of all kinds." *Authorship and Publicity*, 203. Basel was also an important hub for the transmission of mystical texts, such as those of Meister Eckhart and Jan van Ruusbroec, especially through the group known generally as the "Friends of God," who also exchanged texts with the Modern Devotion. See Wybren Scheepsma, "Godsvrienden, Jan van Ruusbroec en de Moderne Devotie: Religieuze Bewegingen van de Veertiende Eeuw en hun Verhouding Tot de Volkstalige Geestelijke Literatuur," *Spiegel de Letteren* 56, no. 4 (2014), and Esther Jonker, "Teksten op reis: Handschriftelijke getuigen van betrekkingen tussen Brabant en Bovenrijn in de veertiende eeuw," *Ons Geestelijk Erf* 83 (2012).

abbot of San Zeno in Verona.[107] Cecilia was the daughter of the first Marquis of Mantua, and she decided in 1445 to enter a Clarissan convent rather than acquiesce to the marriage her father had arranged for her. Cecilia and Gregorio had been educated together at the "Casa Giocosa," a school lead by the prominent humanist Vittorino da Feltre.[108] Gregorio's letter of 1443 is concerned mainly with Cecilia's desire to join a convent, and he offers her lengthy advice on fleeing the world. Near the end of the letter, he comes to the issue of her studies and reading. He forbids her to read secular literature or poetry and urges her to instead read the Psalter and the early Christian fathers. He wonders why some seek out the "alien eloquence" of "heathen" works "when we enjoy such an abundance of our own Christian eloquence?"[109] He then warns her away from another sort of book: "You should also consider alien those trifling songs and the ravings of dreamers, such as that book by an I-don't-know-who silly little woman, which is called *The Mirror of Simple Souls*. Repudiate such books. You should read nothing that is not used and approved by the learned."[110]

A second warning appears in a similar setting in Florence a few years later, sometime between 1449 and 1451, in a letter written by the Observant Dominican, archbishop of Florence, and eventual saint Antonino Pierozzi to the widow Diodata ("Dada") degli Adimari.[111] In his "Letter 14," written in Italian, not Latin, Antonino writes to Dada of the difficulties of pursuing and persevering in goodness. Initially, he says, we may hate the spiritual doctrines that we read, but then, like a sheep, once we ruminate on them through meditation, we want to follow such doctrines. He then goes on: "And if a little book should come into your hands which is entitled *Of the Simple Souls*, which some people have reputed to be spiritual, beware of reading it, because it is dangerous, and has caused many to be ruined."[112]

---

107. Margaret L. King and Albert Rabil, *Her Immaculate Hand: Selected Works by and about the Women Humanists of Quattrocento Italy* (Binghamton: Centre for Medieval and Early Renaissance Studies, 1983), 91.

108. Margaret L. King, *Humanism, Venice, and Women: Essays on the Italian Renaissance* (Aldershot: Ashgate, 2005), 291.

109. Gregorio Correr to Cecilia Gonzaga, trans. in King and Rabil, *Her Immaculate Hand*, 103.

110. "sicut libellum illum nescio cuius mulierculae, qui *Speculum animarum simplicium* intitulatur." Latin from "Opuscula G. Corrarii," *Anecdota Veneta*, vol. 1, ed. Giovanni B. Cantarini (Venice, 1777), 42; cited also in Guarnieri, "Il movimento," 469. The translation is my own partial modification of that from King and Rabil, *Her Immaculate Hand*, 103.

111. On Antonino and Dada's relationship see Judith Bryce, "Dada degli Adimari's Letters from Saint Antonino: Identity, Maternity, and Spirituality," *I Tatti Studies in the Italian Renaissance* 12 (2009).

112. Antonino Pierozzi, Letter 14, in *Lettere di sant'Antonino: Archivescovo di Firenze*, ed. Tommaso Corsetto (Florence: Tipografica Barbèra, 1859), 147. "E se ti venisse alle mani uno libretto, intitolato *Dell'Anima semplice*, il qual sogliono avere persone reputate spirituali, ten' guarda di leggerlo; perocch' è pericoloso, e molti n' ha fatti rovinare."

While brief, these two mentions of the *Mirror* are intriguing, in part for the little extra details they offer but also for the dimensions they add to our view of the *Mirror*'s circulation. The first thing that catches the eye is Gregorio Correr's awareness that the author of the *Mirror* was a woman. How he came to such a conclusion is unknown; it is highly unlikely that he knew of Marguerite Porete specifically. More likely is that he had encountered a copy bearing the name *Margarita*. We know that the name *Margarita* was circulating in some way with the *Mirror* in two cases, one of which is in the Latin tradition. MS Laud Latin 46, the *Mirror* held by the Bodleian Library and discussed in the next chapter, gives *Margarita* as an alternate title for the *Mirror* in its incipit. The second is in the Italian version, where the work was attributed to Margarita of Hungary. In this instance, the former might be more likely. Gregorio's stated ignorance as to the identity of the "silly little woman" makes it seem less likely that he is referring to the Italian attribution, as Margarita of Hungary was well known and popular in Italy. We can assume that Gregorio probably learned of the *Mirror* and its "ravings" through his uncle Antonio. And, again, here we see the *Mirror* coming up in a broader discussion of acceptable and unacceptable books, much like it did in one of Bernardino's sermons. It is worth noting that the *Mirror* is the only spiritual work that Cecilia is warned against here; the others Gregorio mentions are secular or pagan texts. Clearly, Gregorio felt this was the most likely suspect spiritual text to come into Cecilia's hands.

This brings us to Antonino Pierozzi's warning to Dada degli Adimari. He, too, expresses the same belief: the *Mirror* may "come into your hands." Antonino, however, takes a slightly more strident tone than Gregorio: the *Mirror* is "dangerous" and, interestingly, "has caused many to be ruined." One wonders whether Antonino had firsthand knowledge of this "ruin," or if he was merely repeating rumors that he had heard. Antonino, like many of the men in this chapter, was also an associate of Eugenius IV, having hosted him and other attendants of the Council of Florence at his Dominican convent in Florence; Eugenius had also appointed Antonino to be archbishop of Florence.[113] It is possible that Antonino had heard of the events surrounding the *Mirror* in Venice and Padua, hence the "ruin" brought by reading it. But he also likely had seen the *Mirror* circulating himself, given that we know the *Mirror* was present in at least one convent near Florence, at Camaldoli.[114] But however Antonino came to his information, here again is the implication that reading the *Mirror* causes people to fall into its "dangerous" doctrine.

---

113. Ezra Sullivan OP, "Antonino Pierozzi: A *Locus* of Dominican Influence in Late Medieval and Early Renaissance Florence," *Angelicum* 93, no. 2 (2016): 347.

114. More on this later in this chapter.

Both of these instances are another example of the broad range of the *Mirror*'s circulation. Whether or not Cecilia or Dada actually came across the *Mirror*, both Gregorio and Antonino *believed* there was a chance that they would. In other words, the *Mirror* was moving in circles to which these women were connected. Furthermore, Cecilia and Dada themselves add another layer of social diversity. Cecilia was both aristocratic—the daughter of a Marquis—and highly educated, literate in both Latin and Greek; she also eventually entered the religious life.[115] Dada remained in the secular sphere and was more middle class—from a notarial family—and likely not literate in Latin.[116] Yet both are warned away from the same spiritual reading material. Once again, we see evidence of the *Mirror* as a book that cut across multiple levels of class, education, gender, and religious affiliation.

## North of the Alps: Johannes Wenck

While a majority of the events we have seen here took place in Italy, it is worth mentioning one other instance of *Mirror* criticism that took place in the German empire in the 1440s. This is useful in part because the manuscript discussed in chapter 2 may have German connections, but also because this case shares the same characteristics as the criticisms in Italy. The reference is found in a manuscript owned by the fifteenth-century theologian Johannes Wenck (d. 1460), who was based at the University of Heidelberg. Wenck had attended the Council of Basel and was a supporter of the conciliarists against Eugenius IV.[117] The manuscript in question, Vatican City, BAV, MS Pal. lat. 600, is a compilation of texts that Wenck assembled and annotated extensively. Many of them are texts from the Council of Basel; a few others deal with heresy and lay mendicancy. In this latter category is a text found on folios 228r–233r, labeled in the description done by the Universitätsbibliothek Heidelberg as *Questiones de paupertate voluntaria*.[118] This is an anonymous treatise that criticizes beghards and accuses them of fostering mystical errors. In a section discussing the idea of needing only love and being absolved from the use of the virtues, the tract mentions that such topics appear in a certain book called *De simplici anima*.[119] "Out of that book six

115. King, *Humanism, Venice, and Women*, 88.
116. See the details of her life in Bryce, "Dada degli Adinari's Letters."
117. On Wenck see Haubst, *Studien*.
118. MS Pal. lat. 600 is fully digitized on the Universitätsbibliothek's website: https://digi.ub.uni-heidelberg.de/diglit/bav_pal_lat_600/0463 (October 2020).
119. MS Pal. lat. 600, f. 228v. Noted also in Haubst, *Studien*, 119, and in Lerner (citing Haubst), *Heresy of the Free Spirit*, 170. Trombley's "Latin Manuscripts" incorrectly states that the reference appears on f. 229v.

errors burst forth and spread [*pullularent*], which are condemned in [*Ad nostrum*]. And the book is held in Strasbourg, in the Charterhouse."[120] Wenck underlined the title of the book, and in the margin next to this passage he drew a *manicula* pointing to it and wrote underneath, "Ecce librum *de simplici anima*."[121]

Unfortunately the author of this treatise is unknown. But it shows many of the same attitudes we have seen throughout this chapter. First, by being included in a specifically antibeghard treatise, it is explicitly linked with beghards, and with *Ad nostrum*. Here, six errors of *Ad nostrum* "burst forth and spread" from the *Mirror*—another instance in which the *Mirror* is seen as the original source of these errors. But notice that the author is discerning in his allegations: he says only six errors, whereas the decree itself contains eight. Like modern scholars, he, too, saw a match between only some of *Ad nostrum*'s articles and the *Mirror*, and not all. The use of *pullularent* here is also worth noting, as it was a word frequently used when describing the emergence and spread of heretical sects.[122] This again carries the idea that the *Mirror* is a cause of heresy, that it actively *propagates* heresy, a sort of heresy super-spreader. Finally, we are told that the *Mirror* is held by the Carthusians of Strasbourg. Whether this was a Latin version is unknown, but it also shows a Carthusian connection to the *Mirror* on the Continent, showing that its appeal to that order was not confined to the charterhouses of England. But this short passage actually raises more questions than it answers. How does the author know the Carthusians of Strasbourg owned a copy? Did he see it himself, or was it secondhand information? We simply do not know. But it is worth noting that, in the course of criticizing beghards and mystical errors, the author makes a point of mentioning the Carthusians' possession of the *Mirror*, perhaps another glimpse of concern over the popularity of this work. In addition to the Carthusians' known enthusiasm for mystical literature, Strasbourg itself and areas nearby would have been likely places for the *Mirror* to circulate, as Strasbourg was a hub in a robust textual network in which mystical texts with affinities to the *Mirror*'s content—such as those by Meister Eckhart, Johannes Tauler, and Jan van Ruusbroec—circulated widely.[123] Who knows how many other *Mirrors* may have been residing in other monastic houses—or semireligious communities—nearby.

---

120. MS Pal. lat. 600, f. 228v. "Ex quo libro sex errores pullularent qui reprobantur de hereticis, unico capitulo. Et habetur liber Argentine, in cartusia."

121. MS Pal. lat. 600, f. 228v; Lerner, *Heresy of the Free Spirit*, 170.

122. See, for example, the entry for *pullulare* in the *Dictionary of Medieval Latin from British Sources*. Available online at https://logeion.uchicago.edu.

123. For an overview see Geert Warnar, "Prelude: Northern Circulation of Fourteenth-Century Mystical Texts," in *A Companion to Mysticism and Devotion in Northern Germany in the Late Middle Ages*, ed. Elizabeth Anderson, Henrike Lähnemann, and Anne Simon (Leiden: Brill, 2014). Like Basel, Strasbourg was a main center for the Friends of God.

This passage clearly piqued Wenck's interest. Had he, too, encountered the *Mirror*? Or was he merely noting its alleged heretical nature for future reference? Robert Lerner suggests that Wenck recognized the *Mirror* from its use against Eugenius at the Council of Basel.[124] This is entirely possible, if that accusation actually took place; Wenck could also have heard news of the Venetian inquisition through his attendance at Basel. But, given that the *Mirror* seems to have been in Strasbourg, then it was probably circulating elsewhere in German areas as well. It is also likely that news of the *Mirror's* heresy had traveled to Germany from Northern Italy via other routes, which will be discussed in the next chapter.

## Two Faces of the *Mirror*

This chapter began with Bernardino of Siena and the suggestion that he was likely motivated in his attacks on the *Mirror* by fear of its popularity and influence. We have seen that this fear was shared by several others. But how valid were these fears? A striking feature of these events is how heavily concentrated they are within the circle of close friends and allies surrounding Eugenius IV; these men knew each other well and frequently corresponded and worked with one another. Might this give a false impression of how ubiquitous the *Mirror* really was? Did the *Mirror* alarm them because it really was popular and influential, or were these fears merely resounding in an echo chamber, where the same alarm sounded by one or two members of their group came back repeatedly? This was, after all, how the "heresy of the free spirit," the *Mirror's* close sibling, was given a life of its own.[125]

The evidence, however, reveals a striking undercurrent to this atmosphere of suspicion. There is a layer of popularity underlying most of these events. We can see this most clearly in the Venice inquisition, where copies of the *Mirror* were found in the hands of multiple people. It would be to dismiss the integrity of the sources entirely to think that these were complete fabrications by Giovanni of Capestrano and Antonio Zeno. The warnings given by Bernardino of Siena and those given to Cecilia Gonzaga and Dada degli Adimari also reflect this: there was an expectation that those reading or listening to these warnings might encounter the *Mirror*—in both Latin and the vernacular, at that. But we do not only have to read between the lines in order to get a glimpse of the *Mirror's* broad appeal; the manuscripts of the *Mirror* itself tell a similar story. The Italian

---

124. Lerner, *Heresy of the Free Spirit*, 170.
125. Lerner, *Heresy of the Free Spirit*.

copies possibly confiscated by Giovanni of Capestrano have already been mentioned. As we saw in the introduction, several of the Latin copies are also bound with other works of unimpeachable orthodoxy by authors such as Richard of St. Victor, Bonaventure, and St. Bernard. One copy, MS Chigianus C IV 85, was owned by the eminent Sacro Speco Benedictine monastery in Subiaco. Although that particular copy was written in 1521, it is made from an older exemplar, so we can assume it was within Subiaco's orbit in the fifteenth century as well.[126] And, indeed, the high number of continental Latin copies and their geographical diversity, combined with the presence of the Italian version, which was attributed to a saint, demonstrate a fairly robust circulation.

But there is also relatively new evidence from within the manuscript corpus that speaks to the *Mirror*'s popularity. A recently discovered copy throws the complicated atmosphere around the *Mirror* into sharp relief. This is Florence, Biblioteca nazionale centrale, MS Conv. soppr. G.3.1130.[127] It is a codex comprising various spiritual and contemplative works, such as Hugo de Balma's *Theologia mystica* and Bonaventure's *Itinerarium mentis in Deum*, as well as various epistles by Ambrose, Augustine, Bernard of Clairvaux, and William of St. Amour. Among these works is also included a Latin copy of *The Mirror of Simple Souls*. But its importance does not only come from its inclusion alongside so many "classics" of Western Christian spirituality but also from who placed it there alongside them. The manuscript was compiled and mostly copied by John-Jerome of Prague (ca. 1368–1440), who was a monk at the famed monastery of Camaldoli in Tuscany, roughly sixty-three kilometers east of Florence. John-Jerome was not what one would call a "radical" reader or a monk with daring tastes; considered to be "theologically conservative," he preferred simple, straightforward texts and was a fierce opponent of heresy.[128] Yet he seems to have embraced the *Mirror*, a work not usually noted for simplicity or straightforwardness, including it in a manuscript that he intended for his fellow monks. He copied it himself and even bound a copy of one of his own works in the same codex.[129] John-Jerome completed the manuscript in 1425, a scant two years before Bernardino of Siena's first warning against the *Mirror* in Siena.[130] Within the initial "A" of *Anima*, the first word of the text,

---

126. The old exemplar is mentioned in the manuscript itself by the copyist, who on folio 127r notes, "Here mice have nibbled the original." Verdeyen, Introduction to *Speculum CCCM*, xi.

127. On this manuscript see Trombley, "New Frontiers," 164–174.

128. William P. Hyland, "John-Jerome of Prague: Portrait of a Fifteenth-Century Camaldolese," *American Benedictine Review* 46, no. 3 (1995): 313, and Trombley, "New Frontiers," 174.

129. Trombley, "New Frontiers," 166–167.

130. The explicit on folio 124r reads, "Finitus in eremo Camalduli per fratrem Ieronimum reclusum. Sub anno Domini MCCCCXXV die XVIII Octobris." I thank the Biblioteca nazionale centrale for providing me with digital photographs of this manuscript.

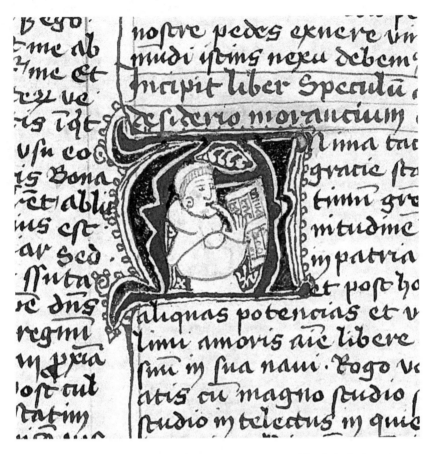

**FIGURE 1.1.** An illustration of a monk happily reading *The Mirror of Simple Souls*, drawn by John-Jerome of Prague in the "A" of the opening word (*Anima*) of the *Mirror*, on folio 103r of MS Conv. soppr. G.3.1130. By permission of the Ministry of Culture/Biblioteca nazionale centrale, Florence.

John-Jerome even drew a picture of a monk—perhaps himself?—reading the *Mirror* with a gentle smile on his face (figure 1.1).

The only acknowledgment that he saw anything amiss in the *Mirror*'s content is a note that John-Jerome inserted after writing the title of the work: "To be read cautiously, and not by everyone."[131] Furthermore, the manuscript itself continued to reside in Camaldoli unscathed; the only hint that any trouble may have brushed against it is the fact that the *simplicium* in the title was scratched out at some point. Whether this was because "simple" itself was problematic (i.e., it was not a text that should be read by "the simple") or because it was an

---

131. MS Conv. soppr. G.3.1130, f. 103r. "Caute legendus, et non ab omnibus."

attempt to conceal the work in light of the controversies that began around the *Mirror* in the 1430s, it is impossible to say for certain. It is, however, a minor erasure; whatever reservations John-Jerome and later readers may have had, these clearly did not override their belief in its usefulness. There is also evidence to suggest that other copies of the *Mirror* were circulating within the Camaldolese Order, particularly in Venice, as indicated by its appearance in an eighteenth-century catalog of San Michele di Murano, the Venetian Camaldolese house, at which John-Jerome was a *visitator*, and at which he resided sometime after 1433, when he was prevented from returning to Camaldoli from the Council of Basel by the then prior, Ambrogio Traversari.[132] This copy also notes an association with John-Jerome, as below the *Mirror*'s title is a note reading, "This book bears the name 'Jerome of Prague,' but it says it should be read cautiously, and not by everyone indiscriminately."[133] This means that it was probably made from the copy John-Jerome himself made at Camaldoli. It is possible, therefore, that John-Jerome himself brought the *Mirror* to the Venice house, either when he went as a *visitator* or when he took up residence there later. Furthermore, if John-Jerome arrived at the Venetian house in 1433 and remained there until his death in 1440, then he, and likely a copy of the *Mirror*, was there during Giovanni and Lorenzo's inquisition in 1437. Word of the inquisition would surely have reached San Michele. And yet it retained its copy of the *Mirror* all the way up to the eighteenth century.

This fits neatly into the fears that the *Mirror*'s critics expressed. Here we have a moderate monk at one of the most respected monastic institutions on the Italian peninsula reading, copying, and possibly circulating the *Mirror* as a useful and beneficial work. Evidence that it was also circulating in other eminent Benedictine institutions such as Santa Giustina and Subiaco—as well as among the Carthusians in Strasbourg—confirms further that this was not merely a case of educated elites worrying about the reading habits of "the simple." This could perhaps be the case if the only evidence we had came from, say, the Venice inquisition, or the letter to Dada degli Adimari. But it is clear that the *Mirror* attracted readers within the ranks of the professed religious *as well as* among the more general reading population. Its appearance in these varied contexts would certainly have caused alarm to those who saw its contents as heretical and dangerous.

---

132. Hyland, "Portrait," 329.

133. Giovanni Benedetto Mittarelli, *Bibliotheca Codicum Manuscriptorum Monasterii S. Michaelis Venetiarum Prope Murianum, una cum Appendice Librorum Impressorum Seculi XV, Opus Posthumum Johannis-Benedicti Mittarelli* (Venice: Typographia Fentiana, 1779), col. 507. "Hic liber nomen fert Hieronymi Pragensis, sed caute legendus dicitur et non ab omnibus indiscriminatim."

*Why* was *The Mirror of Simple Souls* caught up in such a swirling mix of acceptance and suspicion? One could point to the intense currents of reform coursing through most religious orders in the years after the Great Schism, the Observant reform movement. Observant reformers across all orders emphasized obedience, strict adherence to institutional regulations, and stringent moral rectitude. One can see how those intensely focused on institutional obedience and behavior could fear the *Mirror*'s freewheeling, paradoxical, and decidedly anti-institutional approach to spiritual life. Bernardino of Siena provides a particularly good example. Bernardino, a pillar of the Observant Franciscan movement, fiercely admonished and warned his audiences against sin and vice; it was the main overarching theme of most of his sermons.[134] He emphasized constant vigilance against these things, and one can see this underlying his treatment of the *Mirror*, as he repeatedly casts its readers as those who shun the work needed to ward off these threats. The confiscation order issued at Santa Giustina—a key driver of Benedictine Observance—shows a similar clash between a desire for stricter institutional regulation and obedience and the *Mirror*'s ethereal swirl of personal self-negation. An anti-institutional message may also not have sat well within the tense atmosphere of the standoff between councils and the papacy. With the supreme authority of the church in such a contentious state and the chaos of the Great Schism not yet a distant memory, a book that spoke of two churches and the soul seeking God without the aid of reason and church-prescribed practices may have disturbed those locked in such a power struggle. We will see in chapters 3 and 4 a more detailed picture of what specific concerns critics of the *Mirror* had, as we examine texts that refute particular passages taken from its pages.

But, while those texts show us the specific passages from the *Mirror* that alarmed certain readers, when it comes to speculating about what broader spiritual currents might have caused readers to reject the *Mirror*, the point might largely be moot. This is because, as the example of John-Jerome demonstrates, the *exact same* spiritual currents might also have brought people to *embrace* the *Mirror*. John-Jerome, too, was a fierce proponent of reform, advocating strict morality and a purging of vice and sin from the church.[135] He also was a great believer in *sancta simplicitas*, holy simplicity, in which the individual not only

---

134. See the overview in Mormando, *Preacher's Demons*, 14–15.

135. This is exemplified by his biting criticism of prelates in his sermons at the Council of Pavia/Siena, as well as in his other writings. See William Patrick Hyland, "John-Jerome of Prague and Monastic Reform in the Fifteenth Century," *The American Benedictine Review* 47, no. 1 (1996); Hyland, "Reform Preaching and Despair at the Council of Pavia-Siena (1423–1424)," *The Catholic Historical Review* 84, no. 3 (1998); and Hyland, "Giovanni-Girolamo da Praga al Concilio di Basileo: varieta del discorso di riforma," in *Camaldoli e l'ordine Camaldolese dalle origini alla fine del XV secolo*, ed. Cécile Caby and Pierluigi Licciardello (Cesena: Centro Storico Benedetto, 2014).

divests himself of material worldly attachments but also rejects the "distractions" of pagan philosophers and the overly stylized rhetoric of the humanists.[136] Such a worldview could easily fit with the *Mirror* in its rejection of overly learned reason and its "church" of "simple" souls who support and inform the Holy Church.[137] The intense spirituality of the *Mirror* rooted in total rejection of worldly things—be they physical or intellectual—also undoubtedly appealed to many of the brothers of Santa Giustina. This attraction to the *Mirror*, juxtaposed against the alarm that was contemporarily coursing through some of the same circles, emphasizes that we cannot necessarily separate out the *Mirror*'s readers into supporters and detractors based on what we think their milieu would approve or disapprove of.

This contentious, contradictory atmosphere around the *Mirror* sets the stage for the three manuscripts to be discussed next. Some of them, such as those examined in chapters 3 and 4, can be placed directly in the midst of some of the events described in this chapter. The manuscript in the next chapter may not at first appear to fit into it so neatly, but, as we shall see, there is plenty of reason to think that it, too, had connections to this same contested world.

---

136. Hyland, "John-Jerome of Prague and Monastic Reform," 80–87; and Trombley, "New Frontiers," 168. See also the entirety of Hyland, "The Climacteric of Late Medieval Camaldolese Spirituality: Ambrogio Traversari, John-Jerome of Prague, and the *Linea salutis heremitarum*," in *Florence and Beyond: Culture, Society, and Politics in Renaissance Italy: Essays in Honor of John M. Najemy*, ed. D. S. Peterson and D. E. Bornstein (Toronto: Centre for Reformation and Renaissance Studies, 2008).

137. Trombley, "New Frontiers," 170–172.

# CHAPTER 2

# The Excision of Error

## The Fragments of MS Laud Latin 46

The physical destruction of a book is an evocative image. One could imagine, in the aftermath of *The Mirror of Simple Souls'* condemnation in Paris, William of Paris lighting a bonfire of confiscated copies. This is, of course, more an image drawn from the popular imagination than the historical record. Through the work of scholars like Thomas Werner, we know that burning books was often intended not as a way of wiping all copies of a text physically from the earth but rather as a symbolic act representing the destruction of error, meaning that it was often only one or a few copies of a text that were consigned to the flames or otherwise destroyed.[1] The spectacle of this act, however, remains a powerful representation of the efforts some church authorities took to ensure that the pages of heretical books did not find the eyes of any more readers.

The attacks and criticisms on the *Mirror* that we saw in the preceding chapter were relatively light on physical destruction. The only suggestion we have of *Mirror* copies being destroyed is the episode with the hermit James denouncing Eugenius IV, when thirty-six copies were allegedly brought to Basel to be burned. Aside from this, we can only guess as to whether copies of the *Mirror* were destroyed as a result of the various attacks made upon it. It seems likely that the

---

1. Werner documents cases in which books were also lacerated or torn to pieces. *Den Irtumm liquidieren: Bücherverbrennungen im Mittelalter* (Göttingen: Vandenhoeck & Ruprecht, 2007), 21–125.

inquisition of Giovanni of Capestrano may have included such an event, but there is no record if it did. Similarly, we do not know if anyone took Bernardino of Siena's advice that whoever owned the *Mirror* "puts it into the fire". Evidence of verbal attacks on the *Mirror* abound—physical ones, not so much.

This means, then, that Oxford, Bodleian Library, MS Laud Latin 46 is a unique artifact within the *Mirror*'s history. This manuscript not only provides evidence of the intentional destruction of a *Mirror* copy but is the only *physical* evidence we have of the *physical* destruction of one. The Laud codex did, once, contain a complete copy. But all that now remains of the Laud *Mirror* are a few fragments: a single page, seven stubs, and the remains of the final paragraph. While it is more likely that this copy was removed discreetly, rather than being destined for the drama of a public burning, its fragmentary appearance here nonetheless implies a removal based on a less-than-approving attitude toward its contents. Of the three codices examined in this book, MS Laud Latin 46 is the one most familiar to scholars. It has been frequently invoked in passing as an example of the *Mirror* being treated as a suspicious text.[2] Verdeyen also included it in his descriptions of the Latin codices and the edition of the Latin text. The Laud copy has, however, never been investigated in its own right. This is perhaps because the Laud codex initially seems like a dead end. Unlike the other two manuscripts examined here, there are no texts or written attacks that can be read and analyzed. Instead, we are presented with an absence, which, at face value, seems to be self-evident: the absence of the *Mirror* is the evidence of opposition. There is no note from the perpetrator saying why it was done. There is no contemporary document (that we know of) recording the act.

But if we are to chronicle opposition and condemnation of the *Mirror*, there is hardly a stronger statement of opposition than physical destruction. Such an event demands further investigation. Additionally, we have just seen how diverse the *Mirror*'s reception could be; vehement opposition frequently rubbed shoulders with acceptance. No other manuscripts of the *Mirror* show signs of deliberate physical destruction. It seems necessary, then, to further interrogate its excision from the Laud codex. What was it about this *particular* copy of the *Mirror* that made someone cut out its pages? There were plenty of contemporary forces—both directed at the *Mirror* specifically and in the wider religious climate—that could have moved the cutter's hand. The Laud codex takes us to southern Germany, where we have already seen some instances of *Mirror* criticism. As this chapter will demonstrate, there is plenty of reason to think that the climate surrounding the Laud *Mirror* was not unrelated but rather connected to

---

2. See Kerby-Fulton, *Books under Suspicion*, 276; Sargent, "Latin and Italian," 145; and Trombley, "Latin Manuscripts," 198–199.

and grew out of the contentious climate on the Italian peninsula. Furthermore, while the *Mirror* is the only text in this manuscript that was removed, other texts that appeared alongside it also carried their own histories of suspicion or unease, and some also bear physical marks of disapproval or distrust.

Since there is a lack of textual evidence, the story of the Laud *Mirror* has to be pieced together mostly through codicological and paleographical evidence, some of which is new and much of which has not previously been discussed. This chapter, then, is as much about an incarnation of the *Mirror* as a unique object as it is a text. Additionally, when one's main piece of evidence is the evidence of absence, this inevitably involves a great deal of speculation and guesswork. But the evidence is strong enough to make such speculation reasonable—which is really all the historian can hope for. Once we scratch the surface of MS Laud Latin 46, it appears as one of the most mysterious and complex codices of the *Mirror*. While much about the Laud *Mirror* is (for now) still a mystery, by exploring both its textual surroundings and its geographical context, this chapter will for the first time shed new light on some previously dark corners of our knowledge.

## Oxford, Bodleian Library, MS Laud Latin 46

MS Laud Latin 46 is a fifteenth-century mixed parchment and paper manuscript of 110 folios and 7 stubs. It is relatively large in comparison to most of the other Latin *Mirrors*, measuring about 21.2 (W) × 29.1 cm (H) (8.3 × 11.4 in). According to the updated online Bodleian description, it is made up of three distinct sections: section A, which runs from the table of contents up to the first work in the codex; section B, which includes the *Mirror* fragments; and section C, which comprises various patristic and pseudoclassical texts, many of which are copied in the same hand that copied section A.[3] Sections A and C appear to have been added to section B at a later date.[4] Watermark evidence points to a date of origin perhaps sometime between 1430 and 1460. The text is written in two columns throughout the whole manuscript; the one exception is folio 94v, where it is written in a single block. Plain red and blue initials are used to start new texts and new sections within texts. It is a very plain manuscript, with no decoration.

MS Laud Latin 46 was given to the Bodleian by Archbishop William Laud in 1639 as part of his third donation to the library of 559 manuscripts, most

---

3. The newly updated description of the Laud codex can be found at https://medieval.bodleian.ox.ac.uk/catalog/manuscript_7620 (accessed September 2020). See also table 2.1.

4. More on this later.

of which he had acquired from the Continent during the Thirty Years' War.[5] An inscription on the bottom of folio II(b)r denoting Laud's ownership bears the date 1637; this is not the year in which the manuscript was acquired on the Continent but rather refers to the date the manuscript was received and recorded at Laud's palace in London.[6] This means the manuscript's acquisition on the Continent would have been a few years earlier, perhaps sometime between 1631 and 1636.[7] The manuscript is not in its original binding; like all of the manuscripts in the Laud collection, it was rebound in brown leather when it came into the archbishop's possession, and the front cover was stamped with his coat of arms.

It is difficult to say with certainty who owned the codex before it came into Laud's possession. The geographical possibilities are discussed later in this chapter. There are no marks of ownership and no other internal evidence pointing to any specific group or individual owner. One tentative guess might be that it was owned by a Benedictine house, given how frequently the Latin *Mirror* appeared in Benedictine hands in northern Italy, and the fact that one other work in the codex—a collection of Pseudo-Augustinian epistles—also frequently circulated in Benedictine houses.[8] But it could also be the personal property of a Latin-literate reader interested in mysticism and patristic piety. This latter subject could possibly suggest a connection to a reader or readers interested in humanist writings. This is perhaps indicated by the Pseudo-Augustinian epistles and the works by Jerome, and the works found in section C of the manuscript, all of which are either patristic or classical/pseudoclassical. The Latin translation of Chrysostom's *Ad stagirium* that is excerpted on folio 94v was originally done by Ambrogio Traversari, the famed humanist leader of the monastery of Camaldoli.[9] Works such as the Seneca/Pseudo-Seneca texts *De liberalibus studiis* and *De quattuor virtutibus* could also point toward a humanist taste in texts. While it can be risky pigeonholing texts as

---

5. An overview of Laud's manuscript donations can be found in R. W. Hunt's introduction to H. O. Coxe, *Laudian Manuscripts: Reprinted from the Edition of 1858–1885, with Corrections and Additions, and an Historical Introduction by R. W. Hunt*, ed. R. W. Hunt, Quarto Catalogue 2 (Oxford: Bodleian Library, 1973), ix–xxiv. A detailed overview focusing on his German manuscript acquisitions is found in Daniela Mairhofer, *Medieval Manuscripts from Würzburg in the Bodleian Library: A Descriptive Catalogue* (Oxford: Bodleian Library, 2015), 9–36.

6. Mairhofer, *Medieval Manuscripts*, 11.

7. Mairhofer, *Medieval Manuscripts*, 11.

8. See Franz Römer, "A Late Mediaeval Collection of Epistles Ascribed to Saint Augustine," *Augustinian Studies* 2–3 (1971–1972), and Römer, "Notes on the Composition of Some Pseudo-Augustinian Letters," *Studia Patristica* 14 (1976).

9. Charles L. Stinger, *Humanism and the Church Fathers: Ambrogio Traversari (1386–1439) and Christian Antiquity in the Italian Renaissance* (Albany, NY: SUNY Press, 1977), 130. It is worth repeating that, in addition to being another ally of Eugenius IV, Traversari clashed repeatedly with John-Jerome of Prague. See Hyland, "The Climacteric."

being the sole province of any distinct "-ism" or group, these texts' currency within such a group might suggest such a connection.

One of the first things that strikes the reader when examining the Laud codex is how eclectic its contents are in comparison to most other Latin manuscripts containing the *Mirror*, which usually have either one or no other work bound up with it.[10] MS Laud Latin 46 is an interesting mix of complex theological and contemplative texts and simple, instructive works of piety, mostly drawn from the patristic (or pseudopatristic) tradition. There are also several blank pages, places where a work stops abruptly, and places where a spare page or space has been filled with a short extract from a larger work, giving the impression that the manuscript's owner collected and assembled bits and pieces over time as they came across texts that interested them. The later additions of sections A and C reinforce this impression. In order to give a clearer idea of how the manuscript is put together, a brief overview of its contents is presented in table 2.1.[11]

Section B of the manuscript is copied in one hand, the sole exception being the excerpt from Chrysostom's *Ad stagirium monachum* on folio 94v. When this excerpt begins, the manuscript takes on a more haphazard appearance. The excerpt from Chrysostom is written on the verso of folio 94, the last folio of section B, in the same hand that wrote the Letter of Lentulus on folio I(b), showing that it was an addition done when sections A and C were added on. The hand which copied the Seneca / Pseudo-Seneca in section C is the same hand that copied section A, and is also one of the main commenting hands in the margins throughout the codex. This suggests that the separate parts of the manuscript were brought together early and purposefully. In other words, section B, containing the *Mirror*, was deliberately included with the Pseudo-Seneca and Jeromian texts of section C, rather than these being brought together by chance in, say, its seventeenth-century travels. This means that whoever compiled this manuscript initially wanted the *Mirror* to be there as a part of their mystical / patristic collection.

## Origins of MS Laud Latin 46

The origins and provenance of this manuscript prior to its acquisition by William Laud are difficult to pin down. For many years it was described as German in origin; this is how it was described by R. W. Hunt in the Bodleian *Quarto Catalogue*, and Paul Verdeyen, probably following the catalog, also designated it as

---

10. Only two other Latin copies—Bautzen, Domstiftsbibliothek Sankt Petri, MS M I 15 and Florence, Biblioteca nazionale centrale, MS Conv. soppr. G.3.1130—contain multiple other works besides the *Mirror*.

11. The table follows the order in which they appear in the manuscript. The foliation follows that found on the Bodleian online description.

*Table 2.1*   Contents of MS Laud Latin 46

| FOLIO NUMBER(S) | CONTENTS |
| --- | --- |
| **Section A**<br>1* (i[b]r) | In the top left-hand corner is a small table of contents referring to select letters or works of Pseudo-Augustine and Jerome. |
| | Written in a different hand in the top right-hand corner are two sentences taken from Jerome's *Ad Eustochium virginem*: *Patiens enim vir multum prudentia. Qui autem pusillanimis est vehemens insipiens est. Hieronimus. Difficile est modum tenere [in omnibus.]* (The edge of the page has crumbled away here, obscuring most of *in omnibus*.) |
| | In the center of the page, written in the same hand as the Jerome quotation, is the *Letter of Lentulus*, an apocryphal letter supposedly written by the fictional Publius Lentulus, allegedly the governor of Jerusalem before Pontius Pilate. The letter is from Lentulus to the Roman senate, giving a physical description of Jesus.[1] |
| | At the very top of the page are a few words that at the moment are indecipherable. A rough transcription is as follows: *Se no[n] de f[i]nir[e]*. |
| | There are also several squiggly lines on the lower outer edge of the page, which look like pen tests. |
| II(b)r–X(b)r | Table of contents for Ramon Llull's *Disputatio heremite et Raymundi super aliquibus dubiis sententiarum magistri Petri Lombardi*. At the bottom of folio II(b)r is a seventeenth-century *ex libris* designating the manuscript as a possession of Archbishop William Laud: *Liber Guil[lelmi]. Laud Archiepiscopi Cantuarensis et Cancellari universitatis Oxoniensis. 1637.* |
| **Section B**<br>1r-66–70r | Ramon Llull's *Disputatio heremite et Raymundi super aliquibus dubiis sententiarum magistri Petri Lombardi*. |
| 66–70v | The first page of Marguerite Porete's *Speculum simplicium animarum*. It is followed by seven stubs of pages that were intentionally cut out. One stub contains the remnants of marginalia at its top, middle, and bottom. |
| 71r–v | A misbound page of the Pseudo-Augustinian epistles. Folio 71r contains the final quarter of *Ad nembridum*, the entirety of *Ad bonifacium*, and the first three quarters of *Ad cirillum*. Written on folio 71v are the last quarter of *Ad cirillum*, the entirety of *Ad fabianum* and *Ad brisinam*, and the first half of *Ad ualentinum*. (Meant to be between 76v and 77r.)[2] |
| 72r–73r | At the top of folio 72r are the last eight lines of the *Speculum simplicium animarum*. These lines contain the end of Godfrey of Fontaines's appraisal, and the closing lines of the entire work (figure 2.1).[3] Just below this is the beginning of *Libellus de uita, doctrina et reuelationibus beate Angele de Fulgineo* (Angela of Foligno's *Memorial*, which I refer to here as her *Liber*), which includes the paragraph describing the work's examination by Cardinal Giacomo Colonna and the first twelve of her twenty considerations. This copy is unfinished, breaking off suddenly in the second column on folio 73r. It ends at the very beginning of the twelfth consideration: *Duodecimo cum nostro uidetur mihi qui possem cum rebus seculi . . .* The following folios are blank (73v, 73bis, 73ter, and 73quatr). |
| 74r–80r | A collection of Pseudo-Augustinian epistles. Letters of Ps. Jerome and Ps. Bernard of Clairvaux (*Ad Leontinum*) are also a part of this collection and regularly circulated with them.[4] The exception is a single epistle of Jerome, *Ad Eustochium*, which appears on folio 80r and is unfinished—this did not circulate with the collection. |
| 80v–87vb | Jerome, book I of *Contra Jovinianum*. |
| 87vb–88vb | Ps. Jerome, *Ad Pammachium et Oceanum*. |
| 88vb–89vb | Ps. Jerome, *Ad Oceanum de vita clericorum*. |
| 89vb–91va | Jerome, *Ad Heliodorum exhortatoria*. |

*Table 2.1*    (continued)

| FOLIO NUMBER(S) | CONTENTS |
| --- | --- |
| 91vb–93va | Jerome, *Ad Paulinum.* |
| 93bis–94r | Blank |
| 94v | An excerpt from Ambrogio Traversari's Latin translation of John Chrysostom's *Ad Stagirium monachum.* |
| **Section C**<br>95r–96va | Ps. Seneca, *De remediis fortuitorum (Ad gallionem).* |
| 96vb–98vb | Seneca, *De septem artibus liberalibus.* |
| 98vb–100vb | Martin of Braga, *Formula vitae honestae,* attributed here to Seneca. |
| 100vb–101rb | Seneca, *Ad lucilium.* |
| 101rb–102ra | Pelagius (attributed to Jerome), *Libellus fidei ad Innocentium papam.* |
| 102rb–105r | Ps. Jerome, *De essentia divinitatis.* |
| 105r | Jerome, *Ad Marcellam de decem nominibus Dei.* |
| 105v–110v | Blank |

[1] Ernst von Dobschütz, *Christusbilder: Untersuchungen zur christlichen Legende,* in *Texte und Untersuchungen zur Geschichte der altchristlichen Literatur* vol. 3, ed. Oscar Gebhardt and Adolf Harnack (Leipzig: J. C. Hinrichs'sche Buchhandlung, 1899).

[2] An edition of these letters is found in parts I and II of Römer, "A Late Mediaeval Collection," 129–143 (I) and 147–168 (II).

[3] On the appraisal of the *Mirror,* see introduction. For the text, see *Speculum CCCM,* 407–409.

[4] See Römer, "A Late Mediaeval Collection." These epistles circulated as a unit and were immensely popular in Italy and southern Germany in the fifteenth century.

such.[12] In past publications, I have also described this codex as German, based on watermark evidence, which will be discussed shortly. Within the past ten years, however, this designation has been questioned.[13] As recently as September 2020, the Bodleian Library has updated its online catalog entry for this manuscript, which adds further complexity to the issue.[14] Since the geographical location of this manuscript has some bearing on discussions that take place in the next section regarding knowledge of the *Mirror* as a heretical book, let us consider the codicological and paleographical evidence. The updated Bodleian entry suggests that an Italian origin for the manuscript seems more likely than a German one. This is based on mainly paleographical grounds, where the catalogers note some Italian characteristics and the use of some Italian spellings (*sesaginta,* using "x" for "s"—e.g., *concluxiones*). The catalog also suggests Italian watermarks for all three sections of the manuscript. The motif for the Laud manuscript's watermarks is the same throughout: a plain "triple mount" or "Dreiberg" design.[15]

---

12. Hunt, *Quarto Catalogue 2,* 21–22; Verdeyen, Introduction to *Speculum* CCCM, XI–XII.

13. Sargent, "Latin and Italian," 88n8.

14. Bodleian Library, *A Catalogue of Western Manuscripts at the Bodleian Libraries and Selected Oxford Colleges,* https://medieval.bodleian.ox.ac.uk/catalog/manuscript_3358 (accessed September 2020).

15. See Gerhard Piccard, *Die Wasserzeichenkartei in Hauptstaatsarchiv Stuttgart: Dreiberg,* vol. 16 (Stuttgart: Kohlhammer, 1996).

According to the catalog, sections A and C of MS Laud Latin 46 contain watermarks potentially from Udine (Piccard nos. 77–87, ca. 1448–1463), and section B from Ferrara, Urbino, or Pesara (Piccard nos. 73–76, ca. 1433–1436). My own examination of the watermark evidence shows a more mixed picture, and here I modify or correct some of my previous arguments.[16] For watermarks found in all three sections of the Laud codex, I digitally overlayed photographs of the watermarks with the images of the most similar-looking watermarks listed in Piccard. For section A, while two of the Udine watermarks are very close (Piccard nos. 81 and 86), the watermark that matches near perfectly is a watermark from Pappenheim in 1442.[17] Pappenheim lies roughly sixty-five kilometers south of Nuremberg in Bavaria and would have been within the diocese of Eichstätt. In terms of section C, no watermarks matched closely—neither the Udine watermarks suggested by the catalog, nor the Pappenheim watermark. On folio 102 there is a very close match with a watermark from Frankfurt (1450), which is a Dreiberg with the additional motif of a cross above it—although, as the watermark is written over, it is more difficult to discern the shape and it is not as clear a match as that in section A with the Pappenheim watermark. As for section B, none of the catalog's suggested watermarks from the Piccard collection match the watermarks in this section, and I have not yet located any other Piccard watermarks that match closely.[18]

Regarding paleographical elements, there have been varying opinions. As mentioned earlier, R. W. Hunt described it as "written in Germany" in the *Quarto Catalogue*. Nigel Palmer, consulted by Michael Sargent, did not feel that the handwriting was German, though it is unclear whether this was his opinion solely on the hand that wrote the *Mirror* or for all the hands in the manuscript.[19] As mentioned earlier, the Bodleian catalog notes the presence of Italian spellings and characteristics for the whole codex, but particularly for sections A and C; for B, the abbreviations for "qui" and "tur" are noted as Italian. When I did my own consultations several years ago with two Italian paleographers—Attilio Bartoli Langeli and Sandro Bertelli—they did not think the features of the hands for either the *Mirror* or those in section C looked distinctly Italian but suggested the more generic designation of "Northern European."[20]

---

16. Trombley, "Latin Manuscripts," 187n3.

17. The Pappenheim watermark seems to be only in the online Piccard database and not the printed catalog. See *Piccard Wasserzeichen*, Hauptstaatsarchiv Stuttgart, https://www.piccard-online.de/einfueh.php?sprache=, no. 150055 (accessed September 2020).

18. This differs from the comments in Trombley, "Latin Manuscripts," where it says that the Pappenheim watermark can be found throughout. While the Dreiberg motif is used consistently, the particular shape of the Dreiberg differs between sections.

19. Sargent, "Latin and Italian," 88n8.

20. Trombley, "Latin Manuscripts," 187n3.

These contradictory opinions and the tricky watermark evidence make for a slightly confused picture of the Laud manuscript's origins and pre-Bodleian provenance. Absolute certainty either way is likely impossible. There may be, however, a happy medium, and in terms of chronicling opposition to the *Mirror*, this indistinct place of origin, rather than impeding discussion, actually helps to broaden it and raise several interesting scenarios. It is entirely possible that this codex traveled in both areas and therefore contains characteristics from both. This is perhaps made more likely by the fact that the manuscript was not assembled all at once, with sections A and C being added on to B later. The earlier part of the codex (section B, which includes the *Mirror*) could have been copied and acquired in northern Italy. The later sections—which include section A containing the Pappenheim watermark—could then have been added later in Germany, hence the watermark. Regarding the paleographical characteristics, it is possible that the manuscript could have been copied by someone who was trained in Italy but was not necessarily native to or permanently based there. This will be discussed momentarily.

## Connecting the Dots: MS Laud Latin 46 in the Anti-*Mirror* Landscape

The potentially mixed origins of MS Laud Latin 46 enhance, rather than impede, discussion of the history of opposition to the *Mirror*, providing more than one interesting scenario for this manuscript's "life cycle" and the circumstances of the *Mirror*'s excision. First, there is the Italian scenario, where the Laud codex is both written in Italy and still there when the *Mirror* is removed. These circumstances are relatively easy to imagine. We know that, in the north of Italy, copies were likely circulating in the Congregation of Santa Giustina and in certain Camaldolese houses, as well as generally in Venice and probably Padua. There were also public prohibitions of and inquisitions into the *Mirror* in these areas. It is entirely likely that, if this copy was in Italy at the time of its removal, that removal was a direct result of one or more of those events. While there is no hard evidence to prove it, perhaps this copy was one of those circulating in Santa Giustina and was then removed after its prohibition in 1433. It could also be the case that whoever owned the Laud *Mirror* removed it themselves, perhaps out of fear during the inquisition in Venice or confiscations in Padua, or after hearing that it was a suspect text, having not realized it before, similar to Giovanni Tavelli's dealings with the text. Or it could be that the manuscript received scrutiny from a third party who recognized it as a heretical text. One can easily imagine a situation from, for example, the inquisition of

Giovanni Capestrano or Antonio Zeno's actions against the *Mirror* in Padua in which someone fell under suspicion, or was apprehended while fleeing, and their books were either examined or they were caught with the *Mirror* in hand. The text could then have been either confiscated or simply destroyed.

The second scenario, in which the manuscript is in Germany when the *Mirror* is removed, involves a bit more assembly. A location in southern Germany may at first seem to distance it contextually from the other manuscripts examined here, but there is no reason to see it as such. As we saw in chapter 1 with Johannes Wenck and the treatise he owned, negative responses to the *Mirror* occurred in southern Germany as well as in northern Italy. This is more than coincidence. Southern Germany and northern Italy were highly integrated and tightly bound by intellectual and cultural ties, mostly forged through the flow of people to and from northern Italian universities. While the broader persecution of beghardian and Eckhartian errors that took place in Germany could have informed how the Laud copy was treated, there is plenty of reason to believe that it was particular knowledge of the *Mirror* as a "bad book" that caused its destruction. That knowledge, in all likelihood, came from Italy.

The ecclesiastical world of southern Germany was in constant contact with that of northern Italy, and paramount among these connections was the city of Padua, the site of Antonio Zeno's confiscation of the *Mirror* and consultation with the university theologians, and also where Giacomo de Zocchi, the owner of the anti-*Mirror* polemic discussed in chapter 4, taught canon law. There was an almost constant flow of German students to the University of Padua, most drawn to its highly regarded reputation both in medicine and in canon and civil law.[21] Countless German officials—both secular and ecclesiastical—were trained in law there; it produced so many bishops that Monika Fink-Lang dubbed it a *Pflanzstätte der Bischöfe*, a "seeding ground of bishops."[22] A figure such as Johann von Eych (ca. 1404–1464), who was bishop of Eichstätt (the diocese in which Pappenheim was located) between 1445 and 1464, near to the time when the later sections of MS Laud Latin 46 might have been copied, provides a useful example. Von Eych was a well-known reformer, particularly in regard to the major monastic houses of his diocese such as Rebdorf and the nunnery of St. Walburg.[23] Like many other members of his family, von Eych studied law at

---

21. Monika Fink-Lang, *Untersuchungen zum Eichstätter Geistesleben im Zeitalter des Humanismus* (Regensburg: F. Pustet, 1985), 33.

22. Fink-Lang, *Untersuchungen*, 33. See also Melanie Bauer, *Die Universität Padua und ihre fränkischen Besucher: Eine prosopographisch-personengeschichtliche Untersuchung* (Neustadt An der Aisch: Schmidt, 2012), and Agostino Sottili, *Studenti tedeschi e umanesimo italiano nell'Università di Padova durante il Quattrocento* (Padua: Antenore, 1971).

23. See the biography in Alfred Wendehorst, *Germania Sacra: Das Bistum Eichstätt: Die Bischofsreihe bis 1535* (Berlin: Walter De Gruyter, 2006), 202–220, and the essays in Jürgen Dendorfer, ed., *Re-*

the University of Padua, starting in 1429.[24] He was already at the level of "licentiate" in canon law by 1430, and in 1433 he was promoted to doctor of canon law.[25] Von Eych maintained close contacts with Padua after returning to Eichstätt, and the vast majority of officials who served under him were also graduates of the Padua *studium*, both those who had studied contemporaneously with him and others who graduated in later years; in fact von Eych actively favored having such alumni in his circle.[26] He was steeped in humanist piety and culture and actively propagated and cultivated a humanist milieu around him. While von Eych was certainly one of the most prominent "Frankish" students of Padua, he was by no means an exceptional case. Ecclesiastical institutions and courts across southern Germany—in Augsburg, Würzburg, Nuremberg, Bamberg, and so on—were filled with men who had studied law at Padua.[27] This kind of exchange can also be seen through the manuscript holdings of certain German religious institutions. A useful example is the Domstiftsbibliothek of St. Kilian in Würzburg, whose library holdings have been reconstructed digitally by the Universitätsbibliothek in Würzburg and the Bodleian Library. (Worth noting is the fact that William Laud acquired a significant number of manuscripts from Würzburg and included nearly all of them in his third donation of 1639—the same donation that included MS Laud Latin 46.) St. Kilian's cathedral library contains a number of fifteenth-century legal codices—such as *Decretal* commentaries—that were either copied in northern Italy (in some cases by German scribes) or are codices of legal texts from Italian universities that were copied in Germany.[28]

Given the volume of students returning from northern Italy/Padua to southern Germany, it seems highly likely that the hostile attitudes toward the *Mirror* we saw in the previous chapter made their way north of the Alps. We

---

form und früher Humanismus in Eichstätt: Bischof Johann von Eych (1445–1464) (Regensburg: F. Pustet, 2015).

24. Wendehorst, *Bistum Eichstätt*, 203.

25. Caspare Zonta and Iohanne Brotto, eds., *Acta Graduum I*, 243, no. 765. See also Melanie Bauer, "Fränkische Studenten an der Universität Padua: Johann von Eych und seine *comprovinciales*," in Dendorfer, *Reform und früher Humanismus*, 27–46.

26. Dendorfer, *Reform und Früher Humanismus*, 17; Bauer, "Fränkische Studenten," 34–45.

27. Bauer's *Universität Padua* provides a useful prosopography of fifteenth-century German students at Padua and their subsequent careers.

28. See, for example, Würzburg, Universitätsbibliothek Würzburg, MS M.ch.f. 189, a copy made in southern Germany of a *Decretals* commentary by Giacomo de Zocchi, the professor at the University of Padua who owned Padua, Biblioteca universitaria di Padova, MS 1647, the codex discussed in chapter 4; or MS M.ch.f.18, copied in 1433 in Italy by Heinrich Moens and then owned by Johannes von Eyb, who was educated in Padua in the 1430s and who was an episcopal official and vicar in Eichstätt from 1441 to 1445. Klaus Walter Littger, "Ob memoriam quondam venerabilis viri, qui hoc in testamento suo fieri deposuit: Die fata libellorum der frühen Eichstätter Humanisten," in Dendorfer, *Reform und Früher Humanismus*, 388. MS M.ch.f.18 also has one of the same watermarks as MS 1647 (Briquet 10500).

can discern two main points of transmission. First, Padua was the site of two identifiable *Mirror*-related incidents: the proscription against the *Mirror* at the 1433 general chapter of Santa Giustina and the confiscation of *Mirror* copies by Antonio Zeno in 1437.[29] News of Santa Giustina's stance on the *Mirror* could easily have spread through the university, as the two institutions had close ties, with the congregation frequently recruiting monks from the university's ranks.[30] Four years later, Antonio Zeno issued his command that anyone possessing the *Mirror* must turn it over to him under pain of excommunication; this event also resulted in Zeno consulting the faculty of theology at the university on the *Mirror*'s orthodoxy. Knowledge of Zeno's activities against the *Mirror* must surely have circulated among students residing in Padua at the time, particularly if Zeno had made a public command for the *Mirror* to be turned over. News of the inquisition in Venice could also have been circulating.

The second point of transmission comes from within the university itself. As mentioned, Giacomo de Zocchi, a professor of canon law at the university, had copied and owned a polemical text that attacked the *Mirror* as dangerous and heretical and refuted its doctrines using canon legal authorities. De Zocchi clearly considered the text important, as he copied it in his own hand and included it alongside a *Decretals* commentary and a list of Roman *Rota* decisions, both works he would have used in a professional capacity. De Zocchi was a preeminent figure at the University of Padua, and he served as one of the nominators for the degree in canon law to countless students, including many German students; several of the German students he taught would later go on to distinguished ecclesiastical careers.[31] De Zocchi could have been a source of information on the *Mirror* to his students, just as he might have done with Marco Donato in 1437. Given these connections to the *Mirror* in Padua—all of them hostile—it is not unreasonable to suggest that students who graduated from Padua and returned to Germany could have brought with them knowledge of the *Mirror* as a heretical or dangerous book. Adding to this the example of Johannes Wenck and his recognition of the *Mirror* solidifies the argument that, in addition perhaps to the general anxiety over beghardian errors and "free spiritism," hostility toward the *Mirror* in particular could also have led to a removal of the Laud copy if it was in Germany at the time.

---

29. While the prohibition of the *Mirror* within the Santa Giustina congregation was not targeted specifically at Padua, it would certainly have applied to the Paduan house, which was also the mother house.

30. Collet, *Italian Benedictine Scholars*, 4. Giacomo de Zocchi also had close associations with Santa Giustina. See chapter 4.

31. See Zonta and Brotto, *Acta Graduum I*, passim, and Primo Griguolo, "Per la biografica del canonista Ferrarese Giacomo Zocchi († 1457): l'insegnamento, la famiglia, i libri," *Quaderni per la storia dell'Università di Padova* 44 (2011): 187.

It is here that the paleographical evidence comes back into play. The mixed appearance of the hands in the Laud codex could also be a result of this mixed German-Italian environment. It is possible that some parts of the manuscript could have been copied by someone who had been educated in Italy but was not Italian themselves. In her study of German students at the University of Padua in the fifteenth century, Melanie Bauer has noted that several German writers who had been educated in Italy in the mid-to-late fifteenth century sometimes used "hybridized" handwriting styles that exhibited Italian-humanistic characteristics as a result of their training at Italian universities.[32] Examination of the hands that Bauer provides as examples of this mixed hand reveals that some of them have similar characteristics to at least two of the hands that appear in the Laud manuscript, from sections A and C. It is entirely possible, then, that rather than being either distinctly Italian or German, the hands in the manuscript blend characteristics from both, and therefore at least some of the Laud codex could have been copied by a German scholar who had been educated in Italy.

In both scenarios, Italian or German, the *Mirror* was initially brought into the Laud codex as one piece of a spiritual collection geared toward contemplation, mysticism, and patristic piety, but was then rejected. In a sense, then, the Laud codex reflects the *Mirror*'s broader turbulent reception.

## The *Mirror* in MS Laud Latin 46

Let us return to the manuscript itself. What about the codicological evidence for the *Mirror*'s destruction? The question would seem to be self-evident: the stubs show that it was cut out; the *Mirror* was there, and now it is not. But what are the details that accompany that action? What did the *Mirror* in this manuscript look like? How exactly was it removed? How might this action relate to the other works in this manuscript? The codicological details can suggest possibilities that help to paint a fuller picture, beyond just the bare fact of this copy's absence.

The largest remaining piece of the *Mirror*—its first page containing the title, incipit, and roughly the first two chapters—appears on what the Bodleian has labeled 66–70v, a parchment page. It is written in two columns in a rather small, neat *hybrida* hand (which, according to the Bodleian entry, has some humanistic forms), the same hand that copied Llull's *Disputatio*, Angela's *Liber*, the Pseudo-Augustinian epistles, Jerome's *Contra Jovinianum*, and the Jeromian epistles that follow it, up to folio 94r. This *Mirror* also bears a rather interesting incipit. It reads: *Incipit liber qui appellatur speculum animarum simplicium. Aliter vocatur*

---

32. Bauer, *Universität Padua*, 246–251.

*Margarita.* ("Here begins the book that is named *The Mirror of Simple Souls.* It is otherwise called *Margarita.*")[33] This is an intriguing reference to Marguerite Porete's name, however indirect. It is possible that this copy represents a tradition that originally carried a reference to the author's name, which then became garbled over time.[34] It could also be the case that this "Margarita" was given to this *Mirror* from the Italian version, where several copies were attributed to Saint Margarita of Hungary.[35] Perhaps the Margarita here is a garbled reference to that attribution. A hint may come from the Latin used here: *appellatur* refers to its formal title; it is formally "named" *The Mirror of Simple Souls.* But it is then "otherwise <u>called</u> *Margarita*," using *vocatur.* This could tentatively suggest that *Margarita* is an alternate name that the scribe perhaps has only heard given to the work, rather than a name that appeared on the text from which he was copying.

The first page fragment is then followed by seven stubs, showing where the *Mirror* was cut out from the manuscript. The *Mirror's* first page and five of the stubs seem to be part of the same quire as that containing the final pages of Llull's *Disputatio.* The first page of the *Mirror* survives, then, because whoever cut it out wanted to preserve the final pages of Llull's work. For many years, descriptions of the Laud copy have only mentioned the single page and the stubs.[36] There is, however, more to the *Mirror* here than previously thought: other parts of the *Mirror's* text have long hidden in plain sight. When (gently) prized apart, one of the stubs shows fragments of marginalia. More importantly, the *Mirror's* concluding lines have also survived (figure 2.1).[37] As shown in table 2.1, this last new bit of text is found on folio 72r, just above the beginning of Angela of Foligno's *Liber.* This fragment has long been overlooked, and, while small, it has important implications for how we perceive the *Mirror's* inclusion in the Laud codex and gives us a clearer idea of what the intact copy looked like.[38]

---

33. MS Laud Latin 46, f. 70va. The Bodleian entry has "et hec" instead of "Aliter," but although the text in this section is somewhat faded, it is clearly an uppercase "A" rather than an "h" (compare with how "A" is written in the name "Augustine" in the Pseudo-Augustinian epistles). Verdeyen has "alias" instead of "aliter," but a round "r" is used, which could have been mistaken for an "s."

34. Trombley, "Latin Manuscripts," 199–200.

35. Falvay, "Italian Version," 230–232.

36. See Verdeyen, Introduction to *Speculum* CCCM, xi–xii; Kerby-Fulton, *Books under Suspicion,* 276–277; and Sargent, "Latin and Italian," 87–88.

37. I first discovered this and the marginalia while working on my master's dissertation, which focused on MS Laud Latin 46, and then included it in my PhD thesis, Trombley, "The Mirror Broken Anew: The Manuscript Evidence for Opposition to Marguerite Porete's Latin *Mirror of Simple Souls* in the Later Middle Ages" (PhD diss., University of St. Andrews, 2014).

38. The appearance of this extra fragment is now noted in the 2020 update of the Bodleian's description.

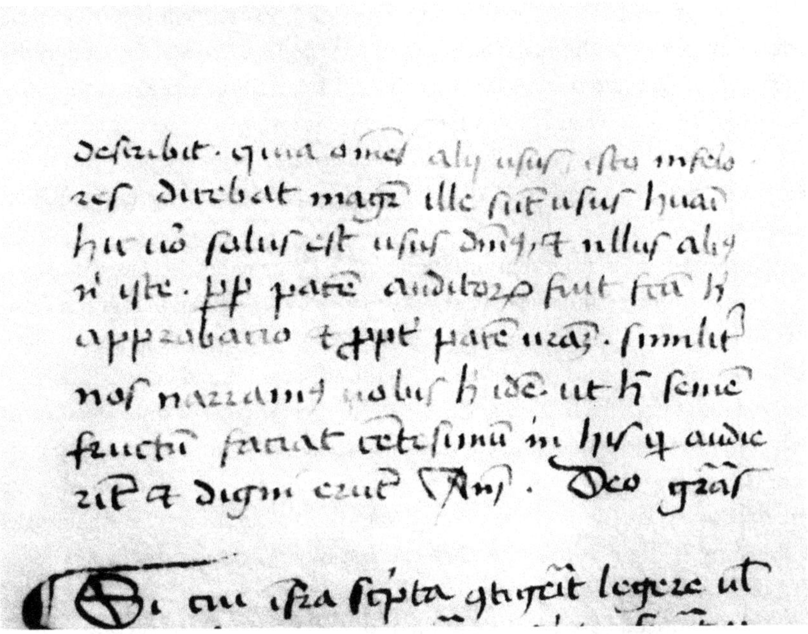

**FIGURE 2.1.**    The final lines of *The Mirror of Simple Souls* on folio 72r of MS Laud Latin 46, with the first line of the appraisal of Angela of Foligno's *Liber* just below. The Bodleian Libraries, University of Oxford, MS Laud Latin 46, f. 72r.

The final paragraph—which contains the last few lines of Godfrey of Fontaines's opinion on the work, and the concluding sentence—is easily missed. It is written at the very top of the first column on folio 72r, in the left-hand corner, immediately above the start of Angela of Foligno's *Liber*. The reason it appears here, and not on folio 71, is due to a mix-up that must have occurred when the manuscript was bound. The single *Mirror* folio on 66–70v is immediately followed by a page of the Pseudo-Augustinian epistles, but this page of the epistle collection is misplaced. It is not the first page of the collection but is instead supposed to appear after folio 76. The formal start of the epistles is in fact on folio 74r, after the blank pages that follow Angela of Foligno's *Liber*. The misplaced page gives the initial impression that the small bit of text above Angela's *Liber* on folio 72r is part of the epistles. All three works are copied in the same hand, and the break between the end of the *Mirror* and the beginning of Angela's *Liber* is not immediately obvious; there are no large initials, just a single blank line and a blue pilcrow at the start of the Angela piece. Even at a more-than-casual glance, there does not appear to be anything amiss.

But, of course, if one were actually reading the manuscript through, this mistake would have been glaringly obvious. One such fifteenth-century reader did notice: the copyist of both section A and folios 95–102, who seems to have left the majority of the marginalia present in the Laud codex. He caught the mistake and directed readers through the mix-up, writing at the bottom of folio 71v, "This follows as below on page 106 [77r], at 'quaerentes docere,' etc."[39] On folio 76v, he writes below the interrupted epistle, "See the end of this above on page 96, at collocatur, etc.," directing the reader back to the first words on folio 71r.[40]

The long-hidden fragment of text on folio 72r provides a clearer image of the Mirror in this manuscript. First, the presence of the final paragraph clarifies how much of the Mirror was present. Previously, most descriptions have said that there are the stubs of thirty folios left in the Laud codex, following the old foliation, which on folio 71r is "96."[41] The remains of only seven stubs would seem to discount a full copy, as that would likely not be enough to contain the entire Mirror. But, since the last few lines of the Mirror on folio 72r are the concluding lines of the entire work, then this demonstrates that it was a full copy. If this was the case, then the rest of the quires, rather than being cut out, must have been removed in their entirety.

Also unnoticed have been the remains of marginalia on the second stub, at the top, middle, and bottom. The fragments contain nothing intelligible, but the distinguishable marks are as follows: q[uia] (top section), q[uam] / i[n] / ip[sum] / assu[-] (middle section), and q[uod] / ir[-] / se[-] (bottom section). The hand of these fragments is the same as that which directed the reader through the folio mix-up, that is, the hand appearing in sections A and C. This hand made both corrections and comments throughout the codex; since there is not enough text here to distinguish what exactly was written, it is difficult to say whether the marginalia was correction, comment, or a mix of the two. Nevertheless, these marginalia do indicate that the Mirror was read through. But if the rest of the Mirror's quires were wholly removed from the manuscript, this suggests either that the manuscript existed in fascicle form at the time, meaning the quires could be easily taken out, or that the manuscript was unbound in order for them to be removed.

The codicological evidence tells us the logistical details of how the Mirror was cut out, but it can also add contextual evidence in explaining why this copy may have found a hostile reader. But first, what tells us that the absence of the Mirror here is due to hostility against it, rather than the loss of its quires through accident? Or perhaps it was taken because someone wanted the work for them-

---

39. MS Laud Latin 46, f. 71v. "Hic sequitur ut infra a carte 106, ibi quarentes docere, etc."
40. MS Laud Latin 46, f. 76v. "Vide finem huius supra a carte 96, ibi collocatur, etc."
41. Verdeyen, Introduction to Speculum CCCM, xii; Kerby-Fulton, Books under Suspicion, 277.

selves, rather than wanting to destroy it? In response to the first question, the fact that the *Mirror* is the only work missing from the codex seems to argue against the disappearance of its remaining quires through mishap. No other works—in either this section of the manuscript or others—are missing folios. It would be strange that a work sandwiched in between two others could disappear in such a targeted and complete way. Regarding the second question, if someone removed the *Mirror* out of a desire to own it themselves, then one would expect them to have taken the first page as well, rather than show concern over preserving the last page of a work they were not interested in taking. Whereas, if someone wanted to get rid of the *Mirror*, they would not want to lose the final pages of Llull's *Disputatio*. The most logical explanation is that the *Mirror* was removed because someone disapproved of its presence there.

If we look at the overall character of the manuscript, the *Mirror* is not the only work here with a checkered history; some of its fellow texts could also have attracted potential scrutiny from those with a suspicious eye. The two works that immediately precede and follow the *Mirror*—Ramon Llull's *Disputatio* and the fragment of Angela of Foligno's *Liber*—both had their share of controversy or suspicion, as did their authors. Out of the two, Llull had the most trouble, both during his lifetime and long after. The end of the fourteenth and first half of the fifteenth centuries in particular saw his substantial corpus of works face suspicion and condemnation. His particular posthumous nemesis was the inquisitor Nicholas Eymerich, who led a fierce campaign against his works and those reading them.[42] In fact, in Eymerich's famous inquisitor's manual, the *Directorium inquisitorum*, completed in Avignon in 1376, he lists over one hundred errors taken from Llull's works and notes the books from which they are taken; several of these errors are said to have come from his *Super sententiarum*, his sentences commentary, which is the *Disputatio*.[43] In addition to this, in the fifteenth century the chancellor of the University of Paris, Jean Gerson, famously

42. On Llull controversies, see J. N. Hillgarth, *Ramon Lull and Lullism in Fourteenth Century France* (Oxford: Clarendon Press, 1971), 56, 213, 269–270, and 286, and Alois Madre, *Die Theologische Polemik gegen Raimundus Lullus: Eine Untersuchung zu den Elenchi Auctorum de Raimundo Male Sententium* (Münster: Aschendorff, 1973). See also Claudia Heimann, *Nicolaus Eymerich (vor 1320–1399): Praedicator viridus, inquisitor intrepidus, doctor egregious: Leben und Werk eines Inquisitors* (Münster: Aschendorff, 2001), 81–86.

43. For an example see the fourth article from the ninth *questio* of the second book of the *Directorium*. There is no modern edition of the *Directorium*, but a sixteenth-century printed edition with commentary by Francisco Peña has been digitized as part of the Cornell Witchcraft Collection. See *Directorivm Inqvisitorvm R. P. F. Nicolai Eymerici, Ord. Præd. S. Theol. Mag. Inquisitoris Hæreticæ Prauitatis in Regnis Regis Aragonum, Denvo Ex Collatione Plvrivm, Exemplarium Emendatum, et Accessione Multarum Literarum, Apostolicarum, Officio Sanctæ Inquisitionis Deseruientium, Locupletatum, Cvm Scholiis Sev Annotationibvs Eruditissimis D. Francisci Pegnæ Hispani, S. Theologiæ et Iuris Vtriusque Doctoris* (Rome, 1585), 189–196, http://ebooks.library.cornell.edu/cgi/t/text/pageviewer-idx?c=witch;cc=witch;idno=wit045;node=wit045%3A7;view=image;seq=217;size=100;page=root. See also Madre, *Theologische Polemik*, 74.

wrote against Llull's writings and declared his writings to be unacceptable at the university.[44] Therefore Llull and his works, much like the *Mirror*, were highly controversial.

While there is no evidence of open criticism or condemnation of Angela's *Liber*, it did perhaps garner some suspicion initially because of her (albeit contested) association with the Spiritual Franciscans.[45] Angela's *Liber*, like the *Mirror*, carries an approbation of its contents by eight Franciscan lectors—two of whom had been inquisitors—and by Cardinal Giacomo Colonna.[46] This approbation in and of itself might have been problematic, since the Colonnas were allies of the Spirituals and mortal enemies of Boniface VIII and were eventually excommunicated by him.[47] Not all of the copies of the *Liber* include this approbation, and in one copy it has been scratched out.[48] The approbation is, however, present in the Laud version, and appears immediately below the final paragraph of the *Mirror*. This means that the *Mirror*'s approbation and the *Liber*'s appeared side-by-side since the approbation appears at the end of the Latin *Mirror* and the beginning of the *Liber*. The *Disputatio* and the *Liber*, however, show no real signs of scrutiny here, and suspicion in one area and at one time does not automatically translate across to another time and place. Angela's *Liber* does stop abruptly in the middle of a sentence on folio 73ra, and the pages following it were left blank. But it is impossible to say whether it was abandoned due to suspicion or to some other factor.

There is, however, evidence for suspicion and scrutiny in other places in this manuscript. It comes not from what would seem to be the most daring works in the collection but instead from the Pseudo-Augustinian epistles, which would be considered among the more innocuous works to appear here. As mentioned, this collection of epistles circulated as a unit and was immensely popular in the fifteenth century, predominantly in northern Italy and southern Germany.[49] Franz Römer notes that the collection is written in "a most simple manner and in a homiletic style," and most of the letters, attributed either to Augustine or Jerome, are standard exhortations for living a virtuous

---

44. See Hillgarth, *Ramon Lull and Lullism*, 269, and also Ruedi Imbach, "Notule sur Jean Gerson, critique de Raymond Lulle," in *Les formes laïques de la philosophie: Raymond Lulle dans l'histoire de la philosophie médiévale*, ed. D. de Courcelles (Turnhout: Brepols, 2018).

45. Angela of Foligno, *Angela of Foligno: Complete Works*, ed. and trans. Paul Lachance (New York: Paulist Press, 1993), 111–112. On the debate over Angela's Spiritual connections, see Burr, *Spiritual Franciscans*, 335–346. On affinities between the *Mirror* and the *Liber*, see Barbara Newman, "Annihilation and Authorship: Three Women Mystics of the 1290s," *Speculum* 91, no. 3 (2016).

46. *Angela of Foligno: Complete Works*, 123.

47. Angela of Foligno, *Angela of Foligno: Memorial*, ed. Cristina Mazzoni and trans. John Cirignano (Cambridge: University of Cambridge Press, 1999), 17.

48. *Angela of Foligno: Complete Works*, 111.

49. Römer, "A Late Mediaeval Collection of Epistles."

life.[50] They touch upon subjects ranging from rejecting worldly goods, to chastity and virginity, to being wary of both physical and intellectual temptation. On the latter subject is an epistle that appears on folios 77v–78r. It is entitled *De divina sapientia*, sent from a certain "Theodore" bishop of Toledo (*Teodorus episcopus Tolletanus*) to the monks of "Saint Rifini," warning them against becoming too enchanted with the ideas of sophists and pagan philosophers. The epistle holds up Origen as an example of a once pious man who fell into error through being overly fond of pagan philosophy. This letter appears in only six other surviving copies of this epistle collection—out of a total of fifty-three—in manuscripts of both German and Italian origin.[51] At the top of the second column on folio 78r, a section of the letter appears to be scratched out. This effacement is different to the slightly faded appearance of certain parts of texts in other sections of the manuscript, in that there are visible scratch marks, suggesting a deliberate (albeit halfhearted-looking) effacement rather than the text merely rubbing off naturally.

Next to this effaced section is a marginal note that reads *Verba Origenis in extremis* ("The words of Origen as he was dying"). In the top margin of this page, above this section, there is a note, written in what seems to be a contemporary hand, but which does not appear anywhere else in the manuscript, which reads *Nota quod penitentia origenis est apocrifa* ("Note that the *Penitence of Origen* is apocryphal"). This is followed by a citation referring the reader to the fifteenth distinction of Gratian (*xv. di[stinctione] lib[ri]*), which, as we heard in the previous chapter, contains a long list of apocryphal works that it declares are not accepted by the church.[52] The *Penitentia Origenis* is indeed included in this list; we saw both this distinction and the *Penitentia* referenced by Bernardino of Siena in his sermon that distinguished between good and bad books. The *Penitentia* purportedly relates the last words of Origen, in which he laments his own wickedness. An examination of other intact copies of this epistle reveals that this is precisely what appears in the letter.[53] Therefore the epistle appears to be quoting from the apocryphal *Penitentia Origenis*. While the whole of the *Penitentia* was not erased,

---

50. Römer, "A Late Mediaeval Collection of Epistles," 115.

51. The German codices are Eichstätt, Universitätsbibliothek Eichstätt, MS Cod. st. 435; Würzburg, Universitätsbibliothek Würzburg, MS M.ch.f. 137; and Copenhagen, Det Kongelige Bibliotek, MS Thott 105. The Italian codices are Gotha, Forschungsbibliothek Gotha, MS Chart.B. 239; Vatican City, BAV, MS Chigianus A.V. 132; and Oxford, Bodleian Library, MS Canon. Pat. Lat. 40. I am grateful to the staff at all of these libraries for allowing me to view these manuscripts in person or providing me with digital photographs of the letter in question. The Eichstätt codex was owned by the parish priest Ulrich Pfeffel. See Matthew Wranovix, "Ulrich Pfeffel's Library: Parish Priests, Preachers, and Books in the Fifteenth Century," *Speculum* 87, no. 4 (2012).

52. D. 15, c. 3 , in Friedberg, *Decretum*, 36.

53. For example in Oxford, Bodleian Library, MS Canon. Pat. Lat. 40, and Gotha, Forschungsbibliothek Gotha, MS Chart.B. 239.

the first half of it—which contains some of the more colorful passages in which it says that God will grant demons eternal life, as well as exclamations that "the fruit-bearing tree is thrown down" (*Ecce arbor fructifera prostrata est*) and "the stars have fallen from the heavens" (*Ecce sidus de celo cecidit*)—is part of the effaced section. The apocryphal *Penitentia*, therefore, was noticed, partially erased, and then the reader was warned that something in this text was considered to be suspect in canon law.

Were any other copies of this letter censored in some way? Did it attract negative attention in other areas where it was circulating? In terms of explicit remarks upon it or deliberate effacement, the answer is "no"; no other copies of the letter exhibit these kinds of marks. But additional modification of this work did occur. In its other various manuscript copies, this letter essentially exists in two versions. One version is shorter, usually ending at the *Hec ille* that appears just after the words *et humilibus*. The other version—the one that appears in the Laud codex—is longer, appending an extra section that contains the *Penitentia Origenis*. This second section starts immediately after the first *Hec ille*, with no noticeable break in the text, beginning with *Jeronimus in quadam epistola* ("Jerome, in a certain letter . . ."). Two other copies of this letter—both in manuscripts of German origin—contain the shorter version, where the epistle ends at the first *Hec ille*.[54] Three other copies—one German and two Italian—do contain the longer version that has the section containing the *Penitentia*.[55] Hence two versions of this epistle were circulating: one with the quotation from the *Penitentia Origenis* and one without. Since it is clearly not a case of the letter being incomplete, as the shorter version does have a formal conclusion, denoted by the *Hec ille*, it seems that these versions of the *Divina sapientia* epistle were purposefully edited, either to include or to exclude the *Penitentia* section. It can be reasonably suggested that the section containing the *Penitentia* was perhaps edited out due to its suspicious apocryphal material, although it is equally possible that this section was added to later copies rather than erased. Nevertheless, the version of this epistle that appears in MS Laud Latin 46 contains the more "suspect" version of this letter, and someone took notice. Though the note and effacement are certainly more measured types of censorship than what the *Mirror* in this codex received, they indicate that other material in the Laud manuscript was scrutinized and modified. If someone felt it necessary to partially efface a small section of apocryphal text then it is easy to imagine someone taking more stringent measures against a text like the *Mirror*. Whether or not this was done by the

---

54. These are Eichstätt, Universitätsbibliothek Eichstätt, MS Cod. st. 435 and Würzburg, Universitätsbibliothek Würzburg, MS M.ch.f. 137.

55. MS Canon. Pat. Lat. 40, MS Chart.B. 239, and MS Thott 105.

same person we cannot say for sure, but it certainly shows that a reader or readers of this manuscript were not entirely comfortable with everything that appeared between its covers, and that they took steps to correct, point out, or remove questionable material.

## Conclusion

While this manuscript perhaps has the least to offer us in terms of textual evidence regarding the *Mirror*, it is still a significant artifact in the history of its reception. Additionally, the Laud manuscript is a useful reminder of manuscripts as unique objects, not just static conduits for texts. This *particular* manuscript shows what happened to a *particular* copy of the *Mirror*. The pieces of codicological evidence that we can glean from MS Laud Latin 46 help to bring this *Mirror* copy out of the margins and into a much bigger conversation about its reception as a whole. When more closely examined, its indistinct origins offer multiple scenarios for the *Mirror*'s treatment in the codex. It could perhaps have fallen afoul of the efforts against the *Mirror* taking place in Venice and Padua, or may have been removed while in southern Germany. The social and intellectual connections between northern Italy and southern Germany—in the form of Italian-educated German scholars, monks, and ecclesiastical officials returning north—meant that knowledge of the *Mirror* as a dangerous or heretical book, which we know was prevalent especially in the environs of the University of Padua, could easily have traveled north and had an impact on the *Mirror* within this manuscript. Therefore, the Laud codex, far from being an outlier, was likely caught up in some of the same currents as those surrounding the Vatican and Paduan codices discussed in chapters 3 and 4. It is evident that there were also broader attitudes of suspicion at work in this codex, as seen in the mild censoring of another work within the manuscript.

In a way, the Laud manuscript shows us opposition to the *Mirror* "in action." That is, when looked at in the context of the manuscript as a whole object, we can see the "life cycle" of this copy unfolding.[56] Its removal emerges as a process of multiple different actions, not just a single moment of destruction frozen in time by the few remaining fragments left behind. Someone copied the *Mirror*—or had it copied for them—because they wanted to have it as a part of their collection of spiritual literature. Its inclusion alongside the works of Ramon Llull

---

56. On the "life cycle" of the medieval manuscript, see Michael Johnston and Michael Van Dussen, "Introduction: Manuscripts and Cultural History," in *The Medieval Manuscript Book: Cultural Approaches*, ed. Michael Johnston and Michael Van Dussen (Cambridge: Cambridge University Press, 2015).

and Angela of Foligno—both of which shared themes with the *Mirror*—shows this preference most clearly, but they also saw a place for it alongside other non-mystical, patristically oriented works. But, eventually, this acceptance of the *Mirror* soured, and it was removed. This moment in the life cycle of MS Laud Latin 46 is, then, a microcosm of the conflicted, contradictory reception of the *Mirror* treated in chapter 1, as we saw John-Jerome of Prague bring the *Mirror* into Camaldoli for his brothers while the monks of Santa Giustina had it confiscated from them, or as Bishop Giovanni Tavelli expressed surprise at its errors while Antonio Zeno confiscated it and commissioned an assessment of its orthodoxy. This assessment is our next focus. Turning now to this theological examination of the *Mirror*, we move from the codicological into the textual, from physical to intellectual destruction.

# CHAPTER 3

# "Against the Foundation of the Faith"

## Theological Refutation in MS Vat. lat. 4953

When the twenty-one Parisian masters of theology delivered their judgment against *The Mirror of Simple Souls* in 1310, it was a pivotal moment in the trial of Marguerite Porete. Having examined the extracts given to them, they declared that "such a book . . . should be exterminated as heretical and erroneous and containing heresy and errors."[1] But this moment has always been frustratingly thin on information. Why did they think the *Mirror* was heretical and erroneous? They do not say. The theologians' pronouncement does not come to us directly from them but rather through the filter of William of Paris's carefully crafted report of their consultation. As a result, there is almost no detail given about the process of deliberation; the document merely provides two of the assessed articles from the *Mirror* and the decision on its orthodoxy. While we know their names, we have nothing from the theologians themselves, whether a collective written judgment or an individually written opinion on the matter; there is very little that allows insight into *how* they came to declare the *Mirror* heretical.[2]

---

1. Verdeyen, "Le procès," 51. English from Field, *The Beguine*, 224.
2. Based on analysis of their careers and writings, speculation can and has been made about what some of the individual theologians might have made of the *Mirror*. See Field, *The Beguine*, 133–143, and Troy J. Tice, "'Containing Heresy and Errors': Thomas of Bailly and the Condemned Extracts of the *Mirror of Simple Souls*," *The Catholic Historical Review* 104, no. 4 (2018).

This gap in knowledge has persisted in the events we have seen so far. Its various Italian critics stated that the *Mirror* was full of errors but did not say what they were; someone cut the *Mirror* from the Laud codex, but we do not know what exactly within its pages worried them. But a four-folio text found in a manuscript held by the Vatican Library can finally provide us with some firm answers to this question. On folios 29r–32r in Vatican City, BAV, MS Vat. lat. 4953 is an incomplete list of thirty extracts from a Latin copy of the *Mirror*, which are presented as errors and followed by theological refutations. As ever, nothing is perfect: the Vatican list is the reverse of what we have in Marguerite's trial. We have the reasons why the *Mirror* might be considered heretical, but the final judgment or action against it is still a matter of speculation. But this list nevertheless offers significant insight into why exactly certain readers of the *Mirror* would find its contents less than acceptable.

This text is not a new discovery. An edited version of the Vatican list has been available in print since 1965, when Romana Guarnieri published her transcription of it in "Il movimento del libero spirito."[3] Paul Verdeyen included a description of the list in his introduction to the Latin edition in 1986.[4] Yet the list has never been subjected to any detailed scrutiny since then, receiving, like the Laud manuscript, only brief mentions.[5] As Guarnieri pointed out back in 1965, the text is probably connected to two events we encountered in chapter 1: the inquisition against the *Mirror* led by Giovanni of Capestrano and the business of Pope Eugenius IV and his interest in it.[6] But it also likely has connections to another event of the 1430s that has never before been discussed in connection with the *Mirror*: negotiations between the Greek and Latin churches at the Council of Ferrara-Florence.

This list is one of two glimpses we have of how the *Mirror*'s critics argued against it, and what specific points within its pages that they found disconcerting— the second glimpse is discussed in chapter 4. The Vatican list demonstrates that real concerns over the theological implications of the *Mirror*'s ideas could underpin the kinds of attacks that we have seen so far. This chapter will first discuss

3. Guarnieri, "Il movimento," 649–660 and 506. The existence of the list was first noted in 1952 by Emmanuel Candal, who identified all the works in the codex and gave a brief overview of its early modern ownership. Candal was not aware of the *Mirror*'s identity in the error list, describing it as "a little work *De amore in animas*" (*Opella De amore in animas*) and "an ascetical-mystical work" (*scriptum ascetico-mysticum*). See Emmanuel Candal's introduction to André de Escobar, *Tractatus Polemico-Theologicus de Graecis Errantibus*, vol. 1, ed. Emmanuel Candal (Rome: Pontificum Institutum Orientalum Studiorum, 1952), cxvii–cxxii, cxix n2.

4. Verdeyen, Introduction to *Speculum CCCM*, xii.

5. Kerby-Fulton, *Books under Suspicion*, 276, and Sargent, "Latin and Italian," 88–89.

6. Guarnieri, "Il movimento," 476 and 649–650.

how the text in MS Vat. lat. 4953 might fit into that broader landscape of hostility. It will then turn to the text itself and present some of the arguments and authorities that these particular critics marshaled against the *Mirror*'s doctrines. What will become clear is that, while the *Mirror* was ridiculed by a few elsewhere for being "foolish" or written by a "silly little woman," here the *Mirror* is taken very seriously as a work that repeated intellectual heresies and warranted academic refutation.

## Vatican City, BAV, MS Vat. lat. 4953

MS Vat. lat. 4953 is a fifteenth-century parchment manuscript of Italian provenance bound in wooden boards covered in red leather. The front board is stamped in gold with the arms of Pope Paul V (1552–1621). It is a relatively large codex, measuring 35.2 × 27.0 cm (13.8 × 10.6 in), but is a slender volume at only sixty-five folios. The parchment is of high quality and the manuscript is carefully and neatly laid out, with faint horizontal ruling in additional to vertical ruling. In other words, there is none of the haphazardness that we saw in MS Laud Latin 46, at least not in appearance. All the texts are copied in a single small, neat, and careful hand, which is eminently legible, and the text is written in a single large block on each page. Despite its refined appearance, there is no decoration to speak of, and there are gaps where initials were never put in. The only color in the manuscript comes from a few rubricated incipits and section headings.

Apart from the list of errors from the *Mirror*, the manuscript is entirely made up of texts concerned with theological disputes between the Greek Church and the Latin Church, including copies of works from the thirteenth and fourteenth centuries as well as the fifteenth. The order of its contents is presented in table 3.1, according to modern BAV foliation.[7]

Previously unnoticed in *Mirror* scholarship is the existence of a second copy of this list in a seventeenth-century manuscript, also held in the Vatican Library, MS Ott. lat. 983. This manuscript was made expressly for the library of Pope Paul V (r. 1605–1621) from MS Vat. lat. 4953, reproducing its contents entirely and in the same order. Therefore the copy of the list in MS Ott. lat. 983 is, unfortunately, merely a reproduction of the one in MS Vat. lat. 4953 and does not

---

7. Compare with Candal, Introduction to *Tractatus*, cxvii–cxxii. I am grateful to the staff at the Vatican Library for allowing me to view this manuscript in person. MS Vat. lat. 4953 is now digitized on the Vatican Library website: https://digi.vatlib.it/view/MSS_Vat.lat.4953. (accessed March 2021).

*Table 3.1*    Contents of MS Vat. lat. 4953

| FOLIO NUMBER(S) | CONTENTS |
| --- | --- |
| 1r–14r | *Contra grecos de processione Spiritus Sancti et de animabus defunctorum, de azimo et de fermentato et de obedientia ecclesie Romane, editus in Constantinopoli*, a Dominican composition originally written in 1252 by Brother Bartholomew of Constantinople.[1] The titles of various sections in this work are rubricated. |
| 15r–23r | *Tractatus contra Grecos.* Anonymous. |
| 23r | *Nota Pantaleonis Constantinopolitani*, a speech given by Michael Caerularios, Patriarch of Constantinople (1043–1058) to the legates of Pope Leo IX. |
| 24r–28v | Compilation of various short documents from the Greek-Latin union attempted at the Second Council of Lyon (1272–1274), including letters between Pope Gregory X (1210–1276) and the Byzantine Emperor Michael Paleologus (1223–1282).[2] |
| 28v | Brief excerpts from Thomas Aquinas's *Quodlibeti* (between 1256 and 1272) and *Summa contra Gentiles* (ca. 1270).[3] |
| 29r–32r | List of thirty extracts from a Latin copy of *The Mirror of Simple Souls*, presented as errors, which are followed by refutations. No incipit or explicit. |
| 32r–33r | An attestation of the legates of Urban V (r. 1362–1370), accepting the profession of faith from John V Palaeologus (1332–1391). Includes the text of his profession. |
| 34r–65v | The treatise *De grecis errantibus et ipsorum erroribus*, a work written by André de Escobar (1348–1448), the bishop of Megara, master of theology and chaplain to Pope Eugenius IV.[4] Written in the context of the Council of Ferrara-Florence. Originally completed on 15 December 1437. |

[1] On its authorship and composition, see R. Loenertz, "Autour du traité de fr. Barthélemy de Constantinople contre les Grecs," *Archivum Fratrum Praedicatorum* 6 (1936).

[2] The letters are in Edmund Martene and Ursini Durand, eds., *Veterum Scriptorum et Monumentorum Historicorum Dogmaticorum Moralium, Amplissima Collectio*, vol. 7 (Paris: Franciscum Montalant, 1733), 218–258. Candal believed that this compilation was originally made for the private study of some of the Council Fathers, as a useful reference for previous deliberations with the Greeks. See Candal, Introduction to *De grecis errantibus*, cxviiin7.

[3] For *Summa contra Gentiles* see Thomas Aquinas, *Summa Contra Gentiles*, ed. Anton C. Pegis, James F. Anderson, and Vernon J. Bourke (South Bend, IN: University of Notre Dame Press, 1955–1957).

[4] For the edition see Candal, *Tractatus Polemico-Theologicus*.

represent a separate witness. Since this is the case, my main focus in this chapter will remain on the text in MS Vat. lat. 4953.[8]

MS Vat. lat. 4953 was once part of the private library of Cardinal Guglielmo Sirleto (1514–1585), as his *ex libris* appears on the front flyleaf.[9] Sirleto was the librarian of the Vatican Library from 1572 until his death in 1585. He was an avid collector of Greek manuscripts and manuscripts that dealt with Greek

---

8. Candal, Introduction to *Tractatus Polemico-Theologicus*, cxxii–cxxiii. Ott. lat. 983 is also mentioned in the dissertation of Johnna Sturgeon, "Cares at the Curia: Andreas de Escobar and Ecclesiastical Controversies at the Time of the Fifteenth-Century Councils" (PhD diss., Northwestern University, 2017), who noted that Ott. lat. 983 "reproduces the same texts [of MS Vat. lat. 4953] in the same order." The manuscript has been digitized on the Vatican Library website: https://opac.vatlib.it/mss/detail/Ott.lat.983 (accessed June 2019). The *Mirror* list appears on ff. 215v–237r.

9. "Emptum ex libri Cardinali Sirleti." MS Vat. lat. 4953, front flyleaf.

subjects.[10] In 1588, the inheritors of his library sold it to Cardinal Ascanio Colonna, who then upon his own death left it to the chapter of St. John Lateran; it was then sold to the Duke of Altemps in 1611.[11] It entered the Vatican Library in the same year when the block of manuscripts including MS Vat. lat. 4953 was bought by Pope Paul V, and it has remained there ever since.[12]

The specifics of this manuscript's ownership before it came into Sirleto's possession are for the moment unknown, as is its exact date of composition. But we are perhaps on firmer ground than we were with the origins of the Laud codex, as its general context can be placed with some certainty. The manuscript was likely put together by or for someone who was participating in the Council of Ferrara-Florence (1438–1449). This council grew out of the power struggle between Pope Eugenius IV and the Council of Basel. As mentioned in chapter 1, Eugenius had tried from the beginning to dissolve or transfer the council to Italy, where he could more easily dominate the proceedings, but was met with years of stanch resistance by those in charge of the council. Finally, in the autumn of 1437—when he also commissioned the inquisition into the *Mirror* in Venice—Eugenius set up his own breakaway council in Ferrara, while the Council of Basel still refused to dissolve. Eugenius then made union between the Eastern and Western churches the centerpiece of his own council. In spring of 1438 the Greek delegation arrived, and debate began on the main theological divides between the two churches. In early 1439 the council was transferred to Florence, where debate continued. In July of 1439 union between the two churches was announced in the bull *Laetentur caeli*, although this turned out to be more or less ineffectual as it was largely rejected in the Eastern Empire.[13]

Since the majority of its contents relates to theological disputes and previous negotiations of union between the Greek Church and the Latin Church, it is almost certain that MS Vat. lat. 4953 was put together in the context of Ferrara-Florence.[14] The earliest possible date would be 1437, when the Portuguese bishop André de Escobar finished his *De grecis errantibus*.[15] Candal believed it was copied shortly after the council was transferred from Ferrara to Florence, as the copy of de Escobar's *De grecis errantibus* in MS Vat. lat. 4953 contains an addition that de Escobar made after the disputations at Ferrara.[16]

---

10. On Sirleto's interest in Greek, see in general Irena Backus and Benoît Gain, "Le cardinal Guglielmo Sirleto (1514–1585), sa bibliothèque et ses traductions de saint Basile," *Mélanges de l'École française de Rome: Moyen-Âge, Temps modernes* 98, no. 2 (1986).

11. Backus and Gain, "Le cardinal," 921.

12. Backus and Gain, "Le cardinal," 921.

13. See Gill, *Council of Florence*, (Cambridge, UK: Cambridge University Press, 1959), passim.

14. Noted by Verdeyen, Introduction to *Speculum CCCM*, xii.

15. Guarnieri, "Il movimento," 649.

16. Candal, Introduction to *Tractatus Polemico-Theologicus*, cxvii–cxviii.

This would place the date of its copying sometime in the first half of 1439, after the council had been moved to Florence.

The manuscript seems to be a reference book or a handbook, a collection of documents that the reader would find useful in navigating the negotiations taking place at the council. Whoever owned this manuscript was a participant in the council on the Latin side of the debate and would have used this manuscript as a "primer" for the debates. It is possible that it was compiled by or for a Dominican, as it contains an anonymous Dominican treatise and also a few excerpts from Aquinas; André de Escobar also had close connections to Dominican circles and took a Thomist approach in his writings.[17] It is also reasonable to assume that the owner was involved in the business of the papal court, given that this council was Eugenius IV's initiative and given the inclusion of works such as de Escobar's *De grecis*, which was dedicated to Eugenius, and the text relating to the *Mirror*, which likely came from Eugenius's commission to Giovanni of Capestrano in Venice.

## The *Mirror* and the Council

The intended purpose of this manuscript makes the appearance of the *Mirror* list here seem slightly mysterious. At first glance, it appears to have little to do with the Greek Church or the negotiations taking place at Ferrara-Florence. This incongruity led me to speculate in a previous publication that the list was possibly included in the manuscript by mistake, and that it ended up here mainly as a result of it being related to "papal business" in general and getting bundled in with other matters of importance at the time.[18] But further investigation has revealed that the *Mirror* list's inclusion here was likely deliberate, and that it was in some way connected to the discussions taking place at the council. This adds an entirely new element to the *Mirror*'s reception history. To my knowledge, while there has been discussion of the *Mirror* at the Council of Basel, there has been no consideration of any connections it may have had to the contemporary Council of Ferrara-Florence, beyond Guarnieri and Verdeyen's brief comments on the contents of MS Vat. lat. 4953. First, a short detour is in order.

The Council of Ferrara-Florence had four main theological disputes between East and West at its heart. The first and arguably dominant one was the long-divisive question of whether the Holy Spirit proceeded from the Father

---

17. Christiaan Kappes, *The Epiclesis Debate at the Council of Florence* (South Bend, IN: University of Notre Dame Press, 2019), 3–4.

18. Trombley, "Latin Manuscripts," 197.

only (the Greek position) or from both the Father *and* the Son (the Latin position), known as the *filioque* controversy. The three other main issues were the Greek rejection of purgatory, the use of unleavened bread in the Eucharist, and the question of papal supremacy. Bubbling under the surface, however, was another controversy that revolved around "Palamism." Taking its name from the Greek theologian Gregory Palamas (1296–1357), Palamism largely revolved around the question of the divine attributes and the nature of union between humans and the divine. To give a heavily simplified description of the tenets most relevant to our discussion here, Palamism made a distinction between God's *essence*, which is incapable of being shared with created beings, and God's *energies*, which can be shared.[19] Following on from this, the Palamite school argued that real transformation of human nature into God could happen *in this life*, in the sense that such a union occurs only with the divine energies but not the divine essence.[20] Opponents to Palamism argued that the distinction between essence and energies compromised divine unity, and that transformation into the divine could only happen "in a manner of speaking" and was not something that could be achieved in this world.[21] While initially the Palamite controversy took place internally within Byzantine circles, it eventually became yet another West versus East bone of contention, coming into particular conflict with Thomistic schools of thought along the way.[22]

In the lead up to the Council of Ferrara-Florence and during the council itself, Palamism became a particular flash point, as several members of the Greek delegation who were to participate in the theological debates there were committed Palamites, something that greatly exercised the (largely Dominican) anti-Palamite camp, who wanted Palamism officially condemned.[23] As part of the preparation for the approaching council, in November 1437 Eugenius IV commissioned a group of Franciscan theological experts to examine two questions: the primacy of the Roman papacy and the Palamite issue of the divine attributes.[24] Whatever their conclusions were on this is unknown, as the report is lost, but in the end it was decided that Palamism would not be made a main

---

19. Norman Russell, "The Hesychast Controversy," in *An Intellectual History of Byzantium*, ed. Anthony Kaldellis and Niketas Siniossoglou (Cambridge: Cambridge University Press, 2017), 494.

20. Russell, "Hesychast Controversy," 506 and 507.

21. Russell, "Hesychast Controversy," 507.

22. Kappes, *Epiclesis Debate*, 2–3. See also Christine Caldwell Ames, *Medieval Heresies* (Cambridge: Cambridge University Press, 2015), 308–311.

23. Kappes, *Epiclesis Debate*, 3.

24. Christiaan Kappes, Foreword to J. Isaac Goff, *Caritas in Primo: A Historical-Theological Study of Bonaventure's "Quaestiones disputate de mysterio Ss. Trinitatis"* (New Bedford, MA: Academy of the Immaculate, 2015), xviii. For the letter itself see Wadding, *Annales Minorum*, 2, and Hüntemann, *Bullarium Franciscanum*, 150.

topic of debate at the council.[25] Nevertheless, aspects of Palamite doctrine hovered in the background of many of the issues that were debated.[26]

What does this have to do with the *Mirror*? It is possible that the list of errors in MS Vat. lat. 4953 is connected to concerns about Palamism and to debates on the council's main issues, and it may even have been a part of the Franciscan consultation that Eugenius IV commissioned. Three kinds of evidence suggest this connection: textual, contextual, and codicological. First, if we examine the passages and refutations in the *Mirror* list, as will be done in detail later, many of them are concerned with issues of divine essence and the nature of union between the human soul and the divine, both of which were points of controversy in Palamite theology and in council discussions on the Trinity more broadly. Certainly, it is risky making judgments on how the *Mirror* may or may not have been interpreted—as we saw with its complex reception in chapter 1—but here is where other evidence comes into play. According to Christiaan Kappes, among the Franciscans whom Eugenius commissioned on the question of the divine attributes were two familiar faces: Bernardino of Siena and Giovanni of Capestrano.[27] Furthermore, the letter in which Eugenius made his request to the Franciscans is dated 23 September 1437, during Giovanni of Capestrano's inquisition into the *Mirror* in Venice. Important to note is Guarnieri's observation that the types of theological authorities used in the list—such as Bonaventure, Alexander of Hales, and Richard of Middleton—point to a Franciscan-Augustinian training.[28] Finally, the other works in MS Vat. lat. 4953 also have anti-Palamite connections. André de Escobar, author of *De grecis errantibus*, which appears at the end of the manuscript, was a committed anti-Palamite and includes Palamite concepts as part of his list of Greek errors.[29] The theological intricacies are beyond this chapter's parameters, but Palamite questions about the divine energies and the divine essence underpinned several of the main issues tackled at Ferrara-Florence, in particular the debates on the procession of the Holy Spirit.[30] The date of origin for MS Vat. lat. 4953—early 1439, after the

---

25. Kappes, *Epiclesis Debate*, 5.

26. For example, see Gill, *Council of Florence*, 205–206, and André De Halleux, "Bessarion et le palamisme au concile de Florence," *Irénikon* 62 (1989).

27. Kappes, Introduction to *Caritas in Primo*, xxi–xxii. While Kappes lists a number of Franciscans whom he says were part of the group of experts, it is unclear where this information comes from, as no specific names are given in Eugenius's letters inviting experts to the council and commissioning the study into the divine attributes. But given Bernardino's and Giovanni's prominence within the Franciscan Order, it seems likely that they would be included in the group of experts invited to provide comment, and both certainly attended the council.

28. Guarnieri, "Il movimento," 650.

29. For example, see de Escobar, *Tractatus Polemico-Theologus de Graecis Errantibus*, 36, 83. See also Kappes, *Epiclesis Debate*, 3.

30. Kappes, *Epiclesis Debate*, 4; Gill, *Council of Florence*, 205–206.

council's transfer to Florence—places it right in the build-up to the substantive theological debates regarding the procession, which began on 2 March.[31]

It is possible, then, that the *Mirror* list is included here because its contents may have been considered useful for the forthcoming debates, particularly on questions of divine essence and unity with the divine. How, then, can we imagine its arrival into this context? There are a couple of options. One is that the list was made, perhaps by Bernardino of Siena or Giovanni of Capestrano, as a part of the process of the Franciscan consultation on the divine attributes. If they were asked to consider questions that had bearing on the divine essence, divine union, and even the supremacy of the Roman pontiff, then they may have been put in mind of the *Mirror*'s content as examples of errors related to those topics. But if it were created explicitly for the council then one might expect the refutations to use more authorities that would be accepted by both parties, such as scripture and certain Eastern/patristic authors, but this is not the case here. While biblical quotations and authorities like Augustine and Jerome are certainly present, much use is also made of Franciscan authorities and decrees/decretals of the Latin church, which presumably would not carry much weight in disputations with the Greeks, particularly since they did not recognize the latter.[32]

What seems more likely is not that the list was created in the immediate council environment but that it was perhaps imported into it from Giovanni of Capestrano's investigation into the *Mirror* in Venice and the events related to it in Padua. As we saw in chapter 1, Antonio Zeno informed Giovanni that he had sent extracts from the *Mirror* to theologians at the University of Padua for assessment. It is probable that the refutation of the *Mirror* found in the Vatican manuscript is a partial copy of the theologians' judgment, a theory that Guarnieri first suggested.[33] The sources cited in the refutations show a distinct theological (as opposed to canon-legal) line of argumentation, and in

31. Gill, *Council of Florence*, 191. The previous debates on the procession, held in 1438, had been more textually focused, focusing on the authenticity or legitimacy of the insertion of the *filioque* clause into the Creed. See Gill, *Council of Florence*, 131–179.

32. In fact, this view is made explicit in MS Vat. lat. 4953 itself, in the Aquinas excerpts included immediately before the beginning of the *Mirror* list. The extract from Aquinas's Quodlibet IV, article 3, explicitly states that in theological debates aiming to remove doubt about something, authorities accepted by both of the parties should be used the most. After listing Jews and Manichees, Aquinas states, "[B]ut if with schismatics, who accept the Old and New Testaments but not the doctrine of our saints, as it is with the Greeks, then one debates them with authorities from the Old and New Testaments and the Doctors that they accept." ("Si autem cum scismaticis, qui recipiunt vetus et novum testamentum, non autem doctrinam sanctorum nostrorum, sicut sunt Graeci, oportet cum eis disputare ex auctoritatibus veteris vel novi testament et illorum doctorum quos recipiunt.") MS Vat. lat. 4953, f. 28v. The other texts in the manuscript that dispute Greek errors take this tack, citing mainly scriptural and Eastern saints/doctors recognized by both churches.

33. Guarnieri, "Il movimento," 650.

terms of the Franciscan-Augustinian character of the work, the University of Padua at the time was an important center of Franciscan thought.[34] Furthermore, the format of the document conforms to such a context. It is very much a list, with numbers in the margins and brief, bullet-point-like refutations. There is no use of the first person and there is almost no elaboration or opinion given outside of the source citations. This mirrors the style of other lists of condemned academic errors.[35]

In other words, an existing list of the *Mirror*'s errors, possibly produced by the Paduan theologians after their consultation by Antonio Zeno, may have been a source used in the Franciscans' deliberation on the matter of divine attributes, brought in perhaps by Giovanni of Capestrano. If we cast our minds back to Antonio Zeno's letter to Giovanni, at the end of it he seemed to write *transmittam*, "I will send over," implying that he would send the theologians' assessment to Giovanni and his fellow investigator Lorenzo Giustiniani. It is almost certain that he did this, as it would have been a key document for Giovanni and Lorenzo in their investigation of the *Mirror*. Then, with such a text in his hand, Giovanni may have considered the *Mirror*'s passages to be apt examples of errors related to the Franciscans' commission from Eugenius and it may have been used as a point of reference. Another possibility is that one of the theologians at the University of Padua who was consulted also attended the council and brought with him the errors from the *Mirror*. Even though Eugenius decided not to include Palamism as a topic for debate, the materials the Franciscans may have included in their study could still have made the rounds at the council, given the Franciscan experts' attendance there.

Another possible scenario is that it is not linked to the Franciscan consultation but that the list was instead circulating within circles around Eugenius IV from the time of the Venice inquisition. Not just Giovanni and Lorenzo, but also Antonio Zeno, as the *vicarius* of the bishop of Padua, would likely have kept a copy of the theologians' assessment for the bishop himself, Pietro Donato. Donato, a close associate of Eugenius IV who had previously represented Eugenius as a papal legate at the Council of Basel, would also participate in the Council of Ferrara-Florence; perhaps a copy of the list traveled there with him.

---

34. Guarnieri, "Il movimento," 650.

35. See, for example, the list of condemned errors issued in Paris in *Chartularium Universitatis Parisiensis*, ed. E. Chatelain and H. Denifle, vol. 1 (Paris: Ex typis fratrum Delalain, 1889), 170–172. English translation in Dana Carleton Munro, ed., *Translations and Reprints from the Original Sources of European History*, vol. 2.3 (Philadelphia: University of Pennsylvania Press, 1895), 17–19. Reprinted online by Fordham University: http://www.fordham.edu/halsall/source/uparis-cond1241.html (last modified 2 January 2020) (hereafter *1241 Errors*). See also in general Thijssen, *Censure and Heresy*, 25–26, and Josef Koch, "Philosophische und Theologische Irrtumslisten von 1270–1329: Ein Beitrag Zur Entwicklung der Theologischen Zensuren," in *Kleine Schriften*, vol. 2 (Rome: Edizioni di storia e letteratura, 1973).

Zeno or Donato could also have decided that such a judgment should be publicly circulated, given their actions against the *Mirror* in Padua. Once Giovanni
of Capestrano had a copy, he may also have sent a copy of it to Eugenius IV,
since Eugenius had commissioned the inquisition against the *Mirror* in the first
place. This provides at least two clear avenues of transmission to the papal
court and those involved with the Council of Ferrara-Florence. From there, it is
easy to imagine it circulating and taken up by someone who saw in it issues that
were relevant to the coming debates with the Eastern Church. It is possible that
whoever compiled the manuscript was a close associate of André de Escobar,
the author of *De grecis errantibus*. The copy of his work in MS Vat. lat. 4953 is a
very early one made from de Escobar's own amanuensis copy; that copy contains annotations and corrections in de Escobar's own hand.[36] Again, this brings
us to those closely connected with Eugenius IV, as well as to circles that may
have been staunchly opposed to Palamite ideas, as de Escobar was. It is possible,
of course, that the *Mirror* was seen as relevant not merely because it *related* to
the topics under discussion, but that it was believed—at least by the compiler of
this manuscript—to be itself a *product* of the Eastern Church, circulating in
Latin, and that its errors were seen as genuine "errors of the Greeks."

Guarnieri also suggested that a copy of this list may have made its way to
Eugenius's rivals at the Council of Basel in October 1437, after the inquisition
against the Gesuati had been brought to a close and in the midst of Eugenius's
struggle with the council over his attempts to transfer it to Ferrara.[37] The list
may have been sent by an individual or group of individuals who felt that the
heresies discovered in Venice had been covered up, since the Gesuati were ex-
onerated.[38] This is not impossible, considering the episode at Basel two years
later in 1439 involved a list of "thirty errors" drawn up against the *Mirror* (although, since the Vatican list is incomplete, we do not know how many errors
may have been in it originally). If a garbled account of the Venice inquisition
was circulating in Basel that cast Eugenius as a *supporter* of the *Mirror*, then this
list would be the perfect demonstration of the *Mirror's* errors and therefore of
Eugenius's status as a heretic. It is entirely possible that a copy did make it to
Basel, but for the origins of MS Vat. lat. 4953 specifically, the more probable
avenue is through those who were close to, rather than set against, Eugenius IV.
The manuscript shows a clear involvement in the events at Ferrara-Florence,
which was Eugenius's endeavor, and the presence of de Escobar's treatise in

---

36. The amanuensis copy is Vatican, BAV, MS Vat. lat. 4067. Candal, Introduction to *Tractatus
Polemico-Theologicus*, cxvii.

37. Guarnieri, "Il movimento," 650.

38. Guarnieri, "Il movimento," 650.

particular, which was dedicated to Eugenius IV, cements its connection to a pro- rather than anti-Eugenius milieu.

As shown in chapter 1, we now know with relative certainty that the extracts in MS Vat. lat. 4953 were taken from MS Rossianus 4. The list mentions the chapters (*capitula*) from which the passages come, and several errors are said to be "in the same chapter" (*in eadem capitulo*) as the preceding ones. As mentioned earlier, no chapter numbers are cited but they are instead identified by their opening sentence; in the Rossianus copy these are marked out by the use of decorated initials. This is unlike the chapters of the Chantilly codex, and those found in another Latin Vatican copy, MS Chigianus B IV 41, which has formal titles and numbers for its chapters. It is also unlike the extracts that are quoted in Padua, Biblioteca universitaria di Padova, MS 1647, examined in chapter 4, which denotes its *Mirror* chapters by number.[39] The extracts cited span almost the full length of the *Mirror*, with the first coming from chapter 5 and the last from chapter 117. They do not, however, always proceed in the order in which certain passages appear in the *Mirror*, with some excerpts that appear later in the book appearing alongside or before earlier passages in the list.[40]

# A Theological Refutation of the *Mirror*

What, then, does this list say? It begins immediately with a *Mirror* quotation at the top of folio 29r. There is no title or introduction, and no mention of the work being refuted. It ends in a similarly abrupt manner—it cuts off in the middle of a sentence, before it finishes the *Mirror* quotation. There are thirty errors in total, although since the thirtieth error is incomplete and is missing its refutation, there is no way of knowing if this was the full number of errors originally intended. The text is set up in a typical list format, with the quotation from the work in question copied out first, immediately followed by the refutation. The number of each extract is written in arabic numerals next to it in the outer margin, followed by the word "error." The errors and refutations are visually separated out from one another as separate blocks of text, and by small and lightly decorated initials at the start of each block, done in plain ink. There is a distinctly "no frills" approach to the refutations, with almost no additional commentary or opinion, and no colorful rhetoric. The aim here is simply to provide clear points of refutation, with little elaboration. The refutations are

---

39. This wide variation indicates that chapters were not an original feature to the *Mirror*.

40. For example, the first error contains passages from both chapter 5 and chapter 11 of the Chantilly reckoning, but then the second and third errors both come from chapter 5. See appendix 1.

more or less a series of quotations from theological and biblical sources, set down one after another, using *Item* to begin each subsequent citation. It is very much a formal, cut-and-dry assessment, methodically laid out. One imagines, then, that this list is the final product of a formal consultation or assessment, rather than one piece from the process leading up to the final judgment. This reinforces the impression that this could be the result of Antonio Zeno's consultation of the theologians at Padua, which would have been circulated.

Scriptural quotations and the usual authorities of Augustine, Ambrose, Jerome, and Gregory the Great are frequently invoked. Boethius makes an appearance, as does Peter Lombard. Three thirteenth-century Franciscan authorities are used: Richard of Middleton, Alexander of Hales, and Bonaventure, each mentioned once. The famous condemnations of theological errors by William Auvergne and Stephen Tempier in Paris—issued in 1241 and 1277, respectively—are cited multiple times. Among these theological and scriptural authorities there are also a few canon-legal sources, namely Gratian's *Decretum*, the *Liber extra*, and *Ad nostrum* from the Clementine decrees.

Overall, there is less focus on "practical" issues, such as the behavior of the Soul and its moral character, although there is certainly concern over the Soul's abandonment of the virtues and the implications this has for topics such as one's culpability for sin. There is much more focus on subjects such as the nature of divine union, the ability of humans to understand the divine and acquire knowledge of God, the nature of the soul's essence and being, and the issue of free will. More broadly, when taken together the errors show a general current of anxiety concerning the nature of the annihilated soul's relationship to God and the implications of that relationship for both the nature of the soul *and* the nature and power of God. In the following section, I will present a sampling of errors and refutations, grouped around particular themes that they address.[41] This will help to give a general idea of the main concerns that this list's compilers had regarding the *Mirror* and convey the flavor of the text's format and style.[42]

One common objection is to the Soul's claim to a "special status" that either exempts it from normal spiritual practice and the tenets of the church or that challenges what is achievable for the human soul in its union with divinity. In this category is the *Mirror*'s famous declaration that the annihilated soul is free from servitude to the virtues, which was one of the two articles mentioned in

---

41. For a full list and translation of the *Mirror* extracts that appear in the list, see appendix 1.

42. Where possible, I have tried to locate the works cited and their modern editions. Corrections to Guarnieri's transcription are noted in square brackets. As a historian, rather than a theologian, my summary of the list is concerned with relating its overall content rather than analyzing the theological concepts and intricacies in-depth.

the Parisian theologians' judgment in 1310.[43] First, it is refuted as a rejection of the proper pursuit of a good spiritual life within the church. The fifth error, which is drawn from chapter 5 of the *Mirror*, where the Soul first proclaims its freedom from the virtues, is refuted with Augustine's *Soliloquies*: "Without these three virtues—faith, hope, and charity—no soul is saved, when it may see God Himself."[44] This is also noted as an "error of the beghards" (*error beguardorum*), condemned in *Ad nostrum*, where it says that "the perfect soul is excused from the virtues."[45] The rejection of virtuous work is refuted again in the interpretation of the eighteenth error, which is taken from chapter 45 of the *Mirror*, wherein the voice of God states that the Soul does nothing and works in the Soul without the Soul herself.[46] The refutation begins by saying this is against Augustine (attributed to Anselm in the manuscript): "He who made you without you will not save you without you."[47] It goes on to say, "That the soul is saved without the work of the virtues is against that of Gregory, 'If you wish to advance in life, you must serve [his] commandments [Matthew 19:17].'"[48] It concludes by quoting the *Sentences* of Peter Lombard: "Therefore these works of virtue are necessary to this mortal life; whence just as *without faith it is impossible to please God* [Hebrews 11:6], so also without works of virtue."[49]

Not only is the Soul seen to deny the value of the virtues, it inverts them, turning them from good into bad. "What is said to be the greatest torment that a creature could endure?" asks Love in the fourth error, an excerpt taken from chapter 8 of the *Mirror*. The answer? "To remain in love and in obedience to the virtues."[50] In the refutation, this is tantamount to denying the threat of hell and its punishments, as is suggested by the use of a quotation from John Chrysostom: "There are two eternal punishments: To be cut down and sent into the

---

43. Verdeyen, "Le procès," 51; Field, *The Beguine*, 223–224.

44. MS Vat. lat. 4953, f. 28v; Guarnieri, "Il movimento," 652. "Sine istis tribus virtutibus, fide, spe, caritate, nulla anima sanatur, ut possit Deum suum videre." Augustine, *Soliloquies*, caput VI. See Augustine, *S. Aurelii Augustini Hipponensis Episcopi Soliloquiorum Libri Duo, Patrologia Latina* 32, col. 0876. All citations from *Patrologia Latina* will hereafter be designated with the abbreviation *PL*. https://patristica.net/latina/.

45. Clem. 5.3.3. Friedberg, *Clementis Papae V Constitutiones*, cols. 1183–1184. "Quod anima perfecta licentiat a se virtutes."

46. See *Speculum CCCM*, 141.

47. MS Vat. lat. 4953, f. 29v; Guarnieri, "Il movimento," 657. "Qui fecit te sine te non salvabit te sine te." See Augustine, *Opera Omnia Augustini Hipponensis: Classa Prima: De Scripturis*, Sermo 169, caput 9, *PL* 38, col. 0923.

48. MS Vat. lat. 4953, f. 29v; Guarnieri, "Il movimento," 657. "Item quod anima salvetur sine [MS and Guarnieri: "suis"] operibus virtutum est contra illud Gregorii, 'Si vis ad vitam ingredi, serva mandata.'"

49. MS Vat. lat. 4953, f. 29v; Guarnieri, "Il movimento," 657. "Ista ergo virtutum opera huic mortali vite necessaria sunt; unde sicut sine fide impossibile est placere Deo ita sine operibus virtutum." Peter Lombard, *Liber Sententiarum*, *PL* 192, 3.33. See *Liber Sententiarum, Liber Tertius: De Incarnatione Verbi*, *PL* 192, col. 0823.

50. MS Vat. lat. 4953, f. 28r; Guarnieri, "Il movimento," 652. "Quod dicitur maius tormentum, quod possit creatura portare? . . . manere in amore et in obedientia virtutum." See *Speculum CCCM*, 31.

fire. Many shrink from hell. . . . It is better to endure ten thousand lightning bolts, than to see the gentle face of Christ turned away in judgment."[51] This point is reinforced with a quotation from Richard of Middleton (ca. 1242–ca. 1302): "The lack of the vision of God is the greatest punishment for all who are in hell."[52] In other words, portraying service to the virtues as the greatest torment lessens the threat of hell, which, to the refuters, should be considered the greatest and most terrifying punishment of all. Additionally, to deny the goodness of the work of the virtues by labeling them a "torment," the Soul is denying the good work of the scholars and saints of the church:

> If it were true that to be in love and obedience to the virtues were the greatest of punishments, then all the saints and doctors, leading men to the virtues and to love of God and neighbors, would be leading [them] to the greatest of punishments. The opposite of this is seen in Proverbs 1[:8]: "Listen, my son, to the discipline of the father," and that is [the discipline] of God himself, says the Gloss, because, as Rabbi Solomon said, "He is the Father of all through creation," and "you should not dismiss the law of your mother," that is, [the law] of the Church, "which Abel began from the first justice."[53] As Gregory [the Great] said, homily VII: "so that grace may be imparted upon your head" [Proverbs 1:9], that is the crown given by grace. And in consequence it is not the greatest of punishments.[54]

To the compilers of the list, the denial of the virtues and the characterization of their practice as a great torment absurdly inverts the proper models of good and evil. It separates the soul from the work that brings one closer to God, places the threat of hell in a less serious light, and discredits the work of all those who, in both the past and the present, guide people toward a virtuous life.

---

51. MS Vat. lat. 4953, f. 28r; Guarnieri, "Il movimento," 652. "Due sunt pene eternales: excidi et in ignem mitti. Multi iehenna, horrent . . . etenim decem milia melius est sustinere fulmina, quam faciem Christi mansuetam adversam videre in judicio." The refuter cites this as John Chrysostomus, *Super Mattheum*.

52. MS Vat. lat. 4953, f. 28r; Guarnieri, "Il movimento," 652. "Carentia visionis dei est maior omnibus penis que sunt in inferno." The refuter notes that this is from Richard of Middleton's commentary on the *Liber sententiarum*, 4th sentence, 3rd distinction.

53. According to Guarnieri, this is from the *Glossa ordinaria*.

54. MS Vat. lat. 4953, f. 28v; Guarnieri, "Il movimento," 652. "Item si esset verum quod esse in amore et obedientia virtutum esset maxima penarum, tunc omnes sancti et doctores, inducentes homines ad virtutes et ad amorem Dei et proximi, inducerent ad maximam penarum. Cuius oppositum videtur Proverbiorum 1[:8]: 'Audi, fili mi, disciplinam patris,' id est ipsius Dei, inquit glossa, quia, ut dicit Rabbi Salomon, 'pater est omnium per creationem,' et 'ne fimittas legem matris tue,' id est Ecclesie, 'que a primo Abel iusto incepit,' ut dicit Gregorius, omelia VII, 'ut addatur gratia capiti tuo,' id est corona gratiosa, et per consequens non penarum maxima." The Gregory reference may be from his *Responsoria de sapientie Salomonis*. See Gregory the Great, *Responsoria de Sapientie Salomonis*, in *Opera Omnia Gregorii Magni*, PL 78, col. 0833C.

It is not just denial of the virtues that appears to be troubling, but also the Soul's proclaimed indifference to all other practices and emotions. At least six different errors include the declaration that the Soul does not desire or does not have use for such intangible things as fear, love, hate, or shame, and has the same indifference toward actions tied to the institutional church, such as masses, sermons, prayers, and fasts. This lack of desire is characterized in the refutations not so much as a turning away from such things to embrace immorality but rather as occupying a state that is unnatural to the human mind and soul. A good example of this view is the response to the sixth error, which is an extract from chapter 7 of the *Mirror* that describes the Soul's lack of care for shame, poverty, riches, joy, sadness, love, hate, hell, paradise, and honor.[55] The refutation begins by saying, "That error is against natural inclination, placed in the human mind supernaturally, and thus is against that of Psalms [41:2]: 'As the hart panteth after the fountains of water, so my soul panteth after thee, God.'"[56] In other words, God meant for man to have such desires, not to deny them. To desire nothing is also to deny one's own human nature, as is reinforced with a quotation from Boethius: "For the desire of true good things is naturally sown in the mind of man."[57] Finally, desiring nothing also denies the soul's own desire for God, as is shown by the citation of Gregory the Great's homily on Ezekiel: "The mind, by which the soul is joined to the visible bridegroom through Love, accepts no consolation from the present world, but sighs for that which is in the marrow, feverish and breathless."[58] This also applies to the desire for blessedness, as shown in the refutation to the tenth error, which again speaks of the Soul's indifference to all things. "Nature drives [us] to seek out blessedness," it reads, quoting Augustine's *De trinitate*.[59] It moves on to the *Sentences* of Peter Lombard: "But to desire to be blessed, this all men have," and then to Boethius: "For natural thoughts induce us to true goodness."[60] For the refuters, the Soul's indifference is unnatural. It is an

55. See *Speculum CCCM*, 25.

56. MS Vat. lat. 4953, f. 28v; Guarnieri, "Il movimento," 653. "Iste error contra inclinationem naturalem inditam menti humane supernaturaliter, et sic est contra illud Psalmi [41:2]: 'Quemadmodum desiderat cervus ad fontes aquarum, ita desiderat anima mea ad te, Deus.'"

57. MS Vat. lat. 4953, f. 28v; Guarnieri, "Il movimento," 653. "Est enim veri boni naturaliter mentibus hominum inserta cupiditas." Boethius, *Consolatio philosophiae*. See *De Consolatione Philosophiae, Liber Tertius*, 176 Prosa II, PL 63, col. 0724A.

58. MS Vat. lat. 4953, f. 28v; Guarnieri, "Il movimento," 653. "Mens, per quam anima per amorem visibili sponso iungitur, nullam presentis seculi consolationem recipit, sed ad illam quam augit medullinis suspirat, fervet et anhelat." Gregory the Great, *Homiliae in Ezechielem: Liber Secundus*, PL 76, col. 0962B.

59. MS Vat. lat. 4953, f. 29r; Guarnieri, "Il movimento," 654. "Ad appetendum beatitudinem natura compellit." Augustine, *De trinitate*. See *De Trinitate Liber Tertius Decimus*, caput VIII, PL 42, col. 1023.

60. MS Vat. lat. 4953, f. 29r; Guarnieri, "Il movimento," 654. "Beatus autem se esse velle, omnium hominum est." Peter Lombard, *Liber sententiarum*. See *Liber Sententiarum, Liber Quartus*, D. 49,

inversion of what one should naturally desire in this life. By desiring nothing, it is negating any essential natural inclination toward goodness and blessedness.

As one might expect, the *Mirror*'s rejection of institutional church-oriented practices such as sermons, masses, fasts, and—in one error—the sacraments is also singled out. The seventh error is another famous passage from the *Mirror*, taken from chapter 9, which states that the Soul "neither desires nor despises" poverty, masses, sermons, fasts, or prayers, and states that the Soul "always gives to Nature whatever it asks, without remorse of its own conscience."[61] This is another article that appeared in the course of Marguerite Porete's trial in 1310.[62] This is one of the few places where canon-legal authorities dominate the refutation, although it is brief, with only two citations. First it says, "This error is condemned in the Clementines, *Ad nostrum, de hereticis*."[63] It then refers the reader to Hostiensis's commentary on the *Decretum*: "Again, it is against that of Hostiensis, who says that on Sunday anyone of the faith is held to hear mass, and in its entirety, in such a way that he receives benediction from the priest, as in *de consecratione*, distinction I, in the chapter *missas*, and in the chapter *omnes fideles*."[64]

The issue comes up again in the twenty-ninth error, which is an extract from chapter 85, where the *Mirror* states that the Soul "does not seek God through penance, nor through any sacrament of the Church," and neither through meditations, words, creatures, justice, mercy, divine knowledge, divine love, or divine praise.[65] The refutation is concerned primarily with the Soul's rejection of penance and the sacraments of the church, and it mixes scriptural exhortations with legal references:

This error is against the word of the Gospel [Matthew 8:4], "Go, show yourself to the priests," as regards [the passage] *she does not seek God through penance.*

Again, it is against: "Go, do penance" [Matthew 3:2].

---

PL 192, col. 0958; "Nos enim ad verum bonum naturalis inducit [Guarnieri: "induit"] intencio." Boethius, *De Consolatione Philosophiae, Liber Tertius*, 186 Prosa III, PL 63, col. 0731B.

61. MS Vat. lat. 4953, f. 29v; Guarnieri, "Il movimento," 653. "semper dat nature quicquid petit, absque omni consciencie proprie remorsu." For the corresponding passage in the *Mirror* see *Speculum* CCCM, 33.

62. It is noted in the account of her trial found in the continuation of Guillaume de Nangis. Verdeyen, "Le procès," 88; Field, *The Beguine*, 234.

63. MS Vat. lat. 4953, f. 29v; Guarnieri, "Il movimento," 653. "Error est dampnatus in Clementinis, 'ad nostrum, de hereticis.'"

64. MS Vat. lat. 4953, f. 29v; Guarnieri, "Il movimento," 653. "Item est contra illud Hostiensis, qui dicit quod die dominico quilibet fidelis tenetur audire missam et totam, ita quod accipiat benedictionem a sacerdote, ut *de consecration*, distinction 1, capitulo 'missas,' et capitulo 'omnes fideles.'" For the canon Hostiensis is commenting on see Friedberg, *Decretum*, 1312.

65. MS Vat. lat. 4953, f. 31v; Guarnieri, "Il movimento," 660. "non querit Deum per penitentiam, nec per aliquod Ecclesie sacramentum." For the corresponding passage in the *Mirror* see *Speculum* CCCM, 243.

Again, it is against *de penitencia et remissione omnis utriusque sextus* [X 5.38.12] as regards [the passage] *she does not seek God through sacrament of the Church.*[66]

The rest of the refutation focuses on those things that urge man to do good and to praise God, citing Psalms 104:2 ("Sing to him from the heart and proclaim all his miracles"), Matthew 7:8 ("Anyone who seeks will find, and to he who knocks it will open"), and Psalms 36:27 ("Shun evil, and do good"). It concludes by noting that "it is an error condemned in the Clementines [*Ad nostrum*]."

As can be seen in the above error, the Simple Soul is believed to set itself apart not only in rejecting practices but also in that it sets its way of life apart from the church. In the seventeenth error, the *Mirror* speaks of the institutional church and describes it as "Holy Church the Lesser" (*Sancta Ecclesia Minor*), because its way of life is based upon Reason and is therefore inferior to the "church" of the Simple Souls, which the *Mirror* elsewhere calls "Holy Church the Greater" (*Sancta Ecclesia Maior*), and which follows the counsel of Love.[67] The passage from the *Mirror* quoted in the seventeenth error makes it very clear that *Ecclesia Minor* is inferior to *Ecclesia Maior*. *Ecclesia Minor* itself speaks and declares that "such Souls are above us in life, because Love remains in them and Reason in us."[68] The refutation portrays this passage as an attempt to set up two separate churches:

This error puts two churches in this life, and that is against *de summa Trinitate et fide catholica*, in the chapter beginning *firmiter* [X 1.1.1.3]: "Truly there is one church of the universal faith, outside which no one at all is saved."[69] Again, it is against the Apostle's Creed: "I believe in the Holy Catholic Church," and it does not say "churches." At which the gloss of the lord Bonaventure in the third [book] of Sentences: "I believe in the holy Church, that is the holy, sanctified, universal Church."[70]

---

66. MS Vat. lat. 4953, f. 31v; Guarnieri, "Il movimento," 660. "Iste error est contra illud verbum evangelicam: 'Ite, ostendite vos sacerdotibus,' quoad 'non querit Deum per penitenciam.' Item est contra illud: 'Agite penitenciam.' Item est contra illud *de penitencia et remissione utriusque sextus*, quoad illud 'non querit per Ecclesie sacramentum Deum.'" The cited decretal can be found in Emil Friedberg, ed., *Decretalium D. Gregorii Papae IX*, in *Corpus Iuris Canonici*, vol. 2. (Leipzig: Bernhard Tauchnitz, 1881), 887–888.

67. For the passage in the *Mirror* see *Speculum CCCM*, 133.

68. MS Vat. lat. 4953, f. 29v; Guarnieri, "Il movimento," 656. "tales Anime sunt supra nos in vita, quia Amor manet in eis et Ratio in nobis."

69. MS Vat. lat. 4953, f. 29v; Guarnieri, "Il movimento," 656. "ponit duplicem ecclesiam in hac vita, et sic est contra illud *de summa Trinitate et fide catholica*, capitulo *firmiter*: 'Una vero est fidelium universalis ecclesia, extra quam nullus omnino salvatur.'" See X 1.1.1.3, in Friedberg, *Decretalium*, 6.

70. MS Vat. lat. 4953, f. 29v; Guarnieri, "Il movimento," 656. . "'Credo sanctam Ecclesiam Catholicam,' et non dicit 'ecclesias.' Ubi glossa domini Bonaventure in 3o Sententiarum: 'Credo sanctam ecclesiam, id est sanctam, santificatem, universalem ecclesiam.'"

The message is clear: there cannot be multiple churches, there can be only one, and thus setting up another contradicts an essential point of doctrine.

The compilers of the list were also concerned about the idea of the soul achieving complete and unmediated union with God, a concern not unfamiliar to the realm of mysticism, and an issue also connected with Greek Palamism. At least five of the errors included in the Vatican list deal specifically with this issue, and it is linked to at least one other error. The fifth error mainly deals with the Soul's retreat from the virtues. But this error's entry in the list is first prefaced with the compilers' stating that it is the soul that "is placed in divine love" (*in amore divino posita*) that recedes from the virtues. By stating that it is both placed in divine love *and* not performing the virtues, the compilers of the list take this to mean that the soul is still living in its present earthly life and is therefore implying a permanent state of union in this lifetime. The refutation states that "this is the error condemned in Paris, from which followed that the soul knows the divine essence through its natural condition, and that it knows it immediately in this life."[71] This is a reference to the list of 219 philosophical errors that were famously condemned in Paris in 1277 by Bishop Stephen Tempier. The reference here is probably to errors eight and nine in that list: "That our intellect by its own natural power can attain to a knowledge of the first cause" (8) and "That we can know God by his essence in this mortal life" (9).[72]

The above point is embedded in an error on the virtues, but there are at least four other errors where this issue takes center stage. The twentieth error, from chapter 64 of the *Mirror*, states explicitly that "there is no mediary between such Souls and the divinity itself, nor do they want there to be any mediary."[73] The refutation again operates from the stance that the Soul is speaking about one's present, human life, and also that the human soul is able to see and know God by its own natural power. It begins by declaring that such an error "nullifies the light of glory"; that is, it renders null and void the necessity of divinely infused power to allow the soul to see God. It again marks it out as an error "condemned in Paris" (*dampnatus Parisius*) in 1277—likely

---

71. MS Vat. lat. 4953, f. 29v; Guarnieri, "Il movimento," 652. "Item est error dampnatus Parisius, eo quod sequitur quod anima cognoscat divinam essentiam per sua naturalia, et quod eam cognoscat immediate in via."

72. English translation in Gyula Klima, Fritz Allhoff, and Anand Jayprakash Vaidya, eds., *Medieval Philosophy: Essential Readings with Commentary* (Oxford: Wiley-Blackwell, 2007), 180–189. Guarnieri says that it is an error from the earlier condemnation of 1241, which condemned ten errors, issued by William of Auvergne, but there are no errors on that list that seem to correspond to what is written in the Vatican list.

73. MS Vat. lat. 4953, f. 31r; Guarnieri, "Il movimento," 657. "nullum medium est inter tales animas et ipsam divinitatem, nec aliquid medium volunt esse." For the corresponding passage in the *Mirror*, see *Speculum CCCM*, 185.

referring again to the ninth error in that list—as well as marking it as an error condemned in *Ad nostrum*, probably referring to errors four and/or five, both of which talk of achieving a state of beatitude in this life and not needing the light of glory.[74] It also notes that it is refuted by the Franciscan Alexander of Hales (ca. 1185–1245) in his *Sentences* commentary: "In the present [life] one does not know God without a mediary."[75] In other words, the compilers of the list see the *Mirror* as arguing that the human soul can see God directly, purely through its own natural power, rather than requiring the divinely bestowed gift of the light of glory. Furthermore, it is clear that this is perceived as occurring not in the afterlife but in one's present life on earth.

There are other passages where the *Mirror* is seen to take this unmediated union even further beyond the bounds of acceptability. At points it is thought to be claiming not just a special status but a status so special as to be divine. That is, the Soul is thought to be claiming powers for itself that should in theory only belong to God. The fourteenth error, from chapter 23 of the *Mirror*, after describing how the Soul has drunk of the "greater part" of divine goodness, then states that "there is not any difference between Him [God] and herself [the Soul]."[76] The refutation responds, "This error . . . is against that of Augustine in *De fide catholica ad Petrum*: 'He who creates and that which is created are not able to be of one substance or nature.'" It is also perceived as an "error of the Manichees" (*error manicheorum*), because it states that that the soul is from God's substance.[77] These same quotations are then recycled to respond to the twenty-fifth error (from chapter 70), which makes a similar claim of the Soul being nothing other than "that which God is" (*Ergo non sum, si aliquid sum, nisi id quod Deus est*).[78] In the thirteenth error, this is stated even more explicitly. The first part of the error comes from chapter 17, where Love states, "Such Souls . . . about whom this book speaks . . . have by righteousness of their being [MS has "actualization" (*effectus*)] that [which] is pure divine being." It then moves to an (in)famous passage taken from chapter 21: "And who are you, Love? says Reason. Are you not one of the Virtues with us, how-

---

74. MS Vat. lat. 4953, f. 31r; Guarnieri, "Il movimento," 657.

75. MS Vat. lat. 4953, f. 29v; Guarnieri, "Il movimento," 657. "In presenti non est recognoscere Deum sine medio."

76. MS Vat. lat. 4953, f. 30r; Guarnieri, "Il movimento," 655. "non est inter eum et ipsam aliqua dissimilitudino." For the passage in the *Mirror* see *Speculum CCCM*, 87.

77. Vat. lat. 4953, f. 30r; Guarnieri, "Il movimento," 655. "Iste error . . . est contra illud Augustini in *de fide catholica ad Petrum*: 'non unius substantie sive nature possunt esse qui fecit et quod factum est." The sentence on the Manichees reads "Item est error manicheorum, ponentium animam esse de Dei substantia."

78. MS Vat. lat. 4953, f. 31r; Guarnieri, "Il movimento," 659. For the corresponding passage in the *Mirror* see *Speculum CCCM*, 197.

ever much you may be above us? *Love*: I am God, says Love, because Love is God and God is Love. And this Soul is God from himself by the condition of Love. And I am God through divine nature, and this [Soul] is God through the righteousness of Love."[79]

The refutation does not mince words: "That error is against the foundation of the faith," it states, "that there is only one God: 'I believe in one God,' in the [Apostle's] Creed."[80] What concerns the refuters here is not necessarily the presumption of the Soul to aspire to such a divine status, but rather that it is setting itself up as a *second* God:

It is against that of Exodus [2:3]: "I am the Lord your God," and "no other came before me." It is against this: "Hear, Israel, the Lord your God is one." [Deuteronomy 6:4]. And it is against that of *De summa trinitate et fide catholica*, "we firmly believe and simply confess that there is only one God."[81]

Therefore the Simple Soul's claim of "I am God" is not necessarily seen as a transformation into God but as setting itself up as a counterpart or even a rival to God. The Soul makes a similar claim in the thirtieth error. That error, taken from chapter 117, is the last one in the list, and it includes the rather startling passage in which the Soul states, "Just as Christ by his death is the redemption of the people and the praise of God the Father, so I am by the reason of my depravity the salvation of the human race and the glory of God the Father."[82] Unfortunately, the text breaks off in the middle of this error, and so we have no idea what the refutation to this passage was. But it can be said with relative certainty that such a statement would have played into the same concerns over the Soul claiming divine status.

The list also shows great concern with another characteristic that the annihilated soul acquires in union: the Soul's claim to a state of "immovability" in which it can only will the divine will, possessing no will of its own. This in a sense is the other side of the coin to the above errors just discussed: while those

---

79. MS Vat. lat. 4953, f. 30r; Guarnieri, "Il movimento," 655. "Et quod estis vos, Amor? dicit Ratio. Nonne estis una de virtutibus nobiscum, quantumcumque sitis superior nobis? *Amor*: Ego sum Deus, dicit Amor, quia Amor est Deus et Deus est Amor. Et ista Anima est Deus ex ipsius amoris conditione. Et ista est Deus per ius amoris." From *Speculum CCCM*, 83.

80. MS Vat. lat. 4953, f. 30r; Guarnieri, "Il movimento," 655. "Iste est error contra fundamentum fidei, quod tantum unus Deus est: 'Credo in unum Deum,' in Symbolo."

81. MS Vat. lat. 4953, f. 30r; Guarnieri, "Il movimento," 655. "Est contra illud Exodi [2:3]: 'Ego sum dominus Deus tuus,' et 'non est alius preter me.' Et contra illud *de summa Trinitate et fide catholica*, 'firmiter credimus et simpliciter confitemur quod unus solus Deus est.'"

82. MS Vat. lat. 4953, f. 32r; Guarnieri, "Il movimento," 660. "Sicut Christus suo [MS: "sua"] morte est redemption populi et laus Dei patris, ita sum [MS: "sunt"] ratione mee pravitatis salus humani generis et Gloria Dei patris."

errors focus on what the Soul claims is possible in the state of annihilation, these errors show concern over what it claims to be *impossible*; it is impossible for the Soul in such a state to will anything other than the divine will. The primary problem with this idea is its perceived negation of free will. Such a worry appears multiple times. We see it first in the third error: "That the Soul, united with God through Love, and resting in him, always remains fixed in the divine goodness."[83] "This article is against free will," is the immediate response.[84] Specifically, it is interpreted as removing man's ability to sin, since if the soul were to always remain in the divine goodness it would never contradict that goodness and therefore could not sin. A quotation attributed to Jerome lays it out for the reader: "It is therefore against the words of Jerome, who, in [his] explanation of the Catholic faith [in] *ad Damasum papam*, begins: 'We therefore profess free will, so that we may always claim to need the help of God. And they err, both those who with the Manichee say that man is unable to avoid sin, and those who with Jovinian assert that man is not able to sin, for both take away free will. We say man is always able to sin or not to sin.'"[85]

It is also marked out as an error from *Ad nostrum*, presumably because of its implication of achieving "impeccability" and earthly beatitude. The refutation concludes by reiterating that it is against Jerome more broadly, because he proves that even the perfect in this life are able to sin.[86]

The issue returns again in the eighth error, where the Soul says that it is unable to do anything, can do nothing against the divine will, and is unable to desire anything. The emphasis in the refutation here is on how denying free will removes man's responsibility for his own actions. The refutation draws on Augustine's *De libero arbitrio*: "But if the impulse, by which the will is moved hither and thither, were not in our own power, man would be neither praiseworthy when he turned to higher things, nor ought to be blamed when he turned to the lower."[87] The *Sentences* of Peter Lombard are also used: "It is

---

83. MS Vat. lat. 4953, f. 29r; Guarnieri, "Il movimento," 651. "Quod anima unita Deo per amorem, ac quiescens in ipso, semper immobilis permanet in divina bonitate." For this passage in the *Mirro*, see *Speculum CCCM*, 23.

84. "Iste articulus est contra liberum arbitrium."

85. MS Vat. lat. 4953, f. 28r; Guarnieri, "Il movimento," 651–652. "Liberum arbitrium sic confitemur, dicamus nos semper indigere auxilio Dei et tam illos errare, qui cum manicheo dicunt hominem peccatum vitare non posse, quam illos qui cum Joviniano asserunt hominem non posse peccari. Uterque enim tollit arbitrii libertatem. Nos vero dicimus hominem peccare semper et non peccare posse." This may be taken from Peter Lombard's *Liber sententiarum*, where it is attributed to Jerome. See *Liber Sententiarum, Liber Secundus*, D. 28, PL 192, col. 0719.

86. MS Vat. lat. 4953, f. 29r; Guarnieri, "Il movimento," 651.

87. MS Vat. lat. 4953, f. 28v; Guarnieri, "Il movimento," 653. "Motus autem, quo huc aut illuc vertitur voluntas, nisi esset in nostra potestate, nec laudabilis homo esset cum ad superiora, nec culpandus cum ad inferiora detorquet." From Augustine, *De Libero Arbitrio Libri Tres*, caput 3, PL 32, col. 1275.

called free will, as it is turned by the will, because it has been moved volun-
tarily and is brought by spontaneous desire to that which it judges or wishes
to judge good or evil."[88] After citing Romans 6:10 ("For in that he died for
sin, he died once"), it provides the following gloss:

"Man is not made degenerate by the authority of God, but it is the fault of
will by which man is degenerate."[89] Therefore, those which are unable to
do good in any way, are not working on behalf of God, but adore another
than God, or blaspheme God, and thus these sinful souls are damned, just
as [in] that of Matthew [25:41]: "Go from me, you accursed, into the eternal fire."[90]

The twenty-second error, in which the Soul declares that it is dissolved into
the Trinity and is unable to do anything other than the divine will through the
works of the Trinity (from chapter 68), is also refuted as negating free will, with
a one-line refutation reading, "This error does away with free will, which is mentioned above."[91]

Clearly, the compilers of this list view the *Mirror* as denying free will and
therefore excusing humans from responsibility for their actions and responsibility for sin. In this view, the *Mirror* is claiming that degeneracy is not an in-
nate, inescapable quality of being human but is something that can be
overcome by achieving the state of annihilation. There seems to be a sense
here as well that this aspect of the *Mirror* removes a fundamental element of
being human. Exempted from its own will, the Soul is separating itself from
the rest of humanity, seeming to give itself license to act and live according to
laws other than those that most of the human race follow.

A final concern revolves around the *Mirror*'s concept of "unknowing" or
the "unknowable" nature of union with the divine in annihilation. Four
errors—the second, ninth, twenty-third, and twenty-fourth—all claim in some
way that man cannot truly have knowledge of God, by denying both internal
acquisition of knowledge through contemplation or revelation and external

88. MS Vat. lat. 4953, f. 28v; Guarnieri, "Il movimento," 653. "Liberum arbitrium dicitur quan-
tum ad voluntatem, quia voluntarie moveri et spontaneo appetitu ferri ad ea que bona vel mala iudi-
cat vel iudicare valet." From Lombard, *Liber Sententiarum, Liber Secundus*, D. 15, PL 192, col. 0706.

89. From Peter Lombard, *In Epistolam ad Romanos*, caput VI, PL 191, col. 1406C.

90. MS Vat. lat. 4953, f. 28v; Guarnieri, "Il movimento," 653; "'Non Deo auctore fit homo deterior,
sed voluntatis vitium [MS and Guarnieri: "initium"] est quo homo est deterior.' Propterea illa que nullo
modo bene fieri possunt, non sunt facienda propter Deum, aut adorare aliud quam Deum, aut blas-
phemando Deum, quoniam his peccatis anima dampnatur, iuxta illud Mathei: 'Ite maledicti in ignem
eternalem.'"

91. MS Vat. lat. 4953, f. 31r; Guarnieri, "Il movimento," 658. "Iste error tollit liberum arbitrium,
de quo superius est mention facta."

acquisition from teachings and writings. The rejection of acquiring knowledge from external sources is dealt with in errors twenty-three and twenty-four. In error twenty-three (taken from chapter 69) the Soul states that God's teaching cannot be found in any writings or in the teachings of men, because his gift cannot be given through any testimony or proof.[92] This is met initially with a quotation from Augustine's *Confessions*: "O Lord, is not your scripture true? O man, truly it is my scripture, for I, Truth, brought it forth."[93] This is then followed by a series of biblical quotations, among them Ecclesiasticus (Sirach) 1:1, "All wisdom is from the Lord God,"; Psalms 118:18, "Open my eyes and I will consider the wonders in your law"; and the pronouncement that "it is against the Gospel, declaring the life of Christ and [his] miracles" (*Est contra Evangelia, declarantia vitam Christi et miracula*).[94] This clearly characterizes the *Mirror* as discounting scriptural truth and authority.

Error twenty-four again demonstrates a rejection of finding God in "created" things. This is also taken from chapter 69 and is the famous passage wherein Marguerite calls those adhering to Reason "beasts and asses" (*bestiales et asinos*) who seek God "in creatures, in churches for praying, in a created paradise, in the words of people, in the Scriptures" (*querunt Deum in creaturis, in templis orando, in paradiso creata, in verbis hominum, in scripturis*).[95] First, the refutation sees a denial of God's presence in his creation, quoting Romans 1:20: "The invisible things of Him from the creation of the world are clearly seen, being understood by the things that are made, even His eternal power and divinity."[96] The refutation also, as it did with the twenty-third error, pushes back at the seeming rejection of scripture, saying it contradicts Augustine in *Ad Paulam de videndo Deo*: "If you ask whether it is possible to see God, I respond: It is possible. If you ask from where I know this, I respond: because in the truest Scripture it is read: 'Blessed are the pure in heart, for they shall see God.'"[97] The

---

92. MS Vat. lat. 4953, f. 31r; Guarnieri, "Il movimento," 658. The corresponding passage can be found in *Speculum CCCM*, 195.

93. MS Vat. lat. 4953, f. 31r; Guarnieri, "Il movimento," 658. "O domine, nonne ista scriptura vera est? O homo, nempe scriptura mea est, quoniam ego, Veritas, edi eam." The quotation is from book XIII of the *Confessions*. See Augustine, *Augustine Confessions: Volume 1: Introduction and Text*, ed. James J. O'Donnell (Oxford: Oxford University Press, 1992), 202.

94. MS Vat. lat. 4953, f. 31r; Guarnieri, "Il movimento," 658.

95. MS Vat. lat. 4953, f. 31r; Guarnieri, "Il movimento," 658.

96. MS Vat. lat. 4953, f. 31r; Guarnieri, "Il movimento," 658. "Invisibilia Dei per ea que facta sunt in intellectu conspiciuntur, sempiterna quoque eius virtus et divinitas."

97. MS Vat. lat. 4953, f. 31r; Guarnieri, "Il movimento," 659. "Si queris utrum Deus possit videri, respondeo: potest. Si queris unde hoc sciam, respondeo: quia in veracissima Scriptura legitur: "Beati mundo corde, quoniam ipsi Deum videbunt." From Augustine, *Ad Paulinum, de videndo Deo*. See *Opera Omnia Augustini Hipponensis: De Videndo Deo Liber, Seu Epistola CXLVII*, caput 3, PL 32, col. 1275.

*Sentences* of Peter Lombard are also brought in, which say that the truth of God can be seen in the greatness of creatures, in a wise disposition, and in good governance.[98]

The second and ninth errors take on the more abstract issue of comprehension and understanding of the divine, as separate from material rituals or writings. Both errors assert that the divine goodness and God cannot be understood by anyone, saying that God's goodness is not comprehended except by himself (second error) and that God cannot be understood perfectly by anyone, not even those in paradise (ninth error).[99] The refutations of both take it as denying the ability of man to come to knowledge of God and see him face-to-face in the afterlife. The refutation to the second error marks it as yet another Parisian error, this time from the condemnation of 1241, "That the divine essence may not be seen by man."[100] The refutation of the ninth error responds, "That error is against that of the Apostle [1 John 3:2]: 'We shall see him just as he is.'"[101] The ninth refutation also takes the view that the *Mirror* is denying any gift of divine knowledge that is given from God, stating, "It is against the Apostle's Creed, which places the unity of God and the Trinity of Persons, and the twelve articles, those of the apostles, not as ignorance but as the enlightened teaching of the Holy Spirit, as Jerome testifies to the bishop Paul in *De institutis clericorum*: 'Accordingly, one does not learn these letters by human reason, but the Holy Spirit of heaven infuses [them] into man.'"[102]

In a similar vein, if this error were true, "all revelations would vanish" (*perirent omnes revelationes*).[103] It is also "against the gospel of John and all the evangelists, and is against any others who speak about God, and is against the entirety of Holy Scripture."[104] It is also another error from the 1241 Parisian list:

---

98. MS Vat. lat. 4953, f. 31r; Guarnieri, "Il movimento," 659. 659. Lombard, *Liber Sententiarum, Liber Primus: De Mysterio Trinitatis*, D. 3, *PL* 192, col. 0530.

99. For the passages in the *Mirror*, see *Speculum CCCM*, 21–23 and 45.

100. MS Vat. lat. 4953, f. 29r; Guarnieri, "Il movimento," 651. "quod divina essentia non videatur ab homine." See *1241 Errors*, first error.

101. MS Vat. lat. 4953, f. 29v; Guarnieri, "Il movimento," 654. "Iste error est contra illud apostoli: 'videbimus eum sicuti est.'"

102. MS Vat. lat. 4953, f. 29v; Guarnieri, "Il movimento," 654. "Item est contra Symbolum Apostolicum, ponentem unitatem Dei et trinitatem Personarum, et XII articulos, quod sancti apostoli, non tanquam ignari sed tanquam illuminati doctrina Spiritus Sancti, ut testatur Jeronimus ad Paulinum episcopum de institutis clericorum: 'Has siquidem litteras non ratio humana reperit, sed hominibus sanctis Spiritus celestis infudit.'" This is not from Jerome, but from Cassiodorus (ca. 485–ca. 585). See *M. Aurelii Cassiodori de Institutione Divinarum Litterarum*, caput 16, *PL* 70, col. 1131D.

103. MS Vat. lat. 4953, f. 29v; Guarnieri, "Il movimento," 654.

104. MS Vat. lat. 4953, f. 29v; Guarnieri, "Il movimento," 654. "Item est contra evangelium Johannis et omnium evangelistarum, ac contra quoscumque alios loquentes de Deo, et contra totam Sacram Scripturam."

"Concerning God nothing is able to be known, except that he was his being."[105] These refutations give a clear signal that if no one is able to understand God, it renders all efforts directed toward God irrelevant; it essentially negates the whole point of scripture and any other theological or spiritual exercise. This error is seen to negate not only man's work but also God's, as is suggested by the quote from Jerome and the comment about revelations. If knowledge and understanding of God is impossible, then all teachings said to come directly from God—through prophets and revelations—are rendered false. It is suggesting that not even God himself can allow man to understand him, not through revelation or infused knowledge. This places limits on God's own abilities. One could perhaps also see in this echoes of controversies over the beatific vision from John XXII's pontificate in the fourteenth century, in which John asserted that the blessed did not immediately see the full divinity of God after death but were rather in an "imperfect" state until the Final Judgment.[106] This was also a matter of controversy between the Greek and Latin churches.[107]

The limiting of God also appears in the sixteenth error, where the Soul states that God cannot love anything else without the Soul, and thus has never been able to love anything without her, nor will ever love anything without her.[108] The refutation states that this was among the propositions condemned in Paris in 1277, "since it places the soul as having existed eternally."[109] The refutation also presents Genesis 2:7: "And I breathed my breath into you," and 1:27: "God created man (that is to say the soul) in his image and likeness." "Therefore," the refutation continues, "it [the soul] was not made from eternity, and yet from eternity He has loved without the soul, which before then was nothing except aptitudinally."[110] Two objections can be seen here. The first is the one plainly stated, that the *Mirror* is asserting that the soul has existed from eternity, which is impossible since it was created by God and was thus preceded by him. The sec-

---

105. MS Vat. lat. 4953, f. 29v; Guarnieri, "Il movimento," 654. "de Deo non posset sciri nisi quod esset suum esse." See *1241 Errors*, second error.

106. A clear and succinct discussion of what was at stake in the beatific vision controversy is given by Michael W. Dunne, "Richard FitzRalph on the Beatific Vision: *Delectatio* and *Beatitudo* in His Oxford Lectures on the Sentences," *Irish Theological Quarterly* 80, no. 4 (2015): 330–331.

107. Dunne, "Richard FitzRalph," 331.

108. MS Vat. lat. 4953, f. 29v; Guarnieri, "Il movimento," 656.

109. MS Vat. lat. 4953, f. 29v; Guarnieri, "Il movimento," 656. "cum ponat animam eternaliter fuisse." The error referenced is "That the substance of the soul is eternal, and that the agent intellect and the possible intellect are eternal," number 129 on the list. English translation from Klima, Allhoff, and Vaidya, *Medieval Philosophy*, 186.

110. MS Vat. lat. 4953, f. 29v; Guarnieri, "Il movimento," 656. "Creavit Deus hominem (scilicet animam) ad ymaginem et similitudinem suam. Ergo non fuit ab eterno, et tamen ab eterno se dilexit sine anima, que pro tunc non erat nisi aptitudinaliter."

ond, though, is the implication of the soul having direct influence on God, and that some of God's actions—namely, his ability to love creation—are somehow dependent upon the soul's presence. This limits God's omnipotence and once again raises the soul to a nonhuman level, existing with God since eternity and not living under him as his creation. Therefore, to the compilers of the list, the Soul in the *Mirror* lays claim to a position of divine influence and power that is beyond what is possible for a human being to achieve.

If we stitch these various refutations together into a whole, the overall picture that this list presents is of the *Mirror* as a work that exalts the human soul above a status that is considered appropriate—or even possible—for it to attain. It portrays the *Mirror* as a book that sets up the Simple Soul as a rival not only to the institutional church but also to God himself. It also denies man's ability to both arrive at and receive divine knowledge and experiences, while simultaneously arguing that it can achieve a state of divinity in this lifetime. The indifference and total absorption into God's will—at the expense of one's own will—that comes with this state is also seen as negating free will and removing man's culpability for sin. In other words, to the authors of this list, the *Mirror* contradicts several foundational points of doctrine. To them, the *Mirror* is clearly a heretical book.

The responses recorded here also reveal how those who compiled the list thought the *Mirror* fitted into the larger landscape of theological error. Most obvious (and unsurprising) are those that reflect the errors that were singled out during Marguerite Porete's trial in 1310: those that addressed the abandonment of the virtues, the license of the Soul to give to nature all that it asks, and an indifference to or lack of need for the gifts and consolations of God. These issues also appear in the errors listed in *Ad nostrum*, but added to them are also questions of the divinization of humans and the attainment of blessedness without the light of glory. As we saw, the Vatican list links *Ad nostrum* and the *Mirror* explicitly regarding these topics. This is in exact accord with what we saw in chapter 1, in the sermons of Bernardino of Siena and the anonymous treatise against the beghards owned by Johannes Wenck: the doctrine of the *Mirror* was linked directly to the errors listed in that decree. Those who responded to the *Mirror* here perceived that same connection, situating it within the broader campaign against beghards and other "free spirits."

That such aspects of the *Mirror* would be singled out is not surprising, as these questions were also hotly contested in other contexts. They were flash points in the condemnation of Meister Eckhart's teachings, promulgated in the bull *In agro dominico* in 1329. In that list of errors, too, are numerous references to humans adopting the same essence as God, the same will as God, and surpassing the need for basic virtuous acts and practices.[111] Various figures, such as the German theologian Heinrich von Friemar, the Flemish mystic Jan van Ruusbroec, and even Eckhart's disciples Heinrich Suso and Johannes Tauler, criticized such ideas.[112] The critics could then become the criticized: in the fifteenth century, Jean Gerson accused Ruusbroec repeatedly of claiming in his writings that humans could share the same essence and being as God.[113] In many of these instances, such errors were often linked to the errors of the beghards; *In agro dominico* was even used at times in conjunction with *Ad nostrum* as an inquisitorial interrogatory into free spirit errors.[114] In an echo of how the *Mirror* is treated in the Vatican list, the fifteenth-century theologian Heinrich von Kamp wrote a short compilation of errors that he reportedly found in two *libelli* owned by a "beghard" in the Rhineland. There, too, we find categories of errors that deal with such assertions as human essence becoming divine essence, man achieving a union with God as perfect as the union Christ had with God, and the eternal existence of the human soul, among other articles that also deal with "impeccability" and the virtues.[115]

The *Mirror* in scholarship has long been associated with these broader troubles over "free spirits" and mysticism, linked to *Ad nostrum* and Eckhartian ideas.[116] But while *Ad nostrum* is the most prominent canon-legal source in the Vatican list, it only accounts for about six out of the twenty-nine refutations that appear in it. It is clear that the refuters saw the *Mirror* as more than just a representation of beghardian errors. They also thought it connected to theological-philosophical errors that had come out of the universities a century earlier. Most interesting are the invocations of the theological errors condemned in Paris in the thirteenth century, both in 1241 and in 1277.[117] These are

111. Edmund Colledge and Bernard McGinn, eds., *Meister Eckhart: The Essential Sermons, Commentaries, and Defense* (New York: Paulist Press, 1981), 77–81.

112. Lerner, *Heresy of the Free Spirit*, 182–199; Jan van Ruusbroec, *John Ruusbroec: The Spiritual Espousals and Other Works*, ed. and trans. James A. Wiseman, OSB (New York: Paulist Press, 1985), 139.

113. Jean Gerson, *Jean Gerson: Early Works*, trans. Brian Patrick Maguire (New York: Paulist Press, 1998), 202–210. For a full study of all of Jean Gerson's attacks on Ruusbroec, see André Combes, *Essai sur la critique de Ruysbroeck par Gerson*, 4 vols. (Paris: Vrin, 1945–1972).

114. Lerner, "Meister Eckhart's Specter: Fourteenth-Century Uses of the Bull *In agro dominico* Including a Newly Discovered Inquisitorial Text of 1337," *Mediaeval Studies* 70 (2008).

115. Wilhelm Preger, "Beiträge zur Geschichte der religiösen Bewegung in den Niederlanden in der 2 Hälfte des 14 Jahrhunderts," *Abhandlungen der historischen Classe der Königlich Bayerischen Akademie der Wissenschaften* 21 (1898): 22–24. The text can also be found in Guarnieri, "Il movimento," 463n2.

116. This can be seen from its inclusion in Lerner, *Heresy of the Free Spirit*, and Guarnieri, "Il movimento," as well as the many studies linking the *Mirror* with Meister Eckhart, noted in the introduction.

117. The literature on the 1277 condemnation is vast. Useful studies are Jan Aertsen, Kent Emery, and Andreas Speer, eds., *Nach der Verurteilung Von 1277/After the Condemnation Of 1277: Philosophie und Theologie an der Universität Paris im Letzten Viertel des 13 Jahrhunderts. Studien und Texte* (Berlin: De Gruyter, 2013); Thijssen, *Censure and Heresy*, 40–56; and Luca Bianchi, *Il vescovo e i filosofi: La condanna parigina del 1277 e l'evoluzione dell'aristotelismo scolastico* (Bergamo: Lubrina, 1990).

mentioned at least five times in total—three times for the 1277 condemnation, and two for that of 1241, and in at least two places in the list these academic errors are cited alongside *Ad nostrum* to refute the same issue. The presence of these condemnations in the refutations here implies that these readers of the *Mirror* saw in it resonances of philosophical ideas that were seen to contradict Christian truths. A studied comparison between the *Mirror*'s ideas and the theological issues raised in these condemnations is far beyond the scope of this book, and so I will not attempt it here.[118] But their use here against the *Mirror* show some basic similarities. The articles taken from the 1277 condemnation are used to address the question of unmediated union and divinization, that God's essence can be known by the human soul in this lifetime; they also refute the idea of the eternity of the soul. Those from 1241 are almost the opposite, addressed to concepts that deal with what is *not* possible, namely, the question of the *Mirror*'s themes of unknowing and inability to understand the divine. By citing these condemnations in their refutations, the compilers of this list are seeing in the *Mirror* not just ideas associated with heretical mysticism but also concepts connected to Aristotelian philosophy that had been current in and provoked censure within academic circles for over a century.[119] This affinity between the *Mirror* and university scholastic concepts has been noted by Danielle Dubois and Peter King in terms of the *Mirror*'s relationship to orthodoxy; the Vatican list shows that it also shared that affinity when it came to heresy. By connecting the *Mirror* to these long-standing controversies within academic circles, the compilers of this list also offer a glimpse into how they approached and perceived such a work, particularly when considered alongside the method of assessment that they deployed against it. Much like the original appraisal of the *Mirror* by Parisian theologians in 1310, the *Mirror* is being treated here as a product of the world that the compilers inhabited, that of the educated university theologian. They are assessing the *Mirror* much as they would the work of an academic peer. By doing so, they gave the *Mirror* a high level of intellectual respect.

A measure of that respect can also be seen in the second interpretive layer of this list: its connection to the theological debates between Latins and Greeks at the Council of Ferrara-Florence. While the list itself is clearly written with

---

118. To my knowledge there has not yet been a consideration of Marguerite's ideas in relation to the academic condemnations of the thirteenth century. There have, however, been interesting comparisons between Marguerite's ideas and scholastic thought, particularly in the work of Danielle Dubois. See Dubois, "Natural and Supernatural Virtues," and also Peter King, "Marguerite Porete and Godfrey of Fontaines: Detachable Will, Discardable Virtue, Transformative Love," *Oxford Studies in Medieval Philosophy* 6, no. 1 (2018).

119. See the essays in Aertsen, Emery, and Speer, *Nach der Verurteilung.*

mostly Western heresies in mind, its inclusion in MS Vat. lat. 4953 indicates that some felt that the *Mirror*'s errors also reflected issues that divided East and West. The topics of divinization, the divine essence, and the human capacity to see God were all contested points between the Latin and Greek churches, particularly in relation to Palamite thought.[120] One could even see how the *Mirror*'s statements on *Ecclesia Maior* and *Ecclesia Minor* could be linked to debates over papal supremacy and, of course, resonate with participants in a council that was trying to bring about union between two acrimoniously divided churches. This connection of the *Mirror* to the debates between East and West is a new facet to the *Mirror*'s reception history. A more in-depth analysis of the theological issues than I am able to provide here would no doubt produce new and interesting intellectual affinities between the *Mirror*'s ideas and Greek doctrine. This manuscript demonstrates the *Mirror* potentially being used as a tool to attack or defend particular points of doctrine, not merely against heresies "at home", but also ones that were part of a deep and centuries-long schism with the East.[121] It shows controversies over the *Mirror* connecting to one another, migrating, and being used in new contexts. The *Mirror* did not disappear into the background after an event like the Venice inquisition but lingered in the minds of those who came across it. Therefore what we have here is a text that has two interpretive levels for the *Mirror*: one that treated the *Mirror* as the product of internal Latin heresies and another that saw in it issues that bitterly divided Latins and Greeks.

## Conclusion

For a long time we have lacked insight into the details behind condemnations of *The Mirror of Simple Souls*. What we find in MS Vat. lat. 4953 fills in some of those gaps. The Vatican text is not a general condemnation of the *Mirror* but a systematic refutation of its key points. It provides in detail some of the theological arguments that were used to denounce the *Mirror*'s doctrines, and it shows quite clearly that a number of particular points were troubling to those who made this list. Clearly, to the compiler or compilers of this list, the *Mirror*

---

120. Kappes, *Epiclesis Debate*, 4–6; De Halleux, "Bessarion et le palamisme."

121. The "errors of the Greeks" were increasingly included in descriptions of heresy and in inquisitors' manuals by the late Middle Ages and were also frequently linked to the Hussites in the fifteenth century. See, for example, Nicholas Eymerich's inclusion of them in his *Directorium inquisitorum*. See also William Hyland, "John-Jerome of Prague (1368–1440) and the *Errores Graecorum*: Anatomy of a Polemic Against Greek Christians," *The Journal of Religious History* 21, no. 3 (1997), and Irene Bueno, "Late Medieval Heresiography and the Categorisation of Eastern Christianity," in Peter Biller and Lucy Sackville, eds., *Inquisition and Knowledge 1200–1700* (York, UK: York Medieval Press, 2022).

was a work that opposed several essential components of Christian life and doctrine. On a worldly level it rejected virtuous practices and the authority of the church. But of much more concern to the authors of this list are the theological tenets that it challenges. To them, it raises troubling questions about free will, the ability of the human soul to see God or become divine, how humans obtain knowledge of God, and humans' ability to know or understand the divine. They saw in the *Mirror* not only the "errors of the beghards" condemned in *Ad nostrum*, which their contemporaries were frequently deploying against it, but also ideas that had roiled their own ranks within universities and other intellectual circles for over a century. The manuscript's connection to the Council of Ferrara-Florence adds a further layer showing that some might have also seen the "errors of the Greeks" within its pages.

This text is also likely connected to the Venice inquisition of 1437, along with (possibly) the accusation against Eugenius IV in 1439. If the list of MS Vat. lat. 4953 is the assessment of the Paduan theologians carried out at Antonio Zeno's request then it provides an additional piece of evidence for the *Mirror*'s treatment in the events surrounding the Venice inquisition. It reinforces the impression that the *Mirror* must have received some type of censure at the end of this episode. Its inclusion in MS Vat. lat. 4953, among documents meant to aid someone in the debates between the Greek and Latin churches at the Council of Florence, also demonstrates how both this list and concerns over the *Mirror* were transmitted and traveled within papally-linked circles, as well as being reused and linked to larger concerns and debates. This is also suggested by the events at Basel, where some form of this list may have been used in the accusation against Eugenius. If this list—or some form of it—was used against Eugenius IV in the 1439 accusation at Basel, it is easy to see why it would have been chosen for such a use. The above errors—with their denial of the institutional church and claims to a divine authority not deemed acceptable for a human soul to make—would have complemented the Council of Basel's characterization of Eugenius as a schismatic and an "obstinate heretic" with no regard for "the peace and unity of God's church."[122] But the context of the Vatican list once again highlights the interesting parallel lives of the *Mirror*. This manuscript was probably put together shortly after the council's transfer to Florence in 1439 and was likely used by someone who participated in the council while it was there. Not far from Florence was, of course, Camaldoli, where John-Jerome of Prague had made his own copy of the *Mirror* fourteen years previously. Although John-Jerome himself was by

---

122. Stieber, *Supreme Authority*, 55.

this time no longer at Camaldoli, the copy he made of the *Mirror* was likely still there and, presumably, still being read.[123]

MS Vat. lat. 4953 was not, however, the first detailed denouncement of the *Mirror*'s errors to have been written. Another text, also connected to the University of Padua, had turned up earlier. Giacomo de Zocchi, professor of canon law at the university in Padua, had become aware of the *Mirror*'s dangers at least eleven years previously. He had come across a document that attacked the *Mirror*'s errors not from a theological but from a canon-legal standpoint. This text, too, cast the *Mirror* in a heretical light, but one that had a much more sinister tint to it. Let us now turn to Giacomo's find.

---

123. It is difficult to know whether news of this list or the controversy that produced it ever made it back to Camaldoli, but it is not impossible—Ambrogio Traversari, a close ally of Eugenius IV and participant in the council, was the minister general of Camaldoli at that time. John-Jerome had attended the Council of Basel in 1433 but had been prevented from returning to Camaldoli by Ambrogio Traversari. He therefore took up residence in the Camaldolese house in Venice. Hyland, "Portrait," 329. Interesting to note is that John-Jerome had himself written a work attacking the Greeks just before the Council of Ferrara-Florence. See Hyland, "Anatomy of a Polemic."

# CHAPTER 4

# Reason Strikes Back

## The Polemic of MS 1647

For all the controversy it stirred up, the responses we have so far seen to the Latin *Mirror of Simple Souls* have been relatively short and to the point. Excised, banned, denounced, and refuted, the *Mirror* was nevertheless not engaged with extensively. Even the refutations of MS Vat. lat. 4953 are more bullet points of scriptural and theological proofs than lengthy diatribes. Furthermore, while these instances clearly show disapproval of, concern over, and opposition to the *Mirror*, most are devoid of any real emotional heft. Even Bernardino of Siena, who perhaps can be named as the fiercest critic of the *Mirror* that we have so far seen, remarked on how the *Mirror* was "dangerous" but mostly left it at that.

This makes the next text to be examined remarkable even among an already crowded field of critics. Copied on the last seven folios of the fifteenth-century codex Padua, Biblioteca universitaria di Padova, MS 1647, it, like MS Vat. lat. 4953, provides verbatim extracts from a Latin *Mirror* followed by refutations. But, unlike the Vatican text, it is more of a treatise and not a list, exhibiting a narrative style and distinct authorial voice. This voice not only denounces the *Mirror*'s doctrines as erroneous but portrays the *Mirror* itself as a dangerous and diabolical influence. This text was long forgotten in *Mirror* scholarship, and its rediscovery adds several new dimensions to the *Mirror*'s reception history. It is the only known polemic written against the *Mirror*. It represents the strongest attack against it outside of its condemnations in Valenciennes and

Paris and, in its rhetoric and detail at least, surpasses even those iconic events in the *Mirror*'s history.

The uniqueness of the text becomes even more important when considered in the context of its origins. While it exists only in a fifteenth-century copy, it was very likely first composed in the early fourteenth century, quite close in time to—perhaps even contemporarily with or before—the *Mirror*'s two condemnations and Marguerite Porete's execution.[1] Among other things, this means that the polemic provides a new window into the *Mirror*'s reception on two fronts: its early reception in the fourteenth century and its controversial fifteenth-century reception. Situating the text within these two contexts, this chapter provides the first in-depth examination of this work, discussing its ownership and context in Bologna and Padua and then providing a detailed description and analysis of its contents.

# Padua, Biblioteca universitaria di Padova, MS 1647

MS 1647 is a fifteenth-century paper codex of 224 folios that retains its original wooden binding.[2] It was compiled no later than 1428, as there is a customs note on the first folio bearing the date 22 December 1428.[3] Its owner was Giacomo de Zocchi, a canon lawyer at the University of Padua who moved there from Bologna in 1429.[4] Watermark evidence suggests that all of the texts in the codex were copied in Bologna sometime between 1396 and 1428.[5] With over two hundred folios and measuring 44.7 × 30.7 cm (ca. 17 × 11 in), it is a hefty tome—in other words, not a book designed with portability in mind. It is bound in two large wooden boards, and there are square spaces on the outer edges of the top, bottom, and right-hand side of the front board where there are remnants of red and blue fabric straps. This is almost certainly the original binding, as in the fifteenth-century catalog of Santa Giustina—where the manuscript was bequeathed after de Zocchi's death—the manuscript is described as a "large paper

1. See the full argument in Trombley, "New Evidence"; a brief recap is given in the section on the text's origins.

2. A description of MS 1647 can also be found in Luigi Montobbio, "I quattro codici di Giacomo Zocchi," *Benedictina* 10 (1956): 55–56.

3. Trombley, "New Evidence," 139. This note meant that de Zocchi could bring his books with him into Padua tax-free. See Luciano Gargan, "L'enigmatico 'conduxit': Libri e dogana a Padova fra Tre e Quattrocento," *Quaderni per la storia dell'università di Padova* 16 (1983).

4. Annalisa Belloni, *Professori giuristi a Padova nel secolo XV: Profili bio-bibliografici e cattedre* (Frankfurt: Klostermann, 1986), 216; Griguolo, "Per la biografia," 184 and 185.

5. Trombley, "New Evidence," 139–140. The three watermark designs present are a rampant lion, a dragon, and a three-mountain design.

*Table 4.1*  Contents of MS 1647

| FOLIO NUMBER(S) | CONTENTS |
| --- | --- |
| 1r–124r | Antonio de Butrio, *Super quarto Decretalium*. A commentary on the fourth book of the *Decretals* by the fourteenth-century Italian canonist Antonio de Butrio (1338–1408). |
| 124v–126v | Blank |
| 127r–131v | Table of contents for William of Horborch (ca. 1320–1384), *Conclusiones seu determinationes quorundam dubiorum per Rotam Romanam*, organized in numerical order. |
| 132r–133v | Blank |
| 134r–202v | William of Horborch's *Conclusiones seu determinationes quorundam dubiorum per Rotam Romanam*. |
| 203r–208r | An index of the *Conclusiones*, ordered by subject, written in the hand of Giacomo de Zocchi. |
| 208v | Blank |
| 209r–215r | A copy of *Impugnacio cathedre sedis Romane ecclesie in concilio Constanciensi eiusdemque defensio*, ca. 1417.[1] |
| 215v–221v | The polemic against the *Speculum simplicium animarum*. Also copied in the hand of Giacomo de Zocchi. |
| 222r–224v | Blank |

[1] Heinrich Finke published an edition of the *Impugnacio* in his *Forschungen und Quellen zur Geschichte des Konstanzer Konzils* (Paderborn: Ferdinand Schöningh, 1889), 288–297.

volume, covered in wooden boards with red straps" (*volumen magnum in papyro, tectum tabulis cum fundello rubeo*).[6] It contains four different works, all of a canon-legal nature, which are outlined in table 4.1 (according to modern foliation).[7]

The codex is clearly a canon lawyer's book, meant to be referenced and used professionally. It appears to be one of a set of four volumes—the other three preserved as MSs 1645, 1646, and 1648 in the Biblioteca universitaria di Padova—each containing a book of Antonio de Butrio's commentary on the *Decretals*.[8] De Zocchi seems to have collected the works together himself and then sent them to a binder.[9] Most of the texts are carefully laid out, written in two neat columns with wide margins, and in legible hands. It is a plain manuscript, with only the de Butrio commentary and the *Roman Rota* decisions featuring lightly decorated red and blue initials. The *Impugnacio* and anti-*Mirror* text have spaces

6. Giovanna Cantoni Alzati, *La biblioteca di S. Giustina di Padova: Libri e cultura presso i Benedettini Padovani in età umanistica* (Padua: Antenore, 1982), 102. There is also a note in a fifteenth-century hand written on the inside of the back board at the bottom left, which is not easily legible but seems to read *Johanes caxinus siculus est ab omnia seruicia vestra et mandata paritus*. This presumably was left by the binder.

7. My layout differs from that of Montobbio, "Quattro codici," as he used the old foliation, which is inconsistent.

8. Montobbio, "Quattro codici." Two of these other volumes—MSs 1645 and 1646—also bear the same customs note. Of the four, only MS 1647 seems to have kept its original binding.

9. Trombley, "New Evidence," 141.

for initials that were never filled in. There are at least five different hands: one for the de Butrio work, one for the *Roman Rota* decisions and its table of contents, two hands for the *Impugnacio cathedre*, and Giacomo de Zocchi's own hand, which copied both the anti-*Mirror* text and the table of contents for the *Roman Rota* decisions.[10] De Zocchi also left numerous notes and comments in the margins throughout the manuscript. The anti-*Mirror* text is the exception to the neat aspect of the manuscript: it is still written in two columns, but the columns are often of different widths from one another, and the lines of text occasionally run on a slant. MS 1647 remained in de Zocchi's possession until his death in November 1457, upon which the codex was bequeathed—along with twelve other books in his possession—to the Benedictine monastery of Santa Giustina in Padua, where de Zocchi was also buried. Three separate notes in the manuscript inform the reader of de Zocchi's bequest, on folios 1r, 123v, and 221v.

## The Lawyer and the *Mirror*

Giacomo de Zocchi was a well-respected and well-known professor of canon law at the University of Padua.[11] Born sometime at the end of the fourteenth century in Massa Fiscaglia—about sixty kilometers northeast of Bologna and thirty-four kilometers east of Ferrara—he grew up in Ferrara and later attended the University of Bologna, receiving a degree in canon law on 20 March 1425.[12] After three and a half years of teaching at Bologna, he moved to the University of Padua sometime in the second half of 1429, where he would spend the rest of his academic career.[13] On 8 May 1439, he received a second degree in civil law.[14] He attracted a large following of students, many of them coming from abroad, especially from Germany. De Zocchi taught law to several students who would go on to illustrious careers in the church, such as Johannes Hinderbach, bishop of Trent (1418–1486); the jurist Bartolomeo Cipolla (1420–1475); and the papal judge Giovanni Francesco Pavini (d. 1485).[15] He was

10. Montobbio describes the hands for the de Butrio commentary and the *Rota* decisions as "bastarda" and "gothic libraria," respectively. "Quattrio codici," 55. On de Zocchi's hand see Trombley, "New Evidence," 140.

11. The most detailed and up to date study of de Zocchi's life is Griguolo, "Per la biografia." Brief biographical notes on de Zocchi have also appeared in Theodor Pyl, *Die Rubenow Bibliothek: Die Handschriften und Urkunden der von Heinrich Rubenow 1456 gestifteten Juristen- und Artisten-Bibliothek zu Greifswald* (Greifswald: Reinhold Scharff, 1865), 115–118; Montobbio, "Quattro codici," 49–50; and Belloni, *Professori giuristi*, 216–218.

12. Griguolo, "Per la biografia," 184.
13. Belloni, *Professori giuristi*, 217.
14. Griguolo, "Per la biografia," 185.
15. Griguolo, "Per la biografia," 187.

an active part of public life, acting as a consultant and an *arbiter causarum,* and oversaw countless degree-conferring ceremonies at the university.[16] He was closely connected with the monastery of Santa Giustina during the course of his life, as evidenced by his bequest to the monks of several of his books upon his death and his request to be buried there, clothed in the habit of the order.[17]

Giacomo de Zocchi seems to have been a high-profile member of the university, perhaps even something of a minor celebrity. Copies of his legal writings—most of them commentaries on collections of canon law or particular legal decrees—survive in numerous manuscripts in libraries all over Europe. We even, remarkably, have a picture of him, although one done posthumously. The Paduan jurist Marco Mantova Benivides (1489–1582) had a collection of forty-seven portraits of famous jurists that were printed and published in two installments; the first was printed and published by Antoine Lafréry in 1566 and the second was printed by the Venetian Domenico Zenoi and published by Bolognino Zaltieri in 1570. Among those published in 1570 is an engraving of Giacomo de Zocchi, one copy of which is held by the British Museum. The caption reads *Jacobus Zochus Ferrariensis i[uris] con[sulti] magni nominis floruit Anno MCCCCXL,* indicating that it depicts de Zocchi as he was in the year 1440 (figure 4.1).[18]

The reason for de Zocchi's interest in the anti-*Mirror* text is not obvious at first glance. He owned many books, mostly the principal collections of canon law (the *Decretum, Decretals, Liber sextus,* and Clementines) and commentaries on them from major figures of the Bolognese school.[19] Nothing, either in this collection or in the details of his life, reveals a particular interest in issues of heresy or mysticism. But this perhaps makes his possession of the anti-*Mirror* text more interesting. If such issues were not of primary interest to de Zocchi, yet he felt that it was worth his time and effort to copy out this *Mirror* polemic—no fast and easy task, as it comprises around 32,000 words—this suggests that something made him feel it was important to have a text like this in his collection. As we have seen, the 1420s and 1430s were the exact time at which negative attention toward the *Mirror* gathered pace on the Italian peninsula. Bernardino of Siena made his first denouncement of the *Mirror* in 1427, a year before de Zocchi moved to Padua, and within the timeframe of MS 1647's creation. But there are also more tangible connections than merely chronological ones. While de Zocchi is best known for his closeness to the

16. Griguolo, "Per la biografia," 191 and 194

17. Griguolo, "Per la biografia," 198 and 199.

18. The image is also digitized on the British Museum's website: https://www.britishmuseum .org/collection/object/P_1873-0510-2945 (accessed March 2021).

19. Griguolo, "Per la biografia," 205.

Iacobus zochus ferrariensis I. con. magni nominis floruit Anno MCCCCXL

**FIGURE 4.1.**    A portrait of Giacomo de Zocchi, published ca. 1570 by Bolognino Zaltieri.
© The Trustees of the British Museum.

monks of Santa Giustina, de Zocchi also seems to have favored the Franciscans, in particular the Observants. One indication of this is in his will, where he left a Bible to the Observant Franciscans of Padua.[20] But, more importantly, de Zocchi had social and spiritual connections to the Observants. He personally knew and listened to the preaching of Alberto of Sarteano, yet another of the "four pillars" of the Observant Franciscans, who had been trained by

---

20. An edition of de Zocchi's will is printed in Montobbio, "Quattro codici." The mention of the Franciscans is on p. 59.

Bernardino of Siena.[21] De Zocchi, perhaps through Sarteano, had spiritual affinities particular to those promoted by Bernardino of Siena, or maybe he had seen Bernardino himself preach. In his will he mentions "Saint Bernardino" as one of the figures to whom he commends his soul.[22] But more interesting are signs of de Zocchi's attraction to Bernardino's signature issue: devotion to the Holy Name of Jesus, which emphasized contemplation and fixation on the Name of Jesus in order to acquire moral and spiritual benefits.[23] Bernardino advocated devotion to the Name in his sermons, during which he held aloft to the crowd a specially designed IHS monogram (the abbreviation for "Jesus"), which would often provoke intense, ecstatic emotional responses from the audience.[24] Bernardino also encouraged his listeners to mark buildings and personal items with the IHS monogram.[25]

De Zocchi appears to have been among those who took up this practice. On the first folio of Padua, Biblioteca universitaria di Padova, MS 1646—which is de Zocchi's copy of de Butrio's commentary on the second volume of the *Decretals*—there is an illuminated IHS monogram at the top of the page. The IHS is written in gold on a red background, with a cross through the top of the "H," set within a sunburst that has rays of gold and blue.[26] This closely resembles descriptions of Bernardino's own famous monogram.[27] The similarity between the monogram in MS 1646 to that carried by Bernardino indicates that its presence in the codex is an example of this "possession marking," and that de Zocchi had seen it himself; it is therefore directly related to Bernardino's preaching and his promotion of the Holy Name.[28] Since this manuscript bears the same customs note as MS 1647—22 December 1428—the monogram must have been placed in it before de Zocchi moved to Padua from Bologna, and therefore around the time he would have found and copied the anti-*Mirror* polemic.[29] De Zocchi's connection to the Holy Name is cemented

---

21. Griguolo, "Per la biografia," 204.

22. Montobbio, "Quattro codici," 59. Bernardino preached a series of Lenten sermons in Padua in 1443, which according to Robert Rusconi are preserved in MS V.23 in the Biblioteca civica Angelo Mai di Bergamo. See "Il sacramento della penitenza nella predicazione di San Bernardino da Siena," *Aevum* 47, no. 3 (1973): 235.

23. For an overview of the cult of the Holy Name, see Rob Lutton, "Devotion to the Holy Name of Jesus in the Medieval West," in *Illuminating Jesus in the Middle Ages*, ed. Jane Beal (Leiden: Brill, 2019).

24. Lutton provides an evocative description in "Devotion to the Holy Name," 146–147.

25. Loman McAodha, "The Holy Name of Jesus in the Preaching of St Bernardine of Siena," *Franciscan Studies* 29 (1969): 40. Bernardino's Holy Name activities would eventually land him in hot water; he was accused of heresy in 1426 but cleared in 1427. Lutton, "Devotion to the Holy Name," 151–152.

26. Padua, Biblioteca universitaria di Padova, MS 1646, f. 1r.

27. McAodha, "The Holy Name of Jesus," 40; Lutton, "Devotion to the Holy Name," 151.

28. I am grateful to Dr. Rob Lutton for consultation on this matter.

29. It is unlikely that the monogram was added later, or by someone else. The same folio also contains an elaborate illuminated initial and an intricate illuminated drawing of de Zocchi's family

further by a printed version of one of his texts, *Canon omnis utriusque sexus de poenitentia et remissione*, made in 1472 in Padua. The front page of this incunable carries various decorative drawings that all represent some aspect of de Zocchi's particular spiritual interests: one of these drawings is of Bernardino of Siena in a pulpit, holding his sun-rayed IHS monogram.[30]

It is possible, then, that de Zocchi heard warnings about the *Mirror*, perhaps through Alberto of Sarteano (who heard them from Bernardino), or perhaps through the preaching of Bernardino of Siena directly. Perhaps de Zocchi even encountered the *Mirror* himself and those who read it in Bologna. However he came to know about it, de Zocchi probably acquired the anti-*Mirror* polemic because he felt that it would be relevant and useful against a dangerous, but popular, text. In other words, this was not a curiosity that he simply wanted to own but a document he considered useful. We can perhaps see another hint of this mindset in the appearance of the text in the manuscript. Unlike the other works in the codex, the anti-*Mirror* text is not neatly copied out, with uneven column width and slanted lines of text. None of the initials were executed. It begins on a verso page and is written on the final folios of the manuscript, with a few blank pages after it. All in all, it looks like a haphazard job, in contrast to the carefully planned quality of the other works. This suggests that it was not originally part of the plan for this manuscript and that de Zocchi included it at the last minute on his own initiative before it went to the binder, copying it in his own hand on spare folios at the back. Therefore, he came across this text and copied it on his own initiative, indicating that he felt it worth the effort to have it at his disposal. As to why it would be useful, it becomes clear upon examining the text that it provides a ready-made legal case against the *Mirror*, demonstrating the many ways in which it contravenes canon law and scripture.

Whether de Zocchi ever had recourse to use it is not clear. But we have seen in previous chapters that, in addition to his Observant Franciscan connections, de Zocchi was also connected to several other figures in Padua involved with the *Mirror*, so it is not unreasonable to think that he may have been indirectly involved in some of the events we have examined.[31] Four years after de Zocchi arrived in Padua, Santa Giustina prohibited the *Mirror* at its general chapter; eight years after his arrival, Antonio Zeno would confiscate the *Mir-*

---

coat of arms: a burning, limbless tree topped by four stars. This shows a deliberate schema of decoration that was probably requested by de Zocchi from the outset, rather than something added as an afterthought. See MS 1646, f. 1r.

30. This incunable is digitized by the Biblioteca civica Angelo Mai in Bergamo: https://www.bdl .servizirl.it/vufind/Record/BDL-OGGETTO-2945 (accessed October 2020).

31. De Zocchi also had connections to Giovanni Tavelli, who had defended the Gesuati during Giovanni of Capestrano's Venice inquisition. Griguolo, "Per la biografia," 189.

REASON STRIKES BACK     133

*ror* from men and women in Padua and send extracts of it to university theologians for assessment. As discussed in chapter 1, de Zocchi could have been a source of information for Zeno, and he surely would have known of the consultation requested of the university theologians, his colleagues. Whether or not de Zocchi had anything to do with the ban at Santa Giustina is less certain, as the congregation at that point spanned several cities outside of Padua.

A sliver of new evidence demonstrates that, however he was involved in those events, the *Mirror* did linger in de Zocchi's mind in other contexts. A fifteenth-century manuscript of Italian origin held in the British Library, MS Arundel 498, contains various commentaries on the major collections of canon law. One of the works in this manuscript is a collection of short glosses on the Clementine decrees done by Giacomo de Zocchi. On folio 140v are his glosses for the decree *Ad nostrum*. The first gloss comments on the first error listed in that decree, which talks about humans acquiring a degree of perfection and "impeccability." De Zocchi comments that it is impossible for humans not to sin in the present life, except through beatification granted by God. After this he says, "That is against the simple souls" (*Quod est contra animas simplices*).[32] There can be no doubt that "simple souls" refers to the *Mirror*. This demonstrates that de Zocchi clearly remembered the *Mirror* and its contents, and that it was the main thing that came to mind for him in connection with perfection and beatitude in the present life. Here again we see the *Mirror* directly linked to *Ad nostrum*, and in a way that perceives it as integral to the heresies condemned there. The use of "simple souls" as a collective also echoes the language used in the *vita* of Giovanni of Capestrano, where he rooted out the "heresy of the simple soul"; they are both entities unto themselves. Except here the phrasing gives even more of an impression of a specific sect, not just a set of doctrines, as if the "Simple Souls" could appear in a catalog of heretics alongside Waldensians and Cathars. Once again, here is an impression of a group following the errors of the *Mirror*. Whether or not such a group was real is immaterial; what matters is that men like de Zocchi thought it was out there, with members wielding copies of *The Mirror of Simple Souls*.

## Origins: The Fourteenth Century

Although de Zocchi copied the anti-*Mirror* polemic, he did not compose it. Instead, he seems to have used an exemplar of a work written much earlier, probably before the year 1317. While the argument establishing the text's origins in

---

32. London, British Library, MS Arundel 498, f. 140r.

the early fourteenth century has been laid out in more detail elsewhere, it merits a brief recap here.[33] The text was likely composed by a canon lawyer, or at least someone who was very familiar with canon-legal sources, vocabulary, and forms, which appear throughout. The author cites legislation from all the major collections of canon law, from Gratian up to the *Liber sextus* of 1298. While he references almost all of the other well-known legal canons and decrees that deal with heresy in both Gratian and the *Decretals*, he makes no mention at all of the Clementine decree *Ad nostrum*, the standard text we have seen used repeatedly against the *Mirror* by most of its late medieval critics and which de Zocchi himself glossed and linked to the *Mirror*.[34] Nor are any other Clementine decrees used or mentioned anywhere in the text. This, for a canon lawyer who used every other antiheretical legal weapon at his disposal, is highly unusual. Such an omission becomes particularly glaring when one compares some of the errors that MS 1647 shares with the list found in MS Vat. lat. 4953. On the extracts that show a clear resemblance to errors found in *Ad nostrum*, MS Vat. lat. 4953 cites that decree; on the same errors, the text in MS 1647 does not. All of these factors make it highly likely that the anti-*Mirror* polemic was written before the publication of the Clementines in 1317, and possibly even before Marguerite's trial.[35]

This makes the text an important addition to the history of the *Mirror*'s reception and raises a whole host of new questions and avenues to pursue. First, it places the origins of the text quite close in time to Marguerite Porete's life and trial and establishes an early date of origin for the Latin translation of the *Mirror*.[36] Such chronological closeness is made more intriguing by the fact that the author of the polemic appears to have had no knowledge of the *Mirror*'s authorship or the fact that it had been condemned elsewhere. This is most clearly demonstrated by the author referring to the work as "apocryphal" (*aprocriphus*) and repeatedly referring to the author as a male, a *hereticus* and not a *heretica*.[37] This apparent ignorance raises the tantalizing possibility that the polemic could even have been written *before* Marguerite's condemnation in Paris, or even before Valenciennes, meaning a very early origin indeed for the Latin translation.[38] Another tempting possibility is that this text is in fact related to the processes against Marguerite. I have considered this point be-

---

33. For the full argument see Trombley, "New Evidence," 147–149.
34. Trombley, "New Evidence," 147–148.
35. Trombley, "New Evidence," 149–150.
36. Trombley, "New Evidence," 149–150.
37. Trombley, "New Evidence," 142.
38. Notably, the author of the polemic also makes no mention of the approbation usually found at the end of the Latin, but this could be due to other reasons, discussed later.

REASON STRIKES BACK 135

fore but will briefly return to it here.[39] It is unlikely that this refutation is connected to the Parisian theologians' judgment of the *Mirror*, as this text takes a clear canon-legal approach to its doctrines. If William of Paris had also given the book to the canon lawyers to look over, one would expect there to be some evidence of this in the trial documents, although it is entirely possible that such evidence may have been lost. But, in Marguerite's sentence, William of Paris only notes that the book was condemned by the "counsel of the masters of theology residing in Paris."[40] Given William's meticulous handling of the case, if he had consulted lawyers about the book who also condemned it as heretical, one would expect him to mention that in the sentence as well.

It is not impossible that this text could be connected to the *Mirror*'s first condemnation in Valenciennes, although that theory, too, has some weaknesses. The bishop of Cambrai, Guido de Collemezzo, was trained in canon law and would have been fully capable of authoring a text like this, but, given the author's apparent ignorance of the *Mirror*'s authorship, it is highly unlikely that he was behind it.[41] Could he have given it to a canonist for assessment and withheld information about the book's author and origins? Perhaps, but even if that were the case, it is questionable whether such a person would have then described the text as "apocryphal" in their assessment, as they would surely have been told that it was authored by a particular living individual, if nothing else.[42]

This text therefore represents a critique of the *Mirror* that was roughly contemporary with the two condemnations of the *Mirror* in Valenciennes and Paris, but was written *entirely in ignorance* of these events. The text also allows insight into how the *Mirror*'s critics attacked its doctrines before a ready-made decree like *Ad nostrum* was available for reference, and it presents a canon-legal take on the *Mirror* rather than a theological one. Finally, on a larger scale, such an early origin places this text right at the dawn of the broader controversies that were brewing over precisely the kinds of mystical concepts found within the *Mirror*'s pages, as we saw in the introduction. This text is therefore an early example of attacks not only specifically against the *Mirror* but also against the type of speculative mysticism it embodied, which later found currency on a larger scale, seen in the creation and use of *Ad nostrum* and the prosecution of a figure like Meister Eckhart. In this sense, the anti-*Mirror* polemic carries significance not only in the history of the *Mirror* itself but also in the broader history of the construction and pursuit of the "heresy of the free spirit" and radical mysticism.

---

39. See Trombley, "New Evidence," 150–151.
40. Field, *The Beguine*, 229; Verdeyen, "Le procès," 82.
41. Trombley, "New Evidence," 150.
42. Trombley, "New Evidence," 151.

## The Shadow of a *Mirror*

Like the errors in the Vatican list, the *Mirror* passages cited in MS 1647 are taken directly from a Latin *Mirror* copy. In one or two places the author seems to be paraphrasing, which sometimes makes a comparison difficult, but where he does quote directly the readings of those passages match the larger group of Latin copies, that is, all of the other copies except Verdeyen's codex **A** (MS Vat. lat. 4355), which he used as the base text for his edition.[43] This means it was part of the Latin version that (seemingly) had the widest circulation.[44] This is significant, given the work's early origins, meaning that the Latin reading found in most of the surviving Latin *Mirror* copies is likely representative of one of the earliest, if not the first, Latin version that was made. It also means that these extracts represent not only the oldest Latin text (textually, if not physically), but also some of the oldest surviving *Mirror* text overall, matched only by the *picard* extracts found in Valenciennes, Bibliothèque municipale, MS 239.[45]

The Paduan polemic provides us with pieces of a now lost Latin copy of the *Mirror*, a "shadow witness," and it offers some clues as to how it was laid out. Of the thirty-five *Mirror* passages presented, twenty-two begin with the author noting where they appear in the book itself. He gives chapter numbers, page numbers, and column numbers, though not always all together and not consistently. He begins with chapter numbers. In the first error he writes that it comes from "the beginning of the third chapter" (*in principio tertii capituli*).[46] He uses chapter designations again in the fourth, sixth, seventh, ninth, seventeenth, and eighteenth errors, naming seven chapters in total.[47] None of the chapter divisions here match up with those of other *Mirror* chapter forms, either in the Latin or in the other linguistic traditions.[48] Each of MS 1647's chapters on average comprise two to three chapters of the Chantilly reckoning, and they are almost comparable in length to the chapters of MS Chigianus B IV 41. This can be best shown with a table, placing the chapters mentioned in MS 1647 in parallel with the chapters they span in Chantilly and Chigianus— see table 4.2. Overall, the chapters cited roughly span nineteen Chantilly chapters and eight Chigianus ones.

---

43. Trombley, "New Evidence," 141–142. See the introduction, as well as the appendix to Trombley, "New Frontiers," 176–177, for a more detailed breakdown of the Latin subgroupings.
44. Another manuscript matching the version of A has yet to be discovered.
45. Trombley, "New Evidence," 150.
46. MS 1647, f. 215v.
47. MS 1647, ff. 216r, 216v, 217r, 217v, 218v, 219r.
48. This is consistent with other *Mirror* copies that contain chapter divisions: no one manuscript's divisions match up with any other.

*Table 4.2*   Comparison of *Mirror* Chapters

| MS 1647 | MS CHANTILLY | MS CHIGIANUS B IV 41 |
|---|---|---|
| 3rd chapter (errors 1, 2, and 3) | Chapters 5–6 | Chapter 2 |
| 4th chapter (errors 4, 5, and 6) | Chapters 7–8 | Chapter 3 |
| 5th chapter (errors 7 and 8) | Chapters 9–10 | Chapters 3–4 |
| 6th chapter (errors 9–16) | Chapter 11 | Chapter 4 |
| 7th chapter (errors 17 and 18) | Chapters 13–19 | Chapters 6–8 |

But the chapter citation strangely comes to an end after the eighteenth error, upon which the author begins to cite only page (*carta*) numbers. The first page cited is the fifth, in the quotation of the eighteenth error, and page citation continues through to the last error, which is said to be taken from the twenty-sixth page. We could speculate, then, that the copy behind this polemic may have been around thirty folios. This may at first seem small for a work that in most of its full extant Latin copies comprises between forty-seven and sixty-two folios.[49] But one manuscript, MS Conv. soppr. G.3.1130—John-Jerome of Prague's copy—contains the entirety of the *Mirror* in only twelve folios, in a codex measuring about 31.0 × 22.0 cm (ca. 12 × 8 in), with the text in two columns per page. We know that the text in this "shadow *Mirror*" was also in two columns, as the polemic author mentions column numbers (*columpna*) in some of the errors as well; for example, an error can be found "in the seventh chapter in the first column."[50] Finally, the *Mirror* is referred to in the polemic as an *opusculum*, a "little work." Since it is doubtful that *opusculum* is being used here as a humility trope, it can only be assumed that the book used by the author of MS 1647's document was a relatively compact copy.

One other possibility worth mentioning is that this *Mirror* might have been missing several chapters at the end. At the beginning of the text the author says that he has examined the *Mirror* from the beginning "all the way up to the end" (*usque in finem*), and yet the last error cited in MS 1647 is taken from chapter 117, leaving the last twenty-two chapters unmentioned. It is possible that the author felt that these chapters contained no errors worth mentioning, but this seems unlikely. Although it is true that chapters 123–139 are considered to be "tamer" in both tone and content than the rest of the work, chapter 118 is the culmination of the entire book, in which Marguerite lays out her famous

---

49. These are, respectively, MS Chigianus C IV 85 and MS Chigianus B IV 41.

50. The column number count goes up to four, which would mean the second column on the recto folio, if the book was lying open.

"seven stages" that the Soul must go through in order to become annihilated.[51] Here she develops and reasserts many previous ideas that receive censure in the MS 1647 document. The author is not averse to attacking the same idea more than once (as is shown in his refutation of both the seventh and seventeenth errors, which are almost identical), so it is difficult to imagine him neglecting this section merely to avoid repetition. He also makes no comment on the approbations from the three churchmen that appear at the end of all the surviving Latin manuscripts, something that surely would have dismayed him and prompted a response. It is possible, therefore, that the copy he possessed ended shortly after chapter 117.[52] This could be simply a case of the final quires being lost. But it could also suggest that this early Latin copy deliberately did not have those chapters and that they appeared only in later versions, meaning that some early Latin copies were perhaps shorter than later incarnations.[53] Such a possibility merits future investigation.

## The Polemic

What, then, is this text that Giacomo de Zocchi found? The work can be characterized as a polemical treatise, similar in many ways to the well-known antiheretical polemics of the thirteenth century but differing from them in others. It also resembles the written assessments that stemmed from papally commissioned textual evaluations in the early fourteenth century, such as those done against Peter of John Olivi's Apocalypse commentary.[54] It seems to mix genres, combining the format of a legal *consilium* with that of a scholarly polemic or opinion, but with added teeth: it has a vitriolic tone and draws upon several famous tropes of antiheretical discourse.[55] The result is a text that seeks to affirm the heresy and illegitimacy of the *Mirror* on many levels and provides a comprehensive demonstration of its danger, bolstered by a fierce sense of outrage from the author.[56]

---

51. See *Speculum CCCM*, 317–333.

52. While the list in MS Vat. lat. 4953 also ends after chapter 117, the list is incomplete and therefore it cannot be determined whether this was the intentional end point.

53. Chapters 121–140 of the *Mirror* are notoriously problematic across the various linguistic versions of the *Mirror*, with lacunae occurring in different places in the French, English, and Latin traditions. See *Speculum CCCM*, 338–409.

54. For example, see Patrick Nold, "New Annotations of Pope John XXII and the Process Against Peter of John Olivi's *Lectura super Apocalipsim*: The Marginalia of MS Paris BnF lat. 3381A," *Oliviana* 4 (2012); or Piron, "A Theological Advice."

55. Trombley, "Text as Heretic." On thirteenth-century polemics see L. J. Sackville, *Heresy and Heretics in the Thirteenth Century: The Textual Representations* (Woodbridge, UK: Boydell and Brewer, 2012).

56. Trombley, "Text as Heretic."

The author also aimed for edification of the reader, using his attacks as opportunities to instruct the reader in the "truth," another common tactic of antiheretical discourses.[57] This is made clear by a line from 1 Corinthians 11:19 written at the very top of folio 215v, above the start of the main text: "For there must also be heresies, so that those who are approved may be made manifest."[58] Whether this was added in by de Zocchi or was original to the text is not certain, but either way this line, a common passage used in antiheretical discourse, denotes an underlying purpose of the text: to use the *Mirror*'s errors to "manifest" the truth. As we will see in the textual analysis, the author takes the opportunity to lay out and reaffirm orthodox basics in the course of his refutations.

The author's approach can be characterized as literal, pedantic, and rigidly rational. Anyone who has read the *Mirror*—or, in fact, any mystical text—knows that such an approach was guaranteed to cause problems. Not only is reason consistently denigrated in the *Mirror*, but Marguerite's text is also virtually stuffed with metaphors, paradoxes, and narrative forms that, when interpreted literally, appear very shocking indeed. Taking such statements at face value, the author certainly felt these shocks and was not going to leave them unanswered.

The author's opening salvo is aimed not at a particular error of the *Mirror* but instead at the work as a whole. The text begins immediately with a quotation from the *Mirror* taken from chapter 5—the same quotation, in fact, that starts off the Vatican list. But instead of immediately refuting this quotation, the polemical author instead starts by addressing the *Mirror* as a whole, in a format quite similar to a legal *consilium*.[59] He begins, "The opinion that must be questioned concerning this little work seems to be whether it should be received by the Church. And without any dispute it should be said that: not only is it apocryphal, since its origins and author are entirely unknown, but even if it may contain some truths, it nevertheless has many falsehoods, and such things are not received, as in the chapter *Sancta Romana ecclesia*, in Gratian, which is called the fifteenth distinction."[60]

---

57. Sackville, *Heresy and Heretics*, 41.

58. MS 1647, f. 215va. "Oportet et hereses esse, ut qui probati sunt manifesti fiat [*sic*]." All translations from MS 1647 are my own unless noted otherwise. On use of this passage in antiheretical discourse see Herbert Grundmann, "'Oportet et haereses esse': Das Problem der Ketzerei im Spiegel der mittelalterlichen Bibelexegese," *Archiv für Kulturgeschichte* 45 (1963). An English translation appears in Jennifer Kolpacoff Deane, ed., *Herbert Grundmann (1902–1970): Essays on Heresy, Inquisition, and Literacy* (Woodbridge, UK: Boydell and Brewer, 2019).

59. Trombley, "Text as Heretic," 141.

60. "De hoc opusculo positio quaerendum uidetur an sit ab ecclesia recipiendum, et sine allia disputatione dicendum quod non nisi apocriphum est, cum eius origo et auctor ponitus ignoretur, quod etsi aliqua uera contineret, falsa tamen multa habet et huiusmodi non recipiuntur, ut in capitulo *Sancta Romana ecclesia*, Gratiano, que uocatur xv distinctione." From f. 215va of MS 1647. A note on

The author begins, then, not with a question of heresy, but with a question of legitimacy and authority, as "apocryphal" did not automatically indicate heresy but merely that a text lacked canonical authority.[61] The question of the *Mirror* being "received" (*recipiendum*) revolves around whether it can be accepted as authoritative or appropriate spiritual reading. Here we again encounter our old friend the fifteenth distinction and its list of rejected apocryphal works. But despite only citing Gratian here, the author actually seems to combine two views on apocryphal works. In saying that whatever truth the *Mirror* may have is overridden by its falsehoods, he appears to echo Isidore of Seville's comments on apocrypha: "Although some truth is found in the apocrypha, nevertheless because of their many falsities there is no canonical authority in them."[62] Therefore, right at the beginning, the author has immediately undermined whatever authority the *Mirror* might claim to have. Crucially, his description of the *Mirror* as apocryphal also makes it clear that the author has no knowledge of the *Mirror*'s origins and authorship, a fact reinforced by his repeated reference to the author of the *Mirror* as male.

The rest of his mini-*consilium* continues to layer arguments for the *Mirror*'s illegitimacy. After the fifteenth distinction, he goes on: "Yet there are other reasons why it should not be received, for it seems [that] if we fully examine this little work from its beginning all the way up to the end, everything that it asserts the author drew himself out of his own head, without any arguments from Scripture or of the Holy Doctors."[63]

The saints and doctors did not draw faith from their heads, he writes, which is made clear by Augustine in Gratian's ninth distinction: "[When] I read the writings of others, however powerful they are in sanctity and teaching, I do not believe them as truth because they [their authors] know so, but because

---

transcription: I have maintained the sometimes idiosyncratic spellings that are common throughout this text.

61. The *glossa ordinaria* to the fifteenth distinction, following Huguccio, notes that an apocryphal work is rejected by the church not necessarily in the sense that it is banned completely but in that it may not be read in church. It could potentially be read elsewhere in private. Thompson and Gordley, *Gratian: The Treatise on Laws*, 57. On the ambiguous treatment of apocryphal texts see Dzon, "The Apocryphal *Liber infantia salvatoris*."

62. "In iis apocryphis etsi invenitur aliqua veritas, tamen propter multa falsa nulla est in eis canonica auctoritas." Isidore of Seville, *Etymologiarum sive Originum Libri XX*, VI:II:51–52, ed. W. M. Lindsay (Oxford: Clarendon Press, 1911). English taken from Isidore of Seville, *Etymologiae*, trans. Stephen A. Barney (Cambridge: University of Cambridge Press, 2006), 138.

63. MS 1647, f. 215va. "Allia tamen ratione recipiendum non, uidetur nam si bene inspiciemus a principio huius opusculi usque in finem, eius quicquid asserit totum, ipsius auctor ex proprio capite traxit, sine ulla allegationem scripturis aut sanctorum doctorum."

they have been able to persuade me through other authors or through canonical or probable arguments that they do not differ from the truth."[64]

In the eyes of the author, the *Mirror* offers no such proof of its truth. He continues in this vein, combining the question of anonymity and illegitimacy with the charge of creating new doctrine. What the *Mirror* puts forth is new doctrine pertaining to the faith, he says, and he demonstrates the unacceptability of that with three biblical quotations: "You shall not add to the word that I speak to you, neither shall you take away from it" (Deuteronomy 4:2); "If any man shall add to these things, God shall add unto him the plagues written in this book" (Revelations 22:18); and "But though we or an angel from heaven proclaim a gospel to you besides that which we have preached to you, let him be anathema" (Galatians 1:8).[65] Anything pertaining to the faith cannot be accepted unless it is approved by the church, and here he cites Gratian's causa 24, question 1, chapter 15: "You may not teach nor think other than that which you have received from Blessed Peter the Apostle and the rest of the apostles and Fathers."[66] This is similar, he says, to how saints cannot be venerated without the sanction of papal authority. Things that pertain to the faith should not be heard or accepted unless they are written "in the law of the Lord" (*nisi scripta in lege domini*) or it is made clear that they are received from God.[67] It is not permitted to anyone to bring forth new opinions or to invent things, as this brings one to heresy. Here for the first time the polemical author links the *Mirror* to the basic definition of a heretic in Gratian, found in causa 24, chapters 27 and 28, which state that a heretic is anyone who understands scripture other than the Holy Spirit requires and who brings forth and follows new opinions.[68] In using these citations, the author is making use of the main canons dealing with heresy in the *Decretum*, which had formed the legal basis of discussions on heresy from the time of their publication in the twelfth century up through the thirteenth century.[69] "We ought not to have recourse to our own selves or our own senses," he writes, "but to prophetic voices and apostolic

---

64. D. 9, c. 5, in Friedberg, *Decretum*, 17. "Aliorum scripta lego ut quantalibet sanctitatem quantalibet doctrina polleant non ideo uerum putem quia ipsi ita seu sciunt sed quia michi per alios auctores uel canonicas uel probabiles rationes quod a uera non aborreat [*sic*] persuadere potuerint." MS 1647, f. 215va.

65. All English renderings of biblical quotations are taken from the Douay-Rheims edition, unless otherwise noted.

66. C. 24, q. 1, c. 15, in Friedberg, *Decretum*, 970. "non alliud doceatis neque sentiatis quam quod a beato petro appostolo et reliquis appostolis et patribus accepistis." MS 1647, f. 215va.

67. MS 1647, f. 215va. The author cites D. 50, c. 27 in Gratian to support this. See Friedberg, *Decretum*, 188.

68. C. 24 , q. 3, c. 27 and 28, in Friedberg, *Decretum*, 997–998. MS 1647, f. 215va.

69. Sackville, *Heresy and Heretics*, 104–107.

letters and evangelical authors, as in Gratian [C. 24, q. 3, c. 30]."⁷⁰ He then
briefly swerves back to the question of authors and texts, noting that (before
it lists rejected books) Gratian's fifteenth distinction also notes texts and
people that *are* named and accepted by the church as authoritative. He then
notes, "But this stranger is not among the designated people, nor is his work
named in the said chapter [D. 15, c. 3], therefore it ought not to be received."⁷¹

He then moves into the final point of his introduction: illicit dissemination.
"Additionally, it is not permitted to spread this doctrine openly, because that is
clearly against the doctrine of the apostle in Romans 10[:15] and against the
doctrine of the Church: *de hereticis, cum ex iniuncto*."⁷² *Cum ex iniuncto*, a decretal
found in the *Liber extra* that was originally a letter from Innocent III to the diocese of Metz, is concerned, among other things, with unlicensed preaching,
and states that anyone preaching without the authority to do so is usurping an
office from the church.⁷³ The author follows with a quotation from the decretal: "For since the order of doctors and preachers is particular to the Church—
that is, preaching—one should not indifferently usurp the office of preaching
for himself, because as the apostle says, 'How shall they preach, unless they be
sent?'"⁷⁴ Therefore, he concludes, the *Mirror* should not be received because it
has not been "sent." He finishes his little *consilium* with a quotation from He-
brews 13:19: "Be not led away by various and strange doctrines."⁷⁵

By using this line, the author offers up a neat cap to the main picture of
the *Mirror* that he has presented in his introduction. The *Mirror* is an apocryphal, unproven work that comes from "a stranger" (*ignotus*). Like a false
preacher, it is usurping an office of the church and disseminating "various and
strange" doctrines illicitly, which could dangerously "lead away" those reading or hearing it. Such a characterization of the *Mirror* right at the beginning
of the text, before even a single error is refuted, makes sure that the book is
seen as entirely illegitimate. It secures an overall legal judgment on the text's

70. MS 1647, f. 215va. "non debemus recurere ad nosmet ipsos nec ad proprium sensum nostrum sed ad propheticas uoces et ad appostolicas litteras atque euangelicas auctores ut in capitulo qui Gratian *iniquius* xxiiii questio ultimum."

71. MS 1647, f. 215va. "sed iste ignotus non est de personis designatis nec eius oposculum est nominatus in dicto capitulo ergo non est recipiendum."

72. "Preterea quod non licentiat huic hanc doctrinam effundere patet, quia aperto est contra doctrinam apostoli ad Romanos.x. et contra doctrinam ecclesie: *de hereticis, cum ex iniuncto*." MS 1647, f. 215va. The verse in Romans is "How shall they preach, unless they be sent?"

73. X 5.7.12, in Friedberg, *Decretales*, 784–787.

74. "Cum enim doctorum et predicatorum ordo sit quasi precipuus in ecclesia, id est, predicationis, non debet quis assumere [*quis assumere* is deleted in the MS] sibi quisque indifferenter officium predicationis usurpare, quia ait appostolus 'quomodo predicabunt nisi mittantur.'" MS 1647, f. 215va, quoting *Cum ex iniuncto*, X. 5.7.12, in Friedberg, *Decretales*, 784–787.

75. "doctrinus variis et peregrinus nollite ab [MS: "ad"] duci." MS 1647, f. 215va.

authority before dispatching the details of its doctrines.[76] The way it begins also suggests that he is perhaps writing on commission, that he is responding to something—more on this later.

What is interesting about this short *consilium*-like introduction is its mingling of judgments on texts and judgments on people. It starts out attacking an apocryphal text with no known author and then finishes with the images of the classic legal heretic and of a false preacher, accusations that carry a more active and personified connotation than simply an anonymous book. The false preacher image is particularly striking, as it specifically invokes the verbal, physical act of preaching. Is "preaching" merely being used here to represent the general idea of dissemination, or did he envision it—or witness it—being circulated or read aloud in some way?[77] It is not entirely clear. The introduction also heavily emphasizes the need for an authority to prove one's truth or legitimacy. Most of the author's judgments hinge on the fact that the *Mirror* has no authority that demonstrates the truth of its statements. It has no known author, it makes up doctrine with no recourse to scripture or other canonical authorities, and it presumes to spread its ideas without being granted the authority to do so by the church. Once established, this fact undermines any further assertions the *Mirror* makes and places the author on firm footing while he moves against the specifics of the work's doctrines.

Having pronounced judgment on the book's overall illegitimacy, the author then turns to the first error with which he began the text. "Now we come to the text of this little work," he writes, and launches into his refutation.[78] In total, he attacks thirty-five direct quotations from a Latin *Mirror*.[79] Although they are not numbered in the text, the author either numbered them in his head, had planned to number them eventually, or perhaps had been given a numbered list of extracts along with a copy of the book, since at one point he refers to articles "2" and "3" as containing the same idea as the error cited in the first column of folio 217r (the seventh error). Visually, the errors are distinguished from the rest of the text by being written in separate blocks in a larger, neater handwriting style than that of the refutations, which are written in a tiny, somewhat spidery hand (see figure 4.2). In the refutations of longer errors, the author breaks down the passage into component parts and refutes each part in turn, writing each line's opening words and then underlining it to show where the next section of refutation begins. It is not clear whether this is how the text appeared originally, or whether

---

76. Trombley, "Text as Heretic," 141.

77. Trombley, "Text as Heretic," 144.

78. "Nunc ad textum huius opusculi ueniamus." MS 1647, f. 215va.

79. For the full list, see the translations in appendix 2. I am currently working on a critical edition of the entire text.

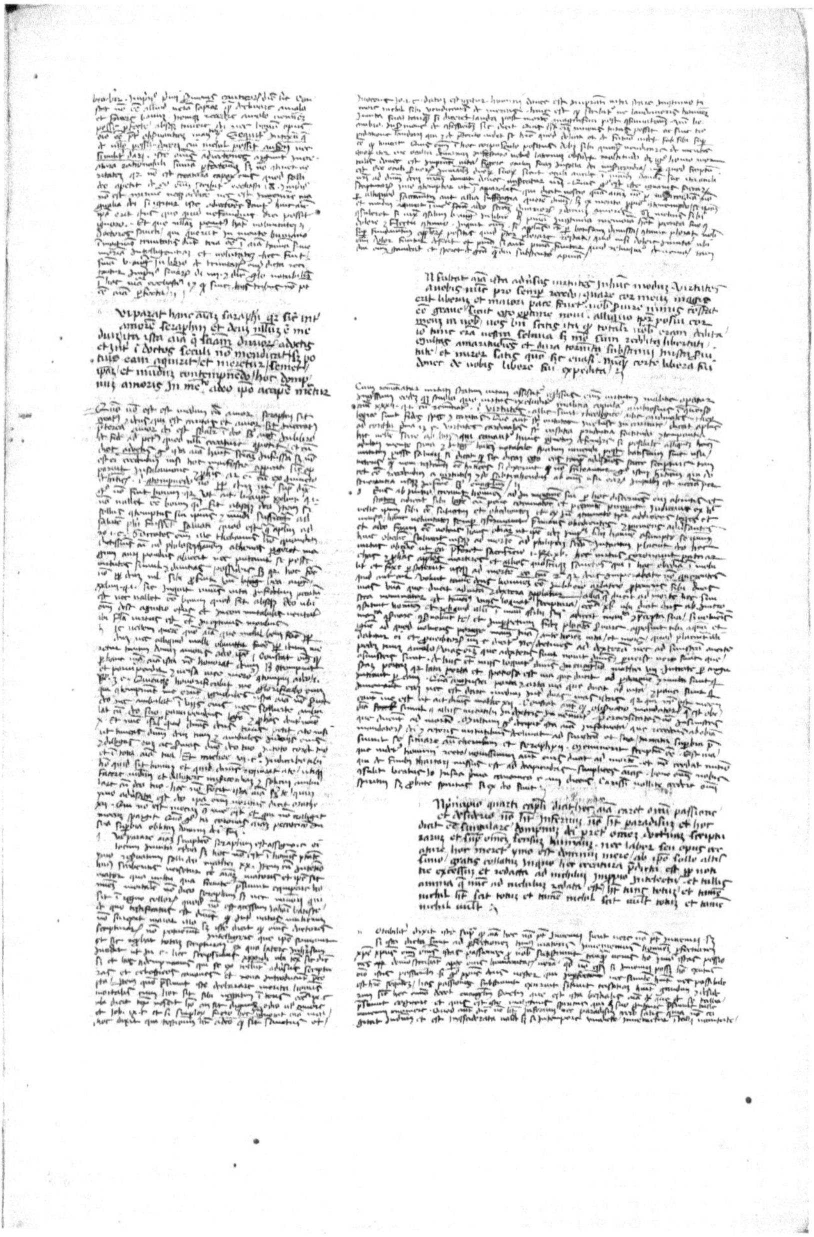

**Figure 4.2.** Folio 216r of MS 1647, showing extracts from *The Mirror of Simple Souls* written in separate blocks of text, which are followed by refutations. Biblioteca universitaria di Padova (MiC), by permission of the Ministry of Culture. Further reproduction by any means is prohibited.

this layout was done by de Zocchi while copying. The polemical author, more so than the Vatican list, intervenes in the *Mirror* text that he excerpts, in that he sometimes mixes verbatim quotation with his own paraphrases of a certain statement, and he occasionally skips over several lines of text from within a single passage.[80] But there is still no doubt that, even if he had a list of extracts given to him, he also had a copy of the Latin *Mirror* in front of him, because within the refutations themselves he occasionally quotes and refers to other passages from the *Mirror* and notes their position in relation to the extracts being refuted.[81]

Looking through the errors, as with the Vatican list, one can distill the concerns of the compiler into broader groups.[82] But, unlike the Vatican list, the author has more distinct and repetitive fixations on specific themes, which can be more clearly sorted into groups. Four in particular dominate. The topics of the *Mirror* that most frequently attract the ire of the polemicist are as follows:

1. The Soul's indifference to any kind of feelings attached to moral guidance—particularly the Virtues (faith, hope, charity), but also shame, honour, fear, hate, love, and the Soul's proclaimed ability to do whatever it pleases.
2. The Soul's rejection of normal Christian practices, i.e. sermons, prayer, fasting, the sacraments, and the belittling of the institutional church by naming it *Ecclesia Minor*.
3. The Soul's self-acquisition of divine knowledge without guidance from or dependence on church teachings, and with no justification given for how this knowledge was acquired.
4. The equation of the Soul with God; the assertion that the annihilated Soul has essentially achieved a status of divinity on a par with God himself.[83]

It is not surprising that these are the main flashpoints. Not only are some of these same concerns present in the Vatican list, as we have seen, but the first two themes also essentially match up with the errors cited in association with Marguerite's trial in 1310. These errors bear repeating:

1. That the annihilated soul gives license to the virtues and is no longer in servitude to them, because it does not have use for them, but rather the virtues obey its command.

---

80. See the translations in appendix 2.
81. Trombley, "New Evidence," 141–142. The extracts from MS 1647 most frequently match Verdeyen's codex B (MS Rossianus 4) and C (MS Chigianus B IV 41) in their readings.
82. For the full list of specific errors see appendix 2.
83. Trombley, "New Evidence," 142–143.

15. That such a soul does not care about the consolations of God or his gifts, and ought not to care and cannot, because such a soul has been completely focused on God, and thus its focus on God would be impeded.[84]

[. . .]

That the Soul annihilated in love of the Creator, without blame of conscience or remorse, can and ought to concede to nature whatever it seeks and desires.[85]

These are also the ideas that can be found in six of the eight errors attributed to the beghards and beguines in the decree *Ad nostrum*. These six also merit repeating:

1. That a person in this present life can acquire a degree of perfection, which renders him utterly impeccable and unable to make further progress in grade.
2. That it is not necessary to fast or pray after gaining this degree of perfection, for then the sensitive appetite has been so perfectly subjected to the spirit and to reason that one may freely grant the body whatever pleases it.
3. That those who have reached the said degree of perfection and spirit of liberty are not subject to human obedience, nor obliged to any commandments of the church.
4. That a person can gain in this life final beatitude in every degree of perfection that he will obtain in the life of the blessed.
5. That any intellectual nature in itself is naturally blessed, and that the soul does not need the light of glory to elevate it to see God and enjoy him blissfully.
6. That the practice of the virtues belongs to the state of imperfection and the perfect soul is free from virtues.[86]

It is clear, then, that the author's concerns in the *Mirror* polemic reflect many of the same concerns we saw in MS Vat. lat. 4953 and in broader controversies. But it focuses more on questions of morality and behavior, on what the soul may *do*, rather than on more abstract questions of being, divine essence, and free will. Its tone, style, and rhetoric are also rather different to what we have

---

84. Verdeyen, "Le procès," 51. English from Field, *The Beguine*, 128. The numbers refer to the numbers they were given in the trial records.

85. Verdeyen, "Le procès," 88. English from Field, *The Beguine*, 234. This is the error noted by the "Continuer of the Chronicle of William of Nangis"; no number was given to it.

86. Clem. 5.3.3. Friedberg, *Clementis Papae V Constitutione*, cols. 1183–1184. The English translations are from Makowski, "When is A Beguine Not a Beguine?", 94–95.

seen so far. In order to examine the author's methods in attacking the *Mirror* here, the four aforementioned groups form the basis of analysis, to allow for a broader presentation of the text as a whole. As was done with MS Vat. lat. 4953, the author's reactions will be selected from several different refutations and grouped together in order to present a composite view of his arguments.

The first group, concerning the alleged immorality of the Simple Soul, was the most troubling for this author. Eighteen of the thirty-five errors contain this theme, and these form some of his longest refutations. Central to his concerns is the Soul's abandonment of the virtues, which also appeared in the Vatican list. It all starts with the third error, which he writes as follows:[87]

> This Soul scoffs at the virtues in this manner: *Virtues, I now recede from you forever, whereby my heart will instead be free, and enjoy greater peace. Everyone knows [that] to serve you is to be much too burdened, as I well know. In another time I placed my heart in you; you know thus that I was wholly given to you. Therefore, I was then your slave, but I have just now been returned to freedom. I endured much bitterness and cruel torments in this service, and I am quite astonished that I have escaped. I was never truly free until I was freely liberated from you.*[88]

Just below the above passage, he begins his refutation by inverting a quotation from Gratian's thirty-second causa: "When virtue is renounced, vice is immediately admitted, for the departure of the virtues works the entry of evil. And with the same determination, where virtue is shut out, it couples with evil."[89]

Here he reflects a broader strain in medieval thought on the virtues, where their absence must attract vice, because vice is defined as a lack of virtue.[90] This concept sets the tone for all other virtue-related refutations that follow.

---

87. Italics indicate where the *Mirror* is being directly quoted.

88. MS 1647, f. 216rb. "Insultat anima ista aduersus uirtutes in hunc modum: 'Uirtutes, a uobis nunc pro semper recedo, quare cor meum magis erit liberum et maiori pace fruetur. Uobis seruire nimis constat essere graue, sicut ego optime noui. Aliquo tempore posui cor meum in uobis, uos bene scitis ita quod totaliter uobis eram dedita. Ideo tunc eram uestra sclaua, sed modo sum reddita libertati. Multas amaritudines et dura tormenta sustinui [MS: "substinui"] in ista seruitute et miror satis quomodo sic euasi. Numquam certe libera fui donec de uobis libere fui expedita.'" For the corresponding passage see *Speculum CCCM*, 25.

89. MS 1647, f. 216rb. "Cum renuntiatur uirtuti, statim uitium asciscitur [MS: "assiscitur"], egressus enim uirtutum malitie operatur ingressum. Eodemque studio quo uirtus excluditur, malitia copulatur." Just after this the author directs the reader to the opposite formula of this in C. 32, q. 1, c. 9: "Cum renunciatur inprobitati, statim asciscitur virtus. Egressus enim maliciae virtutis, operatur ingressum, eodemque studio, quo crimen exlcuditur, innocentia copulatur." See Friedberg, *Decretum*, 1117.

90. István P. Bejczy, *The Cardinal Virtues in the Middle Ages: A Study in Moral Thought from the Fourth to the Fourteenth Century* (Leiden: Brill, 2011), 238–239. Danielle Dubois has recently argued that Marguerite's conception of the role of the virtues in fact reflects certain scholastic concepts of natural and supernatural virtues. See "Natural and Supernatural Virtues," 174–192.

But first, in what is a clear example of using error to remind the reader of orthodox basics, he lays out the seven virtues: "Some are theological, others are cardinal. The theological are Faith, Hope, and Charity. But there are also the virtues included in Charity, [as] the apostle says in first Corinthians 13[:4]. The cardinal virtues are Justice, Wisdom, Strength, and Temperance."[91]

The author makes it quite clear that he does not share Marguerite's view of the Soul's departure from the virtues as a joyous "liberation" but rather views it as a turning away from good to sink into evil. Importantly, the author also targets the qualifications and explanations that Marguerite placed around this concept, presumably because she wanted to ward off the very kinds of interpretations this author placed upon them.[92] In chapter 8 of the *Mirror*, in reaction to Reason's cries of surprise and alarm ("How then does this Soul brazenly recede from the Virtues? Has she not lost her mind to speak so rashly?"),[93] Love steps in to say that the annihilated Soul still *possesses* the Virtues, and the Virtues obey her commands, but she no longer has the *use* of them.[94] But, while Reason may have been calmed by such an explanation, the polemical author was not. This exact passage forms the fifth error in his text. His refutation begins: "He who knows to do good and does not do it, [it] is for him a sin," quoting James 4:17.[95] Either the Simple Souls live temperately or intemperately, for there is no medium between vice and virtue, he says, referring the reader once again to Gratian's thirty-second causa. If they live temperately, then they have the use of the virtues; if they do so intemperately, they are "full of vice, and therefore damned."[96] He goes on: "If the Simple Souls do not have the use of the virtues then they do not have obedience to the commandments of God, which [obedience] is necessary for salvation, Matthew 19[:17]. They also do not have the use of Charity, without which the rest of the virtues are empty, 1 Corinthians 13:[13]. It is clear, therefore, that the Simple Souls are outside the status of salvation. If outside the status of salvation, they are therefore outside the love of God."[97]

---

91. MS 1647, f. 216rb. "Allie sunt theologice, allie sunt cardinales. Theologice sunt fides, spes, et caritas. Que aut sunt uirtutes incluse in caritate, dicat apostolus corinthi prima 13 capitulo. Uirtutes cardinales sunt iustitia, prudentia, fortitudo, et temperantia."

92. On this defensive tactic in the *Mirror*, see Trombley, "Self-Defence."

93. "Quomodo igitur haec anima sic effronte recedit a virtutibus? Amisitne sensum quae sic temerarie loquitur?" *Speculum CCCM*, 29.

94. MS 1647, f. 216va. See *Speculum CCCM*, 29.

95. MS 1647, f. 216va. "Sciente bene facere et non facienti, pecatum est illi."

96. MS 1647, f. 216v. "uitiose, ergo damnate."

97. MS 1647, f. 216v, first column. "Si non habent anime simplices usum uirtutum, non habent usum obedientie mandatorum dei, que necessaria est ad salutem, mathey xix. Non habent usum caritatis sine qua cetere uirtutes casse sunt i. ad corinthy 13 capitulo. Clarum est ergo quod anime simplices sunt extra statum salutis. Si extra statum salutis, ergo extra amorem dei."

The author's lack of a middle ground on this issue is on full display in his refutation of the eighteenth error. Here the characters of Faith, Hope, and Charity ask Love, "Where are the transcendent Souls? Where are they and what are they doing?"[98] After reminding the reader that the Simple Soul has previously declared freedom from the virtues, the polemical author takes the view that, if they have to ask, then Faith, Hope, and Charity do not know the Simple Souls and are therefore estranged from them. This places such souls outside the state of salvation.[99] He then sets out this logical argument: "If, therefore, Charity does not know the Simple Souls, then God does not know them, because God is Charity. If God does not know, then he does not approve, because to be familiar with God is to be approved, as in Psalms 36[:18]: 'The Lord knows the ways of the undefiled.'"[100]

Separation from the virtues also forms the entirety of his response to the seventh error. This passage—much of which is repeated in the seventeenth error—is the passage in which the Soul states she has no desire for masses, sermons, poverty, honor, or shame, and asserts that she "gives to Nature all that it asks without remorse of her own conscience."[101] After the "remorse of conscience" passage, the seventh error then includes a qualifying statement: "*But such a nature is so ordered in herself on account of her full transformation into unity with Love, that she never asks for anything except what is lawful in the highest degree, and what by no means should be denied her.*"[102]

The author, however, finds this qualification utterly unconvincing. In fact, he finds the phrase "without remorse of conscience" itself to be telling:

And so that it does not seem to have erred, it excuses itself, saying *but such a nature is.* To whom is it thus said, if such a Soul is from God, ordered in itself, that it seeks nothing except that which is highly licit? Why was it necessary to say *without remorse of conscience,* since in lawful things remorse of conscience has no place? But here a snake hides in the grass, for

---

98. MS 1647, f. 219r, first column. "Ubi sunt anime transcendentes? Ubi sunt et quid agunt?" This error is not a direct quote from the *Mirror* but is paraphrasing. For the passage in question, see *Speculum CCCM*, 75.

99. MS 1647, f. 219ra.

100. MS 1647, f. 219ra. "Si ergo caritas non nouit animas simplices, ergo deus non nouit eas, quia deus est caritas. Si deus non nouit, ergo non approbat, quia nosce dei est approbare, ut in psalmo 36: *Nouit dominus uias inmaculatorum.*"

101. MS 1647, f. 217ra. "semper dat nature quicquid petit absque omni conscientie proprie remorsu." *Speculum CCCM*, 33.

102. MS 1647, f. 217ra. "Sed tamen tallis natura ita est tantum in se ordinata propter plenam sui transformationem in unitatem amoris, quod numquam alliquid requirit nisi summe licitum, et sibi nullatenus negandum." For the corresponding passage see *Speculum CCCM*, 33–35.

above it had said that it was a great torment for these Souls to be in love and obedience to the virtues, because it required them to give to the virtues whatever they asked, however much it burdened nature. Therefore, it wanted to give to nature that which was *not* allowed according to obedience to the virtues and the order of reason, and in pursuance of this it removed itself from obedience to the virtues, fleeing to another way of transforming this Soul into unity with divine love, in order that, from such a transformation, that which was forbidden and unlawful by the order of reason and obedience to the virtues might become lawful [to it].[103]

A few lines below this, after reiterating that a truly well-ordered soul would not have removed itself from the virtues, he addresses Marguerite's qualifying statement again: "Therefore, let those be silent who try to defend this error on account of this little line: *But yet such a soul*, et cetera. Beware, for he has set this to spring his trap. For, according to the Blessed Leo: 'How else are heretics able to deceive the simple except with poisoned cups smeared with some honey, lest those things which are wholly meant to be deadly might be detected by their sour taste?'"[104]

This same passage from the *Mirror* on remorse of conscience appeared in the Vatican list, but there it was briefly dealt with using *Ad nostrum* and a citation from canon law on the requirement for penance. Here, the refutation digs a bit deeper into the perceived moral failings behind the passage. Throughout his treatment of the *Mirror*, the polemical author uses the virtues issue to craft an image of the Simple Soul not merely as lacking in virtue but as *actively* pursuing vice. To him the Simple Soul is a filthy, lascivious, and devious figure chasing every worldly indulgence and openly scorning virtuousness. This gives rise to some of his most colorful—and vitriolic—statements. The Soul presumes to be

---

103. MS 1647, f. 217ra. "Et ne uideatur errasse se excusat, dicens 'sed tamen tallis natura est.' Cui sic dicitur si talis anima est a deo, in se ordinata, quod non requirit nisi summe licitum? Quid neccessarie fuit dicere 'sine remorsu conscientie,' cum in re licita non habet locum remorsus conscientie? Sed hic latet anguis in herba, supra enim dixerat quod magnum tormentum erat animabus istis esse in amore et obedientia uirtutum, quia opportebat illis uirtutibus dare quicquid petunt, quantumcumque natura grauaretur. Uolebat ergo nature dare illud quod *non* [my emphasis] licebat secundum obedientiam uirtutum et ordinem rationis et ex hoc subtraxit se obedientie uirtutum, fugiens allium modum transformandi hanc animam in unitatem amoris diuini ut ex talli transformatione illud quod erat prohibitum et illicitum ex ordine rationis et obedientia uirtutum fieret licitum." The first part of this passage is also quoted in Trombley, "Self-Defence," 145.

104. MS 1647, 217ra. "Sileant ergo qui conantur hunc errorem defendere propter illum uersiculum: 'Sed tamen tallis anima, et cetera.' Caute, enim posuit illum ad comprehendens decipulam suam. Quomodo enim, secundum Beatum Leonem, 'possent heretici decipere simplices nisi uenenata pocula quodam mele prelinirent, ne usquequaque sentirentur insuauia que essent futura mortifera'?" The quotation is from Leo the Great's letter to Turibius. See Leo the Great, "Letter 15 to Turibius, Bishop of Astorga," in *Leo the Great*, ed. and trans. Bronwen Neil (Abingdon-on-Thames: Routledge, 2009), 91. This quotation also appears in Trombley, "Self-Defence,"146.

in heaven "in the dung of the vices" (*in stercore uitiorum*). It also "roars with laughter over the virtues and at those living virtuously, and wraps itself in carnal desires, wholly manured with vices without number, weight, or measure. As it confesses with a filthy mouth, it dares to say that it is in unity in the divinity. I say it is not in the unity of love, but in the unity of a slave. Those who say such things, may they be confounded and ashamed. May death come upon them, and may they descend living into hell."[105]

This theme also seems to consume the author in a way that other aspects of the *Mirror* do not. For him, the Soul's departure from the virtues ripples through the rest of its ideas and is the crux upon which all its other actions turn. He fixates upon it almost obsessively, to the point where he refers to it even when refuting errors that deal with another topic entirely. He sees it as particularly dangerous in the context of the Soul's claim that the Soul's will has become the same as God's will. A good example of this can be found in his response to the sixteenth error, which deals with precisely this.[106] He begins the refutation by immediately drawing a direct line between the two errors and makes a point of outlining the role of the virtues in man's struggle with his own nature:

> Here there is a need to understand: above the Soul asserted that it did not want to live virtuously and that it had separated from the virtues, saying: "Virtues, I now recede from you for always," et cetera. But we follow according to the apostle in Galatians 5:[22–23],[107] because *there are two [natures] in man*,[108] opposing one another, as one may know: the spirit and the body, of which there are two opposite efforts. The spirit compels man to live virtuously, under the medium of reason, *whose fruits are charity, joy, patience*, et cetera, et cetera. The body draws man to sensuality, which is the longing of the flesh, whose fruits are fornication, wantonness, et cetera.[109]

---

105. MS 1647, f. 220rb. "cachinat de uirtutibus et uiuentibus uirtuose, que se inuoluit concupis- centiis carnalibus, tota stercorata uitiis sine numero, pondere, et mensura. Ut iste fatetur poluto ore presumit dicere se in unitatam in diuininitatem. Non dico unitate amoris sed unitate serue. Confun- dantur et erubescant qui ista dicunt. Ueniat mors super illos et descendant in infernum uiuentes."

106. MS 1647, f. 218v, first column. *Speculum CCCM*, 49.

107. Galatians 5:22–23: "But the fruit of the Spirit is charity, joy, peace, patience, benignity, good- ness, longanimity, mildness, faith, modesty, continency, chastity. Against such there is no law."

108. This is most famously found in Aquinas's *Summa theologica*, II.2, 26.4.

109. MS 1647, f. 218va. "Hic opus est intellectu; supra protestata est ista anima se nolle uiuere uirtu- ose et segregasse a uirtutibus, dicens: 'uirtutes, a uobis nunc pro semper recedo,' et cetera. Nos autem heremus secundum appostolum ad gallatia capitulo v, quia *duo sunt in homine* repugnantia ad inuicem scilicet: spiritus et caro, quorum sunt opera contraria. Spiritus cogit hominem uiuere sub medio rationis uirtuose, cuius fructus sunt caritas, gaudium, patientia, et cetera et cetera que sequuntur. Caro trahit hominem ad sensualitatem, que est concupiscentia carnis, cuius fructus sunt fornicatio, inmunditia, et cetera."

The Soul, he goes on to say, "has receded from the virtues, which are the essential spiritual fruits" (*recessit a uirtutibus que sunt fructus spiritus necessarie*) and therefore has "cleaved to the flesh and its works or fruits" (*adhesit carni et operibus seu fructibus eius*).[110]

The idea of the virtue-less Soul claiming to will the divine will particularly appalled this author. Contemplating the potential of such a union of wills, the author, in a stunning passage, gives us this chilling statement: "This Soul wills not through its own will, but through the divine will, and thus whatever the Soul wills, God wills, whether the Soul wishes to eat or to drink, or even to fornicate, God wants it in its entirety. This is no small offense against the divine majesty, and I do not know how the ears of Catholics are able to hear this and do not instead tear apart these writings, and with their nails gouge out the eyes of the writer."[111]

He resorts to such gruesome imagery again in response to this idea in his refutation of the seventeenth error. He sees the claim to willing God's will as a cover for doing whatever one pleases, and what happens when the Soul claims this and has abandoned both reason and the virtues, "our wisdom may discern." "But," he continues, "I know nothing more, only that this wicked spirit's tongue should be dug out from his throat with a savage hook, if it may be permitted to churchmen to speak of inducing bloodshed."[112]

Gouging out eyes, digging out tongues. No other passages in this polemic so viscerally convey the author's mindset. What this and the other responses demonstrate is his unshakable conviction that, if the soul is departed from the virtues and separated from reason, nothing else that the soul does can possibly contain any goodness or upright intentions; recession from them de facto leads to wickedness. His literal approach to this is particularly evident in his treatment of the questions by Faith, Hope, and Charity. Instead of seeing these questions as merely a mechanism that moves the *Mirror*'s narrative forward, they literally represent to him a total lack of association with these virtues in any way. They are completely absent, and such an absence creates a vacuum into which only base desires can rush. Any attempt at qualification appears to the author as merely a screen, a crafty deception that gives the appearance of goodness but that conceals a more sinister intention beneath it; his images of

---

110. MS 1647, f. 218va.

111. MS 1647, f. 217r, second column. "Ista anima uult, non uoluntatem propria sed uoluntatem diuinam, et sic quicquid anima uult deus uult. Siue anima uellit bibere siue comedere aut fornicari, totam uult deus. Hec non est parua calumpnia aduersus diuinam maiestatem, et nescio quomodo aures catholice possunt ista audire et non potius lacerant ista scripta, et ungulis eruunt oculos scribentis."

112. MS 1647, f. 219r. "discernat prudentia nostra. Ego autem nichil plus scio, nisi quod lingua huius maligni spiritus uncino fereo esset eruenda de guture suo, si liceret uiris eclesiasticis dicere inductum sanguinis."

the lurking snake and the poisoned cup smeared with honey clearly convey this.

The recession from the virtues is one of many instances in the *Mirror* where the annihilated Soul declares herself to be "above" or "free from" actions or feelings that are standard fare for Christian life. Not only do other intangible elements get discarded, such as love, hate, shame, and anxiety, but also both paradise and hell, and physical practices such as good works, penances, masses, prayers, fasting, and sermons. All fall under the category of "creaturely" things, which the Soul must separate from in order to become annihilated. Unsurprisingly, this also attracted the author's attention. Both the seventh and seventeenth errors—which are very similar in content—provide the best examples of this theme in the *Mirror*. A translation of the whole of the seventeenth error will suffice to give the sense of both:

> In the seventh chapter in the first column it says concerning this Soul that: *She has neither concern nor anxiety, nor shame; she does not have honor, she does not have poverty, she does not have riches, she does not have comfort, she does not have sadness, she does not have hate, she does not have love, she does not have hell, she does not have paradise. She has everything and has nothing, she herself knows everything and knows nothing, desires everything and desires nothing. And so the Soul does not desire nor despise poverty, neither martyrdom nor tribulations, neither masses nor sermons, neither fasts nor prayers, and she gives to Nature everything it asks without remorse of conscience.*[113]

First, the author seizes upon the Soul's ambivalence. "He who neither desires nor despises anything," he writes immediately after the seventh error, "is *neither cold nor hot,* and thus is from the number of [those who are] rejected in Apocalypse 3[:15]."[114] In the refutations to both errors seven and seventeen, he attacks the "willing all and willing nothing" of the Soul by comparing it to the sluggard (*piger*) from Proverbs 13:4: "The sluggard wills, and wills not." He takes two more biblical passages to express the evils of ambivalence: "A double-minded man is inconstant in all his ways" (James 1:8) and "Woe to them that are of a double heart and to wicked lips, and to the hands that do evil, and to the sinner

---

113. MS 1647, f. 218va. "In septimo capitulo in prima columpna dicit de ista anima quod non habet curam nec sollicitudinem nec habet uerecundiam non habet honorem non habet paupertatem non habet diuitias, non habet consollationem, non habet tristitiam, non habet odium, non habet amorem, non habet infernum, non habet paradisum, habet totum, habet nichil, ipsa scit omnia et nichil scit, uult omnia et nichil uult. Ista etiam anima non desiderat [MS: "desciderat"] nec despicit nec paupertatem, nec martirium aut tribulationem, nec missas aut sermones, nec ieiunia aut orationes, et dat nature quicquid petit absque omni conscientie remorsu." For the corresponding passage, see *Speculum CCCM,* 55.

114. MS 1647, f. 217ra. "Iste qui nichil appetit nec despicit nec frigidus est nec callidus, et sic est de numero reproborum apocalipsi iii. capitulo."

that goeth on the earth two ways" (Sirach 2:14). This concern is also implied in his response to the Soul's lack of hate, implying that without hate the Soul fails to set itself definitively against the enemies of the Lord, quoting the somewhat chilling passage from Psalms 138:2: "Have I not hated them, O Lord, that hated thee: and I have dwindled away over your enemies. I have hated them with a perfect hatred, and they are become enemies to me." As to not desiring hell or paradise, this means that the Soul does not think of the Final Judgment. "But," the author adds, "if in the time of vengeance he comes enveloped in such vanity, he will without a doubt have hell devouring him with an open mouth."[115] Once again, the author's literal approach crashes headlong into Marguerite's paradoxical language. Such paradoxes are taken here as double-mindedness, with a touch of deceit and hypocrisy, as the image of the "sinner that goeth on the earth two ways" implies.

In showing indifference to all things, the Soul—to the author—displays not only ambivalence but also laziness, which the author invokes first with the image of the sluggard and then pursues further. Using a quotation from Bede's *Commentary on Proverbs*, he states that the Simple Soul "wants to reign with the Lord but does not want to suffer for him."[116] He attacks the lack of desire for poverty, martyrdom, and tribulations, saying, "This Soul wants to eat, to drink, to sleep, and to rest and to go into paradise, but the apostle says 'he who does not work may not eat,' (2 Thessalonians 3:10) and 'he will not be crowned unless he strive lawfully' (2 Timothy 2:5)."[117] This, too, is also colored by the absence of the virtues. The Soul's justification for her indifference—that she is so removed and elevated into contemplation of the divine that she has no need for "creaturely" things—is attacked as making "excuses in sin" (Psalms 140:4), the same argument made by Bernardino of Siena in one of his attacks on the *Mirror*. The author of the Paduan text calls such "excuses" a lie, since the Soul has renounced (*abdicauit*) the virtues and has thus let in base and natural desires, which prevent it from ascending to contemplation of the divine. The answers here differ from that given in the Vatican list. There, the Soul's indifference to shame, poverty, honor, and so on is seen as an "unnatural" state. In the Vatican document, the worry is more over the *lack* of desire, particularly the desire for blessedness. But in MS 1647, the Soul's indifference is painted in a more

---

115. MS 1647, ff. 216r–v. "Sed si in tempore uindicte inuenietur in talis uanitate inuoluta, procul dubio habebit infernum apperto ore uorantem."

116. MS 1647, f. 217ra. "regnare cum domino et non uult pati pro eo." Bede, *Super Parabolas Salomonis Allegorica Expositio*, 2, c. 13, PL 91, 0978A.

117. MS 1647, f. 218vb. "Anima ista uult comedere, bibere, dormire, et quiescere, et in paradissum ire, sed appostolus dicit 'qui non laborat non manducat,' et 'non coronabitur nisi qui legitimis certauerit.'"

sinister light: it is troublesome because it implies deceit, hypocrisy, and laziness, showing more concern over the indifferent Soul's intentions and actions.

Much of the author's concern over the Soul's indifference blends into the second theme, dealing with the *Mirror's* rejection and belittlement of the institutional church. The author makes it clear that the Soul's lack of care for "institutional" things such as masses, sermons, prayers, and fasting immediately marks it as a heretic. He writes in his refutation to the seventeenth error, "Here the author reveals his heresy, for we know that man cannot live the present life without sin, [as in] Ecclesiastes 7[:21]: 'There is no just man upon earth who does good and sinneth not.'"[118] It is sin that primarily concerns the author, as well as the necessary role the church has in cleansing the soul of sin and facilitating its salvation. By rejecting church practices, the Soul is also essentially rejecting its own salvation. His main supporting legal text for this argument is the *Tractatus de penitentia*, found in the third *quaestio* of the thirty-third causa in Gratian's *Decretum*. He repeatedly uses three chapters in particular: *multiplex* (c. 49), *secunda tabula* (c. 72), and *tres actiones* (c. 81), all of which outline the necessity of penitence to receive absolution and divine grace.[119]

The Soul's aforementioned indifference to shame is almost exclusively dealt with in this framework. In the seventeenth error the author refutes it by merely inserting a long quotation from Bernard of Clairvaux's eighty-sixth sermon on the Song of Songs, which outlines the merits of modesty and shame.[120] But in later errors—where lack of shame is the main issue—the author adds his own opinions and brings it into the penitential canon-legal framework. Errors twenty-three and twenty-nine both state that the Soul has no anxiety or shame about sin or any sin that it may commit.[121] The author calls such an assertion "poisonous" (*uenenosa*) because it "induces man towards sinning" and assumes that "an adult sinner can be saved without penitence; that is false and heretical, as in the chapter *ad abolendam de hereticis* [X 5.7.9], for just as a man cannot be saved without the sacrament of baptism, so an adult man who sins after baptism cannot be saved without penitence, as in the chapter *multiplex*, and the chapter *secunda tabula*, and in the chapter *tres actiones*, [in] *de penitentia*, first distinction."[122]

---

118. MS 1647, f. 218vb. "Hic apperit iste auctor heresim suam, scimus enim quod homo iste non uiuit uitam presentem sine pecato, Ecclesiastes vii capitulo: *Non est homo iustus in terra qui faciat bonum et non pecet.*" The MS has "dicit" instead of "uiuit," but this is probably a scribal error as it does not make sense in the sentence.

119. C. 33, q. 3, c. 49, 72, and 81. See Friedberg, *Decretum*, 1170, 1179, 1181–1182.

120. Giacomo de Zocchi, or perhaps another later reader, highlighted this passage by drawing a bracket next to it in the margin.

121. For error 23 see MS 1647, f. 219rb. For error 29 see f. 220rb.

122. MS 1647, f. 219r–v. "inducit hominem ad pecandum"; "presupponitur hominem adultum pecatorem posse saluari sine penitentia; quod est falsum et hereticum in capitulo *ad habolendam de*

Such a rejection of the need for penance is brought about by a "diabolical urge" (*suasione diabolica*) and comes "from tartarean [i.e., demonic] counsel" (*ex consilio tarthareo*). The Simple Soul speaks of having contact with the divine but yet does not seem to desire or experience any of the things that, at least in the eyes of the author, would allow it to get there. "Who is this evil spirit," he asks, "who dares to taste such things for itself, only to vomit out poison?"[123]

Alongside a rejection of specific church practices, the *Mirror* frequently mocks the institutional church—hence the diminutive moniker of *Ecclesia Minor*. *Ecclesia Minor* is ruled by Reason—the ignorant and foolish voice in the *Mirror's* dialogue—and those who follow the counsel of Reason are "beasts and asses" (*bestiae et asini*). Marguerite holds up "Holy Church the Lesser" in contrast to "Holy Church the Greater" (*Ecclesia Maior*), which comprises those Souls who have achieved annihilation in Love and are thus superior to those who have not. The author fixates on this aspect much more so than the Vatican list, and his reaction to such mockery is predictably scathing. "It says this because the number of the Simple Souls is greater than [that of] those who are blessed. But [the Simple Souls'] congregation is not called a 'church,' but [rather] the synagogue of Satan, Apocalypse 3[:9]."[124] It is not to be dismissed, he notes, that the *Mirror's* author invents two churches out of one, and it should be made clear that there is only one true church, per John 10:16 ("And there shall be one fold and one shepherd").[125] The "church" of the Simple Souls—with its plurality of bodies—is characterized as a "chimera" and a "monster."[126]

But the author of the polemic in MS 1647 goes a step further in his response to the twenty-fourth error, which states that the church of the Simple Souls sustains the institutional church. "If this fiction that this heretic makes were true" (*Si uera esset ista fictio quam facit iste hereticus*), it would mean that Christ, who appointed and ordered the one church, was insufficient. But scripture, such as Colossians 2:3 ("In whom are hid all the treasures of wisdom and knowledge") and Luke 9:35 ("This is my beloved son. Hear him"), shows this not to be true, and there is no mention of Christ ordering a second church.[127] Outside of the one church there can be no salvation, as he makes clear with a

---

*hereticis*, sicut enim homo non potest saluari sine sacramento batismi sic non potest homo adultus qui post batismum pecauit sine penitentia saluari, ut in capitulo *multiplex* et in capitulo *secunda tabula* et capitulo *tres actiones de penitentia*, distinctione i."

123. MS 1647, f. 216rb. "Et quis est iste mallignus spiritus qui de suo gustare presumit talle uenenum euomere?"

124. MS 1647, f. 219ra. "Hoc ideo dicit quia maior est numerus animarum simplicium, quam signatarum. Sed earum congregatio non dicitur ecclesia, sed sinagoga satane, apochalipsi iii capitulo."

125. MS 1647, f. 219ra.

126. MS 1647, f. 219ra. MS Vat. lat. 4953 similarly accuses the *Mirror* of setting up two churches.

127. MS 1647, f. 219va.

quotation from Gratian's twenty-fourth causa: "Whoever eats the Lamb of the Lord outside of this [church] is profane. If anyone is not in the Ark of Noah, he will perish in the reigning flood."[128]

The implication is that, by setting itself apart from the institutional church, the Simple Soul is not only rejecting the essential functions that it supplies in regard to salvation but is also rejecting Christ, its founder. Similarly, the author feels that by mocking those who strictly follow the precepts of the church and who actively practice good works and the virtues, the Soul is also mocking all those who have shown such obedience throughout history, such as the prophets or the Church Fathers. The Soul describes those adhering to church works in error twenty-four as "one-eyed" (luscam) and in the twenty-sixth error as a "little owl" (noctue) who thinks it is the most beautiful creature in the forest.[129] Labeling such mockery as "diabolical cunning" (diabolicam astutiam) in his response to the twenty-sixth error, the author defends those who adhere to both faith and works, and holds up the example of Abraham, "who was not vindicated out of faith alone, but out of following faith with works."[130] He then expands his example, saying that "all the rest of the patriarchs and the prophets believed in God and loved God, and although evil men threatened them with death, they did not desist from carrying out the commandments of the Lord up to the point of death."[131] This is true also for the apostles, the holy martyrs, the confessors, and "all those who long to be saved" (uniuersi qui cupiunt saluari). Throughout the entirety of scripture, in both the Old and New Testaments, they labored for nothing else except to bring humans to fear, love, and obedience to God.[132] This is similar in nature to the response given in the Vatican list to the Soul's departure from the virtues, where it notes that, if serving the virtues were a punishment, all of the saints and doctors would be urging men toward torment instead of divine reward. This same sentiment is also seen here, in response to Marguerite's famous characterization of those obedient to Ecclesia Minor as "beasts and asses." "If those who are serving God are beasts and asses," he writes, "[then] the prophets, patriarchs, apostles, evangelists, holy martyrs, and confessors were beasts, who served God to the

---

128. MS 1647, f. 219va. "Quicumque extra hanc domini agnum comederit profanus est; si quis in archa Noe non fuerit peribit regnante diluuio." From C. 24, q. 1, c. 25, in Friedberg, Decretum, 975–976.

129. MS 1647, f. 219va–b. For these passages in the Mirror see Speculum CCCM, 133 and 161, respectively.

130. MS 1647, 219vb. "non ex solla fide iustificatus fuit abraam, sed ex fidem cum opere subsecuto."

131. MS 1647, f. 219vb. "Ceteri patriarche et profete [MS: "profecte"] crediderunt deo et dilexerunt deum et licet malli uiri cominarentur sibi mortem, non desciterunt ab executione dominorum mandatorum usque ad mortem."

132. MS 1647, f. 219vb.

point of death, in many greater and more noble exercises than us."[133] He adds, "But we gladly wish to be associated with these beasts, if the goodness of God Most High and their own [goodness] deems us worthy to be admitted."[134]

There is also clear anxiety here about the Soul's claims to knowledge of or contact with the divine, knowledge that, as the Soul states in the second error, she does not seek "from the learned or from those who do not know the world, but rather acquires it and earns it by scorning herself and the world," and which, in other errors, is also given to her by the Holy Spirit.[135] The author, of course, disbelieves such claims. Not acquiring knowledge from either the learned or the unworldly implies that the Soul "had infused knowledge, but it ought not to be believed unless it is plainly clear, as it was clear in Solomon and the prophets, as is argued in the chapter *cum ex iniuncto, de hereticis.*"[136] Furthermore, "If contempt of oneself and the world sufficed for salvation, then the [pagan] philosophers would have been saved; that is against the apostle in Romans 1[:20]."[137] After error twenty-three, in which the Soul asserts that she had heard from the Holy Spirit that God will put the smallest and lowest in the highest place, he writes, "This assertion is foolish and worthless and nonetheless greatly poisonous. It is foolish and worthless because it is not proved by any jurisdiction or any authority or any reasoning, and therefore ought to be rejected, according to the Blessed Augustine in the chapter *ego solis*, in the ninth distinction. Nor is it to be believed from this Simple Soul that the Holy Spirit was speaking to it, unless it is proved otherwise, as in the chapter *cum ex iniuncto, de hereticis.*"[138]

---

133. MS 1647, f. 220rb. "Si seruentes deo sunt bestiales et asini, bestiales fuerunt prophete, patriarche, apostoli, et euangeliste, sancti martires et confessores, qui seruierunt deo usque ad mortem in multo maiori et meliori exercitio quam nos."

134. MS 1647, f. 220rb. "Sed nos uolumus libenter hiis bestiis assotiari si pietas altissimi dei et ipsorum nos admitere dignatur."

135. MS 1647, f. 216ra. "ista anima que scientiam divinorum a doctis et inter indoctos seculi non mendicat, sed potius eam aquirit et meretur semet ipsam et mundum contempnendo." For the corresponding passage in the *Mirror* see *Speculum CCCM*, 21.

136. MS 1647, f. 216ra. "Ista anima habuit scientiam infussam, sed non est ei credendum, nisi hoc manifeste appareat sicut apparuit in salamone et prophetis, argumentum capitulo *cum ex iniuncto, de hereticis.*"

137. MS 1647, f. 216ra. "si sollus contemptus sui ipsius et mundi sufficeret ad salutem, philosophi fuissent saluati; quod est contra apostolum ad Romanas 1. Capitulo." The Romans verse reads, "For since the creation of the world God's invisible qualities—his eternal power and divine nature—have been clearly seen, being understood from what has been made, so that people are without excuse." I have here used the New International Version translation, as Douay-Rheims does not convey the sense particularly well.

138. MS 1647, f. 219ra. "Ista propositio fatua et uacua est et nichilominus uenenosa ualde. Fatua est et uacua quia nullo iurisdictione, nulla auctoritate, nulla ratione probatur et ideo reicienda, secundum beatum augustinum in capitulo *ego solis* ix. distinctione. Nec est credendum illi anime simplici quod spiritus sanctus fuerit ei locutus, nisi aliter probet, ut in capitulo *cum ex iniuncto, de hereticis.*"

*Ego solis* is the chapter from the *Decretum* cited at the beginning of the text, which asserts the need for scriptural and theological proof when assessing the truth of written works. But here again is also *cum ex iniuncto*, invoked to address questions of authority similar to that in the introductory passage, although here it is not used on the question of illicit preaching but on the claim to possessing divine knowledge. In a similar vein to Augustine's words in *ego solis*, Innocent III writes in this decree that declaring to be sent by God is not enough to give someone spiritual authority, since "any heretic" (*quilibet hereticus*) can claim such a thing.[139] This claim must be supported, either by the testimony of scripture or if he can perform miracles. This is the sense in which the author is applying *cum ex iniuncto* here: the *Mirror* makes claims to divine connection and authority that are simply—in his view, at least—not supported by any proof. By using it in this way, he touches upon the borders of *discretio spirituum*, or distinguishing between true and false revelations.[140] Marguerite is, in fact, famously silent on where her spiritual knowledge comes from. She never says that she had a vision or experienced a moment of revelation. Aside from a few biblical references, she does not refer to any other type of authority upon which her knowledge is based, nor does she mention a confessor or institution that guided her thoughts. This leaves the *Mirror* vulnerable to charges of false revelation, and indeed in the fifteenth century Jean Gerson would make such a connection when he described the writings of a certain "Marie of Valenciennes" (almost certainly Marguerite Porete) as an example of false revelation in his *De distinctione verarum revelationum a falsis*.[141] Remember, too, that one of Bernardino of Siena's attacks on the *Mirror* appeared in a sermon on spiritual discernment. Therefore the author of the Paduan text was not alone in casting the *Mirror* in this light.

But Marguerite's silence on the origins of her divine knowledge is not nearly as striking as her pronouncements on what the Simple Soul becomes in its achievement of annihilation. Above she claimed that the Soul's will becomes God's will, that the Soul mixes in unmediated, indistinct union with the divine.

139. Innocent III, *Cum ex iniuncto*, in *Die Register Innocenz III*, ed. Othmar Hagender, Werner Maleczek, and Alfred A. Strnad (Vienna: Österreichische Akademie der Wissenschaften, 1979), 273.

140. Love Anderson, *Discernment of Spirits*, 48.

141. Jean Gerson, *De Distinctione Verarum Revelationum a Falsis*, in *Jean Gerson: Oeuvres complètes*, ed. Palémon Glorieux, vol. 3 (Paris: Desclée, 1962). Elizabeth A. R. Brown has questioned the identification of Gerson's "Marie" with Marguerite in "Jean Gerson, Marguerite Porete and Romana Guarnieri: The Evidence Reconsidered," *Revue d'histoire ecclésiastique* 108, no. 3–4 (2013). For a reaffirmation of the attribution see Sean L. Field, Robert E. Lerner, and Sylvain Piron, "A Return to the Evidence for Marguerite Porete's Authorship of the *Mirror of Simple Souls*," *Journal of Medieval History* 43, no. 2 (2017): 170–172.

As represented in the nineteenth, twenty-fifth, and thirty-fifth errors, she makes a far bolder statement. The three errors read as follows:

> [19th] On the sixth page in the first column, it discusses how this Soul has been made Lady of the Virtues, *and that Divine Love has transformed her wholly into herself,* and therefore it says that *Love is God Himself, and this Soul is God by the condition of Love itself.* Beneath these words Love says that *Love is God and God is Love, and this Soul is God out of the condition of this Love.*[142]

> [25th] On the twelfth page in the beginning of the first column it says that *it is fitting that this Soul has to be similar to the divinity, because she is transformed into God.*[143]

> [35th] On the twenty-sixth page: *Just as Christ by his death is the redemption of the people, so I am by reason of my depravity the salvation of the human race and the glory of God the Father.*[144]

It is not hard to see how these passages provoked the polemicist's ire. This is the fourth group of error, the Soul's transformation into God and its claiming for itself a role in the salvation of all humanity. These are daring statements, and, unlike with some of her other bold declarations, Marguerite attaches no qualifying explanations to these passages.

We saw the Vatican list address this idea, which it mainly perceived as an example of the Soul setting itself up as a rival to God. The author in the polemical text takes a slightly different route, focusing on the Soul's arrogance and the impossibility of indistinct union without virtue or grace. "In so great a way does this evil spirit elevate itself," the author writes after the nineteenth error.[145] The Soul "is lying prostrate in the filth of the vices, and is fixed deep in the muck, and is stripped naked of the Virtues without any inward cure, without any works of goodness."[146] The Simple Soul claims to be united with God, but "it did not say it has been joined with the bonds of charity, or has

---

142. See MS 1647, f. 219r, first and second columns. "In carta sexta prima columpna tractat quomodo ista anima facta est domina uirtutum et quod diuinus amor totaliter mutauit eam in semetipsum, et ita dicit quod amor est ipse deus et ista anima est deus ex ipsius amoris conditione [MS: "condictione"]. Sub hiis uerbis ait amor qui amor est deus et deus est amor, et ista anima est deus ex ipsius amoris conditione." For this passage in the *Mirror* see *Speculum CCCM*, 81–83.

143. MS 1647, f. 219v, second column. "In duodecima carta in principio prime columpne, dicit quod opportet hanc animam esse simillem diuinitati, quia ipsa est mutata in Deum." Found in *Speculum CCCM*, 151.

144. MS 1647, f. 221r. "In carta uigessima sexta: Sicut christus sua morte est redemptio populi, ita sum ratione mee prauitatis salus humani generis et gloria dei patris." Found in *Speculum CCCM*, 313.

145. MS 1647, f. 219rb. "In tantum se elleuat iste mallignus spiritus."

146. MS 1647, f. 219rb. "iacentem in ceno uitiorum et infixam in limo profundi, et nudatam omnibus uirtutibus sine ullo remedio penitudinis, sine alliquibus operibus bonis."

REASON STRIKES BACK    161

been united [with Him] through the grace of adoption."[147] It cannot be transformed into God, because this was only granted to Christ, and was never
granted nor will ever be granted to anyone else.[148]

By speaking of the Soul "elevating itself" and presuming itself to have acquired a status that was only granted to Christ, the implied allegation here is
of extreme pride and arrogance, that one who, appearing to disdain all other
virtue and goodness, dares to raise itself to the level of God and Christ. This
charge is leveled more overtly in the author's entire response to the twenty-
fifth error, which comprises only four lines but packs a strong rhetorical punch:
"This voice is a diabolical voice, similar to that which prompted Eve to oppose the divine commandment of God: 'You will be as gods, knowing good
and evil' [Genesis 3:5], and to him who dared to want to be equal to the Creator himself, when he said: 'I will soar above the level of the clouds, the rival
of the most High,' Isaiah 14[:14]."[149]

In previous responses, the author has frequently branded the Simple Soul as
"diabolical" and associated it with the general forces of evil. But here, in an inversion of the Soul equating itself with God, the author directly equates the
Simple Soul with Satan. There are two images of arrogance here: one that relates to others—that is, the image of the tempter who is inducing those around
him to commit mortal sin with promises of supreme power—and one that relates to the self, as one being arrogant enough to lay claim to the same place in
the universe as that which is occupied by God.

With error thirty-five—perhaps the most striking statement in the entire
*Mirror*—the author continues his assault in the same vein. This assertion is "stu-
pid" (*stolidus*) and "presumptuous" (*presumptuosus*), he says. By way of elucidat-
ing his point, he first copies out another passage from the *Mirror* that immediately
precedes the one above, in which the Simple Soul describes how she is the
"height and fullness of all evil" (*summa et complementum omnium malorum*) and
that, since God is the height of goodness, he must of necessity give all of his
goodness to her in order to eradicate her wickedness.[150] The author draws on
this passage in order to logically demonstrate the absurdities (*inconuenientes*) of
the Soul's assertion in error thirty-five: "Now it remains to respond to this folly,

---

147. MS 1647, f. 219rb. "Non dixit conexam uinculo caritatis aut per gratiam adoptionis cohadunat."
148. MS 1647, f. 219rb.
149. MS 1647, f. 219vb. "Uox ista uox diabolica est, similis illi qua suggessit eue contrauenire
mandato diuino dei: 'eritis sicut dii, scientes bonum et mallum' et illi que presumpsit uelle se equipe-
rare creatori suo cum dixit 'ascendam super altitudinem [MS: "altitudienem"] nubum et ero similis
altissimo' ysaie xiiii."
150. See *Speculum CCCM*, 311–313.

and we will begin from the absurdities."[151] His argument runs thus: The first absurdity is that if the Soul places itself in such a low state and says that it is the height of all evil, then it must certainly be the devil, since no other could be so supremely evil. And yet, in such evil, the Soul says it preserves divine goodness.[152] The second absurdity follows: If what the Soul asserts were true—that it is the salvation of the human race—then the Soul's wickedness would matter just as much to the redemption of the human race as would Christ's suffering, and the human race would be bound to this "wicked spirit" (*malignus spiritus*) just as much as they would be to Christ. This would therefore mean that Christ had suffered in vain.[153]

"But now," he writes, "we may show all this to be false, deceitful, and heretical" (*Nunc ostendamus omnia ista esse falsa, ficta, et heretica*).[154] Once again taking arrogance as his line of attack, he first cites Isaiah 66:2: "To whom shall I have respect, but to him that is poor and little, and of a contrite spirit, and that trembleth at my words." "Not, then," the author adds almost sarcastically, "to him who is 'the height and fullness' of the vices, but to him that serves the Lord with fear and exults him with trembling. It is written thus in Wisdom 1[:1]: 'Think of the Lord in goodness, and seek him in simplicity of heart.'"[155] To elucidate further the contradictions he outlined above, he quotes 2 Corinthians 6:14–15: "What fellowship has light with darkness? Or what concord has Christ with Belial?" He follows this up with a quotation from Hrabanus Maurus's *Commentary on Wisdom*: "They flatter themselves in vain, the philosophers and the false Christians and the heretics, for only the pure in heart are able to be received by God."[156] He who is "the height and fullness of all evil," who contains in his nature all that is depraved (*pravitas*) and malicious (*malitia*), cannot be received by God. If the things that this Soul "vomits out" (*euomit*) were true, and if God, the greatest goodness, would pour himself into someone who is the height of iniquity, then it would mean God is unjust.[157] But that is against his nature, since it is well known that God is just regarding the sins of man, righteously visiting upon them his vengeful anger and condemnation. If he

---

151. MS 1647, f. 221rb. "Nunc restat respondere huic fatuitati et incipiemus ab inconuenientibus."

152. MS 1647, f. 221rb.

153. MS 1647, f. 221rb.

154. MS 1647, f. 221rb.

155. MS 1647, f 221rb. "Non, ergo, ad eum qui est *sumam et complementum* enim uitiorum, sed ad eum qui seruit domino cum timore et exultat ei cum tremore. Sapientie i. capitulo legitur sic 'sentite de domino in bonitate et in simplicitate cordis querite illum.'"

156. MS 1647, f. 221rb. "Frustra sibi blandiuntur phylosophi et falsi christiani et heretici, solli enim mundi corde sapientie dei possunt accipere." Hrabanus Maurus, *Commentariorum in Librum Sapientiae Libri Tres*, Book 1 c. 1, *PL* 109, col. 0674B.

157. MS 1647, f. 221rb.

were unjust, then he ought to pour his total goodness into the depths of wick-edness of the Simple Soul. However, says the author, this is against the doctrine of Paul in Romans 3:5–6.[158] To imply, as the Simple Soul does, that God allows anyone to commit evil on account of his goodness is "false and damnable" (falsum et damnabile).[159]

In order to prove further that what the Soul claims is impossible, the author then describes through the example of Adam the sinful nature of humanity and quotes from the fourth distinction in the third book of the Decretum, which declares that no person born from the coupling of a man and a woman is free of original sin, and that none can be free of such sin without the mediation of Christ.[160] He reiterates the above argument, that if the Soul's claims were true then it plays just as great a role in human salvation as Christ, making his suffer-ing pointless. This inverts the natural order of things and would mean that worldly desires would matter just as much as the shedding of Christ's blood, and thus "we will be crowned with vice, suppressing the virtues, and it will truly be the grievance of sinners who petition against the divine majesty."[161] He follows this up with a long quotation from Malachi 3:13–15: "Your words have been insufferable to me, said the Lord. And you have said: What have we spo-ken against thee? You have said: He labors in vain that serves God, and what profit is it that we have kept his ordinances, and that we have walked sorrowful before the Lord of hosts? Wherefore now we call the proud people happy, for they that work wickedness are built up, and they have tempted God and are preserved."[162]

"But," writes the author, "let this folly be far from the hearts of the faith-ful, may this disappear from our minds and let us adhere to these [words] that follow," to which he appends an even longer quotation of Malachi 3:16–4:3, which describes how the wicked will be burned and destroyed, and the just raised up.[163] This is the note upon which the author ends his polemic, a note filled with powerful, destructive imagery and a reaffirmation of the idea that the Simple Soul is supremely evil and attempts to invert the natural order of goodness and wickedness. Such a concluding note cements the image of the

---

158. Romans 3:5–6: "But if our injustice commend the justice of God, what shall we say? Is God unjust, who executes wrath? (I speak according to man.) God forbid! Otherwise how shall God judge this world?"

159. MS 1647, f. 221va.

160. MS 1647, f. 221vb. D. 4 de cons. c. 3, in Friedberg, Decretum, 1362.

161. MS 1647, f. 221vb. "et sic coronabimus uitia, uirtutibus depressis et erit uera querela pecato-rum quarum monent aduersus diuinam maiestatem."

162. Malachi 3:13–15. MS 1647, f. 221v, first column.

163. MS 1647, f. 221va–b. "Sed absit stultitia hec a cordibus fidelium, euanescat hoc a mente nos-tra et adhereamus hiis que secuntur."

*Mirror* as an evil text, composed by diabolical impulses of the worst kind. In his view, the *Mirror* is a book that advocates a separation of the soul from the most fundamental elements of goodness and appropriate spiritual practice: it eschews the virtues, ridicules the church, makes false claims to clandestine divine knowledge, and then, laden with all of these "vices," the Simple Soul arrogantly elevates itself to the same height as God.

Having fully demonstrated the demonic nature of the *Mirror*, the author pens a short conclusion. Immediately after the quote from Malachi that describes the destruction of the wicked, he writes,

> We embrace this truth, we pursue it wholeheartedly, and we prosecute this heretic with his work, and we relinquish this heretic with his work to be burned by fire, the power and justice of God having been sufficiently roused [against] anyone who may work any sin whatsoever. For we know because *the wages of sin are death, the grace of God [is] life eternal.*[164] Deo gratias.
>
> I wrote and said this with a clean and pure heart, submitting myself to the sacred and holy Catholic faith and my judgements to the correction of the most sacred and holy mother Church.[165]

This concludes the entire text. It is an intriguing conclusion, for it echoes the language of inquisitorial sentencing. "Relinquish" (*relinquere*) was frequently used in the course of relaxing condemned heretics to the secular arm for execution.[166] Additionally, the formulaic little passage that comes after this implies that this may have been written in or was intended for a more formal context, and the use of *dicta* for "judgments" is a word frequently used in a legal context.[167] It is possible that this text is a product of a commission, that someone was formally tasked with assessing the *Mirror*'s orthodoxy.[168] As mentioned earlier, it has affinities not just with the Vatican *Mirror* list but also with assessments like those of Peter of John Olivi's Apocalypse commentary that were commissioned by Pope John XXII, where excerpts from the text were picked out and submitted to an expert theologian or group of theologians, who then

---

164. Romans 6:23.

165. MS 1647, f. 221vb. "Hanc ueritatem amplectimur, hanc totis precordiis prosequimur, et hunc hereticum cum suo opere prosequimur [MS: "presequimur"] et hunc hereticum cum suo opere relinquimus igne cremandum, instincti sufficienter quidquid operet pecatum quicque uirtus et dei iustitia. Scimus enim stipedia pecati mors est, gratia dei uita eterna. Deo gratias. Hoc scripsi et dixi puro et mero corde sacro sancte fidei catholice, sumitens me et mea dicta coreptioni sacre sancte matris ecclesie."

166. Trombley, "New Evidence," 146.

167. Charles Du Fresne (known as Du Cange), *Glossarium Mediae et Infimae Latinitatis*, 10 vols. (Niort: L. Favre, 1883–1887), 104.

168. This is different to my conclusions in Trombley, "New Evidence," 146.

refuted it at length.[169] It is possible, then, that this document was produced in a similar scenario, although it was clearly given to a canon lawyer rather than a theologian. The possibility of a commission is bolstered by the overview of the text given at the beginning of the assessment, where the author discusses the question of whether the *Mirror* can be accepted as appropriate reading. That section gives the impression that the author is responding to something: the matter that "must be questioned" about the book "seems to be" whether it can be accepted. Such phrasing sounds as though someone wants him to weigh in on the matter, rather than him musing away on his own. But the fury the author brings to his response is remarkable. It goes beyond mere concern; he was clearly deeply disturbed by the implications he saw in the *Mirror*'s doctrines. Again, this is a stark contrast to the fairly dry, to-the-point tone of the Vatican list.

As mentioned earlier, since he notes the specific chapters, pages, and columns in which the excerpted passages appear, and since he brings in additional quotations from the *Mirror* within his refutations, the author clearly had a copy of the *Mirror* in front of him and was not merely working from a list of propositions. This, too, may suggest a commission, similar to Antonio Zeno's provision of a copy to the Paduan theologians in 1437. The references to chapters and pages would then allow anyone reading his refutation to also locate each error within the *Mirror* themselves, should they have a copy. Additionally, he is clearly making a case against the *Mirror*, and his statement that he both wrote *and* said such statements implies that he was arguing this case before others. Giacomo de Zocchi's acquisition of this text fits with this scenario. If he found it in the course of seeking out other legal texts, such as the fourteenth-century *Roman Rota* decisions and the *Impugnacio* of 1417, then it is likely that this text, too, was among such other past judgments and cases. This suggests, then, that this text may represent a canon-legal assessment of the *Mirror* that took place in the early fourteenth century. The author's fierce tone lends a sense of alarm to this judgment. As we have seen in previous chapters, the *Mirror* circulated across a wide range of linguistic, social, and religious circles in the fifteenth century. It is not unreasonable to think that the same was true of its earlier fourteenth-century circulation. In fact, at certain points in the polemical text the author addresses those who would defend certain points in the *Mirror*; whether this is a reference to real people or whether the author is merely constructing a rhetorical opponent himself is difficult to say, but it does suggest

---

169. See Sylvain Piron, "Censures et condamnation de Pierre de Jean Olivi: Enquête dans les marges du Vatican," *Mélanges de l'École française de Rome, Moyen-Âge* 118, no. 2 (2006); Nold, "New Annotations of Pope John XXII," 1–48; Burr, *Olivi's Peaceable Kingdom*, 198–239.

that he had heard support or defenses of the *Mirror* from some others, thereby indicating some degree of popularity. This would help to explain why someone might commission an assessment of its contents. To cite a parallel example, it was not until Olivi's *Lectura super apocalipsim* began to circulate and gain popularity among his increasingly rebellious followers that John XXII commissioned panels of theologians to examine and judge its contents.[170] A similar scenario for the *Mirror* is entirely possible.

As to a more specific time and place for such a commission, there is a tantalizing possibility: the Council of Vienne and the crafting of the Clementine decrees. In other words, this text could be an opinion produced during the process that led to the construction of the decree *Ad nostrum*.[171] I am currently working with Sylvain Piron on a piece investigating this possibility in-depth, so I will only briefly speculate on the matter here. In putting together the list of errors found in *Ad nostrum*, the *Mirror* could have been presented as one piece of evidence for the kinds of heresies thought to be circulating, perhaps brought there by someone who had come upon a Latin copy themselves. It could then have been given to experts, or even one expert, for judgment and assessment, while formulating specific errors to be included in the decree. As mentioned earlier in this chapter, one can easily discern in this text the errors that would eventually be set down in *Ad nostrum*, and we can even see some of the same vocabulary.[172] The text in MS 1647 could have been one opinion involved in the process of creating the decree. Much more remains to be done on this question.

However it originated, this text is an intriguing glimpse into the *Mirror*'s earliest circulation, a time into which we still have very little insight. The trial of Marguerite Porete and the three opinions of the churchmen at the end of the *Mirror* have long been the most evidence we have of reactions to the *Mirror* at that time. This polemical assessment shows a vehement opposition to the *Mirror* that occurred close in time to the *Mirror*'s first condemnations but was made entirely in ignorance of its author and other troubles. This indicates that the *Mirror* took on a life of its own quite early on and began to attract enough notice that someone thought it needed to be dealt with. Marguerite's trial, then, is not necessarily the anomaly that it at first appears. All of the attacks we have seen so far all came over a century after Marguerite's trial and

---

170. Burr, *Olivi's Peaceable Kingdom*, 198–203.

171. I thank Sylvain Piron for first suggesting this possibility and for further discussion on this point.

172. For example, discussion of the earthly human achieving a state of "impeccability" (*impeccabilitas*) in the present life, found on f. 218va.

the *Mirror's* first condemnation. This perhaps makes it more understandable that such attacks show no knowledge of its early history. But here, with its possible pre-1317 origins, we find the *Mirror* receiving the same treatment—indeed, one could argue *worse* treatment—nearly contemporarily with its very public condemnation and the execution of its author but separate from both those events.[173] This shows that the early history of the *Mirror* was not only marked by trouble in tandem with the struggles and actions of Marguerite Porete and the Capetian court but also by those who encountered it anonymously, as a "heretic" in its own right.

## Conclusion

What we have in the Paduan polemic is the most detailed and vehement reaction against the *Mirror* that has yet been found. To the author who wrote this text, the *Mirror* seemed to push Christians away from the mainstays of virtuous life and the path to salvation and instead urged them toward the evils of vice and sin, and encouraged them reject the authority of the institutional church. He also believed it to belittle the importance of Christ and to arrogantly claim for the human soul a state of divinity that no one should be capable of achieving. This is a text that meant to leave no doubt about the *Mirror's* heresy, and, unlike the Vatican list, which merely pointed out error, it makes sure to emphasize the danger and "diabolical cunning" of the *Mirror's* words. It is easy to imagine Giacomo de Zocchi copying it, and subsequently referring to it, in a time when the *Mirror* was being denounced in sermons, banned from the Benedictine Congregation with which he was so close, and confiscated and examined in his adopted hometown of Padua. At a time when the *Mirror* was cropping up in multiple reading circles, a text like this would have proved useful to those looking to highlight its supposed dangers.

Its potential fourteenth-century origins, however, mean that it is also evidence of something we have long been missing: a reaction to the *Mirror's* contents at the time of its earliest circulation that was made *outside* of the experiences of Marguerite Porete. While one can hardly call the Paduan polemic "objective," it was created without the factors that color how we usually talk about the *Mirror's* early treatment: knowledge of its author, its origins, and the circumstances of its condemnations in Valenciennes and Paris. This means that it is the first tangible evidence we have that shows that the *Mirror* in its own

---

173. Trombley, "New Evidence," 151–152.

right was controversial and contested *from the very beginning*, and not necessarily as a result of the circumstances surrounding its author's identity, and her trial and execution. It also means that the *Mirror* was already taking on a life of its own early on and circulating without an immediate link to its author or in circles in which she was known.

This raises another point. With its early origins, this text can be seen as the third condemnation that the *Mirror* received within the first two decades of the fourteenth century. The two in Paris and Valenciennes are, of course, related to each other and certainly took the most dramatic and public turn in the execution of Marguerite Porete. Yet, in terms of their impact on a larger scale, no one who later attacked the *Mirror* remembered and referenced those two events. Their memory did not endure. The polemical text in MS 1647, however, had no such dramatic spectacle and does not seem to have had a broad circulation (that we know of). Yet, in being copied by a canon lawyer over a century after it was composed, this condemnation *did* last and became a standard against which the *Mirror* could potentially be measured, albeit on a small scale. In this sense, the polemical text was a more "successful" condemnation of the *Mirror* than the dramatic trials and burnings of Valenciennes and Paris. It endured to be used again later.

What this text also shows particularly well is the importance of readership and its diversity. It shows the sharpest contrast yet between the positive reception the *Mirror* had on one hand and the antagonism it received on the other. A reader like the Middle English translator M. N., working in the context of Carthusian spirituality largely favorable to mysticism in the vein of the *Mirror*, was perfectly willing to accommodate and explain the *Mirror*'s daring statements as things that needed to be understood "spiritually and divinely" and not literally.[174] John-Jerome of Prague, committed to holy simplicity and church reform and suspicious of overly learned and ornamented expressions of piety, saw his convictions reflected in the *Mirror*'s rejection of reason and mocking of the institutional church, even if its pages should only be "read cautiously, and not by everyone." But the polemical author of the Paduan text, reading these same passages, had no such flexibility or generosity of interpretation. Only once does he say, "I believe this consideration to be true"—and that is when the annihilated Soul declares herself to be the root of all evil and sunk in her horrible defects.[175] This highlights one of the most interesting—and, at times, comical—aspects of this polemic, in that it clearly shows a deep and irreconcilable clash of worldviews. Here we have a canon lawyer approach-

---

174. "goostli and diuineli," *Middle English Mirror*, 259.
175. MS 1647, f. 217va–b. For the passage in the *Mirror* see *Speculum CCCM*, 37–39.

ing the *Mirror* from a literal, legalistic, and rigidly rational viewpoint of what appropriate spiritual life should consist of. The author of this text is, really, exactly the kind of reader that Marguerite believed would struggle with her work: one steeped in reason and operating solely under reason's direction. Love and the Soul relentlessly mocked Reason in the *Mirror*. In this text, Reason strikes back.

# Conclusion

The main goal of this book has been to reveal a new side to the story of *The Mirror of Simple Soul*'s late medieval reception. This new narrative demonstrates that Marguerite Porete's work defied—and continues to defy—categorization and remained controversial well beyond the events of 1310. A detailed examination of manuscript evidence demonstrates that, alongside its widespread positive reception, there was a parallel reception of the *Mirror*—especially in its Latin version—that was one of opposition and condemnation. This is different to the slight feelings of unease that scholarship has noted in the past. Not all criticisms of the *Mirror* seen here take as extreme a stance as calling for the author's eyes to be gouged out or their tongue to be torn out with a hook, but all of them *do* demonstrate that, to many readers, the *Mirror* was a dangerous and heretical book. These attacks came in many forms: public denunciations in sermons; bans, inquisitions, and confiscations; the physical destruction of the *Mirror* in the Laud codex; the theological refutations of the Vatican list; and the viciously expressed legal polemic of the Paduan text. Each case reveals something important about the *Mirror*, and illuminating this dark side of the *Mirror* has crucial implications for how we perceive not just that work but also Marguerite Porete, heretical texts, and the broader landscape of heresy and orthodoxy in the late Middle Ages.

First, this book provides new information on manuscripts that have been little studied and also brings new sources to our attention. It shows the importance of using the manuscripts themselves to tell the story of the *Mirror's* reception. Perhaps best represented by the example of the Laud codex, the uniqueness of the manuscripts as individual physical objects can allow for new considerations even where the text itself is missing. But even the more textually forthcoming Vatican and Paduan manuscripts give us codicological and paleographical information that provides crucial pieces of the puzzle, for instance with the appearance of the *Mirror's* "errors" alongside texts connected to the Council of Ferrara-Florence, or the fact that Giacomo de Zocchi copied the Paduan anti-*Mirror* polemic in his own hand. These are what bring the texts to life, showing how they were read, used, and perceived at specific times and in specific places. In other words, the text must be linked to its physical incarnations in order for us to get the whole picture. It is not just the words of these polemics and refutations that tell the story but also their physical makeup, their tangible existence as unique objects that real humans read and used, that deepens our understanding of the *Mirror's* history and significance to medieval spiritual life. All of the *Mirror's* manuscript traditions, in their number and variety, remain rich resources waiting to be excavated further.

The manuscript evidence presented here, although it comes mostly from texts that were copied in the fifteenth century, has implications for the whole of the *Mirror's* history, including its earliest condemnations. The Vatican and Paduan texts in particular provide answers to questions that have previously been confined to speculation. These two are the only known texts that refute the *Mirror's* doctrines in detail. They show the reasoning behind attacks on the *Mirror* and reveal exactly what scriptural, theological, and canon-legal authorities its critics believed it violated. Up until now, we have had a very limited perspective on this in regard to the *Mirror's* condemnations in Valenciennes and Paris. We have had only the final sentences and the three errors the Parisian theologians' found troubling; we previously have had no specifics telling us *why* they found them troubling and why they drew these conclusions.[1] Now, with the Vatican and Paduan texts, we do. Even better, we have two *different* critiques. The two texts complement one another: one provides a theological refutation and the other a canon-legal one. While we still have to proceed cautiously—the Vatican list was, after all, written over a hundred years after Marguerite Porete's trial—for the first time we can do more than speculate on why the *Mirror* was seen as heretical, both in Marguerite's lifetime and long after.

---

1. As Sean Field has put it, "Caution is required before assuming that specific elements of the way Marguerite constructed or justified her text explain why her work was condemned, since there is no record of any contemporary churchman noting these points, approvingly or disapprovingly." *The Beguine*, 9.

In this vein, it is clear that the *Mirror* provoked negative reactions because it was seen to collide with key views on virtuous living, church authority, and the appropriate limits of the human soul's ability to experience the divine. These were recurring themes when it came to questions of heresy and orthodoxy. Such issues can be found in various incarnations in many of the church's struggles with dissident groups and individuals and were also long-simmering tensions within mystical thought as well. Additionally, repeated reference to prominent antiheretical decrees—*Ad nostrum*, but also *Ad abolendam* and *Cum ex iniuncto*—show that a mental connection was made between the *Mirror* and the broader, more well-known and well-established heresies of the twelfth, thirteenth, and fourteenth centuries. But the Vatican list in particular shows that some also saw connections that were neither mystical nor related to popular heresy. Those critics also saw a very specific kind of heresy in the *Mirror*, that of the academic, Aristotelian heresies and errors that were condemned in Paris in 1241 and 1277. Just like it appealed to a broad spectrum of readers, then, the *Mirror* also touched upon a broad spectrum of errors.

This demonstrates how truly challenging and fluid the *Mirror* was as a text. Its diverse reception lay not only in its ability to be seen as both orthodox or heretical but also in that those who saw it as heretical saw in it many different heresies, both popular and academic. Comparing the Vatican and Paduan texts highlights this nicely. They deal essentially with the same parts of the *Mirror* but see different problems in the same errors. One might fixate on the union of human and divine wills possibly negating free will, while the other could fear divine will being used as a cover for sinful behavior. A reader did not have to dislike the paradoxes of mysticism—like the author of the Paduan text—to find it troubling. They could perhaps be entirely comfortable with paradoxical self-negation but see the *Mirror*'s particular take on it as going beyond what is acceptable. Or they could find other issues just as troubling: its creation of two churches, or its recession from the virtues, or its claims to divinization. Simultaneously, there is also divergence on which errors were selected: the Vatican list addressed *Mirror* passages that the Paduan polemic did not, and vice versa. Therefore, even when it came to having its heresies named, the *Mirror* had considerable depth and could elicit a range of opinions. This in turn highlights yet another way in which heresy could be ambiguous, particularly when it came to books and intellectual heresies in the late Middle Ages: even when the general label of something being "heretical" was agreed upon, the answers to what exactly made it heretical could take many forms.

What is striking about these charges of heresy against the *Mirror* is that, although the *Mirror* was linked to older heresies, it was definitely *not* linked with its first condemnations in Valenciennes and Paris. At no point in any of these attacks are those two events referenced, nor is there any knowledge of who the author was. Indeed, as we saw with the Paduan text, the *Mirror* was called "apocryphal" and it was presumed that the author was a man. This has important implications for how we perceive the *Mirror*, both in its early struggles and later in its reception. In terms of the former, it brings the *Mirror* more fully into the conversation about Marguerite Porete's condemnation. As noted in the introduction, there has been an implied suspicion of the reasons for Marguerite Porete's condemnation, suggesting that it was more to do with political circumstances and manipulation of the evidence by her persecutors than with the actual heresy of her ideas. There is the feeling that her *Mirror* did not get a fair hearing, a feeling that, had the theologians read the entire *Mirror*, with its qualifications and explanations of some of its more shocking statements, it would not necessarily have been judged to be heretical.

That idea is clearly refuted by the evidence presented here. We have seen a series of readers of the *Mirror*—one of whom may have been roughly contemporary with Marguerite's condemnation—encountering its contents in settings entirely separate from those surrounding Marguerite's trial and execution. Yet they came to the same conclusion as the Parisian theologians did in 1310. Furthermore, with the Paduan text, we have seen someone who read some of the *Mirror*'s more shocking statements *in context*, with its attendant qualifications, and still found it dangerous—indeed the qualifications themselves are attacked as errors and viewed as poisonous deceptions. There is no guarantee, then, that had the Parisian theologians been given an entire copy of the *Mirror* to peruse in full, they would have come to a different conclusion.[2] Again, this is not to discount the effects of the other forces surrounding Marguerite Porete's trial in 1310. Rather, it is to argue that the *Mirror*'s content be set alongside these other forces as one that may have had equal power and influence, and that the *Mirror*'s condemnation in 1310 was not necessarily the result of prejudicial judgments based on selective reading, vernacularity, gender, or political circumstances. The *Mirror*'s ideas had the power to provoke, and to provoke in many different times and places. This means that when we discuss the trial and condemnation of Marguerite Porete we should talk as much about the nature and implications of her ideas, about how challenging she was as a thinker, as we do about the schemes of the Capetian court or her refusal to confess. Ultimately, Marguerite Porete died because she refused to give up on her book. It seems important, then, to give prominence to the impact that her book may have had in determining her fate.

The opposition shown to the *Mirror* also cannot be put down as merely a case of academic scholastic theologians being automatically prejudiced against

---

2. This point is also made in Trombley, "Self-Defence," 148.

the *Mirror*'s love-powered, anti-reason, paradoxical mysticism. Certainly, as with the Paduan text, such a clash of worldviews took place. But it is not the only explanation. The work of Danielle Dubois and Peter King has shown intellectual synergies between Marguerite's ideas about virtue and scholastic views of the virtues in the late thirteenth and early fourteenth centuries.[3] Similar synergies can be seen when it comes to those opposed to the *Mirror*. In the case of the Vatican list, the authors there attacked the *Mirror* as if it *were* an academic text—they saw in it the errors of the universities, condemned in Paris in 1241 and 1277. Indeed, the very fact that Antonio Zeno submitted it to the theologians at Padua—in a context different to that which prompted William of Paris to do so—indicates that he thought he was dealing with a theological text that was perhaps a product of their world. This is perhaps partially a consequence of the *Mirror* coming to them in Latin. A Latin text containing the ideas the *Mirror* did would more readily suggest an academic origin than if, say, they encountered a vernacular version, and therefore it was dealt with in the way academic texts were expected to be dealt with. Being in Latin would also have meant that the *Mirror* was more likely to move in circles where readers were trained in disputation and trained to recognize and refute error, so the fact that these condemnations are found mostly in its Latin tradition is perhaps not wholly surprising. But, again, such opposition should not solely or mainly be put down to language, because plenty of its Latin copies were also valued and accepted. Its treatment as an academic heresy also speaks to the sophistication of its content and affinity with multiple intellectual currents.

The introduction to this book noted the seeming disconnect between the *Mirror*'s 1310 condemnation and its subsequent acceptance in the reading circles of late medieval Europe. The evidence examined here helps to resolve that disconnect—or rather shows that there is no disconnect. The good and the bad are two sides to the same coin, not separate entities. Acceptance and rejection do not preclude one another. The *Mirror* could be received as orthodox at the exact same time as it could be condemned as heretical, depending on who was reading it. Chronicling negative reactions to the *Mirror* is not intended to overshadow or negate the positive reception it received in other quarters, or to try and define the *Mirror* solely as a target of persecution. Rather, the negative side of the *Mirror*'s reception complements the positive. As noted before, behind the numerous attacks the *Mirror* endured there must have been a solid level of popularity. Why else would someone like Bernardino of Siena, or the author of the Paduan text, expend such time and energy denouncing

---

3. Dubois, "Natural and Supernatural Virtues"; King, "Godfrey of Fontaines and Marguerite Porete."

it? Revealing the negative side of the *Mirror*'s reception cautions against assuming that there was any single way in which a reader would *have* to consider the *Mirror* either orthodox or heretical. That is, it argues against the notion that there was one "correct" interpretation of the *Mirror*. It is not the case that those who found it heretical merely did not read or understand it properly, and that those who saw it as orthodox knew what it "really" meant. Nor is it a question of the *Mirror* momentarily encountering difficulty and then being freed into the green pastures of orthodoxy. Instead, the reactions chronicled here show that the *Mirror* was an inherently provocative, fascinating, and challenging text. It did not fit neatly into any one definition of "heretical" and "orthodox." Where one person saw a text that championed ascetic simplicity, or blissful mystical union, someone else saw a book that dealt in condemned theological novelties, or that diabolically deceived and tempted the reader into abandoning a virtuous life. This diversity in turn serves as yet another example of the spiritual and intellectual vibrancy of the late Middle Ages. The "multiple options" for spiritual life are reflected in the multiple options for interpreting the *Mirror*'s words.[4]

The multifaceted story of the *Mirror* also points to new ways of thinking about late medieval heresy and the condemnation of texts. In general, it perhaps stands as one of the strongest proofs yet for the statement that "heresy is in the eye of the beholder." As scholars have noted many times, heresy and orthodoxy were rarely divided along clear lines but instead wrangled with one another in a gray, indistinct, and uncertain landscape. More specifically, however, it raises questions about the meaning of textual condemnation in the Middle Ages. As mentioned previously, none of the criticisms and condemnations of the *Mirror* that we have seen throughout this book ever reference the condemnations in Valenciennes and Paris. Yet those two events are often perceived as the "official" condemnations of the *Mirror*. But what exactly did "official" mean in practice when it came to the medieval condemnation of texts?

Obviously, an event like Marguerite's execution in 1310 was official in the sense of being decided by those invested with the institutional power to make such judgments. That decision, however, came from local ecclesiastical and secular officials and was not directed by the papacy, nor was such an event reported back to the papal court. This was of course normal for inquisition, given that there was no centralized office of inquisition in the Middle Ages. But more important to the discussion here is what "official" means in terms of the impact of condemnation on the *Mirror* itself and its circulation, because whereas the condemnation of a person for heresy is generally the end of the process of persecution, the condemnation of a *text* for heresy is often the beginning. Although

---

4. John Van Engen, "Multiple Options."

there were some common tactics that were used, there was no single centralized procedure for condemning texts in the Middle Ages and no unique office tasked with the organization and enforcement of such acts. "Official," when applied to a textual condemnation, implies something that is definitive and centralized and that becomes the standard against which other decisions are measured. Yet, in terms of their impact on a larger scale, the Valenciennes and Parisian judgments did not endure as that standard. This is not just in the sense of the failure to physically exterminate the *Mirror* itself—something that rarely happened as a result of any textual condemnation—but rather in the sense that the *knowledge* of them as acts of condemnation did not survive and continue to have an impact on the *Mirror's* circulation. This means that, beyond the immediate time in which they were carried out, these condemnations ceased to be authoritative and effective events in that sense. If we then look at some of the attacks on the *Mirror* documented here, we see something different. Knowledge of the *Mirror* as a heretical text does seem to have been communicated on a broader level— we can see this knowledge circulating through Bernardino of Siena's sermons, or in the circulation of the Vatican list, or the Paduan polemic being copied into MS 1647, or perhaps in the circles in which the Laud *Mirror* may have traveled. But even these depended on specific networks and came from individuals, and they did not emanate from the same single and central point of authority. The *Mirror* was a heretical text because it was called heretical at certain times and by certain people, but it was not set down as heretical in the sense of being on a widely used list, like the fifteenth distinction in Gratian's *Decretum*, or as would later become the case with the Index of Prohibited Books in the sixteenth century.

This suggests a need to reconsider textual condemnation in the later Middle Ages. Rather than a single judgment or event handed down from a central power that then endured and defined all other assessments that came afterward, textual condemnation could instead take different forms and comprised many different factors that could play out as a process over time. In the example of the *Mirror*, the public spectacle of an author's execution and a text's burning did not necessarily have a more lasting influence over time on the text's reception than did a written condemnation that could be circulated and copied, or a sermon that could be publicly preached. Rather than giving these different methods equal weight, we perhaps need to distinguish between them in order to more fully understand and analyze textual repression and regulation in the late Middle Ages. It is clear, looking at other texts and authors who endured censure and condemnation, such as Peter of John Olivi, Meister Eckhart, or Ramon Llull, that there was by no means a uniform outcome when condemnation took place. Their cases differed from Marguerite's in many and important ways. A broader examination of textual condemnation, focusing on a variety of heretical texts, remains a future project.

Finally, a study of *The Mirror of Simple Souls* should not be concluded without considering the implications for its author, Marguerite Porete. A clearer view of the *Mirror*'s complex reception history also adds another layer to how Marguerite is discussed. As a recent volume on medieval women intellectuals has pointed out, scholarship is beginning to shift away from a dichotomy of specifically feminine or masculine forms of mysticism and spirituality.[5] This same publication also argues that, while we need to acknowledge women's experience of victimhood, we should not "let victimhood have the last word."[6] Both are borne out in the case of Marguerite. The *Mirror* is often defined primarily as a work of beguine spirituality and "female" mysticism. While this is certainly not wrong—Marguerite Porete was a beguine and was, of course, female—it is clear from the evidence presented here that those categories do not adequately cover her ideas and the place that she and the *Mirror* had in the Middle Ages. That is, they describe part, but not all, of the kind of thinker Marguerite was and the way in which medieval readers perceived her book. In addition, because we know very little about Marguerite herself and she is mainly visible to us through the distorted lens of her trial—the most tragic part of her life—Marguerite runs the risk of largely being seen as a victim. Cataloging as it does the repeated and at times vicious condemnation of her work, this book might seem to risk cementing this image of victimhood further.

I would argue, however, that it does the opposite. It can be said with relative certainty that no other text written by a woman in the Middle Ages caused as much controversy or provoked as many different and strong reactions as did *The Mirror of Simple Souls*. This on its own speaks to the singularity and power of Marguerite Porete's intellectual and spiritual concepts and expressions. But the negative treatment of the *Mirror* is not the story of a female-authored text being persecuted at the hands of the patriarchal church. Instead, it is the story of a theologically daring text that caused controversy in the tumultuous late medieval religious landscape, both with and without its author. It can certainly be said that, had Marguerite put forward her ideas as a man, within the sphere of the universities, she may not have been executed but would likely have been accorded the privilege of having her life preserved while her ideas were condemned, as frequently happened with erring scholars. It cannot, however, be said that the *Mirror* would not have been condemned at all if

---

5. Kathryn Kerby-Fulton (quoting Katie Bugyis), "Introduction: Taking Early Women and Intellectuals Seriously," in *Women Intellectuals and Leaders in the Middle Ages*, ed. Kathryn Kerby-Fulton, Katie Anne-Marie Bugyis, and John Van Engen (Woodbridge, UK: Boydell and Brewer, 2020), 5.

6. Kerby-Fulton, "Taking Early Women and Intellectuals Seriously," 11.

it had been authored by a man, for this is precisely what happened in its later circulation. The men who attacked the *Mirror*—theologians, canon lawyers, preachers—all (with the exception of Gregorio Correr) attacked it under the assumption that it *was* written by a man. Their disagreement with it, their fear over it, and their arguments against it all demonstrate that they took Marguerite's ideas seriously and engaged with them on a serious intellectual level. Her ideas were inherently challenging and controversial, touching upon hotly contested topics that reached beyond the realm of mysticism and well beyond controversies surrounding beguines. While the theologians who compiled the Vatican list saw in the *Mirror* the "errors of the beghards," they also saw ideas that had roiled the intellectual world of the universities over a century earlier. They refuted the *Mirror* as if it had come from their own ranks. Such intellectual respect, however couched it is in criticism, is perhaps as much of an accolade for the *Mirror* as its acceptance and popularity.

The story of Marguerite Porete and *The Mirror of Simple Souls*, then, represents not only the increasing suspicion surrounding beguines, women's spiritual experiences, and mysticism in the fourteenth century but also broader intellectual conflicts and debates taking place among the educated elite of that same period. In this way, Marguerite was an intellectual force to be reckoned with, an innovative thinker and writer whose concepts drew her and her work into conflict with a church that was broadening its definition of heresy and narrowing its leeway for dissent. Looked at in this way, Marguerite Porete can and should be included just as readily alongside figures like Peter of John Olivi as she can alongside Joan of Arc. As with the legacies of those figures, Marguerite's own legacy was a shifting mixture of admiration and condemnation. This book began with Marguerite numbering her critics and wondering what "the religious" would say "when they shall hear the excellence of your divine song." The rich complexity of *The Mirror of Simple Souls* meant that many readers did indeed hear in it a sweet divine song, while others heard only the sound of a diabolical voice.

# APPENDIX 1

# Extracts from a Latin *Mirror of Simple Souls* in MS Vat. lat. 4953

These are English translations of the extracts that are presented as errors in MS Vat. lat. 4953, on folios 28r-32r. All translations are my own. The Latin text of these errors—along with their refutations—are published in Guarnieri, "Il movimento," 650–660. Nonitalic text indicates words written by the compiler(s) of the list. Italic text indicates where the *Mirror* is being quoted directly. I have used quotation marks where several sections of the *Mirror* appear one after another in the extract but do not follow on from one another in the *Mirror* itself. In addition to correcting genuine mistakes, there are many places in Guarnieri's edition where she has changed certain words to match what appears in other Latin manuscripts of the *Mirror*. Where it is not a matter of sense or grammar, I have chosen to keep the readings as found in MS Vat. lat. 4953, in order to preserve some of the unique variations found in that text and to preserve how those compiling the list initially may have (mis)read it.

1. *We wish to speak, asking whether there is a Soul who is unable to be found, who is saved through faith without works, who may only be in Love, who does nothing good on God's account, who neglects to do nothing evil on his account, to whom nothing can be taught, from whom nothing can be taken away, nor similarly given.*[1]

---

1. MS Vat. lat. 4953, f. 28r; Guarnieri, "Il movimento," 651; for this passage in the *Mirror* see *Speculum CCCM*, 19–21 (chapter 5).

*The first point is, Love, says [Reason], because you have said that such a Soul is unable to be found.*

*It is true, says Love, this means that she knows in herself only one thing, that is the root of all evils, and the abundance of all sins without number, without measure, and without weight; and sin is nothing and less than nothing; and this [Soul] is sunk deep in her horrible defects, she may be beneath less than nothing.*[2] This is the declaration set down in the book.

2. The second error [is] in the same chapter: *That this Soul, however much more she has of knowledge, or the more she knows of the divine goodness, the more she truly realizes she knows nothing regarding one spark, as I said, of the divine goodness, which cannot be comprehended except by Himself alone.*[3]

3. The third error is in the same chapter: *That the Soul united to God through Love, and resting in Him, remains fixed always in the divine goodness.*[4]

4. The fourth error is: *Love: What, it is said, is the greatest torment that a creature can bear? They may certainly say that [it is] to remain in love and in obedience to the Virtues.*[5]

5. The fifth error is in the same chapter, that the Soul, placed in divine Love, recedes from the Virtues, whence it says: *I depart, says this Soul, to sweet Love. Your carnality liberated me from such servitude,*[6] *on account of which I can say to the Virtues: I am now gone from you always,*[7] *because my heart will be more free, and enjoy greater peace.*[8]

6. The sixth error is in the same chapter, when it says: *This Soul has no care for anything, not shame, nor does she have fear or honor, she does not have poverty nor riches, she does not have joy nor sadness, she does not have love nor hate, not hell nor paradise.*[9]

---

2. MS Vat. lat. 4953, f. 28r; Guarnieri, "Il movimento," 651; *Speculum CCCM*, 37–39 (chapter 11).

3. MS Vat. lat. 4953, f. 28r; Guarnieri, "Il movimento," 651; *Speculum CCCM*, 21–23 (chapter 5).

4. MS Vat. lat. 4953, f. 28r; Guarnieri, "Il movimento," 651; *Speculum CCCM*, 23 (chapter 5).

5. MS Vat. lat. 4953, f. 28r; Guarnieri, "Il movimento," 652; *Speculum CCCM*, 31 (chapter 8).

6. "Carnality": this is the reading in the manuscript (*carnalitas*). In all other *Mirror* copies, it is *curialitas*, "courtliness" (quite a difference). Guarnieri corrects this to *curialitas* in her edition. I maintain *carnalitas* here, as it is difficult to determine whether this was a scribal error on the part of the person writing up this copy of the list or whether this was what was written in the original list. It is *curialitas* in MS Rossianus 4, but it is easy to see how it could have been misread as *carnalitas*. (See MS Rossianus 4, f. 6r.) One can see how *carnalitas* might provoke a more alarmed reaction than *curialitas*.

7. "Gone from you always": here again Guarnieri corrects to what appears in the Latin manuscripts, from *semper* to *prosper* and from *incedi* to *recede*. I have only corrected *incedi* to *incedo*, as the infinitive does not make sense here. I have left the vocabulary as is.

8. MS Vat. lat. 4953, f. 28v; Guarnieri, "Il movimento," 652; *Speculum CCCM*, 25 (chapter 6).

9. MS Vat. lat. 4953, f. 28v; Guarnieri, "Il movimento," 652–653; *Speculum CCCM*, 25 (chapter 7).

7. The seventh error is in the same chapter. This annihilated Soul *neither desires nor despises poverty, tribulations, nor masses, fasts, prayers or sermons, and always gives to Nature whatever it asks, without any remorse of her own conscience.*[10]

8. The eighth error is in the chapter that begins *"The fourth point is, that this Soul does nothing on account of God." "This means, says Love, that God does not care for her work. This Soul does not care about herself. God may not care if He wishes."* And in the chapter immediately following, that begins: *"The fifth point is that the Soul neglects to do nothing evil on account of God." "This means, says Love, that this Soul is able to do nothing contrary to or against the divine will, nor is she able to will anything else."*[11]

9. The ninth error is in the chapter that begins *"The eighth point . . ."* *Sweet Love, says the Soul, there is no other God except He about whom nothing is able to be known, not truly nor certainly. He alone is my God, about whom no one is able to speak nor say any words, nor even those who are in paradise are able to attain a single point, whatever great, clear, and direct knowledge they have of God.*[12]

10. The tenth error is in the chapter that begins *"Now, therefore, Intellect of Reason . . ."* *I assure you, says Love, that those who are led by pure and sincere Love, they have indifference, and therefore desire shame just as honor, and poverty just as riches, and torment from God and His creation, just as consolation from God and His creation, and thus desire to hate as much as to love, and to love just as to hate, hell just as paradise.*[13]

11. The eleventh error is in the chapter that begins *"Do not be amazed . . ."* *This Soul wills all and wills nothing. This Daughter of Sion does not desire to hear masses nor sermons, nor does she care about fasting or prayers.* It is similarly put in the same chapter, that this Soul *does not have thought, nor word, nor work, except the practice of the divine Trinity. This [Soul] does not have sadness about any sin that she may have committed at any time, nor about anything that God may have sustained for her, nor about any sin or defect of her neighbors.*[14]

12. The twelfth error is in the same chapter: *"This Soul gives to Nature whatever it asks."*[15] *"This is true, says Love, because this Soul does not so*

10. MS Vat. lat. 4953, f. 28v; Guarnieri, "Il movimento," 653; *Speculum* CCCM, 33 (chapter 9).
11. Vat. lat. 4953, f. 28v; Guarnieri, 'Il movimento,' 653; *Speculum* CCCM, 41 (chapter 11).
12. Vat. lat. 4953, f. 28v; Guarnieri, 'Il movimento,' 653–654; *Speculum* CCCM, 45 (chapter 11).
13. Vat. lat. 4953, f. 29r; Guarnieri, 'Il movimento,' 654; *Speculum* CCCM, 59 (chapter 13).
14. Vat. lat. 4953, f. 29r; Guarnieri, 'Il movimento,'" 654; *Speculum* CCCM, 67 (chapter 16).
15. "Nature": the MS has *vere*; I follow Guarnieri's correction to *nature*.

*much value or esteem temporal things that she would know how to gain in denying Nature what it asks. On the contrary, she would have guilt over denying it that which is its own." "For who would have guilt in taking from the four elements, for her own necessity, in all the ways that Nature requires from them, without the murmur of Reason?"*[16]

13. The thirteenth error is that: *Such Souls, who are such a kind about which this book speaks, which touches upon some things that they practice, have from the righteousness of their being,*[17] *that which is pure divine essence.*[18]
    This error is placed in the following chapter, that begins: *"O Holy Trinity, many openly . . ." And who are you, Love? says Reason. Are you not one of the Virtues with us, however much you are superior to us? Love: I am God, says Love, because Love is God and God is Love. And this Soul is God from Himself by the righteousness of the condition of Love. And I am God through divine nature, and [this Soul] is God through the righteousness of Love.*[19]

14. The fourteenth error is: *It is right, says Love, that the greater part makes her obedient,*[20] *not because she drank from that greater part, as was said. She drank so much from it because her Beloved has [drunk from it], because between Him and her there is no difference.*[21]
    This error is in the chapter that begins *"O Holy Trinity . . ."*

15. The fifteenth error is in the same chapter. *This Soul, says Love, is submerged in the Sea of Joy, that is in the sea of delights flowing from the Divinity itself. And therefore she feels no joy, because she abides in joy itself, and is submerged in joy, not keeping joy,*[22] *because she abides in joy itself, and joy in her. Indeed, she is joy itself, through the virtue of Joy, which transforms her into itself. Therefore it is one and indivisible, just as fire from flame, the will of the Lover and the will of the Soul.*[23]

16. The sixteenth error is: *Love, says the Soul, you have told me that He who is without beginning from Himself in Himself, never loves anything else without me, nor I without Him. Love: This is true, I decree it, says Love. Soul: Therefore, from now, that is, in eternity, He will never love anything without me. It necessarily follows, that He will never love anything without me.*[24]

---

16. MS Vat. lat. 4953, f. 29r; Guarnieri, "Il movimento," 655; *Speculum* CCCM, 69 and 73 (chapter 17).

17. "Being": the MS has *effectus*; I follow Guarnieri's correction to *esse*.

18. MS Vat. lat. 4953, f. 29r; Guarnieri, "Il movimento," 655; *Speculum* CCCM, 71 (chapter 17).

19. MS Vat. lat. 4953, f. 29r; Guarnieri, "Il movimento," 655; *Speculum* CCCM, 83 (chapter 21).

20. "Obedient": This is the reading in the MS (*obedientiam*); Guarnieri corrected to *ebriam* ("intoxicated").

21. MS Vat. lat. 4953, f. 29r; Guarnieri, "Il movimento," 655; *Speculum* CCCM, 87 (chapter 23).

22. "Keeping": the MS has *servando*; Guarnieri corrects to *sentiendo*. I maintain the MS reading.

23. MS Vat. lat. 4953, f. 29v; Guarnieri, "Il movimento," 656; *Speculum* CCCM, 97 (chapter 28).

24. MS Vat. lat. 4953, f. 29v; Guarnieri, "Il movimento," 656; *Speculum* CCCM, 115 (chapter 35).

17. The seventeenth error is in the same chapter. *O true God, Holy Spirit, says Church. Love: Certainly, Holy Church, says Love, that is, the one below this Holy Church, because these Souls are properly called Holy Church, that they sustain, teach, and nourish the entire Holy Church. Not themselves, I say, but the entire Trinity within themselves. This is true, says Love, there is no doubt. Therefore, says Holy-Church-Below-This-Holy-Church, you may say, says Love, what you want to say about those who are beyond and commended above you, you who ever follow the counsel of Reason. Holy Church the Lesser: We wish to speak, says Holy Church the Lesser, because such Souls are above us in life, because Love abides in them and Reason in us.*[25]

18. The eighteenth error is: *Alas, alas Lord, says the Soul, what will the Soul do who believes this about you? God: She will do nothing, says God, but I will do my work in her without her, because the knowledge of her nothingness and belief in me has reduced her to nothing, thus she is able to do nothing.*[26]

19. The nineteenth error is: *But how the Trinity works the showing of its glory to this Soul, certainly no one knows how to speak about this, except only the Divinity, because the Soul, to whom this Far-Nearness gives Himself, has therefore great knowledge about God,*[27] *about herself and about all other things, which the Soul herself sees in God Himself through divine knowledge, that light of this understanding takes from her knowledge of herself and of God and of all other things.*[28]

20. The twentieth error is in the same chapter: *This life is not understood by anyone, except he who has died this death. This [life], says Love, has the rich/divine flower,*[29] *[there is] no medium between such Souls and the Divinity itself, nor do they wish there to be any medium.*[30]

21. The twenty-first error is in the same chapter: *Now I tell you who it is who sits upon the mountain,*[31] *above the winds and rain: They are those who on earth do not have shame, nor fear, nor honor about anything that might happen to them. Such people are secure, because their doors are open,*

---

25. "Love": the MS has *Ratio*; I follow Guarnieri's correction to *Amor*. MS Vat. lat. 4953, f. 29v; Guarnieri, "Il movimento," 656; *Speculum CCCM*, 133 (chapter 43).

26. MS Vat. lat. 4953, f. 29v; Guarnieri, "Il movimento," 656–657; *Speculum CCCM*, 141 (chapter 45).

27. "Knowledge": the MS has *potenciam*. I have followed Guarnieri's correction to *noticiam*, as *power* would not make sense with "about God, about herself, and about all things."

28. MS Vat. lat. 4953, f. 29v; Guarnieri, "Il movimento," 657; *Speculum CCCM*, 179 (chapter 61).

29. "Rich/divine": *divitem* is what appears in the MS. Guarnieri corrects to *divinitatis*. I supply both here, as it is possible either that this was in the original or that the scribe simply misread an abbreviation of *divinitatem* (or intended *divinitatem* and forgot the abbreviation mark).

30. MS Vat. lat. 4953, f. 29v; Guarnieri, "Il movimento," 657; *Speculum CCCM*, 185 (chapter 64).

31. "You": the MS has *verbo*. I follow Guarnieri's correction to *vobis*.

*and yet nothing can harm them, no work of charity dares to enter. Such people are seated on the mountain and none but these [are seated there].*[32]

22. The twenty-second error is: *This Soul, says Love, is melted, drunk, dissolved, drawn, joined, and united into the highest Trinity. Therefore she cannot will except only the divine will through the divine working of the entire Trinity.*[33]

23. The twenty-third error: *Therefore, now you, Reason, ask where and how we love,*[34] *and on whose account? In Him and through Him alone, who is so strong that He can never die, whose doctrine is not written, nor is had through the works of exemplars, nor through human teachings, because His gift cannot be defrauded.*[35] *He without beginning knows that I may well believe Him without a witness.*[36] *Is there no greater boorishness, than to wish to have a witness in Love?*[37]

24. The twenty-fourth error is: *Lady Soul, says Reason, you have two laws, that is to say, ours and yours. Ours is to believe, yours is to love. Therefore you say what you will, and you call my disciples beasts and asses. Such people, says the Soul, whom I call asses and beasts, seek God in creatures, in churches for praying, in a created paradise, in the words of people, in the Scriptures.*[38]

25. The twenty-fifth error is: *I am, says this Soul, what I am by the grace of God. I am only that which God is in me, and nothing else, and God is the same that He is in me, because nothing is nothing, something is something. I am not, if I am something, except that which God is, and He is not anything else, except only God. And therefore I do not find anything except God alone, wherever I may have gone, because He is nothing at all, except Himself, to speak the truth.*[39]

26. The twenty-sixth error is: *She has no shame from anyone, except from those whom she had offended, because she was kindled and love-captured; therefore she does not care about anything other than Him.*[40]

27. The twenty-seventh error is that *no one loves the humanity of the Son of God, who loves the temporality. No one loves the divinity, who loves*

---

32. MS Vat. lat. 4953, f. 30r; Guarnieri, "Il movimento," 657; *Speculum CCCM*, 187 (chapter 65).

33. MS Vat. lat. 4953, f. 30r; Guarnieri, "Il movimento," 658; *Speculum CCCM*, 193 (chapter 68).

34. "We love": the reading in all the other Latin manuscripts is *dirigimur*, "we are guided." I have maintained the reading in the MS, *diligimus*.

35. "Defrauded": *fraudari*. All other Latin *Mirror* manuscripts except B (MS Rossianus 4) have *forma dari*, "given form."

36. "Knows": the MS has *scitur*; I follow Guarnieri's correction to *scit*.

37. MS Vat. lat. 4953, f. 30r; Guarnieri, "Il movimento," 658; *Speculum CCCM*, 195 (chapter 69).

38. MS Vat. lat. 4953, f. 30r; Guarnieri, "Il movimento," 658; *Speculum CCCM*, 195–197 (chapter 69).

39. MS Vat. lat. 4953, f. 30r; Guarnieri, "Il movimento," 659; *Speculum CCCM*, 197 (chapter 70).

40. MS Vat. lat. 4953, f. 30v; Guarnieri, "Il movimento," 659; *Speculum CCCM*, 211 (chapter 76). In the context of the *Mirror*, it is Mary Magdalene who is being described here, but she is being used as an analogy for the Soul.

*anything corporally. Those who truly love the divinity do not equally feel the humanity.*[41]

28.  The twenty-eighth error is in the chapter that begins *The first aspect from which this Soul is free is that she is [not] rebuked by conscience, nor by God, even if she does not do the work of the Virtues.*[42]

29.  The twenty-ninth error is: *This Soul, that is such a kind, does not seek God through penance, nor through any other sacrament of the Church, nor through meditations, nor through words, nor through works, nor through any superior creature, nor through justice, nor through mercy, nor through divine knowledge, nor through divine love, nor through divine praise.*[43]

30.  The thirtieth error is: *And therefore I say (that is the Soul) that I am the salvation of all creatures and the glory of God. Just as Christ by His death is the redemption of the people and the praise of God the Father, therefore I am by reason of my depravity the salvation of the human race and the glory of God the Father,*[44] *because God the Father gave to His Son His entire goodness, and the goodness of God is made known to the human race through the death of Jesus Christ His son, who is the eternal praise of the Father, and the redemption of the human creature. Therefore I say to you, says this Soul, God the Father gives and unfolds in me His total goodness, which the goodness of God is given to the human race to understand . . .* [45]

---

41.  MS Vat. lat. 4953, f. 30v; Guarnieri, "Il movimento," 659; *Speculum* CCCM, 225 (chapter 79).

42.  MS Vat. lat. 4953, f. 30v; Guarnieri, "Il movimento," 660; *Speculum* CCCM, 233 (chapter 82).

43.  MS Vat. lat. 4953, f. 30v; Guarnieri, "Il movimento," 660; *Speculum* CCCM, 243 (chapter 85).

44.  "Am": the MS has *sunt*. I follow Guarnieri's correction to *sum*.

45.  MS Vat. lat. 4953, ff. 30v–31r; Guarnieri, "Il movimento," 660; *Speculum* CCCM, 313–315 (chapter 117). The text breaks off here, at *cognoscendum humano generis*.

# Appendix 2

# Extracts from a Latin *Mirror of Simple Souls* Appearing in MS 1647

These are English translations of the extracts from a Latin *Mirror* that are presented as errors in MS 1647, on folios 215v-221r. As with MS Vat. lat. 4953, nonitalic text indicates the words of the compiler of the list. Italic text indicates where the *Mirror* is quoted directly. This text mixes paraphrasing and direct quotation much more than the Vatican list. All translations are my own.

1. In a certain book that is entitled *The Mirror of Simple Souls* it is proposed in the beginning of the third chapter a Soul that, as it says there, *is unable to be found, that is saved by faith without works, that is only in Love, that does nothing good on account of God, nor neglects to do any evil on account of God, to whom nothing can be taught, from whom nothing can be taken, nor similarly given, and that inwardly has no will.*[1]

2. The Soul is compared to the seraphim, because *there is no medium in the love between the seraphim and God. Therefore this Soul does not seek knowledge of the divine from the learned or from those who do not know the world, but rather acquires it and earns it by scorning herself and the world. This gift of Love deserves to be received immediately from God Himself.*[2]

---

1. MS 1647, f. 215va; *Speculum CCCM*, 19–21 (chapter 5).
2. MS 1647, f. 216ra; *Speculum CCCM*, 21 (chapter 5).

3. This Soul scoffs at the virtues in this manner: *Virtues, I now recede from you forever, whereby my heart will instead be free, and enjoy greater peace. Everyone knows [that] to serve you is to be much too burdened, as I well know. In another time I placed my heart in you; you know thus that I was wholly given to you. Therefore, I was then your slave, but I have just now been returned to freedom. I endured much bitterness and cruel torments in this service, and I am quite astonished that I have escaped. I was never truly free until I was freely liberated from you.*[3]

4. In the beginning of the fourth chapter it says that this Soul is freed from all passions and desires. *She does not have hell nor does it have paradise*, and this it says is the singular gift of God, more than all the teaching of Scripture and above all human sense. *Nor does creaturely labor or works deserve this, no indeed it is the gift you earn only from Him who is the Most High, into whom this creature is carried by grace. She is lost on account of surpassing knowledge and she is reduced to nothing in her own intellect.*[4] *And such a Soul who has now truly been reduced to nothing has, then, everything, and yet has nothing, knowing everything and yet knowing nothing, willing everything and yet willing nothing.*[5]

5. It says that the Simple Souls have the virtues, but do not have the use of them, because *such Souls are not subject to the Virtues as they used to be. For they were servants long enough, it is right that from now they have full liberty, because*[6] *Love abides in them, and the Virtues serve them without contradiction and without resistance, and without any burden on such Souls.*[7]

6. Likewise below, in the same chapter, it says that it is a great torment for these Souls *to be in love and in obedience to the Virtues, because he who remains in obedience to the Virtues must necessarily give to them whatever they ask, however much it burdens Nature. For the Virtues ask for honors, body, and life.* That is to say, according to the author, *that the Soul, considering all of the aforesaid things, abandons the Virtues. And with all this thus far, such Souls say to the Virtues, who retain for themselves nothing of the necessities of Nature, they say "the just are saved with difficulty."*[8] *Love says: In such debt and obligation these [Souls] live, those over whom the*

---

3. MS 1647, f. 216rb; *Speculum CCCM*, 25 (chapter 6).
4. "Lost": I correct the MS reading of *predicta* to *perdita*, as the former does not make sense.
5. MS 1647, f. 216rb; *Speculum CCCM*, 27 (chapter 7).
6. In the other Latin *Mirror* manuscripts, there are several lines between these two passages (roughly lines 15–21 in *Speculum CCCM*, 29) which here are omitted.
7. MS 1647, f. 216va; *Speculum CCCM*, 29 (chapter 8).
8. 1 Peter 4:18.

*Virtues have power.*[9] *But the Souls about which we speak have brought the Virtues to heel, because they do nothing at all for them. But instead, and conversely, the Virtues yield to a command from these Souls,*[10] *and without hardship and rebellion, because these Souls are the mistresses of the Virtues, and by no means the opposite.*[11]

7. In the fifth chapter, near the beginning, it says that: *Such Souls are unable to be found. They do not have any knowledge of good or evil about themselves, nor can they judge from anything whether they are converted or perverted. Such a Soul, as it is taken [as an example] for all, neither desires nor despises poverty, tribulation, masses, sermons, fasts, or prayers, and always gives to Nature whatever it asks without any remorse of her own conscience. But such a nature is so ordered in herself on account of her full transformation into unity with Love, that she never asks for anything except what is lawful in the highest degree, and what by no means should be denied her. This Soul is not worried or anxious about anything that she may lack, except in the moment of extreme necessity, because only one who is entirely innocent is suitable.*[12]

8. And it says that: *[No] masters in the natural sense, nor doctors of scripture nor those who remain in love or in obedience to the Virtues understand this, nor will they understand that which ought to be understood. Only those alone that Pure Love seeks [will understand it].*[13] *And Love says that this gift is given any time in a moment of one instant, and God gives no higher gift to this creature in life. And it says that this Soul is the Discipline of the Divinity,*[14] *she sits in the Valley of Humility in the Plain of Truth, and rests on the Mountain of Love.*[15] *And she is called the Very Marvelous One, the Unknown One, and the More Innocent of the Daughters of Jerusalem, She Upon Whom the Church is Founded, Illuminated by Understanding, Adorned by Love, Decorated by Praise, Annihilated in All Things by the Highest Humility, Making Peace in the Divine Being through the Divine Will, She Who Is Complete and Perfect without any lack by Divine Goodness through the work of the Trinity, her name is Oblivion. These 12 Names Love gives to her.*[16]

---

9. A few lines are missing here, namely lines 36–38 in *Speculum CCCM*, 31.

10. "To a command": *Ad nutum*. The MS has *ad nuptum*, but this does not make sense.

11. MS 1647, f. 216vb; *Speculum CCCM*, 31 (chapter 8).

12. MS 1647, f. 217ra; *Speculum CCCM*, 33–35 (chapter 9).

13. A few lines are omitted here, lines 31–34 in *Speculum CCCM*, 35.

14. "Discipline": the reading in the *Mirror* is *discipula* (student/disciple), but the MS has *disciplina*. However, rather than a typo, the author in MS 1647 seems to have understood it as *disciplina*, since in his refutation of this point he discusses discipline. I have therefore preserved the reading in the MS.

15. After these three lines are omitted, lines 1–3 of chapter 10 in *Speculum CCCM*, 35.

16. MS 1647, f. 217rb; *Speculum CCCM*, 35–37 (chapters 9–10).

9. In the sixth chapter it makes nine considerations about the Simple Soul.[17] The first is that *such a Soul is not able to be found*. And if there is a reason, it is because *such a Soul knows only one thing, that is the root of all evils and the abundance of all sins without number, without weight, and without measure. And sin is nothing, and less than nothing, and this [Soul] is sunk deep in her horrible defects, she may be beneath less than nothing*. By this understanding it says she is unable to be found.[18]

10. *The second consideration is that such a Soul is saved by faith without works.* The reason: *Because such an Annihilated Soul has so great an understanding from her interior person through the virtue of faith, that she is therefore sustained firmly and sufficiently [with] that faith ministered to her by the Power of the Father, and the Wisdom of the Son, and the Goodness of the Holy Spirit.* And it says other fantastical things that have no foundation.[19]

11. The third consideration is that this Soul is alone in Love, because it does not have affection except only in the Goodness of God. And it is another phoenix, thus it is said: The phoenix is a bird alone in its splendor. How, then, it understands the many living beneath the name.[20]

12. *The fourth is that this Soul does nothing good on account of God.* The reason, according to him [the author], *because God does not care for her work for Him*, about which God Himself does not care.[21]

13. *The fifth consideration is that this Soul does not neglect to do anything evil on account of God.* The reason: *Because this Soul is able to do nothing except only the divine will. She cannot will something else. And therefore she neglects to do nothing evil on account of God.*[22]

14. *The sixth is that this Soul cannot be taught anything for God.* The reason: *If this Soul had all understanding of every creature who was, who will be, and who are, to her would be nothing in comparison to that which she loves from God, that certainly was never known by any creature.*[23]

15. *The seventh is that nothing is able to be taken from this Soul, because whatever may be taken, if only God remained, nothing would be taken from*

---

17. "Considerations": The other Latin MSs have *punctus* rather than *conscideratio*.
18. MS 1647, f. 217va–b; *Speculum CCCM*, 37–39 (chapter 11).
19. MS 1647, f. 217vb; *Speculum CCCM*, 39 (chapter 11).
20. MS 1647, f. 218ra; *Speculum CCCM*, 41 (chapter 11). This is heavily paraphrased but using the same vocabulary as is found in the *Mirror*. I have therefore not used italics as it is mostly the author's arrangement of a passage. The last line is also the author's interpolation, and its meaning is unclear, as the writing is difficult to decipher.
21. MS 1647, f. 218rb; *Speculum CCCM*, 41 (chapter 11). Like the preceding error, this is mostly paraphrased, but using the *Mirror*'s vocabulary.
22. MS 1647, f. 218rb; *Speculum CCCM*, 41–43 (chapter 11).
23. MS 1647, f. 218va; *Speculum CCCM*, 43 (chapter 11).

her.[24] *The eighth is that one cannot give anything to this Soul.* The reason: Because whatever can be given to her is nothing in comparison to that which she loves in herself.[25]

16. *The ninth consideration is that this Soul does not have any will. Because whatever she wills in consent of the will is only that which God wills for her to will, and that from herself and about herself, she is not able to will except that, and the will of God that she wills in herself. Therefore this Soul does not have anything outside the divine will that makes her will whatever she ought to will.*[26]

17. In the seventh chapter in the first column it says concerning this Soul that: *She has neither concern nor anxiety, nor shame; she does not have honor, she does not have poverty, she does not have riches, she does not have comfort, she does not have sadness, she does not have hate, she does not have love, she does not have hell, she does not have paradise. She has everything and has nothing, she herself knows everything and knows nothing, desires everything and desires nothing. And so the Soul does not desire nor despise poverty, neither martyrdom nor tribulations, neither masses nor sermons, neither fasts nor prayers, and she gives to Nature everything that it asks without remorse of conscience.*[27]

18. In the same chapter, on the fifth page in the third column, it introduces Faith, Hope, and Charity, who are in astonishment, asking *Where are the transcendent Souls? Where are they, and what are they doing?* It says that the Lesser Church, which is ruled through these Virtues,[28] *is amazed by this, but not the Greater Church, which is ruled through Love.*[29]

19. On the sixth page, in the first column, it discusses how this Soul has been made the Lady of the Virtues, *and that Divine Love has transformed her completely into herself,* and therefore it says that *Love is God Himself, and this Soul is God by the condition of Love itself.* Beneath these

---

24. MS 1647, f. 218va; *Speculum CCCM*, 43.

25. MS 1647, f. 218va; *Speculum CCCM*, 45 (chapter 11). This line is also heavily paraphrased.

26. MS 1647, f. 218va; *Speculum CCCM*, 49 (chapter 11).

27. MS 1647, f. 218va; *Speculum CCCM*, 55 (chapter 13). This is essentially the same error as number 7.

28. "Ruled through these Virtues": in one *Mirror* manuscript, Verdeyen's manuscript A, this passage says that the Lesser Church is ruled by Reason. But in Verdeyen's manuscripts BCD, as well as Florence, Biblioteca nazionale centrale, MS Conv. soppr. G.3.1130 (here referred to as manuscript J), it reads that the Lesser Church is ruled "by you" (*per vos regitur*), addressing Faith, and in both C and J *virtus fidei* is added after *regitur*. This is a small but substantial change, since criticizing the church for being ruled by the virtue of faith is surely a more daring criticism than for being ruled by reason.

29. MS 1647, f. 219ra; *Speculum CCCM*, 75 (chapter 19). Missing from this passage are lines 3–8 in *Speculum CCCM*.

words Love says that *Love is God and God is Love, and this Soul is God by the condition of Love itself.*[30]

20. On the same page, in the fourth column, it says that *in the cask of divine enjoyment there are many openings. The Humanity of Christ knows this, to which the Person is united by the Word, who tastes from the more noble part after the Trinity, and the Virgin Mother of God, who drinks from the one following, and from the higher one is this Soul intoxicated. And afterward the burning Seraphim drink, and the rest of the holy orders, each according to their own degree, upon whom these Souls fly.*[31]

21. On the seventh page, in the third column, in the beginning, it says that *this Soul feels no joy, because she abides in joy and is submerged in joy, not feeling joy, because she abides in joy and joy in her. Indeed, she is joy itself through the virtue of Joy, which has transformed her into itself. Therefore it is one and indivisible, just as fire and flame, the will of the Lover and the will of the Soul, which is loved because Love has transformed this Soul into herself.*[32]

22. On the same page it compares this Soul to an innocent child, *who does not do anything for the sake of anything, nor does she allow to be done anything except that which pleases her.*[33]

23. On the tenth page, at the end of the first column, it says that this Soul *has heard from the Holy Spirit that God, solely by His goodness, will put the smallest and lowest in the highest place, and therefore such a Soul does not have sorrow over any sin whatsoever that she may have committed, nor does she have hope in something that she might be able to do, except only the goodness of God.*[34]

24. On the same page in the third column, it says that *these Souls are properly called Holy Church, because they sustain and teach and nourish the entire Holy Church, not [only] them but the entire Holy Trinity within them.* It says that to be true and indisputable. It calls the inferior Church— which we say is the militant [Church]—lesser and blind and one-eyed, because it is set beneath the use of Reason.[35]

25. On the twelfth page in the beginning of the first column, it says that *it is fitting that this Soul has to be similar to the Divinity, because she is transformed into God.*[36]

30. MS 1647, f. 219ra–b; *Speculum CCCM*, 83 (chapter 21).
31. MS 1647, f. 219rb; *Speculum CCCM*, 89 (chapter 23).
32. MS 1647, f. 219rb; *Speculum CCCM*, 97 (chapter 28).
33. MS 1647, f. 219rb; *Speculum CCCM*, 99 (chapter 29).
34. MS 1647, f. 219rb; *Speculum CCCM*, 127–129 (end of chapter 40–start of chapter 41).
35. MS 1647, f. 219va; *Speculum CCCM*, 134, lines 1–11 and line 19 (chapter 43).
36. MS 1647, f. 219vb; *Speculum CCCM*, 151 (chapter 51).

26. On the same page in the final column and in the beginning of the following page it demonstrates that *those who live in the work of the Virtues and mortify their body through the work of charity*, believing this to be the perfect life, *with the desire to persevere in this through the help of prayer full of devout entreaties, [and] in the multiplication of goodwill*, believing this to be the sweetest life from all others. It says that *such people are in good works but are lost in their work on account of the sufficiency that they value having in this. Such people are called kings in a country in which everyone is a squinter and sees badly. But those who have two eyes regard them as servants and compare them to little owls, who believe that there may be no more beautiful bird in the forest than their nestlings.* And it says many other foolish things destructive to the foundation of the Church militant, which was founded upon faith and works of charity.[37]

27. On the fourteenth page, at the end and in the first column, it says it is *the one who sits upon the mountain, above the winds and the rain.* And it says that *it is those who on this earth do not have shame nor honor, nor fear on account of anything that may happen to them*, and it says many things which are empty enough, and it calls our Church *little in worth, speedily coming to an end, about which she will have great joy.* And it recapitulates [the Soul's] recession from the works of the Virtues, and it draws from another teaching, and at length it says *this Soul is liquefied, drunk, dissolved, drawn, united, and joined in the Highest Trinity.* Next the Simple Soul jeers against those who live according to Reason: *O most worthless people, rude and incapable.* To whom, responds Reason, are you speaking? The Soul responds: *To all who live by your counsel, who are therefore beasts and asses, that require me to hide my own language on account of their coarseness, lest they should receive death in that being of life in which I am at peace, begging for nothing.* Next it brings in Reason to speak and interrogate as it follows below: *O, for God, sweetest Flower without blemish, how does our practice seem to you?* And it responds: *Yours [seems] to me labor full of occupation, yet one is able to win bread and a daily living through labor, by the many means of this occupation. Christ exalted this by His own body, seeing the bestiality of those who in this labor may be saved, for whom some certainty was necessary, and therefore He who did not wish to lose them assured them through His death and through His Gospels and His Scriptures, through which those laboring people are guided.*[38]

---

37. MS 1647, f. 219vb; *Speculum CCCM*, 159–161 (chapter 55).

38. MS 1647, f. 220ra; *Speculum CCCM*, 187–195 (containing passages from chapters 65, 66, 68, and 69).

28. On the fifteenth page, in the final column, it says that this Soul is interrogated by Reason about why she calls those [people] asses who are the militant [Church] beneath Reason, *those who seek God in creatures, that is to say, in churches for praying, in a created paradise, in the words of humans, in the Scriptures.* She is asked by Reason who this Soul is. She responds that she is that which God is in herself and God is in Himself, that God is in her.[39] And she adds that *it is enough that yours are such people who seek God in mountains and valleys, holding and believing that God may be subject to their sacraments and their works. But those are in a good and profitable time who do not adore God in manufactured temples, but in all places through unity with the divine will.*[40]

29. On the seventeenth page in the first column it says that [the Soul] ought not to be ashamed about sin.[41]

30. On the nineteenth page, in the third column, it says at the end that *this Soul does not seek God through mercy, nor through any sacrament of the Church, nor through meditations, words, works, nor through any creature above, nor through justice, nor through glory of glory, nor through divine knowledge, divine love, nor divine praise.* Next it brings in Reason in amazement, and it contrives that Reason says *What will my children say to me? I do not know what to say to them, nor how to respond in order to excuse this.* And the Soul responds *What a surprise!*[42] *For such people are those who have feet but no path, and hands without work, and mouths without speech, and eyes without sight, and ears without hearing, and reason without reasoning, and body without life, and heart without intellect, as long as they are at this stage. And on account of this they are amazed and beyond amazed about such marvels and are well and truly astonished.*[43]

31. On the 20th page in the first column this Soul speaks about herself:[44] *I was, I am, and I will be always without defect, because Love has no beginning, nor understanding, nor end, and I am not anything other than Love alone.*[45]

32. In the final column of the same [page], in referring to an earlier discussion about *the sad and sorrowful life*, that it calls *the life of the*

---

39. In the other Latin *Mirror* manuscripts, this sentence comes after the one that follows, but here it is cited before.

40. MS 1647, f. 220rb; *Speculum* CCCM, 195–197 (chapter 69).

41. MS 1647, f. 220rb; *Speculum* CCCM, 211. This is a summary of the entirety of chapter 76, which uses Mary Magdalene as an analogy for the Soul.

42. Mystical sarcasm?

43. MS 1647, f. 220va; *Speculum* CCCM, 243 (end of chapter 85 and beginning of chapter 86).

44. "20th": The MS uses Arabic numerals here.

45. MS 1647, f. 220vb; *Speculum* CCCM, 247 (chapter 87).

spirit, [and] places underneath. *Now I say it is the opposite in the life of the Free Soul. The life about which we have spoken, that we call the life of the spirit, is not able to have peace unless the body continuously does the opposite of its desire. That is to say, that such people who live this life, that is the life of the spirit, it is necessary that they do the opposite of sensuality, or else they would fall into perdition from such a life, unless they live according to the opposite of the gratification of their own sensuality. Yet those who are free do the complete opposite, because in the life of the spirit it is necessary that one does everything contrary to their own will, lest they lose peace, so [those who are free] do whatever they wish if they want to retain peace, if they have arrived at the state of freedom. That is, they have fallen from the Virtues into Love, and from Love into Nothingness. They do nothing unless it pleases them, and if they do anything that is not pleasing to them, they take themselves from the peace of freedom and from their nobility, because the Soul is not rightly brought to perfection until she does that which pleases her, and that she is held back by doing the opposite to her pleasure.* And about this it brings in Love as a witness, who above it called God, who thus speaks: *This is true, if your will is ours. She has crossed the Red Sea, and her enemies remain within it. Her pleasure is our will, on account of the purity of unity of the will of the Divinity where we have enclosed her. Her will is ours, because she has fallen from grace into the perfection of the work of the Virtues, and from the Virtues into Love, and from Love into Nothingness, and from Nothingness into Glorification, because there He sees Himself with the eyes of the divine majesty, who has glorified her from Himself in this point. And she is so dissolved in Him, that she sees neither herself nor Him.*[46]

33. On the twenty-first page, in the third column, it says concerning her consorts that *they are naked. They have nothing to hide. All hide themselves. All those, I say, in that place, they do not have another sin, except only from the Annihilated.*[47] *They do not have anything to hide. It is very far from the land of the Virtues, which is worked by the sad and the sorrowful, to the land of the forgotten ones, and the naked and annihilated ones, the glorified ones, who are in the higher status, where Beloved God is in Himself and from Himself.* The same is said on the third page at the end of the fourth column.[48]

---

46. MS 1647, f. 220vb–221ra; *Speculum CCCM*, 255–259 (chapters 90–91).

47. This passage is confusing, due to the fact that in the *Mirror* it is the sin of Adam that is being discussed; Adam makes no such appearance here.

48. MS 1647, f. 221ra–b; *Speculum CCCM*, 265 (chapter 94–95).

34. On the twenty-second page, in the beginning of the third column, it says that *there is as great a difference between the angels and their respective characteristics, as there is between men and brute animals. And angels differ as much from [other] angels as those who are annihilated differ from those about whom we speak, from others who are not this [kind].*[49]

35. On the twenty-sixth page: *Just as Christ by His death is the redemption of the people, so I am by reason of my depravity the salvation of the human race and the glory of God the Father.*[50]

49. MS 1647, f. 221rb; *Speculum CCCM*, 275, lines 1–2 and 5–8 (chapter 100). Lines 3–4 are omitted in the MS.

50. MS 1647, f. 221rb; *Speculum CCCM*, 313 (chapter 117).

# BIBLIOGRAPHY

## Manuscript Sources

*Manuscripts of* The Mirror of Simple Souls

Continental Latin Codices

Bautzen, Domstiftsbibliothek Sankt Petri, MS M I 15

Florence, Biblioteca nazionale centrale, MS Conv. soppr. G.3.1130

Oxford, Bodleian Library, MS Laud Latin 46

Padua, Biblioteca universitaria di Padova, MS 1647

Vatican City, Biblioteca apostolica vaticana

    MS Chigianus B IV 41

    MS Chigianus C IV 85

    MS Ott. lat. 983

    MS Rossianus 4

    MS Vat. lat. 4355

    MS Vat. lat. 4953

French Codices

Chantilly, Musée Condé, MS F XIV 26

Valenciennes, Bibliothèque municipale, MS 239

Italian Codices

Budapest, Országos Széchényi Könyvtár, MS Oct. Ital. 15

Florence, Biblioteca Riccardiana, MS 1468

Naples, Biblioteca nazionale, MS XII F 5

Vienna, Österreichische Nationalbibliothek, MS Palatino 15093

Latin Codex Made from Middle English

Cambridge, Pembroke College, MS 221

Middle English Codices

Cambridge, St John's College, MS 71

London, British Library, MS Additional 37790

Oxford, Bodleian Library, MS Bodley 505

*Other Manuscripts*

Capestrano, Biblioteca Ordini Frati Minori, MS 19

Copenhagen, Det Kongelige Bibliotek, MS Thott 105

Eichstätt, Universitätsbibliothek Eichstätt, MS Cod. st. 435

Gotha, Forschungsbibliothek Gotha, MS Chart.B. 239
London, British Library, MS Arundel 498
Oxford, Bodleian Library, MS Canon. Pat. Lat. 40
Padua, Biblioteca universitaria di Padova
   MS 1645
   MS 1646
   MS 1648
Vatican City, Biblioteca apostolica vaticana
   MS Chigianus A.V. 132
   MS Pal. lat. 600
   MS Vat. lat. 4067
Würzburg, Universitätsbibliothek Würzburg
   MS M.ch.f. 137
   MS M.ch.f. 189
   MS M.ch.f.18

## Printed Primary Sources

*Acta Graduum Academicorum Gymnasii Patavini: Ab Anno 1406 A.D. Annum 1450:*
   *1406–1434.* Vol. 1.1. Edited by Iohanne Brotto and Caspare Zonta. Padua:
   Antenore, 1970.
*Acta Graduum Academicorum Gymnasii Patavini: Ab Anno 1406 A.D. Annum 1450:*
   *1435–1450.* Edited by Iohanne Brotto and Caspare Zonta. Vol. 1.2. Padua:
   Antenore, 1970.
Aeneas Sylvius Piccolomini. *De Gestis Concilii Basiliensis Commentarium Libri II.*
   Edited by Denys Hay and W. K. Smith. Oxford: Oxford University Press,
   1967.
Alzati, Giovanna Cantoni. *La biblioteca di S. Giustina di Padova: Libri e cultura presso i*
   *Benedettini Padovani in età umanistica.* Padua: Antenore, 1982.
Ambrose. *S. Ambrosii Opera Omnia: Expositio Evangelii Secundum Lucam. Patrologia*
   *Latina* 15. https://patristica.net/latina/.
André de Escobar. *Tractatus Polemico-Theologicus de Graecis Errantibus.* Edited by
   Emmanuel Candal. Vol. 1. Rome: Pontificum Institutum Orientalum
   Studiorum, 1952.
Angela of Foligno. *Angela of Foligno: Complete Works.* Edited and translated by Paul
   Lachance. New York: Paulist Press, 1993.
——. *Angela of Foligno: Memorial.* Edited by Cristina Mazzoni. Translated by John
   Cirignano. Cambridge: Cambridge University Press, 1999.
——. *Il libro della beata Angela Da Foligno.* Edited by Ludger Thier and Abul Calufetti.
   Rome: Editiones Collegii san Bonaventurae ad Claras Aquas, 1985.
Antonino Pierozzi. *Lettere di sant'Antonino: Archivescovo di Firenze.* Edited by Tom-
   maso Corsetto. Florence: Tipografica Barbèra, 1859.
Augustine. *Augustine Confessions: Volume 1: Introduction and Text.* Edited by James J.
   O'Donnell. Oxford: Oxford University Press, 1992.
——. *De Libero Arbitrio Libri Tres. Patrologia Latina* 32, https://patristica.net/latina/.
——. *Opera Omnia Augustini Hipponensis: Classa Prima: De Scripturis. Patrologia Latina*
   38. https://patristica.net/latina/.

——. *Opera Omnia Augustini Hipponensis: Classa Prima: S. Aurelii Augustini Hipponensis Episcopi Soliloquiorum Libri Duo. Patrologia Latina* 32. https://patristica.net /latina/.

——. *Opera Omnia Augustini Hipponensis: De Videndo Deo Liber, Seu Epistola CXLVII. Patrologia Latina* 32. https://patristica.net/latina/.

——. *S. Aurelii Augustini Hipponensis Episcopi Soliloquiorum Libri Duo. Patrologia Latina* 32. https://patristica.net/latina/.

Bede. *Super Parabolas Salamonis Allegorica Expositio. Patrologia Latina* 91. https:// patristica.net/latina/.

Bernard of Clairvaux. *Sancti Bernardi Abbatis Claraevallensis Operum Tomus Quartus Complectens Sermones in Cantica Canticorum. Patrologia Latina* 183. https:// patristica.net/latina/.

Bernardino of Siena. *Opera Omnia I: Quadragesimale de Christiana Religione (Sermones I–XLVI)* Edited by Pacifico Perantoni and Agostino Sepinski. Florence: Quaracchi, 1950.

——. *Opera Omnia III: Quadragesimale de Evangelio Aeterno.* Edited by Pacifico Perantoni and Agostino Sepinski. Florence: Quaracchi, 1956.

——. *Prediche volgari sul Campo die Siena.* Edited by Carlo Delcorno. Predica XXIX. Milan: Rusconi, 1989.

——. *Sancti Bernardini Senensis Ordinis Seraphicis Minorum: Opera Omnia.* Edited by Jean de la Haye. Vol. 1. Venice, 1745.

——. *Sancti Bernardini Senensis Ordinis Seraphici Minorum Sermones Eximii de Christo Domino, Augustissimo Eucharistiae Sacramento Deipara Virgine, de Tempore Necnon de Sanctis.* Edited by Jean de la Haye. Vol. 1–5. Venice, 1745.

Boethius. *De Consolatio Philosophiae, Liber Tertius. Patrologia Latina* 63. https:// patristica.net/latina/.

Briquet, Charles Moise. *Les filigranes dictionnaire historique des marques du papier dès leur apparition vers 1282 jusqu'en 1600.* Vol. 3. Paris: Karl W. Hiersemann, 1907. Digitized online as *Briquet Online* by the Österreichische Akademie der Wissenschaften: http://www.ksbm.oeaw.ac.at/_scripts/php/loadRepWmark .php?rep=briquet&refnr=10500&lang=f.

Cassiodorus. *M. Aurelii Cassiodori de Institutione Divinarum Litterarum. Patrologia Latina* 70. https://patristica.net/latina/.

Chatelain, Émile and Heinrich Denifle, eds. *Chartularium Universitatis Parisiensis.* Vol. 1. Paris: Ex typis fratrum Delalain, 1889.

*Congregationis S. Iustinae de Padua O.S.B. Ordinationes Capitulorum Generalium.* Edited by T. Leccisotti. Vol. 1. Montecassino: Badia di Montecassino, 1939.

Contarini, Giovanni B., ed. "Opuscula G. Corrarii." In *Anecdota Veneta*, vol. 1. Venice, 1777.

*Die Register Innocenz III.* Edited by Othmar Hagender, Werner Maleczek, and Alfred A. Strnad. Vienna: Österreichische Akademie der Wissenschaften, 1979.

Eymerich, Nicolaus. *Directorivm Inqvisitorvm R. P. F. Nicolai Eymerici, Ord. Præd. S. Theol. Mag. Inquisitoris Hæreticæ Prauitatis in Regnis Regis Aragonum, Denvo Ex Collatione Plvrivm, Exemplarium Emendatum, et Accessione Multarum Literarum, Apostolicarum, Officio Sanctæ Inquisitionis Deseruientium, Locupletatum, Cvm Scholiis Sev Annotationibvs Eruditissimis D. Francisci Pegnæ Hispani, S. Theologiæ et Iuris Vtriusque Doctoris.* Rome, 1585.

Friedberg, Emil, ed. *Decretum Magistri Gratiani*. In *Corpus Iuris Canonici*. Vol. 1. Leipzig: C. Focke, 1879. Digitized on the *Münchener DigitalisierungZentrum* by the Bayerische Staatsbibliothek: http://geschichte.digitale-sammlungen.de /decretum-gratiani/online/angebot.

———. *Clementis Papae V Constitutiones*. In *Corpus Iuris Canonici*. Vol. 2. Leipzig: C. Focke, 1881.

———. *Liber Extravagantium Decretalium*. In *Corpus Iuris Canonici*. Vol. 2. Leipzig: Bernhard Tauchnitz, 1881.

Gerson, Jean. *De Distinctione Verarum Revelationum a Falsis*. In *Jean Gerson: Oeuvres complètes*, edited by Palémon Glorieux, vol. 3. Paris: Desclée, 1963.

Gratian. *Gratian: The Treatise on Laws, Decretum DD. 1–20, with the Ordinary Gloss*. Translated by James Gordley and Augustine Thompson. Washington, DC: Catholic University of America Press, 1993.

Gregory the Great. *Homiliarum in Evangelia*. Patrologia Latina 76. https://patristica .net/latina/.

———. *Homilia in Ezechielem: Liber Secundus*. Patrologia Latina 76. https://patristica.net /latina/.

———. *Responsoria de Sapientie Salomonis*. Patrologia Latina 78. https://patristica.net /latina/.

Hauptstaatsarchiv Stuttgart. *Wasserzeichensammlung Piccard*. http://www.piccard -online.de/sitemap.php?sprache=.

Hrabanus Maurus. *Beati Rabani Mauri Operum Pars Prima*. Patrologia Latina 109. https://patristica.net/latina/.

———. *Commentariorum in Librum Sapientiae Libri Tres*. Patrologia Latina 109. https:// patristica.net/latina/.

Hüntemann, Ulricus, ed. *Bullarium Franciscanum: Continens Constitutiones, Epistolas, et Diplomata Romanorum Pontificum: Eugenii IV et Nicolai V, ad Tres Ordines S.P.N. Francisci Spectantia: 1431–1455*. Vol. 1. Florence: Quaracchi, 1929.

Isidore of Seville. *Etymologiae*. Translated by Stephen A. Barney. Cambridge: Cambridge University Press, 2006.

———. *Etymologiarum sive Originum Libri XX*. Edited by W. M. Lindsay. Oxford: Clarendon Press, 1911.

Jan van Ruusbroec. *John Ruusbroec: The Spiritual Espousals and Other Works*. Edited and translated by James A. Wiseman OSB. New York: Paulist Press, 1985.

Jerome. *Opera Omnia S. Hieronymi: Complectens Epistolas Ab Anno 386*. Patrologia Latina 22. https://patristica.net/latina/.

John of Segovia. *Monumenta Conciliorum Generalium Seculi Decimi Quinti: Concilium Basiliense*. Edited by F. Palacky and E. von Birk. Vol. 3.3. Vienna: C. R. Officinae Typographicae aulae et status, 1873.

Leo the Great. *Opera Omnia Leonis Magni*. Patrologia Latina 54. https://patristica.net /latina/.

———. *Leo the Great*. Edited and Translated by Bronwen Neil. Abingdon-on-Thames: Routledge, 2009.

Maximus Taurinensis. *Opera Omnia S. Maximi Taurinensi*. Patrologia Latina 57. https://patristica.net/latina/.

Meister Eckhart. *Meister Eckhart: The Essential Sermons, Commentaries, Treatises, and Defense*. Edited by Edmund Colledge and Bernard McGinn. Translated by Bernard McGinn. New York: Paulist Press, 1981.

Munro, Dana Carleton, ed. *Translations and Reprints from the Original Sources of European History*. Vol. 2.3. Philadelphia: University of Pennsylvania Press, 1895.

Nicolo de Fara. *Vita Clarissimi Viri Fratris Joannis de Capistrano*. In *Acta Sanctorum*, edited by Johannes Bolland, Godefridus Henschenius, and Daniel Papebrochius, vol. 10, 439–483. Brussels: Societé des Bollandistes, 1861.

Pelagius. *Libellus Fidei Ad Innocentium*. *Patrologia Latina* 48. https://patristica.net/latina/.

Peter Lombard. *Collectanea in Epistolas Pauli*. *Patrologia Latina* 191 and 192. https://patristica.net/latina/.

———. *In Epistolam ad Romanos*. *Patrologia Latina* 191. https://patristica.net/latina/.

———. *Liber Sententiarum*. *Patrologia Latina* 192. https://patristica.net/latina/.

Marguerite Porete. *Lo specchio delleanime semplici*. Translated by Giovanna Fozzer. Milan: San Paolo, 1994.

———. *Le mirouer des simples âmes anienties et qui seulement demeurent en vouloir et désir d'amour*. Edited by Romana Guarnieri. Rome: Edizioni di storia e letteratura, 1961.

———. *Le mirouer des simples âmes/Speculum Simplicium Animarum*. Edited by Romana Guarnieri and Paul Verdeyen. In *Corpus Christianorum: Continuatio Mediaevalis* 69 (Turnhout: Brepols, 1986).

———. *The Mirror of Simple Souls*. Translated by Ellen L. Babinsky. New York: Paulist Press, 1993.

———. *The Mirror of Simple Souls*. Translated by Edmund Colledge, Judith Grant, and J. C. Marler. South Bend, IN: University of Notre Dame Press, 1999.

———. *The Mirror of Simple Souls: A Middle English Translation*. Edited by Marilyn Doiron. *Archivio italiano per la storia della pietà* 5 (1968): 243–382.

———. *The Mirror of Simple Souls, by an Unknown French Mystic of the Thirteenth Century, Translated into English by M.N.* Edited by Clare Kirchberger. London: Orchard Books, 1927.

———. *Speculum Animarum Simplicium: A Glossed Latin Version of "The Mirror of Simple Souls."* Edited by John Clark. Translated by Richard Methley. In *Analecta Cartusiana* 266. Salzburg: Institut für Anglistik und Amerikanistik, 2010.

Martene, Edmund and Ursini, Duran, eds. *Veterum Scriptorum et Monumentorum Historicorum Dogmaticorum, Moralium, Amplissima Collectio*. Vol. 7. Paris: Franciscum Montalant, 1733.

Thomas Aquinas. *Summa Contra Gentiles*. Edited by Anton C. Pegis, James F. Anderson, and Vernon J. Bourke. South Bend, IN: University of Notre Dame Press, 1955–1957.

Verdeyen, Paul, ed. "Le procès d'inquisition contre Marguerite Porete et Guiard de Cressonessart." *Revue d'histoire ecclésiastique* 81 (1986): 47–94.

Wadding, Luke. *Annales Minorum seu Trium Ordinum a S. Francisco Institutorum*. Edited by Rocco Bernabo and José María Fonseca y Ebora. Vol. 11. Rome, 1734.

## Secondary Sources

Acosta García, Pablo. "Forgotten Marginalia and the French and Latin Manuscript Tradition." *Anuario de estudios medievales* 44, no. 1 (2014): 413–431.

——. "The Marginalia of Marguerite Porete's *Le Mirouer des simple âmes*: Towards a History of the Reading of the Chantilly Manuscript." *Critica del testo* 15, no. 1 (2012): 245–269.

——. "'Notez bien, bonnes pucelles': A Complete Transcription of the French and Continental Latin Annotations of the *Mirror of Simple Souls*." *Sacris Erudiri: Journal of Late Antique and Medieval Christianity* 56 (2017): 347–394.

Aertsen, Jan A., Emery, Kent, and Speer, Andreas. *Nach der Verurteilung Von 1277/ After the Condemnation Of 1277: Philosophie und Theologie an der Universität Paris im Letzten Viertel des 13 Jahrhunderts. Studien und Texte.* Berlin: De Gruyter, 2013.

Arblaster, John. "Iste liber aliter intitulatur Russhbroke: Unanswered Questions Concerning Marguerite Porete and John of Ruusbroec in England." *Ons Geestelijk Erf* 90 (2020): 258–278.

Axters, Stephanus. *Geschiedenis van de Vroomheid in de Nederlanden.* Vol. 2. Antwerp: De Sikkel, 1953.

Backus, Irena, and Gain, Benoît. "Le cardinal Guglielmo Sirleto (1514–1585), sa bibliothèque et ses traductions de Saint Basile." *Mélanges de l'École française de Rome: Moyen-Âge, Temps modernes* 98, no. 2 (1986): 889–955.

Bailey, Michael D. "Magic, Mysticism, and Heresy in the Early Fourteenth Century." In *Late Medieval Heresy: New Perspectives: Studies in Honor of Robert Lerner,* edited by Michael D. Bailey and Sean L. Field, 56–75. Woodbridge, UK: Boydell and Brewer, 2018.

Banfi, Florio. *"Lo specchio delle anime semplici* dalla B. Margarita d'Ungaria scripto." *Memorie Domenicanae* 57 (1940): 3–10, 133–139.

Bauer, Melanie. *Die Universität Padua und ihre fränkischen Besucher: Eine prosopographisch-personengeschichtliche Untersuchung.* Neustadt an der Aisch: Schmidt, 2012.

——. "Fränkische Studenten an der Universität Padua: Johann von Eych und seine *comprovinciales.*" In *Reform und früher Humanismus in Eichstätt: Bischof Johann von Eych (1445–1464).* Edited by Jürgen Dendorfer, 27–46. Regensburg: F. Pustet, 2015.

Bejczy, István P. *The Cardinal Virtues in the Middle Ages: A Study in Moral Thought from the Fourth to the Fourteenth Century.* Leiden: Brill, 2011.

Belloni, Annalisa. *Professori giuristi a Padova nel secolo XV: Profili bio-bibliografici e cattedre.* Frankfurt: Klosterman, 1986.

Bianchi, Luca. *Il vescovo e il filosofi: La condanna parigina del 1277 e l'evoluzione dell'aristotelismo scolastico.* Bergamo: Lubrina, 1990.

Biller, Peter. *The Waldenses: 1170–1530.* Aldershot: Ashgate, 2001.

Blumenfeld-Kosinski, Renate. *Poets, Saints, and Visionaries of the Great Schism, 1378–1417.* Philadelphia: University of Pennsylvania Press, 2006.

Boulnois, Olivier. "Qu'est-ce que la liberté de l'esprit?" In *Marguerite Porete et le "Miroir des simple âmes": Perspectives historiques, philosophiques et littéraires.*

Edited by Sean L. Field, Robert E. Lerner, and Sylvain Piron, 127–154. Paris: Vrin, 2013.

Brown, Elizabeth A. R. "Jean Gerson, Marguerite Porete and Romana Guarnieri: The Evidence Reconsidered." *Revue d'histoire ecclésiastique* 108, no. 3–4 (2013): 693–734.

——. "Marguerite Porète, une béguine brûlée pour hérésie." In *L'affaire des Templiers, du procès au mythe*. Paris, 2011.

——. "Veritas à la cour de Philippe le Bel de France: Pierre Dubois, Guillaume de Nogaret et Marguerite Porete." In *La vérité: Vérité et crédibilité: Construire la vérité dans le système de communication de l'Occident (XIIIᵉ–XVIIᵉ siècle)*. Edited by Jean-Philippe Genet.425–445 Paris: Éditions de la Sorbonne, 2015.

Bryce, Judith. "Dada degli Adimari's Letters from Saint Antonino: Identity, Maternity, and Spirituality." *I Tatti Studies in the Italian Renaissance* 12 (2009): 11–53.

Bueno, Irene. "Late Medieval Heresiography and the Categorisation of Eastern Christianity." In *Inquisition and Knowledge 1200–1700*. Edited by Peter Biller and Lucy Sackville, 135–156. York, UK: York Medieval Press, 2022.

Burnham, Louisa. *So Great a Light, So Great a Smoke: The Beguin Heretics of Languedoc*. Ithaca, NY: Cornell University Press, 2008.

Burr, David. *Olivi's Peaceable Kingdom: A Reading of the Apocalypse Commentary*. Philadelphia: University of Pennsylvania Press, 1993.

——. *The Spiritual Franciscans: From Protest to Persecution in the Century After Saint Francis*. University Park: Penn State University Press, 2001.

Bynum, Caroline Walker. *Resurrection of the Body*. New York: Columbia University Press, 1995.

Caciola, Nancy. *Discerning Spirits: Divine and Demonic Possession in the Middle Ages*. Ithaca, NY: Cornell University Press, 2003.

Caldwell Ames, Christine. *Medieval Heresies*. Cambridge: Cambridge University Press, 2015.

Cocci, Alfredo. "Alvaro Pais e il Libero Spirito: i capitoli 51 e 52 del libro secondo del 'De statu et planctu Ecclesiae.'" *L'Italia francescana: rivista trimestrale di cultura francescana* 58 (1983): 256–310

Colledge, Edmund, and Guarnieri, Romana. "The Glosses by 'M.N.' and Richard Methley to 'The Mirror of Simple Souls.'" Appendix to *The Mirror of Simple Souls: A Middle English Translation*. Edited by Marilyn Doiron. *Archivio italiano per la storia della pietà* 5 (1968): 357–382.

Colledge, Edmund, and Marler, J. C. "'Poverty of the Will': Ruusbroec, Eckhart, and *The Mirror of Simple Souls*." In *Jan van Ruusbroec: The Sources, Content, and Sequels of His Mysticism*, edited by Paul Mommaers and N. De Paepe, 14–47. Leuven: Leuven University Press, 1984.

Collette, Barry. *Italian Benedictine Scholars and the Reformation*. Oxford: Clarendon Press, 1985.

Combes, André. *Essai sur la critique de Ruysbroeck par Gerson*. 4 vols. Paris: Vrin, 1945–1972.

Corbellini, Sabrina. "Beyond Orthodoxy and Heterodoxy: A New Approach to Late Medieval Religious Reading." In *Cultures of Religious Reading in the Late Middle Ages: Instructing the Soul, Feeding the Spirit, and Awakening the Passion*, edited by Sabrina Corbellini, 33–53. Turnhout: Brepols, 2013.

Courtenay, William. "Inquiry and Inquisition: Academic Freedom in Medieval Universities." *Church History* 58 (1989): 168–181.

———. "Marguerite's Judges: The University of Paris in 1310." In *Marguerite Porete et le "Miroir des simple âmes": Perspectives historiques, philosophiques et littéraires*, edited by Sean L. Field, Robert E. Lerner, and Sylvain Piron, 215–248. Paris: Vrin, 2013.

Coxe, H. O., and Hunt, R. W. *Laudian Manuscripts: Reprinted from the Edition of 1858–1885, with Corrections and Additions, and an Historical Introduction by R. W. Hunt*. Edited by R. W. Hunt. Quarto Catalogues, vol. 2. Oxford: Bodleian Library, 1973.

Cracco, Giorgio. "La fondazione dei canonici secolari di S. Giorgio in Alga." *Rivista di storia della chiesa in Italia* 13 (1959): 71–81.

Cré, Marleen. "Contexts and Comments: The Chastising of God's Children and Marguerite Porète's *Mirour of Simple Souls* in Oxford, MS Bodley 505." In *Medieval Texts in Context*, edited by Graham D. Caie and Denis Reveney. 122–135. London: Routledge, 2008.

———. *Vernacular Mysticism in the Charterhouse: A Study of London, British Library, MS Additional 37790*. Turnhout: Brepols, 2006.

———. "Women in the Charterhouse? Julian of Norwich's Revelations of Divine Love and Marguerite Porete's *Mirror of Simple Souls* in British Library, MS Additional 37790." In *Writing Religious Women: Female Spiritual and Textual Practices in Late Medieval England*, edited by Deni Renevey and Christina Whitehead, 43–62. Toronto: University of Toronto Press, 2000.

Dando, Marcel. "L'adaptation provençale de l'Elucidarium d'Honoré d'Autun et le catharisme." *Cuadernos de Estudios Gallegos* 28 (1977): 3–34.

Dendorfer, Jürgen. "Einleitung." In *Reform und früher Humanismus in Eichstätt: Bischof Johann von Eych (1445–1464)*, edited by Jürgen Dendorfer, 27–46. Regensburg: F. Pustet, 2015.

Dubois, Danielle. "Natural and Supernatural Virtues in the Thirteenth Century: The Case of Marguerite Porete's *Mirror of Simple Souls*." *Journal of Medieval History* 43, no. 2 (2017): 174–192.

———. "Transmitting the Memory of a Medieval Heretic: Early Modern French Historians on Marguerite Porete." *French Historical Studies* 41, no. 4 (2018): 579–610.

Du Fresne, Charles [Du Cange]. *Glossarium Mediae et Infimae Latinitatis*. Niort: L. Favre. Vol. 1-10.1883–1887.

Dunne, Michael W. "Richard FitzRalph on the Beatific Vision: *Delectatio* and *Beatitudo* in His Oxford Lectures on the Sentences." *Irish Theological Quarterly* 80, no. 4 (2015): 327–341.

Dzon, Mary. "Cecily Neville and the Apocryphal *Infantia Salvatoris* in the Middle Ages." *Mediaeval Studies* 71 (2009): 235–300.

Elliott, Dyan. *Proving Woman: Female Spirituality and Inquisitional Culture in the Later Middle Ages*. Princeton: Princeton University Press.

Epiney-Burgard, Georgette, and Zum Brunn, Emilie. *Women Mystics in Medieval Europe*. Translated by Sheila Hughes. New York: Paragon, 1989.

Falvay, Dávid. "The Italian Version of the *Mirror*: Manuscripts, Diffusion and Communities in the 14–15th Century." In *A Companion to Marguerite Porete and*

*"The Mirror of Simple Souls,"* edited by Robert Stauffer and Wendy R. Terry, 218–239. Leiden: Brill, 2017.

Falvay, Dávid, and Konrád, Eszter. "Osservanza francescana e letteratura in volgare dall'Italia all'Ungheria: Richerche e perspettive." In *Osservanza francescana e cultura tra Quattrocento e primo Cinquecento: Italia e Ungheria a confronto: [Atti del Convegno (Macerata-Sarnano, 6–7 dicembre 2013)]*, edited by Francesca Bartolacci and Roberto Lambertini, 161–186. Rome: Viella, 2014.

Field, Sean L. *The Beguine, the Angel, and the Inquisitor: The Trials of Marguerite Porete and Guiard of Cressonessart.* South Bend, IN: University of Notre Dame Press, 2012.

——. "Debating the Historical Marguerite Porete." In *A Companion to Marguerite Porete and "The Mirror of Simple Souls,"* edited by Robert Stauffer and Wendy R. Terry, 9–37. Leiden: Brill, 2017.

——. "The Inquisitor Ralph of Ligny, Two German Templars, and Marguerite Porete." *Journal of Medieval Religious Cultures* 39, no. 1 (2013): 1–22.

——. "The Master and Marguerite: Godfrey of Fontaines's Praise of the 'Mirror of Simple Souls.'" *Journal of Medieval History* 35 (2009).

Field, Sean L., Lerner, Robert E., and Piron, Sylvain. "Marguerite Porete et son *Miroir*: Perspectives historiographiques." In *Marguerite Porete et le "Miroir des simple âmes": Perspectives historiques, philosophiques et littéraires*, edited by Sean L. Field, Robert E. Lerner, and Sylvain Piron, 9–23. Paris: Vrin, 2013.

Field, Sean L., Lerner, Robert E., and Piron, Sylvain. "A Return to the Evidence for Marguerite Porete's Authorship of *The Mirror of Simple Souls,*" *Journal of Medieval History* 43, no. 2 (2017): 153–173.

Finke, Heinrich. *Forschungen und Quellen zur Geschichte des Konstanzer Konzils.* Paderborn: Ferdinand Schöningh, 1889.

Fink-Lang, Monica. *Untersuchungen zum Eichstätter Geistesleben im Zeitalter des Humanismus.* Regensburg: F. Pustet, 1985.

Gagliardi, Isabella. *I Pauperes Yesuati: Tra esperienze religiose e conflitti istituzionali.* Rome: Herder, 2004.

Gargan, Luciano. "L'enigmatico 'conduxit': Libri e dogana a Padova fra Tre e Quattrocento." *Quaderni per la storia dell'università di Padova* 16 (1983): 1–41.

Gill, Joseph. . Eugenius IV: Pope of Christian Union. Westminster, MD: Newman Press, 1961.

Gill, Joseph. 'The Council of Florence.' Cambridge, UK: Cambridge University Press, 1959.

Griguolo, Primo. "Per la biografia del canonista ferrarese Giacomo Zocchi († 1457): L'insegnamento, la famiglia, i libri." *Quaderni per la storia dell'università di Padova* 44 (2011): 181–209.

Grundmann, Herbert. "'Oportet et haereses esse': Das Problem der Ketzerei im Spiegel der mittelalterlichen Bibelexegese." *Archiv für Kulturgeschichte* 45 (1963): 129–164.

Guarnieri, Romana. "Il movimento del libero spirito." *Archivio italiano per la storia della pietà* 4 (1965): 353–708.

——. "Lo *specchio delle anime semplici* e Margherita Porete." *L'Osservatore Romano,* 16 June 1946.

Hasenohr, Geneviève. "La seconde vie du *Miroir des simples âmes* en France: Le livre de la discipline d'amour divine (XVᵉ–XVIIIᵉ s.)." In *Marguerite Porete et le "Miroir des simple âmes": Perspectives historiques, philosophiques et littéraires*, edited by Sean L. Field, Robert E. Lerner, and Sylvain Piron, 263–288. Paris: Vrin, 2013.

———. "La tradition du *Miroir des simples âmes* au XVᵉ siècle: De Marguerite Porete (†1310) à Marguerite de Navarre." *Comptes rendus des séances de l'Académie des Inscriptions et Belles-Lettres* 143, no. 4 (1999): 1347–1366.

———. "Retour sur les caractères linguistiques du manuscrit de Chantilly et de ses ancêtres." In *Marguerite Porete et le "Miroir des simples âmes": Perspectives historiques, philosophiques et littéraires*, edited by Sean L. Field, Robert E. Lerner, and Sylvain Piron.103–126. Paris: Vrin, 2013.

———. "The Tradition of the *Mirror of Simple Souls* in the Fifteenth Century: From Marguerite Porete (†1310) to Marguerite of Navarre (†1549)." Translated by Zan Kocher. In *A Companion to Marguerite Porete and "The Mirror of Simple Souls,"* edited by Robert Stauffer and Wendy R. Terry, 155–185. Leiden: Brill, 2017.

Haubst, Rudolf. *Studien zu Nikolaus von Kues und Johannes Wenck aus Handschriften der Vatikanischen Bibliothek*. Münster: Aschendorff, 1955.

Heimann, Claudia. *Nicolaus Eymerich (vor 1320–1399): Praedicator viridus, inquisitor intrepidus, doctor egregious: Leben und Werk eines Inquisitors*. Münster: Aschendorff, 2001.

Hillgarth, J. N. *Ramon Lull and Lullism in Fourteenth-Century France*. Oxford: Clarendon Press, 1971.

Hobbins, Daniel. *Authorship and Publicity in the Age Before Print: Jean Gerson and the Transformation of Late Medieval Learning*. Philadelphia: University of Pennsylvania Press, 2009.

———. "The Schoolman as Public Intellectual: Jean Gerson and the Late Medieval Tract." *The American Historical Review* 108 (2003): 1308–1335.

Huizinga, Johan. *The Autumn of the Middle Ages*. Translated by Rodney J. Payton and Ulrich Mammitzsch. Chicago: University of Chicago Press, 1996.

Hussey, S. S. "Latin and English in the Scale of Perfection." *Mediaeval Studies* 35 (1973): 456–476.

Hyland, William P. "The Climacteric of Late Medieval Camaldolese Spirituality: Ambrogio Traversari, John-Jerome of Prague, and the *Linea salutis heremitarum*." In *Florence and Beyond: Culture, Society, and Politics in Renaissance Italy: Essays in Honor of John M. Najemy*, edited by D. S. Peterson and D. E. Bornstein, 107–120. Toronto: Centre for Reformation and Renaissance Studies, 2008.

———. "Giovanni-Girolamo da Praga al Concilio di Basileo: Varieta del discorso di riforma." In *Camaldoli e l'ordine Camaldolese dalle origini alla fine del XV secolo*, edited by Cécile Caby and Pierluigi Licciardello, 473–484. Cesena: Centro Storico Benedetto, 2014.

———. "John-Jerome of Prague and Monastic Reform in the Fifteenth Century." *The American Benedictine Review* 47, no. 1 (1996): 58–98.

———. "John-Jerome of Prague (1368–1440) and the *Errores Graecorum*: Anatomy of a Polemic Against Greek Christians." *The Journal of Religious History* 21, no. 3 (1997): 249–267.

——. "John-Jerome of Prague: Portrait of a Fifteenth-Century Camaldolese." *American Benedictine Review* 46, no. 3 (1995): 308–334.

——. "Reform Preaching and Despair at the Council of Pavia-Siena (1423–1424)." *The Catholic Historical Review* 84, no. 3 (1998): 409–430.

Imbach, Ruedi. "Notule sur Jean Gerson, critique de Raymond Lulle." In *Les formes laïques de la philosophie: Raymond Lulle dans l'histoire de la philosophie médiévale*, edited by D. de Courcelles, 139–157. Turnhout: Brepols, 2018.

Izbicki, Thomas M., and Bancroft, Luke. "A Difficult Pope: Eugenius IV and the Men Around Him." In *Nicholas of Cusa and the Making of the Early Modern World*, edited by Simon J. G. Burton, Joshua Hollman, and Eric M. Parker, 49–73. Leiden: Brill, 2019.

Johnston, Michael, and Van Dussen, Michael. "Introduction: Manuscripts and Cultural History." In *The Medieval Manuscript Book: Cultural Approaches*, edited by Michael Johnston and Michael Van Dussen, 1–16. Cambridge: Cambridge University Press, 2015.

Jonker, Esther. "'Teksten op reis': Handschriftelijke getuigen van betrekkingen tussen Brabant en Bovenrijn in de veertiende eeuw." *Ons Geestelijk Erf* 83 (2012): 243–263.

Kaminsky, Howard. "From Lateness to Waning to Crisis: The Burden of the Middle Ages." *Journal of Early Modern History* 4, no. 1 (2000): 85–125.

Kappes, Christiaan. *The Epiclesis Debate at the Council of Florence.* South Bend, IN: University of Notre Dame Press, 2019.

——. Foreword to J. Isaac Goff, *Caritas in Primo: A Historical-Theological Study of Bonaventure's "Quaestiones disputate de mysterio Ss. Trinitatis,"* xvii–xxxii. New Bedford, MA: Academy of the Immaculate, 2015.

Kelly, Henry Ansgar. "Inquisitorial Deviations and Cover-Ups: The Prosecutions of Margaret Porete and Guiard of Cressonessart, 1308–1310." *Speculum* 89 (2014): 936–973.

Kerby-Fulton, Kathryn. *Books under Suspicion: Censorship and Tolerance of Revelatory Writing in Late Medieval England.* South Bend, IN: University of Notre Dame Press, 2006.

——. "Introduction: Taking Early Women Intellectuals Seriously." In *Women Intellectuals and Leaders in the Middle Ages*, edited by Kathryn Kerby-Fulton, Katie Anne-Marie Bugyis, and John Van Engen, 1–18. Woodbridge, UK: Boydell and Brewer, 2020.

Kieckhefer, Richard. *Repression of Heresy in Medieval Germany.* Liverpool: University of Liverpool Press, 1979.

King, Margaret L. *Humanism, Venice, and Women: Essays on the Italian Renaissance.* Aldershot: Ashgate, 2005.

——. *Venetian Humanism in an Age of Patrician Dominance.* Princeton: Princeton University Press, 1986.

King, Margaret L., and Rabil, Albert. *Her Immaculate Hand: Selected Works by and about the Women Humanists of Quattrocento Italy.* Binghamton, NY: Center for Medieval and Early Renaissance Studies, 1983.

King, Peter. "Marguerite Porete and Godfrey of Fontaines: Detachable Will, Discardable Virtue, Transformative Love." *Oxford Studies in Medieval Philosophy* 6, no. 1 (2018): 168–188.

Klaniczay, Gábor. *Holy Rulers and Blessed Princesses: Dynastic Cults in Medieval Central Europe.* Translated by Éva Pálmai. Cambridge: Cambridge University Press, 2000.

Klima, Gyula, Allhoff, Fritz, and Vaidya, Anand Jayprakash, eds., *Medieval Philosophy: Essential Readings with Commentary.* Oxford: Wiley-Blackwells, 2007.

Koch, Josef. "Philosophische und Theologische Irrtumslisten von 1270–1329: Ein Beitrag zur Entwicklung der Theologischen Zensuren." In *Kleine Schriften,* vol. 2, 423–450. Rome: Edizioni di storia e letteratura, 1973.

Kocher, Zan [Suzanne]. *Allegories of Love in Marguerite Porete's "Mirror of Simple Souls."* Turnhout: Brepols, 2009.

———. "The Apothecary's Mirror of Simple Souls: Circulation and Reception of Marguerite Porete's Book in Fifteenth-Century France." *Modern Philology* 111, no. 1 (2013): 23–47.

Kolpacoff Deane, Jennifer. "Did Beguines Have a Late Medieval Crisis? Historical Models and Historiographical Martyrs." *Early Modern Women* 8 (2013): 275–288.

Kolpacoff Deane, Jennifer, ed. *Herbert Grundmann (1902–1970): Essays on Heresy, Inquisition, and Literacy.* Woodbridge, UK: Boydell and Brewer, 2019.

Lefèvre, Yves. *L'Elucidarium et les Lucidaires: Contribution, par l'histoire d'un texte, à l'histoire des croyances religieuses en France au moyen âge.* Paris: E. de Boccard, 1954.

Lerner, Robert E. "Addenda on an Angel." In *Marguerite Porete et le "Miroir des simples âmes": Perspectives historiques, philosophiques et littéraires,* edited by Sean L. Field, Robert E. Lerner, and Sylvain Piron, 197–213. Paris: Vrin, 2013.

———. "An 'Angel of Philadelphia' in the Reign of Philip the Fair: The Case of Guiard of Cressonessart." In *Order and Innovation in the Middle Ages: Essays in Honor of Joseph Strayer,* edited by William Chester Jordan and Teofilo F. Ruiz, 343–364. Princeton: Princeton University Press, 1976.

———. *The Heresy of the Free Spirit in the Later Middle Ages.* Berkeley: University of California Press, 1972.

———. "Meister Eckhart's Specter: Fourteenth-Century Uses of the Bull *In agro dominico* Including a Newly Discovered Inquisitorial Text of 1337." *Mediaeval Studies* 70 (2008): 115–134.

———. "New Light on *The Mirror of Simple Souls.*" *Speculum* 85 (2010): 91–116.

Lester, Anne E. "Women Behind the Law: Lay Religious Women in Thirteenth-Century France and the Problem of Textual Resistance." In *Jews and Christians in Thirteenth-Century France,* edited by Elisheva Baumgarten and Judah D. Galinsky, 183–202. New York: Palgrave Macmillan, 2015.

Littger, Klaus Walter. "Ob memoriam quondam venerabilis viri, qui hoc in testamento suo fieri deposuit: Die fata libellorum der frühen Eichstätter Humanisten." In *Reform und früher Humanismus in Eichstätt: Bischof Johann von Eych (1445–1464),* edited by Jürgen Dendorfer, 383–403. Regensburg: F. Pustet, 2015.

Loenertz, R. "Autour du traité de Fr. Barthélemy de Constantinople contre les Grecs." *Archivum Fratrum Praedicatorum* 6 (1936): 361–371.

Love Anderson, Wendy. *The Discernment of Spirits: Assessing Visions and Visionaries in the Late Middle Ages.* Tübingen: Mohr Siebeck, 2011.

Lu, Huanan. "Marguerite Porete et l'enquête de 1323 sur le béguinage Sainte-Élisabeth de Valenciennes." *Revue du Nord* 440 (2021): 451–485.

Lutton, Rob. "Devotion to the Holy Name of Jesus in the Medieval West." In *Illuminating Jesus in the Middle Ages*, edited by Jane Beal, 129–153. Leiden: Brill, 2019.

Madre, Alois. *Die Theologische Polemik gegen Raimundus Lullus: Eine Untersuchung zu den Elenchi auctorum de Raimundo male sentientium*. Münster: Aschendorff, 1973.

Maguire Robinson, Joanne. *Nobility and Annihilation in Marguerite Porete's "Mirror of Simple Souls."* New York: SUNY Press, 2001.

Mairhofer, Daniela. *Medieval Manuscripts from Würzburg in the Bodleian Library: A Descriptive Catalogue*. Oxford: Bodleian Library, 2015.

Makowski, Elizabeth. *A Pernicious Sort of Woman: Quasi-Religious Women and Canon Lawyers in the Later Middle Ages*. Washington, DC: Catholic University of America Press, 2005.

——. "When Is a Beguine Not a Beguine?" In *Labels and Libels: Naming Beguines in Northern Medieval Europe*, edited by Letha Böhringer, Jennifer Kolpacoff Deane, and Hildo van Engen, 83–98. Turnhout: Brepols, 2014.

McAodha, Loman. "The Holy Name of Jesus in the Preaching of St Bernardine of Siena." *Franciscan Studies* 29 (1969): 37–65.

McGinn, Bernard. *The Flowering of Mysticism: Men and Women in the New Mysticism, 1200–1350*. New York: Crossroad, 1998.

Mittarelli, Giovanni Benedetto. *Bibliotheca Codicum Manuscriptorum Monasterii S. Michaelis Venetiarum Prope Murianum, una cum Appendice Librorum Impressorum Seculi XV, Opus Posthumum Johannis-Benedicti Mittarelli*. Venice: Typographia Fentiana, 1779.

Mixson, James D. *Poverty's Proprietors: Ownership and Mortal Sin at the Origins of the Observant Movement*. Leiden: Brill, 2009.

Mixson, James D., and Roest, Bert. *A Companion to Observant Reform in the Late Middle Ages and Beyond*. Leiden: Brill, 2015.

Montobbio, Luigi. "I quattro codici di Giacomo Zocchi." *Benedictina* 10 (1956): 49–60.

Mormando, Franco. *The Preacher's Demons: Bernardino of Siena and the Social Underworld of Early Renaissance Italy*. Chicago: University of Chicago Press, 1999.

Newman, Barbara. "Annihilation and Authorship: Three Women Mystics of the 1290s." *Speculum* 91, no. 3 (2016): 591–630.

——. *Medieval Crossover: Reading the Secular against the Sacred*. South Bend, IN: University of Notre Dame Press, 2013.

——. "The Mirror and the Rose: Marguerite Porete's Encounter with the Dieu d'Amours." In *The Vernacular Spirit: Essays on Medieval Religious Literature*, edited by Renate Blumenfeld-Kosinski, Duncan Robertson, and Nancy Bradley, 105–123. New York: Palgrave Macmillan, 2002.

Nieto Isabel, Delfi I. "Beliefs in Progress: The Beguins of Languedoc and the Construction of a New Heretical Identity." *SUMMA: Revista de Cultures Medievals* 15 (2020): 95–117.

——. "Communities of Dissent: Social Network Analysis of Religious Dissident Groups in Languedoc in the Thirteenth and Fourteenth Centuries." PhD diss., University of Barcelona, 2018.

——. "Overlapping Networks: Beguins, Franciscans, and Poor Clares at the Crossroads of a Shared Spirituality." In *Clarisas y dominicas: Modelos de implantación, filiación, promoción y devoción en la Península Ibérica, Cerdeña, Nápoles y Sicilia*, edited by Gemma Teresa Colesanti, Blanca Garì, and Núria Jornet-Benito, 429–448. Florence: Firenze University Press, 2017.

Nold, Patrick. "New Annotations of Pope John XXII and the Process Against Peter of John Olivi's *Lectura super Apocalipsim*: The Marginalia of MS Paris BnF lat. 3381A." *Oliviana* 4 (2012): 1–48.

O'Sullivan, Robin Anne. "The School of Love: Marguerite Porete's *Mirror of Simple Souls*." *Journal of Medieval History* 32 (2006): 143–162.

Orcibal, Jean. "Le 'Miroir des simples âmes' et la 'secte' du libre esprit." *Revue d'histoire des religions* 176 (1969): 35–60.

Ozment, Steven. *The Age of Reform (1250–1550): An Intellectual and Religious History of Late Medieval and Reformation Europe*. New Haven, CT: Yale University Press, 1980.

Penco, Gregorio. "Lo *Speculum simplicium animarum* al S. Speco di Subiaco." *Benedictina* 34 (1987): 529–30.

Pesce, Luigi. *Ludovico Barbo: Vescovo di Treviso (1437–1443)*. Padova: Antenore, 1969.

Piccard, Gerhard. *Die Wasserzeichenkartei in Hauptstaatsarchiv Stuttgart: Dreiberg*. Vol. 16. Stuttgart: Kohlhammer, 1996.

Pinel, Élodie. "Forme et sens chez Eckhart et Marguerite Porete." In *Maître Eckhart, une écriture inachevée: Nouvelles perspectives théologiques, philosophiques et littéraires*, edited by Élisabeth Boncour, 147–166. Grenoble: Jérôme Millon, 2017.

Piron, Sylvain. "Censures et condamnation de Pierre de Jean Olivi: Enquête dans les marges du Vatican." *Mélanges de l'École française de Rome: Moyen-Âge* 118, no. 2 (2006): 313–373.

——. "Marguerite, entre les béguines et les maîtres." In *Marguerite Porete et le "Miroir des simples âmes": Perspectives historiques, philosophique, et littéraires*, edited by Sean L. Field, Robert E. Lerner, and Sylvain Piron, 69–102. Paris: Vrin, 2013.

——. "Marguerite in Champagne." *Journal of Medieval Religious Cultures* 43 (2017): 135–156.

——. "Recovering a Theological Advice by Jacques Fournier." In *Pope Benedict XII (1334–1342): The Guardian of Orthodoxy*, edited by Irene Bueno, 57–80. Amsterdam: Amsterdam University Press, 2018.

Polecritti, Cynthia. *Preaching Peace in Renaissance Italy: Bernardino of Siena and His Crowd*. Washington, DC: Catholic University of America Press, 2000.

Preger, Wilhelm. "Beiträge zur Geschichte der religiösen Bewegung in den Niederlanden in der 2 Hälfte des 14 Jahrhunderts." *Abhandlungen der historischen Classe der Königlich Bayerischen Akademie der Wissenschaften* 21 (1898): 1–63.

Pyl, Theodor. *Die Rubenow Bibliothek: Die Handschriften und Urkunden der von Heinrich Rubenow 1456 Gestifteten Juristen- und Artisten-Bibliothek zu Greifswald*. Greifswald: Reinhold Scharff, 1865.

Robson, Michael J. P. *The Franciscans in the Middle Ages*. Woodbridge, UK: Boydell and Brewer, 2006.

Römer, Franz. "A Late Mediaeval Collection of Epistles Ascribed to Saint Augustine." *Augustinian Studies* 2 and 3 (1971–1972): 115–154 and 147–189.

——. "Notes on the Composition of Some Pseudo-Augustinian Letters." *Studia Patristica* 14 (1976): 487–495.

Ruh, Kurt. "Beginenmystik: Hadewijch, Mechthild von Magdeburg, Marguerite Porete." *Zeitschrift für deutsches Altertum und deutsche Literatur* 106 (1977): 265–277.

Rusconi, Robert. "Il sacramento della penitenza nella predicazione di San Bernardino da Siena." *Aevum* 47, no. 3 (1973): 235–286.

Russell, Norman. "The Hesychast Controversy." In *An Intellectual History of Byzantium*, edited by Anthony Kaldellis and Niketas Siniossoglou, 494–508. Cambridge: Cambridge University Press, 2017.

Sackville, L. J. *Heresy and Heretics in the Thirteenth Century: The Textual Representations.* Woodbridge, UK: Boydell and Brewer, 2011.

Sargent, Michael. "The Annihilation of Marguerite Porete." *Viator* 28 (1997): 253–280.

———. "'Le Mirouer des simples âmes' and the English Mystical Tradition." In *Abendländische Mystik im Mittelalter*, edited by Kurt Ruh, 443–465. Stuttgart: Springer, 1986.

———. "Medieval and Modern Readership of Marguerite Porete's *Mirouer des simples âmes anienties*: The French and English Traditions." In *English Religious Writing in Practice: Texts, Readers, and Transformations*, edited by Nicole Rice, 47–89. Turnhout: Brepols, 2013.

———. "Medieval and Modern Readership of Marguerite Porete's *Mirouer des simples âmes anienties*: The Manuscripts of the Continental Latin and Italian Tradition." In *The Medieval Translator/Traduire Au Moyen Age 15: In Principio Fuit Interpres*, edited by Alessandra Petrina, 85–96. Turnhout: Brepols, 2013.

Scheepsma, Wybren. "Godsvrienden, Jan van Ruusbroec en de Moderne Devotie: Religieuze Bewegingen van de Veertiende Eeuw en hun Verhouding Tot de Volkstalige Geestelijke Literatuur." *Spiegel de Letteren* 56, no. 4 (2014): 477–509.

Shaw, Robert L. J. *The Celestine Monks of France: Observant Reform in an Age of Schism, Council, and War.* Amsterdam: Amsterdam University Press, 2018.

Simons, Walter. *Cities of Ladies: Beguine Communities in the Medieval Low Countries, 1200–1565.* Philadelphia: University of Pennsylvania Press, 2001.

Skårup, Povl. "La langue du *Miroir des simples âmes* attribué à Marguerite Porete." *Studia Philologica* 60, no. 2 (1988): 231–236.

Solvi, Daniele. "Giovanni of Capestrano's Liturgical Office for the Feast of Saint Bernardino of Siena." *Franciscan Studies* 75 (2017): 49–71.

Sottili, Agostino. *Studenti tedeschi e umanesimo italiano nell'Università di Padova durante il Quattrocento.* Padua: Antenore, 1971.

Stabler Miller, Tanya. *The Beguines of Medieval Paris: Gender, Patronage, and Spiritual Authority.* Philadelphia: University of Pennsylvania Press, 2014.

Stauffer, Robert. "Possibilities for the Identity of the English Translator of *The Mirror of Simple Souls.*" In *A Companion to Marguerite Porete and "The Mirror of Simple Souls,"* edited by Robert Stauffer and Wendy R. Terry, 264–288. Leiden: Brill, 2017.

Stieber, Joachim. *Pope Eugenius IV, The Council of Basel, and the Secular and Ecclesiastical Authorities in the Empire: The Conflict over Supreme Authority and Power in the Church.* Leiden: Brill, 1978.

Stinger, Charles L. *Humanism and the Church Fathers: Ambrogio Traversari (1386–1439) and Christian Antiquity in the Italian Renaissance.* Albany, NY: SUNY Press, 1977.

Sturgeon, Johnna. "Cares at the Curia: Andreas de Escobar and Ecclesiastical Controversies at the Time of the Fifteenth-Century Councils." PhD diss., Northwestern University, 2017.

Sullivan, Ezra, OP. "Antonino Pierozzi: A *Locus* of Dominican Influence in Late Medieval and Early Renaissance Florence." *Angelicum* 93, no. 2 (2016): 345–358.

Tarrant, Jacqueline. "The Clementine Decrees on the Beguines: Conciliar and Papal Versions." *Archivum Historiae Pontificae* 12 (1974): 300–308.

Tassi, Ildefonso. *Ludovico Barbo (1381–1443)*. Rome: Edizioni di storia e letteratura, 1952.

Terry, Wendy R. *Seeing Marguerite in the Mirror: A Linguistic Analysis of Porete's "Mirror of Simple Souls."* Leuven: Peeters, 2011.

Thijssen, J. M. M. H. *Censure and Heresy at the University of Paris, 1200–1400*. Philadelphia: University of Pennsylvania Press, 1998.

Tice, Troy J. "'Containing Heresy and Errors': Thomas of Bailly and the Condemned Extracts of the *Mirror of Simple Souls*." *The Catholic Historical Review* 104, no. 4 (2019): 614–635.

Tramontin, Silvio. "La cultura monastica del Quattrocento dal primo patriarca Lorenzo Giustiniani ai Camaldolesi Paolo Giustiniani e Pietro Quirini." *Storia della cultura veneta* 3, no. 1 (1980): 431–457.

Trombley, Justine L. "The Latin Manuscripts of *The Mirror of Simple Souls*." In *A Companion to Marguerite Porete and "The Mirror of Simple Souls*," edited by Robert Stauffer and Wendy R. Terry, 186–217. Leiden: Brill, 2017.

———. "The Master and the Mirror: The Influence of Marguerite Porete on Meister Eckhart." *Magistra: A Journal of Women's Spirituality in History* 16, no. 1 (2010): 60–102.

———. "The Mirror Broken Anew: The Manuscript Evidence for Opposition to Marguerite Porete's Latin *Mirror of Simple Souls* in the Later Middle Ages." PhD diss., University of St Andrews, 2014.

———. "New Evidence on the Origins of the Latin *Mirror of Simple Souls* from a Forgotten Paduan Manuscript." *Journal of Medieval History* 43, no. 2 (2017): 137–152.

———. "New Frontiers in the Late Medieval Reception of a Heretical Text: The Implications of Two New Latin Copies of Marguerite Porete's *Mirror of Simple Souls*." In *Late Medieval Heresy: New Perspectives: Studies in Honor of Robert E. Lerner*, edited by Michael D. Bailey and Sean L. Field, 157–177. Woodbridge, UK: Boydell and Brewer, 2018.

———. "Self-Defence and Its Limits in Marguerite Porete's *Mirror of Simple Souls*." *Nottingham Medieval Studies* 63 (2019): 129–151.

———. "The Text as Heretic: Mixed Genres and Polemical Techniques in a Refutation of the *Mirror of Simple Souls*." *Medieval Worlds* 7 (2018): 137–152.

Trusen, Winfried. *Der Prozess Gegen Meister Eckhart: Vorgeschichte, Vorlauf, und Folgen*. Paderborn: F. Schöningh, 1988.

Välimäki, Reima. *Heresy in Late Medieval Germany: The Inquisitor Petrus Zwicker and the Waldensians*. Woodbridge, UK: Boydell and Brewer, 2019.

Van Engen, John. "Marguerite of Hainaut and the Low Countries." In *Marguerite Porete et le "Miroir des simple âmes": Perspectives historiques, philosophiques et littéraires*, edited by Sean L. Field, Robert E. Lerner, and Sylvain Piron, 25–68. Paris: Vrin, 2013.

——. "Multiple Options: The World of the Fifteenth Century Church." *Church History* 77, no. 2 (2008): 257–284.

——. *Sisters and Brothers of the Common Life: The Devotio Moderna and the World of the Later Middle Ages.* Philadelphia: University of Pennsylvania Press, 2008.

——. "A World Astir: Europe and Religion in the Early Fifteenth Century." In *Europe After Wyclif,* edited by J. Patrick Hornbeck II and Michael Van Dussen, 11–45. Fordham, NY: Fordham University Press, 2016.

Voigt, Jörg. "Margarete Porete als Vertreterin eines freigeistig-häretischen Beginentums? Das Verhältnis zwischen den Bischöfen von Cambrai und den Beginen nach dem Häresieprozess gegen Margarete Porete (+1310)." In *Meister Eckhart und die Freiheit,* edited by Janina Franzke, Christine Büchner, and Freimut Löser, 31–54. Stuttgart: Verlag W. Kohlhammer, 2018.

Von Dobschütz, Ernst. Christusbilder: Untersuchungen zur christlichen Legende. *Texte und Untersuchungen zur Geschichte der Altchristlichen Literatur* Vol. 3. edited by Oscar Gebhardt and Adolf Harnack. Leipzig: J. C. Hinrichs'sche Buchhandlung, 1899.

Warnar, Geert. "Prelude: Northern Circulation of Fourteenth-Century Mystical Texts." In *A Companion to Mysticism and Devotion in Northern Germany in the Late Middle Ages,* edited by Elizabeth Anderson, Henrike Lähnemann, and Anne Simon, 159–177. Leiden: Brill, 2014.

Watson, Nicholas. "Melting into God the English Way: Deification in the Middle English Version of Marguerite Porete's *Mirouer des simples âmes anienties.*" In *Prophets Abroad: The Reception of Continental Holy Women in Late-Medieval England,* edited by Rosalynn Voaden, 19–49. Cambridge: Cambridge University Press, 1996.

Wegener, Lydia. "Freiheitsdiskurs und Beginenverfolgung um 1308—der Fall der Marguerite Porete." In *1308: Eine Topographie historischer Gleichzeitigkeit,* edited by Andreas Speer and David Wirmer, 199–236. Berlin: De Gruyter, 2010.

Wendehorst, Alfred. *Germania Sacra: Das Bistum Eichstätt: Die Bischofsreihe bis 1535.* Berlin: Walter De Gruyter, 2006.

Werner, Thomas. *Den Irtumm liquidieren: Bücherverbrennungen im Mittelalter.* Göttingen: Vandenhoeck & Ruprecht, 2007.

Wiberg Pedersen, Else Marie. "Heterodoxy or Orthodoxy of Holy Women's Texts: What Makes a Holy Woman's Text Holy?" In *Cultures of Religious Reading: Instructing the Soul, Feeding the Spirit, and Awakening the Passion,* edited by Sabrina Corbellini, 13–32. Turnhout: Brepols, 2013.

Wranovix, Matthew. "Ulrich Pfeffel's Library: Parish Priests, Preachers, and Books in the Fifteenth Century." *Speculum* 87, no. 4 (2012): 1125–1155.

# INDEX

CPSIA information can be obtained
at www.ICGtesting.com
Printed in the USA
LVHW041602050523
746220LV00016B/1000/J